ADOBE PHOTOSHOP CS4 REVEALED

ELIZABETH EISNER REDING

ADOBE PHOTOSHOP CS4 REVEALED

ELIZABETH EISNER REDING

DELMAR
CENGAGE Learning™

Australia • Brazil • Japan • Korea • Mexico • Singapore • Spain • United Kingdom • United States

DELMAR
CENGAGE Learning

Adobe Photoshop CS4 Revealed
Elizabeth Eisner Reding

Vice President, Career and Professional Editorial:
Dave Garza

Director of Learning Solutions: Sandy Clark

Senior Acquisitions Editor: Jim Gish

Managing Editor: Larry Main

Product Managers: Jane Hosie-Bounar,
Nicole Calisi

Editorial Assistant: Sarah Timm

Vice President Marketing, Career and
Professional: Jennifer McAvey

Executive Marketing Manager:
Deborah S. Yarnell

Marketing Manager: Erin Brennan

Marketing Coordinator: Jonathan Sheehan

Production Director: Wendy Troeger

Senior Content Project Manager:
Kathryn B. Kucharek

Developmental Editor: Karen Stevens

Technical Editor: Susan Whalen

Art Director: Bruce Bond, Joy Kocsis

Cover Design: Lisa Kuhn, Curio Press, LLC

Cover Art: Lisa Kuhn, Curio Press, LLC

Text Designer: Ann Small

Proofreader: Kim Kosmatka

Indexer: Alexandra Nickerson

Technology Project Manager:
Christopher Catalina

Production Technology Analyst:
Tom Stover

For product information and technology
assistance, contact us at
**Cengage Learning Customer & Sales Support,
1-800-354-9706**

For permission to use material from this text or
product, submit all requests online at
www.cengage.com/permissions
Further permissions questions can be emailed to
permissionrequest@cengage.com

Adobe® Photoshop®, Adobe® InDesign®, Adobe®
Illustrator®, Adobe® Flash®, Adobe® Dreamweaver®,
Adobe® Fireworks®, and Adobe® Creative Suite® are
trademarks or registered trademarks of Adobe Systems,
Inc. in the United States and/or other countries. Third
party products, services, company names, logos, design,
titles, words, or phrases within these materials may be
trademarks of their respective owners.

The Adobe Approved Certification Courseware logo is a
proprietary trademark of Adobe. All rights reserved.
Cengage Learning and *Adobe Photoshop CS4—Revealed* are
independent from ProCert Labs, LLC and Adobe Systems
Incorporated, and are not affiliated with ProCert Labs and
Adobe in any manner. This publication may asssist students
to prepare for an Adobe Certified Expert exam, however,
neither ProCert Labs nor Adobe warrant that use of this
material will ensure success in connection with any exam.

Library of Congress Control Number: 2008935174

Hardcover edition:
ISBN-13: 978-1-4354-8277-7
ISBN-10: 1-4354-8277-8

Soft cover edition:
ISBN-13: 978-1-4354-4187-3
ISBN-10: 1-4354-4187-7

Delmar
5 Maxwell Drive
Clifton Park, NY 12065-2919
USA

Cengage Learning is a leading provider of customized
learning solutions with office locations around the globe,
including Singapore, the United Kingdom, Australia,
Mexico, Brazil, and Japan. Locate your local office at:
international.cengage.com/region

Cengage Learning products are represented in
Canada by Nelson Education, Ltd.

To learn more about Delmar, visit
www.cengage.com/delmar

Purchase any of our products at your local college
store or at our preferred online store
www.ichapters.com

Notice to the Reader

Publisher does not warrant or guarantee any of the products
described herein or perform any independent analysis in
connection with any of the product information contained
herein. Publisher does not assume, and expressly disclaims,
any obligation to obtain and include information other
than that provided to it by the manufacturer. The reader
is expressly warned to consider and adopt all safety
precautions that might be indicated by the activities
described herein and to avoid all potential hazards. By
following the instructions contained herein, the reader
willingly assumes all risks in connection with such instructions. The publisher makes no representations or warranties
of any kind, including but not limited to, the warranties
of fitness for particular purpose or merchantability, nor are any
such representations implied with respect to the material
set forth herein, and the publisher takes no responsibility
with respect to such material. The publisher shall not be
liable for any special, consequential, or exemplary damages
resulting, in whole or part, from the readers' use of, or
reliance upon, this material.

Some of the images used in this book are royalty-free and the
property of Getty Images, Inc. and Morguefile.com. The Getty
images include artwork from the following royalty-free CD-ROM
collections: Education Elements, Just Flowers, Portraits of
Diversity, Sports and Recreation, Texture and Light, Tools of the
Trade, Travel Souvenirs, Travel & Vacation Icons, and Working
Bodies. Morguefile images include artwork from the following
categories: Objects, Scenes, Animals, and People. Figures 17, 18,
and 19 in the Appendix used with permission from Big
Brothers/Big Sisters of America.

Printed in the United States of America
2 3 4 5 6 7 13 12 11 10 09

Revealed Series Vision

The Revealed Series is your guide to today's hottest multimedia applications. These comprehensive books teach the skills behind the application, showing you how to apply smart design principles to multimedia products such as dynamic graphics, animation, web sites, software authoring tools, and digital video.

A team of design professionals including multimedia instructors, students, authors, and editors worked together to create this series. We recognized the unique learning environment of the multimedia classroom and created a series that:

◾ Gives you comprehensive step-by-step instructions

◾ Offers in-depth explanation of the "Why" behind a skill

◾ Includes creative projects for additional practice

◾ Explains concepts clearly using full-color visuals

It was our goal to create a book that speaks directly to the multimedia and design community—one of the most rapidly growing computer fields today. We think we've done just that, with a sophisticated and instructive book design.

—The Revealed Series

Author's Vision

The Revealed Series is different from some other textbooks in that its target audience is a savvy student who wants important information and needs little hand-holding. This student has a sense of adventure, an interest in design, and a healthy dose of creativity. This person is fun to write for because he or she wants to learn.

Special thanks to the following team members:

Another 18 months, another version of the Adobe Create Suite. While it might seem unusual to some, this is what we in the computer textbook publishing biz have come to call normal. It seems as though we thrive on this hurry-up-and-wait syndrome otherwise known as a new product release. To the reader, a book magically appears on the shelf with each software revision, but to those of us "making it happen" it means not only working under ridiculous deadlines (which we're used to), but it also means working with slightly different teams with slightly different ways of doing things. Karen Stevens, Susan Whalen, Jane Hosie-Bounar and I have all worked together before on a variety of projects that have spanned more years than we care to admit. Added to the mix are Jim Gish, Sarah Timm and

Tintu Thomas. The majority of us have never met face-to-face, yet once again we managed to work together in a professional manner, while defying the time-space continuum with its many time zones, cultural holidays, and countless vacation plans.

I would also like to thank my husband, Michael, who is used to my disappearing acts when I'm facing deadlines, and to Phoebe, Bix, and Jet, who know when it's time to take a break for some good old-fashioned head-scratching.

—Elizabeth Eisner Reding

Introduction to Adobe Photoshop CS4

Welcome to *Adobe Photoshop CS4—Revealed*. This book offers creative projects, concise instructions, and complete coverage of basic to advanced Photoshop skills, helping you to create polished, professional-looking artwork. Use this book both in the classroom and as your own reference guide.

This text is organized into 16 chapters, plus an appendix, "Portfolio Projects and Effects." In these chapters, you will learn many skills, including how to work with layers, make selections, adjust color techniques, use paint tools, work with filters, transform type, liquify an image, annotate and automate a Photoshop document, and create Photoshop images for the web. The appendix provides additional practice in creating projects and effects suitable for use in a design portfolio.

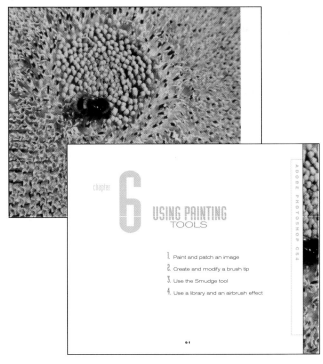

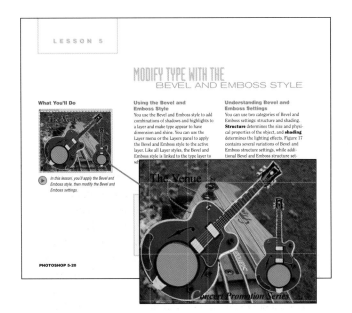

What You'll Do

A What You'll Do figure begins every lesson. This figure gives you an at-a-glance look at what you'll do in the chapter, either by showing you a file from the current project or a tool you'll be using.

Comprehensive Conceptual Lessons

Before jumping into instructions, in-depth conceptual information tells you "why" skills are applied. This book provides the "how" and "why" through the use of professional examples. Also included in the text are tips and sidebars to help you work more efficiently and creatively, or to teach you a bit about the history or design philosophy behind the skill you are using.

Step-by-Step Instructions

This book combines in-depth conceptual information with concise steps to help you learn Photoshop CS4. Each set of steps guides you through a lesson where you will create, modify, or enhance a Photoshop CS4 file. Step references to large colorful images and quick step summaries round out the lessons. The Data Files for the steps are provided on the CD at the back of this book.

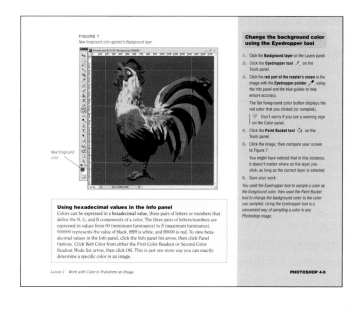

FIGURE 7
New foreground color applied to Background layer

New foreground color

Change the background color using the Eyedropper tool

1. Click the **Background layer** on the Layers panel.
2. Click the **Eyedropper tool** 🖋 on the Tools panel.
3. Click the **red part of the rooster's crown** in the image with the **Eyedropper pointer** 🖋, using the Info panel and the blue guides to help ensure accuracy.

   The Set foreground color button displays the red color that you clicked (or sampled).

   TIP Don't worry if you see a warning sign on the Color panel.

4. Click the **Paint Bucket tool** 🪣 on the Tools panel.
5. Click the image, then compare your screen to Figure 7.

   You might have noticed that in this instance, it doesn't matter where on the layer you click, as long as the correct layer is selected.

6. Save your work.

You used the Eyedropper tool to sample a color as the foreground color, then used the Paint Bucket tool to change the background color to the color you sampled. Using the Eyedropper tool is a convenient way of sampling a color in any Photoshop image.

Using hexadecimal values in the Info panel

Colors can be expressed in a hexadecimal value, three pairs of letters or numbers that define the R, G, and B components of a color. The three pairs of letters/numbers are expressed in values from 00 (minimum luminance) to ff (maximum luminance). 000000 represents the value of black, ffffff is white, and ff0000 is red. To view hexadecimal values in the Info panel, click the Info panel list arrow, then click Panel Options. Click Web Color from either the First Color Readout or Second Color Readout Mode list arrow, then click OK. This is just one more way you can exactly determine a specific color in an image.

Lesson 1 Work with Color to Transform an Image

PHOTOSHOP 4-9

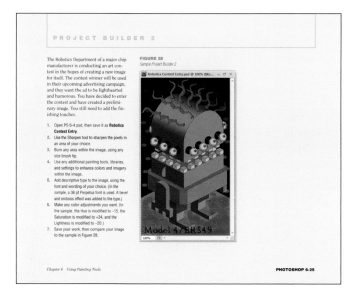

PROJECT BUILDER 2

The Robotics Department of a major chip manufacturer is conducting an art contest in the hopes of creating a new image for itself. The contest winner will be used in their upcoming advertising campaign, and they want the ad to be lighthearted and humorous. You have decided to enter the contest and have created a preliminary image. You still need to add the finishing touches.

1. Open PS 6-4.psd, then save it as **Robotics Contest Entry**.
2. Use the Sharpen tool to sharpen the pixels in an area of your choice.
3. Burn any area within the image, using any size brush tip.
4. Use any additional painting tools, libraries, and settings to enhance colors and imagery within the image.
5. Add descriptive type to the image, using the font and wording of your choice. (In the sample, a 36 pt Perpetua font is used. A bevel and emboss effect was added to the type.)
6. Make any color adjustments you want. (In the sample, the Hue is modified to −15, the Saturation is modified to +34, and the Lightness is modified to −20.)
7. Save your work, then compare your image to the sample in Figure 28.

FIGURE 28
Sample Project Builder 2

Chapter 6 Using Painting Tools

PHOTOSHOP 6-25

Projects

This book contains a variety of end-of-chapter materials for additional practice and reinforcement. The Skills Review contains hands-on practice exercises that mirror the progressive nature of the lesson material. The chapter concludes with four projects; two Project Builders, one Design Project, and one Portfolio Project. The Project Builders and the Design Project require you to apply the skills you've learned in the chapter. Portfolio Projects encourage students to use their resources to address and solve challenges based on the content explored in the chapter and to create portfolio-worthy projects.

What Instructor Resources Are Available with this Book?

The Instructor Resources CD-ROM is Delmar's way of putting the resources and information needed to teach and learn effectively into your hands. All the resources are available for both Macintosh and Windows operating systems.

Instructor's Manual

Available as an electronic file, the Instructor's Manual includes chapter overviews and detailed lecture topics for each chapter, with teaching tips. The Instructor's Manual is available on the Instructor Resources CD-ROM.

PowerPoint Presentations

Each chapter has a corresponding PowerPoint presentation that you can use in lectures, distribute to your students, or customize to suit your course.

Data Files for Students

To complete most of the chapters in this book, your students will need Data Files. The Data Files are available on the CD at the back of this text book. Instruct students to use the Data Files List at the end of this book. This list gives instructions on organizing files.

Solutions to Exercises

Solution Files are Data Files completed with comprehensive sample answers. Use these files to evaluate your students' work. Or distribute them electronically so students can verify their work. Sample solutions to all lessons and end-of-chapter material are provided.

Test Bank and Test Engine

ExamView is a powerful testing software package that allows instructors to create and administer printed and computer (LAN-based) exams. ExamView includes hundreds of questions that correspond to the topics covered in this text, enabling students to generate detailed study guides that include page references for further review. The computer-based and LAN-based/online testing component allows students to take exams using the EV Player and also save the instructor time by grading each exam automatically.

CHAPTER 2 — WORKING WITH LAYERS

CHAPTER 3 — MAKING SELECTIONS

CONTENTS

xv

CHAPTER 8 CREATING SPECIAL EFFECTS WITH FILTERS

CONTENTS

CHAPTER 12 TRANSFORMING TYPE

CHAPTER 13 LIQUIFYING AN IMAGE

CHAPTER 14 PERFORMING IMAGE SURGERY

CHAPTER 15 ANNOTATING AND AUTOMATING AN IMAGE

CONTENTS

APPENDIX | **PORTFOLIO PROJECTS AND EFFECTS**

Intended Audience

This text is designed for the beginner or intermediate student who wants to learn how to use Adobe Photoshop CS4. The book is designed to provide basic and in-depth material that not only educates but encourages the student to explore the nuances of this exciting program.

File Identification

Instead of printing a file, the owner of a Photoshop image can be identified by reading the File Info dialog box. Use the following instructions to add your name to an image:

1. Click File on the Application bar, then click File Info.
2. Click the Description tab, if necessary.
3. Click the Author text box.
4. Type your name, course number, or other identifying information.
5. Click OK.

There are no instructions with this text to use the File Info feature other than when it is introduced in Chapter 1. It is up to each user to use this feature so that his or her work can be identified.

Measurements

When measurements are shown, needed, or discussed, they are given in pixels. Use the following instructions to change the units of measurement to pixels:

1. Click Edit (Win) or Photoshop (Mac) on the Application bar, point to Preferences, then click Units & Rulers.
2. Click the Rulers list arrow, then click pixels.
3. Click OK.

You can display rulers by clicking View on the Application bar, then clicking Rulers, or by pressing [Ctrl][R] (Win) or ⌘ [R] (Mac). A check mark to the left of the Rulers command indicates that the Rulers are displayed. You can hide visible rulers by clicking View on the Application bar, then clicking Rulers, or by pressing [Ctrl][R] (Win) or ⌘ [R] (Mac).

Icons, Buttons, and Pointers

Symbols for icons, buttons, and pointers are shown each time they are used.

Fonts

Data and Solution Files contain a variety of fonts, and there is no guarantee that all of these fonts will be available on your computer. The fonts are identified in cases where less common fonts are used in the files. Every effort has been made to use commonly available fonts in the lessons. If any of the fonts in use are not available on your computer, please make a substitution.

Menu Commands in Tables

In tables, menu commands are abbreviated using the following format: Edit ➢ Preferences ➢ Units & Rulers. This command translates as follows: Click Edit on the Application bar, point to Preferences, then click Units & Rulers.

Skills Reference

As a bonus, a Power User Shortcuts table is included at the end of every chapter. This table contains the quickest method of completing tasks covered in the chapter. It is meant for the more experienced user, or for the user who wants to become more experienced. Tools are shown, not named.

Grading Tips

Many students have web-ready accounts where they can post their completed assignments. The instructor can access the student accounts using a browser and view the images online. Using this method, it is not necessary for the student to include his/her name on a type layer, because all of their assignments are in an individual password-protected account.

Creating a Portfolio

One method for students to submit and keep a copy of all of their work is to create a portfolio of their projects that is linked to a simple web page that can be saved on a CD-ROM. If it is necessary for students to print completed projects, work can be printed and mounted at a local copy shop; a student's name can be printed on the back of the image.

GETTING STARTED WITH
ADOBE
PHOTOSHOP CS4

1. Start Adobe Photoshop CS4

2. Learn how to open and save an image

3. Use organizational and management features

4. Examine the Photoshop window

5. Use the Layers and History panels

6. Learn about Photoshop by using Help

7. View and print an image

8. Close a file and exit Photoshop

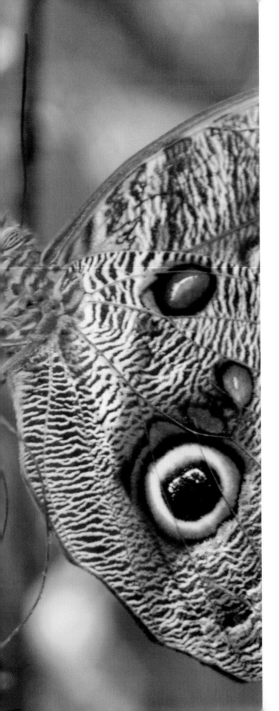

GETTING STARTED WITH
ADOBE
PHOTOSHOP CS4

Using Photoshop

Adobe Photoshop CS4 is an image-editing program that lets you create and modify digital images. 'CS' stands for Creative Suite, a complete design environment. Although Adobe makes Photoshop available as a standalone product, it also comes bundled with all of their Creative Suite options, whether your interests lie with print design, web design, or multimedia production. A **digital image** is a picture in electronic form. Using Photoshop, you can create original artwork, manipulate color images, and retouch photographs. In addition to being a robust application popular with graphics professionals, Photoshop is practical for anyone who wants to enhance existing artwork or create new masterpieces. For example, you can repair and restore damaged areas within an image, combine images, and create graphics and special effects for the web.

> QUICKTIP
>
> In Photoshop, a digital image may be referred to as a file, document, graphic, picture, or image.

Understanding Platform User Interfaces

Photoshop is available for both Windows and Macintosh platforms. Regardless of which platform you use, the features and commands are very similar. Some of the Windows and Macintosh keyboard commands differ in name, but they have equivalent functions. For example, the [Ctrl] and [Alt] keys are used in Windows, and the [⌘] and [option] keys are used on Macintosh computers. There are also visual differences between the Windows and Macintosh versions of Photoshop due to the user interface differences found in each platform.

Understanding Sources

Photoshop allows you to work with images from a variety of sources. You can create your own original artwork in Photoshop, use images downloaded from the web, or use images that have been scanned or created using a digital camera. Whether you create Photoshop images to print in high resolution or optimize them for multimedia presentations, web-based functions, or animation projects, Photoshop is a powerful tool for communicating your ideas visually.

Tools You'll Use

New...	Ctrl+N
Open...	Ctrl+O
Browse in Bridge...	Alt+Ctrl+O
Open As...	Alt+Shift+Ctrl+O
Open As Smart Object...	
Open Recent	▶
Share My Screen...	
Device Central...	
Close	Ctrl+W
Close All	Alt+Ctrl+W
Close and Go To Bridge...	Shift+Ctrl+W
Save	Ctrl+S
Save As...	Shift+Ctrl+S
Check In...	
Save for Web & Devices...	Alt+Shift+Ctrl+S
Revert	F12
Place...	
Import	▶
Export	▶
Automate	▶
Scripts	▶
File Info...	Alt+Shift+Ctrl+I
Page Setup...	Shift+Ctrl+P
Print...	Ctrl+P
Print One Copy	Alt+Shift+Ctrl+P
Exit	Ctrl+Q

Arrange	▶
Workspace	▶
Extensions	▶
3D	
Actions	Alt+F9
✔ Adjustments	
Animation	
Brushes	F5
Channels	
Character	
Clone Source	
✔ Color	F6
Histogram	
History	
Info	F8
Layer Comps	
✔ Layers	F7
Masks	
Measurement Log	
Navigator	
Notes	
Paragraph	
Paths	
Styles	
Swatches	
Tool Presets	
✔ Options	
✔ Tools	
✔ 1 PS 1-1.psd	

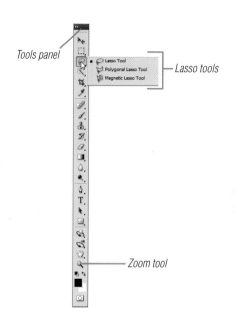

Tools panel

Lasso tools

Zoom tool

Options bar

START ADOBE
PHOTOSHOP CS4

What You'll Do

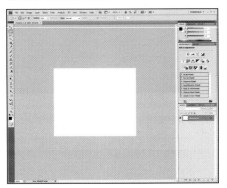

In this lesson, you'll start Photoshop for Windows or Macintosh, then create a file.

Defining Image-Editing Software

Photoshop is an image-editing program. An **image-editing** program allows you to manipulate graphic images so that they can be reproduced by professional printers using full-color processes. Using panels, tools, menus, and a variety of techniques, you can modify a Photoshop image by rotating it, resizing it, changing its colors, or adding text to it. You can also use Photoshop to create and open different kinds of file formats, which enables you to create your own images, import them from a digital camera or scanner, or use files (in other formats) purchased from outside sources. Table 1 lists some of the graphics file formats that Photoshop can open and create.

Understanding Images

Every image is made up of very small squares, which are called **pixels**, and each pixel represents a color or shade. Pixels within an image can be added, deleted, or modified.

Using Photoshop Features

Photoshop includes many tools that you can use to manipulate images and text. Within an image, you can add new items and modify existing elements, change colors, and draw shapes. For example, using the Lasso tool, you can outline a section of an image and drag the section onto another area of the image. You can also isolate a foreground or background image. You can extract all or part of a complex image from nearly any background and use it elsewhere.

You can also create and format text, called **type**, in Photoshop. You can apply a variety of special effects to type; for example, you can change the appearance of type and increase or decrease the distance between characters. You can also edit type after it has been created and formatted.

Adobe Dreamweaver CS4, a web production software program included in the Design Suite, allows you to optimize, preview, and animate images. Because Dreamweaver is part of the same suite as Photoshop, you can jump seamlessly between the two programs.

Using these two programs, you can also quickly turn any graphics image into a gif animation. Photoshop and Dreamweaver let you compress file size (while optimizing image quality) to ensure that your files download quickly from a web page. Using Photoshop optimization features, you can view multiple versions of an image and select the one that best suits your needs.

Starting Photoshop and Creating a File

The specific way you start Photoshop depends on which computer platform you are using. However, when you start Photoshop in either platform, the computer displays a **splash screen**, a window that contains information about the software, and then the Photoshop window opens.

After you start Photoshop, you can create a file from scratch. You use the New dialog box to create a file. You can also use the New dialog box to set the size of the image you're about to create by typing dimensions in the Width and Height text boxes.

TABLE 1: Some Supported Graphic File Formats

file format	filename extension	file format	filename extension
3D Studio	.3ds	Photoshop PDF	.pdf
Bitmap	.bmp	PICT file	.pct, .pic, or .pict
Cineon	.cin		
Dicom	.dcm	Pixar	.pxr
Filmstrip	.flm	QuickTime	.mov or .mp4
Google Earth	.kmz		
Graphics Interchange Format	.gif	Radiance	.hdr
		RAW	varies
JPEG Picture Format	.jpg, .jpe, or .jpeg	Scitex CT	.sct
		Tagged Image Format	.tif or .tiff
PC Paintbrush	.pcx		
Photoshop	.psd	Targa	.tga or .vda
Photoshop Encapsulated PostScript	.eps	U3D	.u3d
		Wavefront	.obj

Start Photoshop (Windows)

1. Click the **Start button** 🔵 on the taskbar.

2. Point to **All Programs**, point to **Adobe Photoshop CS4**, as shown in Figure 1, then click **Adobe Photoshop CS4**.

   TIP   The Adobe Photoshop CS4 program might be found in the Start menu (in the left pane) or in the Adobe folder, which is in the Program Files folder on the hard drive (Win).

3. Click **File** on the Application bar, then click **New** to open the New dialog box.

4. Double-click the number in the Width text box, type **500**, click the **Width list arrow**, then click **pixels** (if it is not already selected).

5. Double-click the number in the Height text box, type **400**, then specify a resolution of **72** pixels/inch (if necessary).

6. Click **OK**.

   TIP   By default, the document window (the background of the active image) is gray. This color can be changed by right-clicking the background and then making a color selection.

7. Click the **arrow** ▶ at the bottom of the image window, point to **Show**, then click **Document Sizes** (if it is not already displayed).

You started Photoshop in Windows, then created a file with custom dimensions. Setting custom dimensions lets you specify the exact size of the image you are creating. You changed the display at the bottom of the image window so the document size is visible.

FIGURE 1
Starting Photoshop CS4 (Windows)

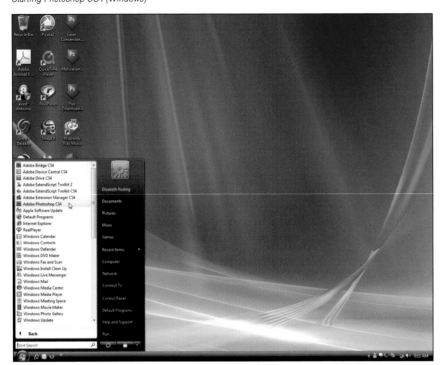

Understanding hardware requirements (Windows)

Adobe Photoshop CS4 has the following minimum system requirements:

- Processor: Intel Xeon, Xeon Dual, Centrino, or Pentium 4 processor
- Operating System: Microsoft® Windows XP SP2 or higher, or Windows Vista
- Memory: 320 MB of RAM
- Storage space: 650 MB of available hard-disk space
- Video RAM: 64 MB; Monitor with 1024 × 768 resolution
- 16-bit video card and Quick Time 7 for Multimedia features

FIGURE 2
Starting Photoshop CS4 (Macintosh)

Items as icons view

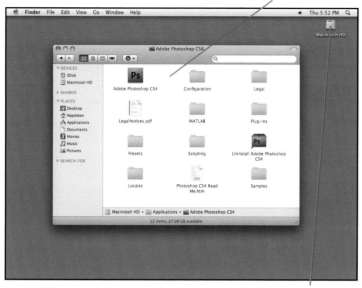

Hard drive icon

Understanding hardware requirements (Macintosh)

Adobe Photoshop CS4 has the following minimum system requirements:

- Processor: G4, G5, or Intel-based
- Operating System: Mac OS X version 10.3 through 10.5
- Memory: 320 MB of RAM (384 MB recommended)
- Storage space: 1.5 GB of available hard-disk space
- Monitor: 1024 × 768 or greater monitor resolution with 16-bit color or greater video card
- PostScript Printer PostScript Level 2, Adobe PostScript 3
- Video RAM: 64 MB
- CD-ROM Drive: CD-ROM Drive required

1. Double-click the **hard drive icon** on the desktop, double-click the **Applications folder**, then double-click the **Adobe Photoshop CS4 folder**. Compare your screen to Figure 2.

2. Double-click the **Adobe Photoshop CS4 program icon**.

3. Click **File** on the Application bar, then click **New**.

    TIP If the Color Settings dialog box opens, click No. If a Welcome screen opens, click Close.

4. Double-click the number in the Width text box, type **500**, click the **Width list arrow**, then click **pixels** (if necessary).

5. Double-click the number in the Height text box, type **400**, click the **Height list arrow**, click **pixels** (if necessary), then verify a resolution of **72** pixels/inch.

6. Click **OK**.

    TIP The gray document window background can be turned on by clicking Window on the Application bar, then clicking Application frame.

7. Click the **arrow** ▶ at the bottom of the image window, point to **Show**, then click **Document Sizes** (if it is not already checked).

You started Photoshop for Macintosh, then created a file with custom dimensions. You verified that the document size is visible at the bottom of the image window.

LEARN HOW TO OPEN AND
SAVE AN IMAGE

What You'll Do

In this lesson, you'll locate and open files using the File menu and Adobe Bridge, flag and sort files, then save a file with a new name.

Opening and Saving Files

Photoshop provides several options for opening and saving a file. Often, the project you're working on determines the techniques you use for opening and saving files. For example, you might want to preserve the original version of a file while you modify a copy. You can open a file, then immediately save it with a different filename, as well as open and save files in many different file formats. When working with graphic images you can open a Photoshop file that has been saved as a bitmap (.bmp) file, then save it as a JPEG (.jpg) file to use on a web page.

Customizing How You Open Files

You can customize how you open your files by setting preferences. **Preferences** are options you can set that are based on your work habits. For example, you can use the Open Recent command on the File menu to instantly locate and open the files that you recently worked on, or you can allow others to preview your files as thumbnails. Figure 3 shows the Preferences dialog box options for handling your files.

TIP   In cases when the correct file format is not automatically determined, you can use the Open As command on the File menu (Win) or Open as Smart Object (Mac).

FIGURE 3
Preferences dialog box

Option for thumbnail preview

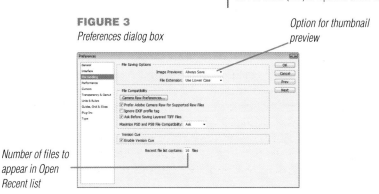

Number of files to appear in Open Recent list

Browsing Through Files

You can easily find the files you're looking for by using **Adobe Bridge**, a stand-alone application that serves as the hub for the Adobe Creative Suite. See the magnifying loupe tool in the Filmstrip view in Figure 4. You can open Adobe Bridge (or just Bridge) by clicking the Launch Bridge button on the Application bar. You can also open Bridge using the File menu in Photoshop.

When you open Bridge, a series of panels allows you to view the files on your hard drive as hierarchical files and folders. In addition to the Favorites and Folders panels in the upper-left corner of the Bridge window, there are other important areas. Directly beneath the Favorites and Folders panels is the Filter panel which allows you to review properties of images in the Content panel. In the (default) Essentials view, the Preview panel displays a window containing the Metadata and Keywords panels, which stores information about a selected file (such as keywords) that can then be used as search parameters. You can use this tree structure to find the file you are seeking. When you locate a file, you can click its thumbnail to see information about its size, format, and creation and modification dates. (Clicking a thumbnail selects the image. You can select multiple non-contiguous images by pressing and holding [Ctrl] (Win) or ⌘ (Mac) each time you click an image.) You can select contiguous images by clicking the first image, then pressing

TIP Click a thumbnail while in Filmstrip view and the pointer changes to a Loupe tool that magnifies content. Drag the loupe over the filmstrip image to enlarge select areas. The arrowhead in the upper-left corner of the window points to the area to be magnified. Clicking the arrowhead closes the loupe.

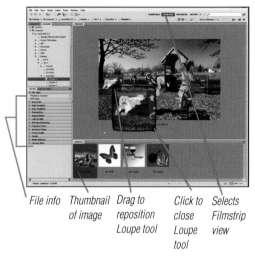

FIGURE 4
Adobe Bridge window

File info Thumbnail Drag to   Click to Selects
         of image   reposition close   Filmstrip
                    Loupe tool Loupe   view
                                tool

Using the Photoshop File Info dialog box

You can use the File Info dialog box to identify a file, add a caption or other text, or add a copyright notice. The Description section allows you to enter printable text, as shown in Figure 5. For example, to add your name to an image, click File on the Application bar, click File Info, then click in the Description text box. (You can move from field to field by pressing [Tab] or by clicking in individual text boxes.) Type your name, course number, or other identifying information in the Description text box, or click stars to assign a rating. You can enter additional information in the other text boxes, then save all the File Info data as a separate file that has an .xmp extension. To print selected data from the File Info dialog box, click File on the Application bar, then click Print. Click the Color Management list arrow, then click Output. Available options are listed in the right panel. To print the filename, select the Labels check box. You can also select check boxes that let you print crop marks and registration marks. If you choose, you can even add a background color or border to your image. After you select the items you want to print, click Print.

Type information to
be printed here

FIGURE 5
File Info dialog box

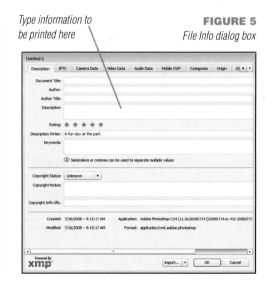

and holding [Shift] and clicking the last image
in the group. You can open a file using Bridge
by double-clicking its thumbnail, and find out
information such as the file's format, and
when it was created and edited. You can
close Bridge by clicking File (Win) or Bridge
CS4 (Mac) on the (Bridge) Application bar,
then clicking Exit (Win) or Quit Adobe
Bridge CS4 (Mac) or by clicking the window's
Close button.

Understanding the Power of Bridge

In addition to allowing you to see all your
images, Bridge can be used to rate (assign
importance), sort (organize by name, rating, and
other criteria), and label your images. Figure 4,
on the previous page, contains images that are
assigned a rating and shown in Filmstrip view.
There are three views in Bridge (Essentials,
Filmstrip, and Metadata) that are controlled by
tabs to the left of the search text box. To assist in
organizing your images, you can assign a color
label or rating to one or more images regardless
of your current view. Any number of selected
images can be assigned a color label by clicking
Label on the Application bar, then clicking one
of the six options.

Creating a PDF Presentation

Using Bridge you can create a PDF
Presentation (a presentation in the PDF file
format). Such a presentation can be viewed
full-screen on any computer monitor, or in
Adobe Acrobat Reader as a PDF file. You can
create such a presentation by opening
Bridge, locating and selecting images using
the file hierarchy, then clicking the Output
button on the Bridge Application bar. The
Output panel, shown in Figure 6, opens and
displays the images you have selected. You
can add images by pressing [Ctrl] (Win) or
[⌘] (Mac) while clicking additional images.

FIGURE 6
Output panel in Bridge

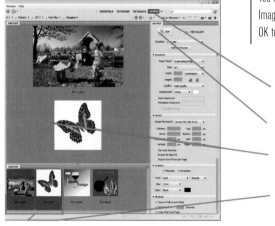

Click to create
output

Click to create
PDF

Output
preview

Selected
thumbnails

Using Save As Versus Save

Sometimes it's more efficient to create a new
image by modifying an existing one, especially if it contains elements and special
effects that you want to use again. The Save
As command on the File menu (in
Photoshop) creates a copy of the file,
prompts you to give the duplicate file a new
name, and then displays the new filename in
the image's title bar. You use the Save As
command to name an unnamed file or to
save an existing file with a new name. For
example, throughout this book, you will be
instructed to open your Data Files and use
the Save As command. Saving your Data
Files with new names keeps the original files
intact in case you have to start the lesson
over again or you want to repeat an exercise.
When you use the Save command, you save
the changes you made to the open file.

FIGURE 7
Open dialog box for Windows

Look in list arrow displays list of available drives

Available folders and files may differ from your list

Selected filename

FIGURE 7
Open dialog box for Macintosh

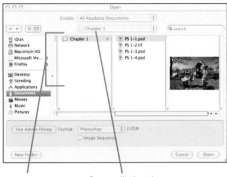

Available folders and files

Current file location list arrow

FIGURE 8
Adobe Bridge window

Essentials button

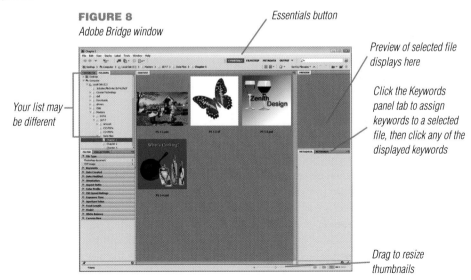

Your list may be different

Preview of selected file displays here

Click the Keywords panel tab to assign keywords to a selected file, then click any of the displayed keywords

Drag to resize thumbnails

Open a file using the Application bar

1. Click **File** on the Application bar, then click **Open**.

2. Click the **Look in list arrow** (Win) or the **Current file location list arrow** (Mac), then navigate to the drive and folder where you store your Data Files.

3. Click **PS 1-1.psd**, as shown in Figure 7, then click **Open**.

   TIP   Click Update, if you receive a message stating that some text layers need to be updated.

You used the Open command on the File menu to locate and open a file.

Open a file using the Folders panel in Adobe Bridge

1. Click the **Launch Bridge button** ▶Br on the Application bar, then click the **Folders panel tab** FOLDERS (if necessary).

2. Navigate through the hierarchical tree to the drive and folder where you store your Chapter 1 Data Files, then click the **Essentials button** if it is not already selected.

3. Drag the **slider** (at the bottom of the Bridge window) a third of the way between the Smaller thumbnail size button ▫ and the Larger thumbnail size button ▭. Compare your screen to Figure 8.

4. Double-click the **image of a butterfly** (PS 1-2.tif). Bridge is no longer visible.

5. Close the butterfly image in Photoshop.

You used the Folders panel tab in Adobe Bridge to locate and open a file. This feature makes it easy to see which file you want to use.

Use the Save As command

1. Verify that the **PS 1-1.psd window** is active.

2. Click **File** on the Application bar, click **Save As**, then compare your Save As dialog box to Figure 9.

3. If the drive containing your Data Files is not displayed, click the **Save in list arrow** (Win) or the **Where list arrow** (Mac), then navigate to the drive and folder where you store your Chapter 1 Data Files.

4. Select the current filename in the File name text box (Win) or Save As text box (Mac) (if necessary); type **Playground**, then click **Save**.

   TIP Click OK to close the Maximize Compatibility dialog box (if necessary).

You used the Save As command on the File menu to save the file with a new name. This command makes it possible for you to save a changed version of an image while keeping the original file intact.

Change from Tabbed to Floating Documents

1. Click the **Arrange Documents button** 　 ▾ on the Application bar, then click **2 Up**.

   TIP The Arrange Documents button is a temporary change to the workspace that will be in effect for the current Photoshop session.

2. Click 　 ▾ , then click **Float All in Windows**. Compare your Playground image to Figure 10.

You changed the arrangement of open documents from consolidation to a 2 Up format to each image displaying in its own window.

FIGURE 9
Save As dialog box

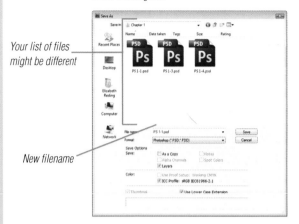

Your list of files
might be different

New filename

FIGURE 10
Playground image

Duplicate file has
new name

Changing file formats

In addition to using the Save As command to duplicate an existing file, it is a handy way of changing one format into another. For example, you can open an image you created in a digital camera, then make modifications in the Photoshop format. To do this, open the .jpg file in Photoshop, click File on the Application bar, then click Save As. Name the file, click the Format list arrow, click Photoshop (*.psd, *.pdd) (Win) or Photoshop (Mac), then click Save. You can also change formats using Bridge by selecting the file, clicking Tools on the Application bar, pointing to Photoshop, then clicking Image Processor. Section 3 of the Image Processor dialog box lets you determine the new file format.

Getting photos from your camera

You can use Bridge to move photos from your camera into your computer by plugging your camera into your computer, opening Adobe Bridge, clicking File on the (Bridge) Application bar, then clicking Get Photos from Camera. Once you do this, the Adobe Bridge CS4 Photo Downloader dialog box opens. This dialog box lets you decide from which device you'll download images, where you want to store them, and whether or not you want to rename them, among other options.

Rated and
Approved file

FIGURE 11
Images in Adobe Bridge

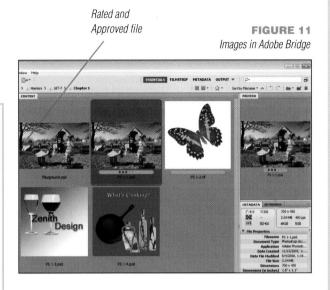

FIGURE 12
Sorted files

Rate and filter with Bridge

1. Click the **Launch Bridge button** ▶Br on the Application bar.
2. Click the **Folders panel tab** FOLDERS if it is not already selected, then click the drive and folder where you store your Chapter 1 Data Files on the File Hierarchy tree (if necessary).
3. Click the butterfly image, file **PS 1-2.tif** to select it.
4. Press and hold **[Ctrl]** (Win) or ⌘ (Mac), click **PS 1-1.psd** (the image of the playground), then release **[Ctrl]** (Win) or ⌘ (Mac).
5. Click **Label** on the Application bar, then click **Approved**.
6. Click **PS 1-1.psd**, click **Label** on the Application bar, then click ✱✱✱. See Figure 11.
7. Click **View** on the Application bar, point to **Sort**, then click **By Type**. Compare your screen to Figure 12.

   The order of the files is changed.

   TIP   You can also change the order of files (in the Content panel) using the Sort by Filename list arrow in the Filter panel. When you click the Sort by Filename list arrow, you'll see a list of sorting options. Click the option you want and the files in the Content panel will be rearranged.

8. Click **View** on the Application bar, point to **Sort**, then click **Manually**.

   TIP   You can change the Bridge view at any time, depending on the type of information you need to see.

9. Click **File** (Win) or **Adobe Bridge CS4** (Mac) on the (Bridge) Application bar, then click **Exit** or **Quit Adobe Bridge CS4** (Mac).

You labeled files using Bridge, sorted the files in a folder, then changed the sort order. When finished, you closed Bridge.

USE ORGANIZATIONAL AND
MANAGEMENT FEATURES

What You'll Do

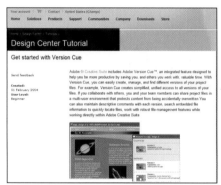

In this lesson, you'll learn how to use Version Cue and Bridge.

Learning about Version Cue

Version Cue is a file versioning and management feature of the Adobe Creative Suite that can be used to organize your work whether you work in groups or by yourself. Version Cue is accessed through Bridge. You can see Version Cue in Bridge in two different locations: the Favorites tab and the Folders tab. Figure 13 shows Version Cue in the Favorites tab of Bridge. You can also view Version Cue in the Folders tab by collapsing the Desktop, as shown in Figure 14.

Understanding Version Cue Workspaces

Regardless of where in Bridge you access it (the Favorites or Folders tab), Version Cue installs a **workspace** in which it stores projects and project files, and keeps track of file versions. The Version Cue workspace can be installed locally on your own computer and can be made public or kept private. It can also be installed on a server and can be used by many users through a network.

FIGURE 13
Favorites tab in Adobe Bridge

Your list of Favorites may differ ———

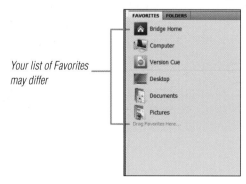

FIGURE 14
Folders tab in Adobe Bridge

Using Version Cue's Administrative Functions

Once you log into Version Cue using Adobe Drive (shown in Figure 15), you can control who uses the workspace and how it is used with the tabs at the top of the screen. Adobe Drive, which you use to connect to Version Cue, lets you open your server, browse projects and other servers, and perform advanced tasks.

Making Use of Bridge

You've already seen how you can use Bridge to find, identify, and sort files. But did you know that you can use Bridge Center to organize, label, and open files as a group? First you select one or more files, right-click the selection (Win) or [control]-click the selection (Mac), then click Open, or Open With, to display the files in your favorite CS4 program. You can apply labels, and ratings, or sort the selected files.

QUICKTIP

You can use Bridge to stitch together panoramic photos, rename images in batches, or automate image conversions with the Tools menu. Select the file(s) in Bridge you want to modify, click Tools on the Application bar, point to Photoshop, then click a command and make option modifications.

FIGURE 15
Adobe Drive and Version Cue

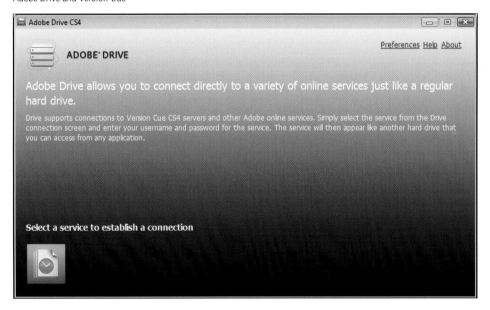

EXAMINE THE
PHOTOSHOP WINDOW

What You'll Do

 In this lesson, you'll arrange documents and change the default display, select a tool on the Tools panel, use a shortcut key to cycle through the hidden tools, select and add a tool to the Tool Preset picker, use the Window menu to show and hide panels in the workspace, and create a customized workspace.

Learning About the Workspace

The Photoshop **workspace** is the area within the Photoshop program window that includes the entire window, from the command menus at the top of your screen to the status bar (Win) at the bottom. Desktop items are visible in this area (Mac). The (Windows) workspace is shown in Figure 16.

In Windows, the area containing the menu bar (containing Photoshop commands) and the title bar (displaying the program name) is called the **Application bar**. These two areas have been combined to use space more efficiently. On the Mac, the main menus are at the top of the screen, but not on the Application bar. If the active image window is maximized, the filename of the open unnamed file is **Untitled-1**, because it has not been named. The Application bar also contains the **workspace switcher**, a Close button, and Minimize/Maximize, and Restore buttons (Win).

You can choose a menu command by clicking it or by pressing [Alt] plus the underlined letter in the menu name (Win). Some commands display shortcut keys on the right side of the menu. Shortcut keys provide an alternative way to activate menu commands. Some commands might appear dimmed, which means they are not currently available. An ellipsis after a command indicates additional choices.

DESIGNTIP **Overcoming information overload**

One of the most common experiences shared by first-time Photoshop users is information overload. There are just too many places and things to look at! When you feel your brain overheating, take a moment and sit back. Remind yourself that the active image area is the central area where you can see a composite of your work. All the tools and panels are there to help you, not to add to the confusion. The tools and features in Photoshop CS4 are designed to be easier to find and use, making any given task faster to complete.

Finding Tools Everywhere

The **Tools panel** contains tools associated with frequently used Photoshop commands. The face of a tool contains a graphical representation of its function; for example, the Zoom tool shows a magnifying glass. You can place the pointer over each tool to display a tool tip, which tells you the name or function of that tool. Some tools have additional hidden tools, indicated by a small black triangle in the lower-right corner of the tool.

The **options bar**, located directly under the Application bar, displays the current settings for each tool. For example, when you click the Type tool, the default font and font size appear on the options bar, which can be changed if desired. You can move the options bar anywhere in the workspace for easier access. The options bar also contains the Tool Preset picker. This is the left-most tool on the options bar and displays the active tool. You can click the list arrow on this tool to select another tool without having to use the Tools panel. The options bar also contains the panel well, an area where you can assemble panels for quick access.

Panels, sometimes called palettes, are small windows used to verify settings and modify images. By default, panels appear in stacked groups at the right side of the window.

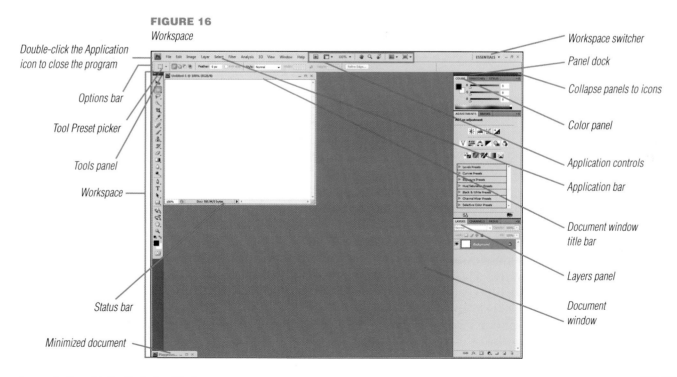

FIGURE 16
Workspace

Double-click the Application icon to close the program

Options bar

Tool Preset picker

Tools panel

Workspace

Status bar

Minimized document

Workspace switcher

Panel dock

Collapse panels to icons

Color panel

Application controls

Application bar

Document window title bar

Layers panel

Document window

Lesson 4 Examine the Photoshop Window

A collection of panels usually in a vertical orientation is called a **dock**. The dock is the dark gray bar above the collection of panels. The arrows in the dock are used to maximize and minimize the panels. You can display a panel by simply clicking the panel tab, making it the active panel. Panels can be separated and moved anywhere in the workspace by dragging their tabs to new locations. You can dock a panel by dragging its tab in or out of a dock. As you move a panel, you'll see a blue highlighted drop zone. A **drop zone** is an area where you can move a panel. You can also change the order of tabs by dragging a tab to a new location within its panel. Each panel contains a menu that you can view by clicking the list arrow in its upper-right corner.

The **status bar** is located at the bottom of the program window (Win) or work area (Mac). It displays information, such as the file size of the active window and a description of the active tool. You can display other informa-tion on the status bar, such as the current tool, by clicking the black triangle to view a pull-down menu with more options.

Rulers can help you precisely measure and position an object in the workspace. The rulers do not appear the first time you use Photoshop, but you can display them by clicking Rulers on the View menu.

Using Tool Shortcut Keys

Each tool has a corresponding shortcut key. For example, the shortcut key for the Type tool is T. After you know a tool's shortcut key, you can select the tool on the Tools panel by pressing its shortcut key. To select and cycle through a tool's hidden tools, you press and hold [Shift], then press the tool's shortcut key until the desired tool appears.

Customizing Your Environment

Photoshop makes it easy for you to position elements you work with just where you want them. If you move elements around to make your environment more convenient, you can always return your workspace to its original appearance by resetting the default panel locations. Once you have your work area arranged the way you want it, you can create a customized workspace by clicking the workspace switcher on the Application bar, then clicking Save Workspace. If you want to open a named workspace, click the workspace switcher, then click the name of the workspace you want to use. In addition, Photoshop comes with many customized workspaces that are designed for specific tasks.

FIGURE 17
Keyboard Shortcuts and Menus dialog box

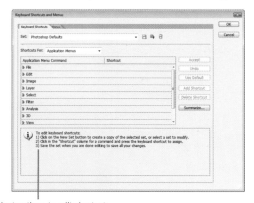

Instructions to edit shortcuts

Creating customized keyboard shortcuts

Keyboard shortcuts can make your work with Photoshop images faster and easier. In fact, once you discover the power of keyboard shortcuts, you may never use menus again. In addition to the keyboard shortcuts that are preprogrammed in Photoshop, you can create your own. To do this, click Edit on the Application bar, then click Keyboard Shortcuts. The Keyboard Shortcuts and Menus dialog box opens, as shown in Figure 17.

DESIGNTIP Composition 101

What makes one image merely okay and another terrific? While any such judgement is subjective, there are some rules governing image composition. It goes without saying that, as the artist, you have a message you're trying to deliver … something you're trying to say to the viewer. This is true whether the medium is oil painting, photography, or Photoshop imagery.

Elements under your control in your composition are tone, sharpness, scale, and arrangement. (You may see these items classified differently elsewhere, but they amount to the same concepts.)

Tone is the brightness and contrast within an image. Using light and shadows you can shift the focus of the viewer's eye and control the mood.

Sharpness is used to direct the viewer's eye to a specific area of an image. **Scale** is the size relationship of objects to one another, and **arrangement** is how objects are positioned to one another.

Are objects in your image contributing to clarity or clutter? Are similarly-sized objects confusing the viewer? Would blurring one area of an image change the viewer's focus?

These are tools you have to influence your artistic expression. Make sure the viewer understands what you want seen.

FIGURE 18
Hidden tools

Shortcut key

Select a tool

1. Click the **Lasso tool** ⟨⟩ on the Tools panel, press and hold the mouse button until a list of hidden tools appears, then release the mouse button. See Figure 18. Note the shortcut key, L, next to the tool name.

2. Click the **Polygonal Lasso tool** ⟨⟩ on the Tools panel.

3. Press and hold **[Shift]**, press **[L]** three times to cycle through the Lasso tools, then release **[Shift]**. Did you notice how the options bar changes for each selected Lasso tool?

   TIP You can return the tools to their default setting by clicking the Click to open the Tool Preset picker list arrow on the options bar, clicking the list arrow, then clicking Reset All Tools.

You selected the Lasso tool on the Tools panel and used its shortcut key to cycle through the Lasso tools. Becoming familiar with shortcut keys can speed up your work and make you more efficient.

Learning shortcut keys

Don't worry about learning shortcut keys. As you become more familiar with Photoshop, you'll gradually pick up shortcuts for menu commands, such as saving a file, or Tools panel tools, such as the Move tool. You'll notice that as you learn to use shortcut keys, your speed while working with Photoshop will increase and you'll complete tasks with fewer mouse clicks.

Select a tool from the Tool Preset picker

1. Click the **Click to open the Tool Preset picker list arrow** on the options bar.

   The name of a button is displayed in a tool tip, the descriptive text that appears when you point to the button. Your Tool Preset picker list will differ, and may contain no entries at all. This list can be customized by each user.

2. Deselect the **Current Tool Only check box** (if necessary). See Figure 19.

3. Double-click **Magnetic Lasso 24 pixels** in the list.

You selected the Magnetic Lasso tool using the Tool Preset picker. The Tool Preset picker makes it easy to access frequently used tools and their settings.

FIGURE 19
Using the Tool Preset picker

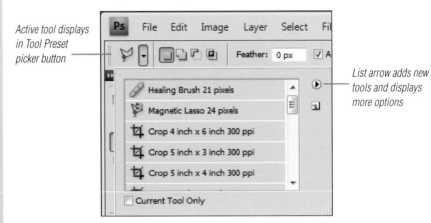

Active tool displays in Tool Preset picker button

List arrow adds new tools and displays more options

FIGURE 20
Full screen mode with Application bar

Using the Full Screen Mode

By default, Photoshop displays images in consolidated tabs. This means that each image is displayed within its own tab. You can choose from three other modes: Maximized Screen Mode, Full Screen Mode with Application Bar, and Full Screen Mode. And why would you want to stray from the familiar Standard Screen Mode? Perhaps your image is so large that it's difficult to see it all in Standard Mode, or perhaps you want a less cluttered screen. Maybe you just want to try something different. You can switch between modes by clicking the Change Screen Mode button (located in the Application controls area of the Application bar) or by pressing the keyboard shortcut F. When you click this button, the screen displays changes. Click the Hand tool (or press the keyboard shortcut H), and you can reposition the active image, as shown in Figure 20.

Use hand pointer to reposition image

Click to change screen modes

Arranging elements

The appearance of elements in an image is important, but of equal importance is the way in which the elements are arranged. The components of any image should form a cohesive unit so that the reader is unaware of all the different parts, yet influenced by the way they work together to emphasize a message or reveal information. For example, if a large image is used, it should be easy for the reader to connect the image with any descriptive text. There should be an easily understood connection between the text and the artwork, and the reader should be able to seamlessly connect them.

FIGURE 21
Move tool added to preset picker

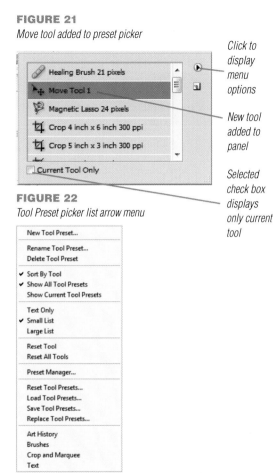

Click to display menu options

New tool added to panel

Selected check box displays only current tool

FIGURE 22
Tool Preset picker list arrow menu

Modifying a tool preset

Once you've created tool presets, you'll probably want to know how they can be deleted and renamed. To delete any tool preset, select it on the Tool Preset picker panel. Click the list arrow on the Tool Preset picker panel to view the menu, shown in Figure 22, then click Delete Tool Preset. To rename a tool preset, click the same list arrow, then click Rename Tool Preset.

Add a tool to the Tool Preset picker

1. Click the **Move tool** on the Tools panel.
2. Click the **Click to open the Tool Preset picker list arrow** on the options bar.
3. Click the **list arrow** on the Tool Preset picker.
4. Click **New Tool Preset**, then click **OK** to accept the default name (Move Tool 1). Compare your list to Figure 21.

   TIP   You can display the currently selected tool alone by selecting the Current Tool Only check box.

You added the Move tool to the Tool Preset picker. Once you know how to add tools to the Tool Preset picker, you can quickly and easily customize your work environment.

Change the default display

1. Click **Edit** (Win) or **Photoshop** (Mac) on the Application bar, then click **Preferences** (Win) or point to **Preferences,** then click **Interface** (Mac).
2. Click **Interface** in the left panel (Win), click the **Open Documents in Tabs check box** to deselect it, then click **OK**.

You changed the default display so that each time you open Photoshop, each image will display in its own window rather than in tabs.

Show and hide panels

1. Click **Window** on the Application bar, then verify that **Color** has a check mark next to it, then close the menu.

2. Click the **Swatches tab** next to the Color tab to make the Swatches panel active, as shown in Figure 23.

3. Click the **Collapse to Icons arrow** to collapse the panels.

4. Click the **Expand Panels arrow** to expand the panels.

5. Click **Window** on the Application bar, then click **Swatches** to deselect it.

   TIP You can hide all open panels by pressing [Shift], then [Tab], then show them by pressing [Shift], then [Tab] again. To hide all open panels, the options bar, and the Tools panel, press [Tab], then show them by pressing [Tab] again.

6. Click **Window** on the Application bar, then click **Swatches** to redisplay the Swatches panel.

You collapsed and expanded the panels, then used the Window menu to show and hide the Swatches panel. You might want to hide panels at times in order to enlarge your work area.

FIGURE 23
Active Swatches panel

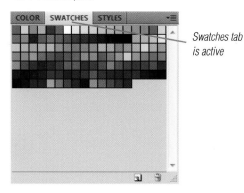

Swatches tab is active

DESIGNTIP **Balancing objects**

The **optical center** occurs approximately three-eighths from the top of the page and is the point around which objects on the page are balanced. Once the optical center is located, objects can be positioned around it. A page can have a symmetrical or asymmetrical balance relative to an imaginary vertical line in the center of the page. In a **symmetrical balance**, objects are placed equally on either side of the vertical line. This type of layout tends toward a restful, formal design. In an **asymmetrical balance,** objects are placed unequally relative to the vertical line. Asymmetrical balance uses white space to balance the positioned objects, and is more dynamic and informal. A page with objects arranged asymmetrically tends to provide more visual interest because it is more surprising in appearance.

DESIGNTIP **Considering ethical implications**

Because Photoshop enables you to make so many dramatic changes to images, you should consider the ethical ramifications and implications of altering images. Is it proper or appropriate to alter an image just because you have the technical expertise to do so? Are there any legal responsibilities or liabilities involved in making these alterations? Because the general public is more aware about the topic of **intellectual property** (an image or idea that is owned and retained by legal control) with the increased availability of information and content, you should make sure you have the legal right to alter an image, especially if you plan on displaying or distributing the image to others. Know who retains the rights to an image, and if necessary, make sure you have written permission for its use, alteration, and/or distribution. Not taking these precautions could be costly.

FIGURE 24
Save Workspace dialog box

FIGURE 25
Image Size dialog box

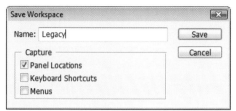

Save Workspace

Name: Legacy

Capture
☑ Panel Locations
☐ Keyboard Shortcuts
☐ Menus

Save
Cancel

Image Size

Pixel Dimensions: 922.9K
Width: 700 pixels
Height: 450 pixels

Document Size:
Width: 1.75 inches
Height: 1.125 inches
Resolution: 400 pixels/inch

☑ Scale Styles
☑ Constrain Proportions
☑ Resample Image:
Bicubic (best for smooth gradients)

OK
Cancel
Auto...

Create a customized workspace

1. Click **Window** on the Application bar, click **History**, then drag the newly displayed panel in the gray space beneath the Swatches panel. (*Hint:* When you drag one panel into another, you'll see a light blue line, indicating that the new panel will dock with the existing panels.)

2. Click **Window** on the Application bar, point to **Workspace**, then click **Save Workspace**.

3. Type **Legacy** in the Name text box, then verify that only **Panel Locations** has a check mark beside it, as shown in Figure 24.

4. Click **Save**.

5. Click **Window** on the Application bar, then point to **Workspace**.

   The name of the new workspace appears on the Window menu.

   TIP You can use the Rotate View tool on the Application bar to *non-destructively* change the orientation of the image canvas. Click the Reset View button on the options bar to restore the canvas to its original angle.

6. Click **Essentials (Default)**.

7. Click the **workspace switcher** on the Application bar, then click **Legacy**.

8. Click the **workspace switcher** on the Application bar, then click **Essentials**.

You created a customized workspace, reset the panel locations, tested the new workspace, then reset the panel locations to the default setting. Customized workspaces provide you with a work area that is always tailored to your needs.

Resizing an image

You may have created the perfect image, but the size may not be correct for your print format. Document size is a combination of the printed dimensions and pixel resolution. An image designed for a website, for example, might be too small for an image that will be printed in a newsletter. You can easily resize an image using the Image Size command on the Image menu. To use this feature, open the file you want to resize, click Image on the Application bar, then click Image Size. The Image Size dialog box, shown in Figure 25, opens. By changing the dimensions in the text boxes, you'll have your image resized in no time. Note the check mark next to Resample Image. With resampling checked, you can change the total number of pixels in the image and the print dimensions independently. With resampling off, you can change either the dimensions or the resolution; Photoshop will automatically adjust whichever value you ignore.

USE THE LAYERS AND HISTORY PANELS

What You'll Do

 In this lesson, you'll hide and display a layer, move a layer on the Layers panel, and then undo the move by deleting the Layer Order state on the History panel.

Learning About Layers

A **layer** is a section within an image that can be manipulated independently. Layers allow you to control individual elements within an image and create great dramatic effects and variations of the same image. Layers enable you to easily manipulate individual characteristics within an image. Each Photoshop file has at least one layer, and can contain many individual layers, or groups of layers.

You can think of layers in a Photoshop image as individual sheets of clear plastic that are in a stack. It's possible for your file to quickly accumulate dozens of layers. The **Layers panel** displays all the layers in an open file. You can use the Layers panel to create, copy, delete, display, hide, merge, lock, group or reposition layers.

QUICKTIP

In Photoshop, using and understanding layers is the key to success.

Setting preferences

The Preferences dialog box contains several topics, each with its own settings: General; Interface; File Handling; Performance; Cursors; Transparency & Gamut; Units & Rulers; Guides, Grid, & Slices; Plug-Ins; Type; and Camera Raw. To open the Preferences dialog box, click Edit (Win) or Photoshop (Mac) on the Application bar, point to Preferences, then click a topic that represents the settings you want to change. If you move panels around the workspace, or make other changes to them, you can choose to retain those changes the next time you start the program. To always start a new session with default panels, click Interface on the Preferences menu, deselect the Remember Panel Locations check box, then click OK. Each time you start Photoshop, the panels will be reset to their default locations and values.

Understanding the Layers Panel

The order in which the layers appear on the Layers panel matches the order in which they appear in the image; the topmost layer in the Layers panel is the topmost layer on the image. You can make a layer active by clicking its name on the Layers panel. When a layer is active, it is highlighted on the Layers panel, and the name of the layer appears in parentheses in the image title bar. Only one layer can be active at a time. Figure 26 shows an image with its Layers panel. Do you see that this image contains six layers? Each layer can be moved or modified individually on the panel to give a different effect to the overall image. If you look at the Layers panel, you'll see that the Finger Painting text layer is dark, indicating that it is currently active.

QUICKTIP

Get in the habit of shifting your eye from the image in the work area to the Layers panel. Knowing which layer is active will save you time and help you troubleshoot an image.

Displaying and Hiding Layers

You can use the Layers panel to control which layers are visible in an image. You can show or hide a layer by clicking the Indicates layer visibility button next to the layer thumbnail. When a layer is hidden, you are not able to merge it with another, select it, or print it. Hiding some layers can

make it easier to focus on particular areas of an image.

Using the History Panel

Photoshop records each task you complete in an image on the **History panel**. This record of events, called states, makes it easy to see what changes occurred and the tools or commands that you used to make the modifications. The History panel, shown in Figure 26, displays up to 20 states and automatically updates the list to display the most recently performed tasks. The list contains

the name of the tool or command used to change the image. You can delete a state on the History panel by selecting it and dragging it to the Delete current state button. Deleting a state is equivalent to using the Undo command. You can also use the History panel to create a new image from any state.

QUICKTIP

When you delete a History state, you undo all the events that occurred after that state.

FIGURE 26
Layers and History panels

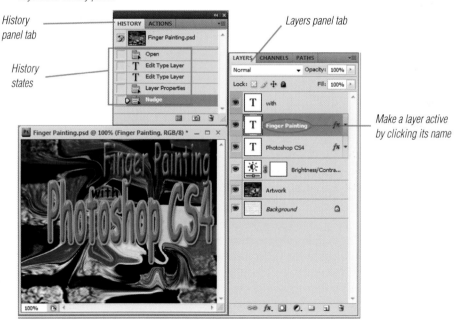

History panel tab

History states

Layers panel tab

Make a layer active by clicking its name

Hide and display a layer

1. Click the **Toddler layer** on the Layers panel.

   TIP   Depending on the size of the window, you might only be able to see the initial characters of the layer name.

2. Verify that the **Show Transform Controls check box** on the options bar is not checked, then click the **Indicates layer visibility button** on the Toddler layer to display the image, as shown in Figure 27.

   TIP   By default, transparent areas of an image have a checkerboard display on the Layers panel.

3. Click the **Indicates layer visibility button** on the Toddler layer to hide the layer.

You made the Toddler layer active on the Layers panel, then clicked the Indicates layer visibility button to display and hide a layer. Hiding layers is an important skill that can be used to remove distracting elements. Once you've finished working on a specific layer, you can display the additional layers.

FIGURE 27
Playground image

Visible Toddler layer

Indicates layer visibility button

Toddler layer

DESIGNTIP   **Overcoming the fear of white space**

One design element that is often overlooked is *white space*. It's there on every page, and it doesn't seem to be doing much, does it? Take a look at a typical page in this book. Is every inch of space filled with either text or graphics? Of course not. If it were it would be impossible to read and it would be horribly ugly. The best example of the use of white space are the margins surrounding a page. This white space acts as a visual barrier—a resting place for the eyes. Without white space, the words on a page would crowd into each other, and the effect would be a cramped, cluttered, and hard to read page. Thoughtful use of white space makes it possible for you to guide the reader's eye from one location on the page to another. For many, one of the first design hurdles that must be overcome is the irresistible urge to put too much *stuff* on a page. When you are new to design, you may want to fill each page completely. Remember, less is more. Think of white space as a beautiful frame setting off an equally beautiful image.

FIGURE 28

Layer moved in Layers panel

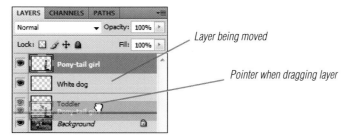

Layer being moved

Pointer when dragging layer

FIGURE 29

Result of moved layer

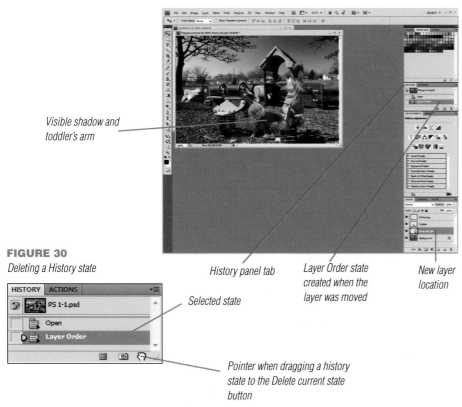

Visible shadow and toddler's arm

FIGURE 30

Deleting a History state

History panel tab

Selected state

Layer Order state created when the layer was moved

New layer location

Pointer when dragging a history state to the Delete current state button

Move a layer on the Layers panel and delete a state on the History panel

1. Click the **Indicates layer visibility button** on the Toddler layer on the Layers panel.

2. Click the **workspace switcher list arrow** on the Application bar, then click **Legacy**.

3. Click and drag the **Pony-tail girl layer** on the Layers panel, beneath the Toddler layer in the panel, as shown in Figure 28.

   The shadow of the toddler is now visible. See Figure 29.

4. Click **Layer Order** on the History panel, then drag it to the **Delete current state button** on the History panel, as shown in Figure 30.

   TIP Each time you close and reopen an image, the History panel is cleared.

   The shadow of the toddler is now less visible.

5. Click **File** on the Application bar, then click **Save**.

You moved the Pony-tail girl layer so it was behind the Toddler layer, then returned it to its original position by dragging the Layer Order state to the Delete current state button on the History panel. You can easily use the History panel to undo what you've done.

LEARN ABOUT PHOTOSHOP
BY USING HELP

What You'll Do

 In this lesson, you'll open Help, then view and find information from the list of topics and the Search feature.

Understanding the Power of Help

Photoshop features an extensive Help system that you can use to access definitions, explanations, and useful tips. Help information is displayed in a browser window, so you must have web browser software installed on your computer to view the information; however, you do not need an Internet connection to use Photoshop Help.

Using Help Topics

The Home page of the Help window has links in the right pane that you can use to retrieve information about Photoshop commands and features. In the left pane is a list of topics from which you can choose. Help items have a plus sign (+) to the left of the topic name. The plus sign (+) indicates that there are subtopics found within. To see the subtopics, click the plus sign (+). Topics and subtopics are links, meaning that the text is clickable. When you click any of the links, the right pane will display information (which may also contain links). The Search feature is located in a tab on the toolbar (above the left and right panes) in the form of a text box. You can search the Photoshop Help System by typing in the text box, then pressing [Enter] (Win) or [return] (Mac).

FIGURE 31
Topics in the Help window

Help links

FIGURE 32

Contents section of the Help window

Choosing
Colors topic in
Contents

Subtopic

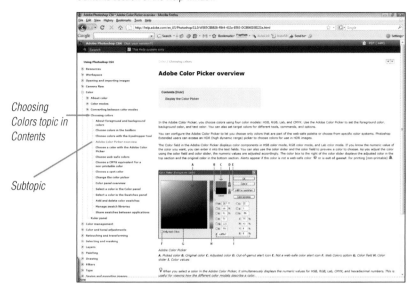

Find information in Contents

1. Click **Help** on the Application bar, then click **Photoshop Help**.

    TIP   You can also open the Help window by pressing **[F1]** (Win) or ⌘ **[/]** (Mac).

2. Click the **plus sign (+)** to the left of the word **Color**.

3. Click **the plus sign (+)** to the left of **Choosing colors**, then click **Adobe Color Picker overview** in the left pane. See Figure 32.

    TIP   You can maximize the window (if you want to take advantage of the full screen display).

    Bear in mind that Help is web-driven and, like any web site, can change as errors and inconsistencies are found.

You used the Photoshop Help command on the Help menu to open the Help window and view a topic in Contents.

Understanding the differences between monitor, images, and device resolution

Image resolution is determined by the number of pixels per inch (ppi) that are printed on a page. Pixel dimensions (the number of pixels along the height and width of a bitmap image) determine the amount of detail in an image, while image resolution controls the amount of space over which the pixels are printed. High resolution images show greater detail and more subtle color transitions than low resolution images. Device resolution or printer resolution is measured by the ink dots per inch (dpi) produced by printers. You can set the resolution of your computer monitor to determine the detail with which images will be displayed. Each monitor should be calibrated to describe how the monitor reproduces colors. Monitor calibration is one of the first things you should do because it determines whether your colors are being accurately represented, which in turn determines how accurately your output will match your design intentions.

Get help and support

1. Click **Help** on the Application bar, then click **Photoshop Help**.

2. Click the **link** beneath the Community Help icon (*http://www.adobe.com/go/lr_Photoshop_community*). Compare your Help window to Figure 33.

You accessed the Community Help feature.

FIGURE 33
Community Help window

Using How-To Help features

Using Help would always be easy if you knew the name of the feature you wanted up look up. To help you find out how to complete common tasks, Photoshop has a listing of "How-To's" in the Help menu. Click Help on the Application bar, point to the How-To you'd like to read, as shown in Figure 34, then click the item about which you want more information.

FIGURE 34
How-To Help topics

Getting Started with Adobe Photoshop CS4

FIGURE 35
Search text box in Help

Search text box

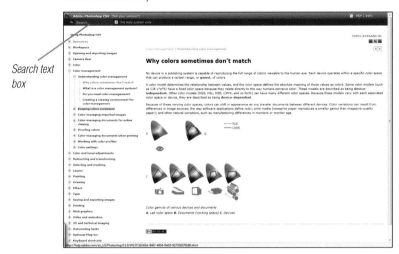

FIGURE 36
Additional keyboard shortcuts

Keys for using panels

This is not a complete list of keyboard shortcuts. This table lists only those shortcuts that are not displayed in menu commands or tool tips.

Result	Windows	Mac OS
Set options (except for Actions, Animation, Styles, Brushes, Tool Presets, and Layer Comps panels)	Alt-click New button	Option-click New button
Delete without confirmation (except for the Brushes panel)	Alt-click Delete button	Option-click Delete button
Apply value and keep text box active	Shift + Enter	Shift + Return
Load as a selection	Control-click channel, layer, or path thumbnail.	Command-click channel, layer, or path thumbnail.
Add to current selection	Control + Shift-click channel, layer, or path thumbnail.	Command + Shift-click channel, layer, or path thumbnail.
Subtract from current selection	Control + Alt-click channel, path, or layer thumbnail.	Command + Option-click channel, path, or layer thumbnail.
Intersect with current selection	Control + Shift + Alt-click channel, path, or layer thumbnail.	Command + Shift + Option-click channel, path, or layer thumbnail.
Show/Hide all panels	Tab	Tab
Show/Hide all panels except the toolbox and options bar	Shift + Tab	Shift + Tab
Highlight options bar	Select tool and press Enter	Select tool and press Return
Increase/decrease units by 10 in a pop-up menu	Shift + Up Arrow/Down Arrow	Shift + Up Arrow/Down Arrow

Find information using Search

1. Click the **Search text box** in the Help window.

2. Type **print quality**, then press **[Enter]** (Win) or **[return]** (Mac).

   TIP   You can search for multiple words by inserting a space; do not use punctuation in the text box.

3. Scroll down the left pane (if necessary), click **2** or **Next** to go to the next page, scroll down (if necessary), click **Why colors sometimes don't match**, then compare your Help screen to Figure 35.

4. Click the **Close box** on your browser window or tab when you are finished reading the topic.

You entered a search term, viewed search results, then closed the Help window.

Finding hidden keyboard shortcuts

There are oodles of keyboard shortcuts in Photoshop, and not all of them are listed in menus. Figure 36 contains a table of additional keyboard shortcuts that are not available on menus or ScreenTips. You can find this help topic by searching on keyboard shortcuts.

VIEW AND PRINT
AN IMAGE

What You'll Do

In this lesson, you'll use the Zoom tool on the Application bar and Tools panel to increase and decrease your views of the image. You'll also change the page orientation settings in the Page Setup dialog box, and print the image.

Getting a Closer Look

When you edit an image in Photoshop, it is important that you have a good view of the area that you are focusing on. Photoshop has a variety of methods that allow you to enlarge or reduce your current view. You can use the Zoom tool by clicking the image to zoom in on (magnify the view) or zoom out of (reduce the view) areas of your image. Zooming in or out enlarges or reduces your *view*, not the actual image. The maximum zoom factor is 1600%. The current zoom percentage appears in the document's title bar, on the Navigator panel, on the status bar, and on the Application bar. When the Zoom tool is selected, the options bar provides additional choices for changing your view, as shown in Figure 37. For example, the Resize Windows To Fit check box automatically resizes the window whenever you magnify or reduce the view. You can also change the zoom percentage using the Navigator panel and the status bar by typing a new value in the zoom text box.

Printing Your Image

In many cases, a professional print shop might be the best option for printing a Photoshop image to get the highest quality. Lacking a professional print shop, you can print a Photoshop image using a standard black-and-white or color printer from within Photoshop, or you can switch to Bridge and then choose to send output to a PDF or Web Gallery. The printed image will be a composite of all visible layers. The quality of your printer and paper will affect the appearance of your output. The Page Setup dialog box displays options for printing, such as paper orientation. **Orientation** is the direction in which an image appears on the page. In **portrait orientation**, the image is printed with the shorter edges of the paper at the top and bottom. In **landscape orientation**, the image is printed with the longer edges of the paper at the top and bottom.

Use the Print command when you want to print multiple copies of an image. Use the Print One Copy command to print a single copy without making dialog box selections, and use the Print dialog box when you want to handle color values using color management.

Understanding Color Handling in Printing

The Print dialog box that opens when you click Print on the File menu lets you determine how colors are output. You can click the Color Handling list arrow to choose whether to use color management, and whether Photoshop or the printing device should control this process. If you let Photoshop determine the colors, Photoshop performs any necessary conversions to color values appropriate for the selected printer. If you choose to let the printer determine the colors, the printer will convert document color values to the corresponding printer color values. In this scenario, Photoshop does not alter the color values. If no color management is selected, no color values will be changed when the image is printed.

Viewing an Image in Multiple Views

You can use the New Window command (accessed by pointing to Arrange on the Window menu) to open multiple views of the same image. You can change the zoom percentage in each view so you can spotlight the areas you want to modify, and then modify the specific area of the image in each view. Because you are working on the same image in multiple views, not in multiple versions, Photoshop automatically applies the changes you make in one view to all views. Although you can close the views you no longer need at any time, Photoshop will not save any changes until you save the file.

FIGURE 37
Zoom tool options bar

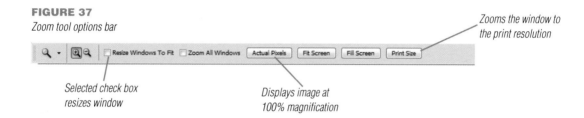

Zooms the window to the print resolution

Selected check box resizes window

Displays image at 100% magnification

Choosing a Photoshop version

You may have noticed that the title bar on the images in this book say 'Adobe Photoshop CS4 Extended'. What's that about? Well, the release of the Adobe Creative Suite 4 offers two versions of Photoshop: Adobe Photoshop CS4 and Adobe Photoshop CS4 Extended. The Extended version has additional animation and measurement features and is ideal for multimedia creative professionals, film and video creative professionals, graphic and web designers who push the limits of 3D and motion, as well as those professionals in the fields of manufacturing, medicine, architecture, engineering and construction, and science and research. Photoshop CS4 is ideal for professional photographers, serious amateur photographers, graphic and web designers, and print service providers.

Use the Zoom tool

1. Click the **Indicates layer visibility button** 👁 on the Layers panel for the Toddler layer so the layer is no longer displayed.

2. Click the **Zoom tool** 🔍 on the Application bar.

   TIP You can also click the Zoom tool on the Tools panel.

3. Select the **Resize Windows To Fit check box** (if it is not already selected) on the options bar.

4. Position the **Zoom In pointer** ⊕ over the center of the image, then click the **image**.

   TIP Position the pointer over the part of the image you want to keep in view.

5. Press **[Alt]** (Win) or **[option]** (Mac), then when the Zoom Out pointer appears, click the center of the image twice with the **Zoom Out pointer** ⊖.

6. Release **[Alt]** (Win) or **[option]** (Mac), then compare your image to Figure 38.

   The zoom factor for the image is 66.7%. Your zoom factor may differ.

You selected the Zoom tool on the Tools panel and used it to zoom in to and out of the image. The Zoom tool makes it possible to see the detail in specific areas of an image, or to see the whole image at once, depending on your needs.

FIGURE 38
Reduced image

Zoom tool options

Zoom percentage changed

Zoom tool on Tools panel

FIGURE 39
Navigator panel

Viewed area of image

Using the Navigator panel

You can change the magnification factor of an image using the Navigator panel or the Zoom tool on the Tools panel. You can open the Navigator panel by clicking Window on the Application bar, then clicking Navigator. By double-clicking the Zoom text box on the Navigator panel, you can enter a new magnification factor, then press [Enter] (Win) or [return] (Mac). The magnification factor—shown as a percentage—is displayed in the lower-left corner of the Navigator panel, as shown in Figure 39. The red border in the panel, called the Proxy Preview Area, defines the area of the image that is magnified. You can drag the Proxy Preview Area inside the Navigator panel to view other areas of the image at the current magnification factor.

Getting Started with Adobe Photoshop CS4

FIGURE 40
Page Setup dialog box

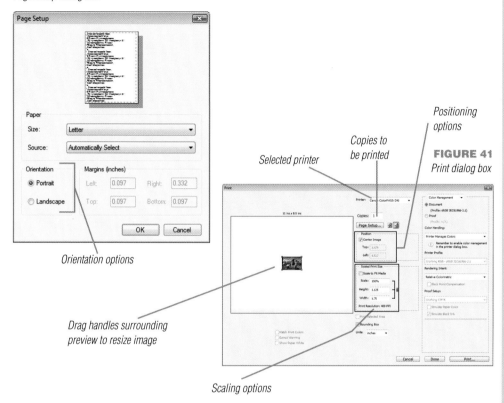

Orientation options

Drag handles surrounding
preview to resize image

Scaling options

Selected printer

Copies to
be printed

Positioning
options

FIGURE 41
Print dialog box

Modify print settings

1. Click **File** on the Application bar, then click **Page Setup** to open the Page Setup dialog box, as shown in Figure 40.

   TIP If you have not selected a printer using the Print Center, a warning box might appear (Mac).

   Page setup and print settings vary slightly in Macintosh.

2. Click the **Landscape option button** in the Orientation section (Win) or **Click the Landscape icon** (Mac), then click **OK**.

   TIP Choose either Landscape option (Mac).

3. Click **File** on the Application bar, click **Print**, then click **Proceed** in the message box that opens. If a PostScript dialog box opens, click **OK** (Mac).

4. Make sure that **1** appears in the Copies text box, then click **Print**. See Figure 41.

   TIP You can use the handles surrounding the image preview in the Print dialog box to scale the print size.

You used the Page Setup command on the File menu to open the Page Setup dialog box, changed the page orientation, then printed the image. Changing the page orientation can make an image fit better on a printed page.

Previewing and creating a Proof Setup

You can create and save a Proof Setup, which lets you preview your image to see how it will look when printed on a specific device. This feature lets you see how colors can be interpreted by different devices. By using this feature, you can decrease the chance that the colors on the printed copy of the image will vary from what you viewed on your monitor. Create a custom proof by clicking View on the Application bar, pointing to Proof Setup, then clicking Custom. Specify the conditions in the Customize Proof Condition dialog box, then click OK. Each proof setup has the .psf extension and can be loaded by clicking View on the Application bar, pointing to Proof Setup, clicking Custom, then clicking Load.

Create a PDF with Bridge

1. Click the **Launch Bridge button** 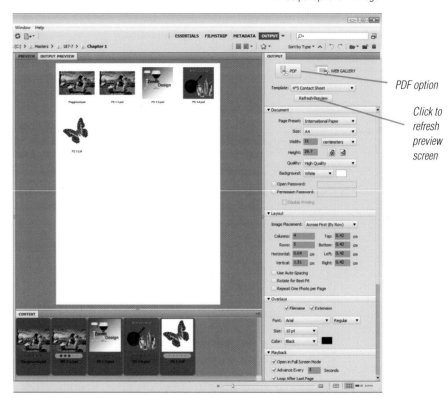 on the Application bar.

2. Click the **Folders tab** (if necessary), then click **Chapter 1** in the location where your Data Files are stored in the Folders tab (if necessary).

3. Click the **Output button** in the Bridge options bar.

4. Click the **PDF button** in the Output tab.

5. Click **Playground.psd,** hold [**Shift**], click **PS 1-4.psd** in the Content tab, then release [**Shift**].

6. Click the **Template list arrow**, click ***5 Contact Sheet**, click **Refresh Preview**, then compare your screen to Figure 1-42.

7. Scroll down the Output panel, click **Save,** locate the folder where your Data Files are stored, type **your name Chapter 1 files** in the text box, then click **Save.** You may need to click OK to close a warning box.

You launched Adobe Bridge, then generated a PDF which was printed using Adobe Acrobat.

FIGURE 42
PDF Output options in Bridge

PDF option

Click to refresh preview screen

DESIGNTIP   **Using contrast to add emphasis**

Contrast is an important design principle that uses opposing elements, such as colors or lines, to produce an inten-sified effect in an image, page, or publication. Just as you can use a font attribute to make some text stand out from the rest, you can use contrasting elements to make certain graphic objects stand out. You can create contrast in many ways: by changing the sizes of objects; by varying object weights, such as making a line heavier surrounding an image; by altering the position of an object, such as changing the location on the page, or rotating the image so it is positioned on an angle; by drawing attention-getting shapes or a colorful box behind an object that makes it stand out (called a **matte**); or by adding carefully selected colors that emphasize an object.

FIGURE 43

Web Gallery options in Bridge

Web Gallery
button

Create a Web Gallery with Bridge

1. Verify that Bridge is open.

2. Click the **Web Gallery button** in the Output tab, click **Refresh Preview**, then compare your screen to Figure 43.

3. Click the **View Slideshow button** in the Output Preview window, then click the **Play Slideshow button**.

4. Scroll down the Output panel, click the **Save to Disk option button**, click the **Browse button**, locate the folder where your Data Files are stored, then click **OK** (Win) or **Choose** (Mac).

5. Click **Save** in the Create Gallery section of the Output panel, then click **OK** when the Gallery has been created.

6. Click **File** on the Bridge menu, then click **Exit** (Win) or click **Adobe Bridge CS4**, then click **Quit Adobe Bridge CS4** (Mac).

You launched Adobe Bridge, then generated a Web Gallery.

CLOSE A FILE
AND EXIT PHOTOSHOP

What You'll Do

New...	Ctrl+N
Open...	Ctrl+O
Browse in Bridge...	Alt+Ctrl+O
Open As...	Alt+Shift+Ctrl+O
Open As Smart Object...	
Open Recent	▸
Share My Screen...	
Device Central...	
Close	Ctrl+W
Close All	Alt+Ctrl+W
Close and Go To Bridge...	Shift+Ctrl+W
Save	Ctrl+S
Save As...	Shift+Ctrl+S
Check In...	
Save for Web & Devices...	Alt+Shift+Ctrl+S
Revert	F12
Place...	
Import	▸
Export	▸
Automate	▸
Scripts	▸
File Info...	Alt+Shift+Ctrl+I
Page Setup...	Shift+Ctrl+P
Print...	Ctrl+P
Print One Copy	Alt+Shift+Ctrl+P
Exit	Ctrl+Q

 In this lesson, you'll use the Close and Exit (Win) or Quit (Mac) commands to close a file and exit Photoshop.

Concluding Your Work Session

At the end of your work session, you might have opened several files; you now need to decide which ones you want to save.

QUICKTIP

If you share a computer with other people, it's a good idea to reset Photoshop's preferences back to their default settings. You can do so when you start Photoshop by clicking Window on the Application bar, pointing to Workspace, then clicking Essentials (Default).

Closing Versus Exiting

When you are finished working on an image, you need to save and close it. You can close one file at a time, or close all open files at the same time by exiting the program. Closing a file leaves Photoshop open, which allows you to open or create another file. Exiting Photoshop closes the file, closes Photoshop, and returns you to the desktop, where you can choose to open another program or shut down the computer. Photoshop will prompt you to save any changes before it closes the files. If you do not modify a new or existing file, Photoshop will close it automatically when you exit.

QUICKTIP

To close all open files, click File on the Application bar, then click Close All.

Using Adobe online

Periodically, when you start Photoshop, an Update dialog box might appear, prompting you to search for updates or new information on the Adobe website. If you click Yes, Photoshop will automatically notify you that a download is available; however, you do not have to select it. You can also obtain information about Photoshop from the Adobe Photoshop website (*www.adobe.com/products/photoshop/main.html*), where you can link to downloads, tips, training, galleries, examples, and other support topics.

FIGURE 44
Closing a file using the File menu

Workspace
switcher

Close command

Exit command

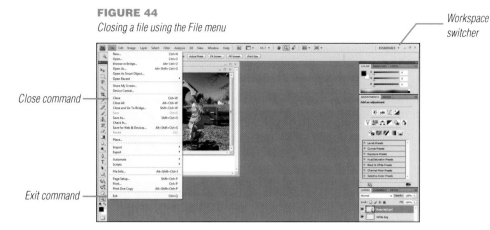

Close a file and exit Photoshop

1. Click the **workspace switcher**, then click **Essentials**.

2. Click **File** on the Application bar, then compare your screen to Figure 44.

3. Click **Close**.

   TIP   You can close an open file (without closing Photoshop) by clicking the Close button in the image window. Photoshop will prompt you to save any unsaved changes before closing the file.

4. If asked to save your work, click **Yes** (Win) or **Save** (Mac).

5. Click **File** on the Application bar, then click **Exit** (Win) or click **Photoshop** on the Application bar, then click **Quit Photoshop** (Mac).

   TIP   To exit Photoshop and close an open file, click the Close button in the program window. Photoshop will prompt you to save any unsaved changes before closing.

6. If asked to save your work (the untitled file), click **No**.

You closed the current file and exited the program by using the Close and Exit (Win) or Quit (Mac) commands.

DESIGNTIP   **Using a scanner and a digital camera**

If you have a scanner, you can import print images, such as those taken from photographs, magazines, or line drawings, into Photoshop. Remember that images taken from magazines are owned by others, and that you need permission to distribute them. There are many types of scanners, including flatbed or single-sheet feed. You can also use a digital camera to create your own images. A digital camera captures images as digital files and stores them on some form of electronic medium, such as a SmartMedia card or memory stick. After you upload the images from your camera to your computer, you can work with images in Photoshop.

You can open a scanned or uploaded image (which usually has a .jpg extension or another graphics file format) by clicking File on the Application bar, then clicking Open. All Formats is the default file type, so you should be able to see all available image files in the Open dialog box. Locate the folder containing your scanned or digital camera images, click the file you want to open, then click Open. A scanned or digital camera image contains all its imagery in a single layer. You can add layers to the image, but you can only save these new layers if you save the image as a Photoshop image (with the extension .psd).

Power User Shortcuts

Key: Menu items are indicated by ➤ between the menu name and its command. Blue bold letters are shortcuts for selecting tools on the Tools panel.

to do this:	use this method:
Close a file	[Ctrl][W] (Win) ⌘[W] (Mac)
Create a new file	[Ctrl][N] (Win), ⌘[N] (Mac)
Create a workspace	Window ➤ Workspace ➤ Save Workspace
Drag a layer	✋
Exit Photoshop	[Ctrl][Q] (Win), ⌘[Q] (Mac)
Hide a layer	👁
Lasso tool	🔗 or L
Modify workspace display	ESSENTIALS ▾
Open a file	[Ctrl][O] (Win), ⌘[O] (Mac)
Launch Bridge	Br
Open Help	[F1] (Win), ⌘ [/] (Mac)
Open Preferences dialog box	[Ctrl][K] (Win) ⌘[K] (Mac)
Page Setup	[Shift][Ctrl][P] (Win) [Shift]⌘[P] (Mac)
Print File	File ➤ Print or, [Ctrl][P] (Win) ⌘[P] (Mac)

to do this:	use this method:
Reset preferences to default settings	[Shift][Alt][Ctrl] (Win) [Shift] option ⌘ (Mac)
Save a file	[Ctrl][S] (Win) ⌘[S] (Mac)
Show a layer	☐
Show hidden lasso tools	[Shift] L
Show History panel	🔳
Show or hide all open panels	[Shift][Tab]
Show or hide all open panels, the options bar, and the Tools panel	[Tab]
Show or hide Swatches panel	Window ➤ Swatches
Use Save As	[Shift][Ctrl][S] (Win) [Shift]⌘[S] (Mac)
Zoom in	🔍 [Ctrl][+] (Win), ⌘[+] (Mac)
Zoom out	[Alt] 🔍 (Win) [Ctrl][−] (Win), ⌘[−] (Mac)
Zoom tool	🔍 or Z

Getting Started with Adobe Photoshop CS4

Start Adobe Photoshop CS4.

1. Start Photoshop.
2. Create a new image that is 500 × 500 pixels, accept the default resolution, then name and save it as **Review**.

Open and save an image.

1. Open PS 1-3.psd from the drive and folder where you store your Data Files, and if prompted, update the text layers.
2. Save it as **Zenith Design Logo**.

Use organizational and management features.

1. Open Adobe Bridge.
2. Click the Folders tab, then locate the folder that contains your Data Files.
3. Close Adobe Bridge.

Examine the Photoshop window.

1. Locate the image title bar and the current zoom percentage.
2. Locate the menu you use to open an image.
3. View the Tools panel, the options bar, and the panels that are showing.
4. Click the Move tool on the Tools panel, then view the Move tool options on the options bar.
5. Create, save and display a customized workspace (based on Essentials) called History and Layers that captures panel locations and displays the History panel above the Layers panel.

Use the Layers and History panels.

1. Drag the Wine Glasses layer so it is above the Zenith layer, then use the History panel to undo the state.

2. Drag the Wine Glasses layer above the Zenith layer again.
3. Use the Indicates layer visibility button to hide the Wine Glasses layer.
4. Make the Wine Glasses layer visible again.
5. Hide the Zenith layer.
6. Show the Zenith layer.
7. Show the Tag Line layer.

Learn about Photoshop by using Help.

1. Open the Adobe Photoshop CS4 Help window.
2. Using the Index, find information about resetting to the default workspace.

3. Print the information you find.

4. Close the Help window.

View and print an image.

1. Make sure that all the layers are visible in the Layers panel.

2. Click the Zoom tool, then make sure the setting is selected to resize the window to fit.

3. Zoom in on the wine glasses twice.

4. Zoom out to the original perspective.

5. Print one copy of the image.

6. Save your work.

Close a file and exit Photoshop.

1. Compare your screen to Figure 45, then close the Zenith Design Logo file.

2. Close the Review file.

3. Exit (Win) or Quit (Mac) Photoshop.

FIGURE 45
Completed Skills Review

Getting Started with Adobe Photoshop CS4

As a new Photoshop user, you are comforted knowing that Photoshop's Help system provides definitions, explanations, procedures, and other helpful information. It also includes examples and demonstrations to show how Photoshop features work. You use the Help system to learn about image size and resolution.

1. Open the Photoshop Help window.
2. Click the Workspace topic in the topics list.
3. Click the Panels and menus subtopic, in the left pane, then click Enter values in panels, dialog boxes, and the options bar topic.
4. Click the Display context menus topic, then read this topic.
5. Click the Opening and importing images topic in the left pane.
6. Click the Image size and resolution topic in the left pane, then click About monitor resolution. Print out this topic, then compare your screen to the sample shown in Figure 46.

FIGURE 46
Sample Project Builder 1

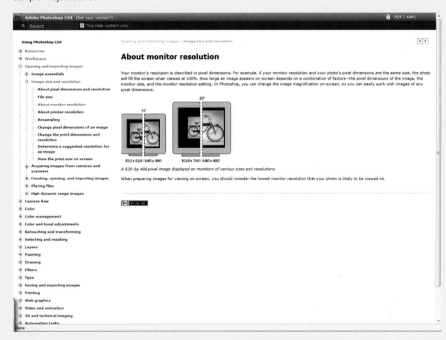

Kitchen Experience, your local specialty cooking shop, has just added herb-infused oils to its product line. They have hired you to draft a flyer that features these new products. You use Photoshop to create this flyer.

1. Open PS 1-4.psd, then save it as **Cooking**.
2. Display the Essentials workspace (if necessary).
3. Make the Measuring Spoons layer visible.
4. Drag the Oils layer so the content appears behind the Skillet layer content.
5. Drag the Measuring Spoons layer above the Skillet layer.
6. Save the file, then compare your image to the sample shown in Figure 47.

FIGURE 47
Sample Project Builder 2

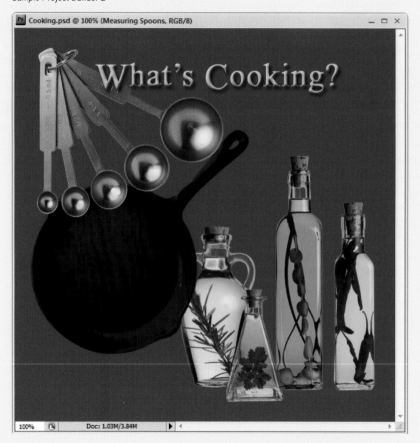

DESIGN PROJECT

As an avid, albeit novice Photoshop user, you have grasped the importance of how layers affect your image. With a little practice, you can examine a single-layer image and guess which objects might display on their own layers. Now, you're ready to examine the images created by Photoshop experts and critique them on their use of layers.

1. Connect to the Internet, and use your browser to find interesting artwork located on at least two websites.
2. Download a single-layer image (in its native format) from each website.
3. Start Photoshop, then open the downloaded images.
4. Save one image as **Critique-1** and the other as **Critique-2** in the Photoshop format (use the .psd extension).
5. Analyze each image for its potential use of layers.

6. Open the File Info dialog box for Critique-1.psd, then type in the Description section your speculation as to the number of layers there might be in the image, their possible order on the Layers panel, and how moving the layers would affect the image.

7. Close the dialog box.

8. Compare your image to the sample shown in Figure 48, then close the files.

FIGURE 48
Sample Design Project

You are preparing to work on a series of design projects to enhance your portfolio. You decide to see what information on digital imaging is available on the Adobe website. You also want to increase your familiarity with the Adobe website so that you can take advantage of product information and support, user tips and feedback, and become a more skilled Photoshop user.

1. Connect to the Internet and go to the Adobe website at *www.adobe.com.*
2. Point to Products, then find the link for the Photoshop family, as shown in Figure 49.
3. Use the links on the web page to search for information about digital imaging options.
4. Print the relevant page(s).
5. Start Photoshop and open the Photoshop Help window.

6. Search for information about Adjusting the Monitor Display, then print the relevant page(s).

FIGURE 49
Completed Portfolio Project

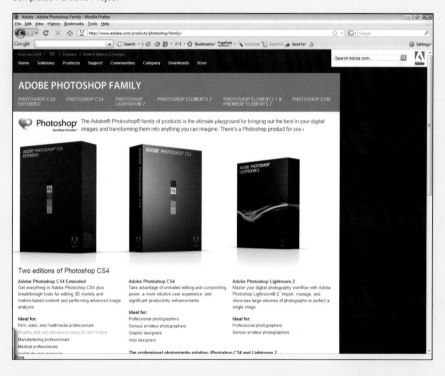

7. Evaluate the information in the documents, and then compare any significant differences.

2

WORKING
WITH LAYERS

1. Examine and convert layers

2. Add and delete layers

3. Add a selection from one image to another

4. Organize layers with layer groups and colors

2 WORKING
WITH LAYERS

Layers Are Everything

You can use Photoshop to create sophisticated images in part because a Photoshop image can contain multiple layers. Each object created in Photoshop can exist on its own individual layer, making it easy to control the position and quality of each layer in the stack. Depending on your computer's resources, you can have a maximum of 8000 layers in each Photoshop image with each layer containing as much or as little detail as necessary.

QUICKTIP

The transparent areas in a layer do not increase file size.

Understanding the Importance of Layers

Layers make it possible to manipulate the tiniest detail within your image, which gives you tremendous flexibility when you make changes. By placing objects, effects, styles, and type on separate layers, you can modify them individually *without* affecting other layers. The advantage to using multiple layers is that you can isolate effects and images on one layer without affecting the others. The disadvantage of using multiple layers is that your file size might become very large. However, once your image is finished, you can dramatically reduce its file size by combining all the layers into one.

Using Layers to Modify an Image

You can add, delete, and move layers in your image. You can also drag a portion of an image, called a **selection**, from one Photoshop image to another. When you do this, a new layer is automatically created. Copying layers from one image to another makes it easy to transfer a complicated effect, a simple image, or a piece of type. You can also hide and display each layer, or change its opacity. **Opacity** is the ability to see through a layer so that layers beneath it are visible. The more opacity a layer has, the less see-through (transparent) it is. You can continuously change the overall appearance of your image by changing the order of your layers, until you achieve just the look you want.

Tools You'll Use

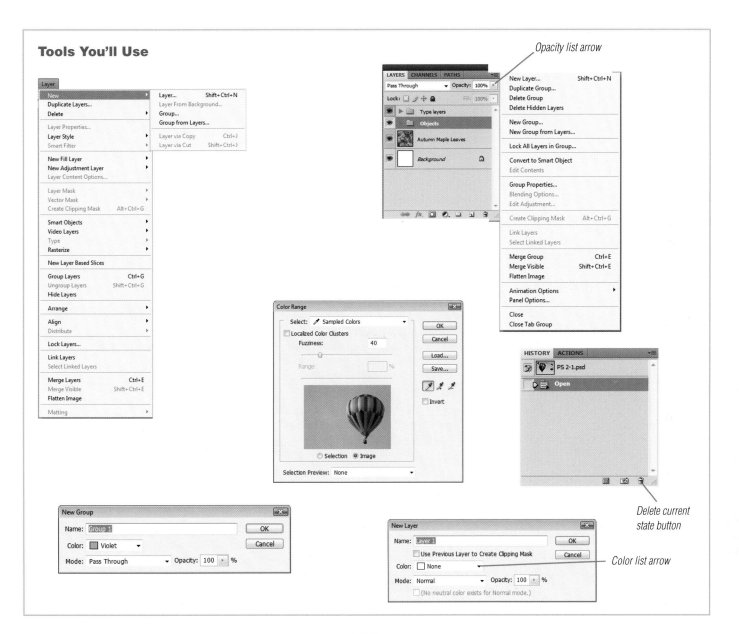

Opacity list arrow

Delete current state button

Color list arrow

EXAMINE AND
CONVERT LAYERS

What You'll Do

 In this lesson, you'll use the Layers panel to delete a Background layer and the Layer menu to create a Background layer from an image layer.

Learning About the Layers Panel

The **Layers panel** lists all the layers within a Photoshop file and makes it possible for you to manipulate one or more layers. By default, this panel is located in the lower-right corner of the screen, but it can be moved to a new location by dragging the panel's tab. In some cases, the entire name of the layer might not appear on the panel. If a layer name is too long, an ellipsis appears, indicating that part of the name is hidden from view. You can view a layer's entire name by holding the pointer over the name until the full name appears. The **layer thumbnail** appears to the left of the layer name and contains a miniature picture of the layer's content, as shown in Figure 1. To the left of the layer thumbnail, you can add color, which you can use to easily identify layers. The Layers panel also contains common buttons, such as the Delete layer button and the Create new layer button.

Recognizing Layer Types

The Layers panel includes several types of layers: Background, type, adjustment, and image (non-type). The Background layer—whose name appears in italics—is always at the bottom of the stack. Type layers—layers that contain text—contain the type layer icon in the layer thumbnail, and image layers display a thumbnail of their contents. Adjustment layers, which make changes to layers, have a variety of thumbnails, depending on the kind of adjustment. Along with dragging selections from one Photoshop image to another, you can also drag objects created in other applications, such as Adobe

Dreamweaver, Adobe InDesign, or Adobe Flash, onto a Photoshop image, which creates a layer containing the object you dragged from the other program window.

Organizing Layers

One of the benefits of using layers is that you can create different design effects by rearranging their order. Figure 2 contains the same layers as Figure 1, but they are arranged differently. Did you notice that the yellow-striped balloon is partially obscured by the black-striped balloon and the lighthouse balloon? This reorganization was created by dragging the layer containing the yellow balloon below the Black striped balloon layer and by dragging the Lighthouse balloon layer above Layer 2 on the Layers panel. When organizing layers, you may find it helpful to resize the Layers panel so you can see more layers within the image.

FIGURE 1
Image with multiple layers

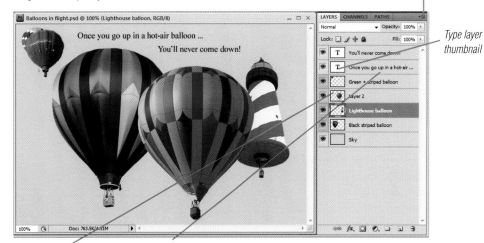

Layers panel list arrow

Type layer thumbnail

Image layer thumbnail

Position mouse over layer name to display full title

FIGURE 2
Layers rearranged

Guide

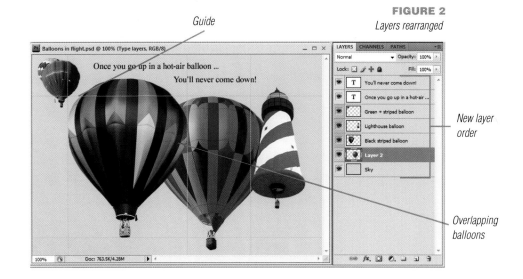

New layer order

Overlapping balloons

Converting Layers

When you open an image created with a digital camera, you'll notice that the entire image appears in the Background layer. The Background layer of any image is the initial layer and is always located at the bottom of the stack. You cannot change its position in the stack, nor can you change its opacity or lighten or darken its colors. You can, however, convert a Background layer into an image layer (non-type layer), and you can convert an image layer into a Background layer. You need to modify the image layer *before* converting it to a Background layer. You might want to convert a Background layer into an image layer so that you can use the full range of editing tools on the layer content. You might want to convert an image layer into a Background layer after you have made all your changes and want it to be the bottom layer in the stack.

Using rulers and changing units of measurement

You can display horizontal and vertical rulers to help you better position elements. To display or hide rulers, click View on the Application bar, then click Rulers. (A check mark to the left of the Rulers command indicates that the rulers are displayed.) In addition to displaying or hiding rulers, you can also choose from various units of measurement. Your choices include pixels, inches, centimeters, millimeters, points, picas, and percentages. Pixels, for example, display more tick marks and can make it easier to make tiny adjustments. You can change the units of measurement by clicking Edit [Win] or Photoshop [Mac] on the Application bar, pointing to Preferences, then clicking Units & Rulers. In the Preferences dialog box, click the Rulers list arrow, click the units you want to use, then click OK. The easiest way to change units of measurement, however, is shown in Figure 3. Once the rulers are displayed, right-click (Win) or [Ctrl]-click (Mac) either the vertical or horizontal ruler, then click the unit of measurement you want. When displayed, the Info panel, displays the current coordinates in your image. Regardless of the units of measurement in use, the X/Y coordinates are displayed in the Info panel.

FIGURE 3
Changing units of measurement

Right-click (Win) or [Ctrl]-click (Mac) to display measurement choices

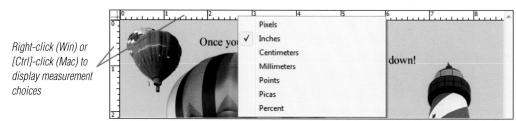

Yout title bar may differ (Mac)

FIGURE 4
Warning box

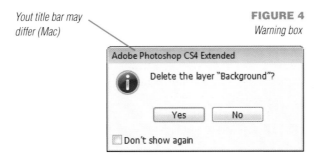

FIGURE 5
Background layer deleted

Background layer no longer present

FIGURE 6
New Background layer added to Layers panel

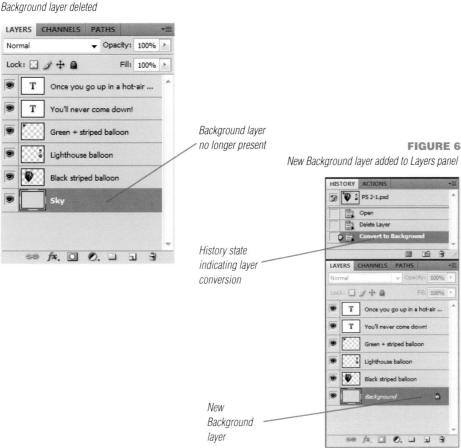

History state indicating layer conversion

New Background layer

Convert an image layer into a Background layer

1. Open PS 2-1.psd from the drive and folder where you store your Data Files, then save it as **Balloons in flight**.

   TIP If you receive a warning box about maximum compatibility, or a message stating that some of the text layers need to be updated before they can be used for vector-based output, and/or a warning box about maximum compatibility, click Update and/or click OK.

2. Click **View** on the Application bar, click **Rulers** if your rulers are not visible, then make sure that the rulers are displayed in pixels.

   TIP If you are unsure which units of measurement are used, right-click (Win) or [Ctrl]-click (Mac) one of the rulers, then verify that Pixels is selected, or click Pixels (if necessary).

3. Click the **workspace switcher** on the Application bar, then click **History and Layers** (created in the Skills Review in Chapter 1).

4. On the Layers panel, scroll down, click the **Background layer**, then click the **Delete layer button** 🗑 .

5. Click **Yes** in the dialog box, as shown in Figure 4, then compare your Layers panel to Figure 5.

6. Click **Layer** on the Application bar, point to **New**, then click **Background From Layer**.

   The Sky layer has been converted into the Background layer. Did you notice that in addition to the image layer being converted to the Background layer that a state now appears on the History panel that says Convert to Background? See Figure 6.

7. Save your work.

You displayed the rulers and switched to a previously created workspace, deleted the Background layer of an image, then converted an image layer into the Background layer. You can convert any layer into the Background layer, as long as you first delete the existing Background layer.

Lesson 1   Examine and Convert Layers

ADD AND DELETE LAYERS

What You'll Do

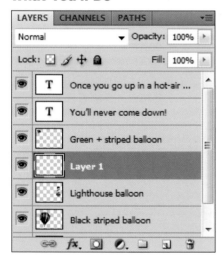

In this lesson, you'll create a new layer using the New command on the Layer menu, delete a layer, and create a new layer using buttons on the Layers panel.

Adding Layers to an Image

Because it's so important to make use of multiple layers, Photoshop makes it easy to add and delete layers. You can create layers in three ways:

- Use the New command on the Layer menu.
- Use the New Layer command on the Layers panel menu.
- Click the Create a new layer button on the Layers panel.

QUICKTIP

See Table 1 for tips on navigating the Layers panel.

Objects on new layers have a default opacity setting of 100%, which means that objects on lower layers are not visible. Each layer

Merging layers

You can combine multiple image layers into a single layer using the merging process. Merging layers is useful when you want to combine multiple layers in order to make specific edits permanent. (This merging process is different from flattening in that it's selective. Flattening merges *all* visible layers.) In order for layers to be merged, they must be visible and next to each other on the Layers panel. You can merge all visible layers within an image, or just the ones you select. Type layers cannot be merged until they are **rasterized** (turned into a bitmapped image layer), or converted into uneditable text. To merge two layers, make sure that they are next to each other and that the Indicates layer visibility button is visible on each layer, then click the layer in the higher position on the Layers panel. Click Layer on the Application bar, then click Merge Down. The active layer and the layer immediately beneath it will be combined into a single layer. To merge all visible layers, click the Layers panel list arrow, then click Merge Visible. Most layer commands that are available on the Layer menu, such as Merge Down, are also available using the Layers panel list arrow.

has the Normal (default) blending mode applied to it. (A **blending mode** is a feature that affects a layer's underlying pixels, and is used to lighten or darken colors.)

Naming a Layer

Photoshop automatically assigns a sequential number to each new layer name, but you can rename a layer at any time. So, if you have four named layers and add a new layer, the default name of the new layer will be Layer 1. Although calling a layer "Layer 12" is fine, you might want to use a more descriptive name so it is easier to distinguish one layer from another. If you use the New command on the Layer menu, you can name the layer when you create it. You can rename a layer at any time by using either of these methods:

- Click the Layers panel list arrow, click Layer Properties, type the name in the Name text box, then click OK.
- Double-click the name on the Layers panel, type the new name, then press [Enter] (Win) or [return] (Mac).

Deleting Layers from an Image

You might want to delete an unused or unnecessary layer. You can use any of four methods to delete a layer:

- Click the name on the Layers panel, click the Layers panel list arrow, then click Delete Layer, as shown in Figure 7.
- Click the name on the Layers panel, click the Delete layer button on the Layers panel, then click Yes in the warning box.
- Click the name on the Layers panel, press and hold [Alt] (Win) or [option]

(Mac), then click the Delete layer button on the Layers panel.

- Drag the layer name on the Layers panel to the Delete layer button on the Layers panel.
- Right-click a layer (Win) or [Ctrl]-click a layer (Mac).

You should be certain that you no longer need a layer before you delete it. If you delete a layer by accident, you can restore it during the current editing session by deleting the Delete Layer state on the History panel.

QUICKTIP

Photoshop always numbers layers sequentially, no matter how many layers you add or delete.

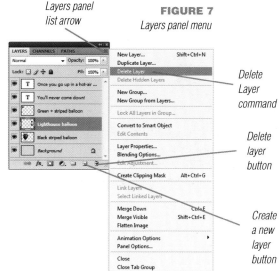

Layers panel list arrow

FIGURE 7
Layers panel menu

Delete Layer command

Delete layer button

Create a new layer button

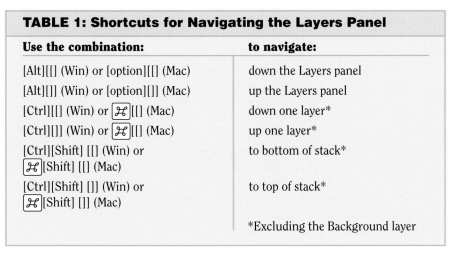

TABLE 1: Shortcuts for Navigating the Layers Panel

Use the combination:	to navigate:
[Alt][[] (Win) or [option][[] (Mac)	down the Layers panel
[Alt][]] (Win) or [option][]] (Mac)	up the Layers panel
[Ctrl][[] (Win) or ⌘[[] (Mac)	down one layer*
[Ctrl][]] (Win) or ⌘[]] (Mac)	up one layer*
[Ctrl][Shift] [[] (Win) or ⌘[Shift] [[] (Mac)	to bottom of stack*
[Ctrl][Shift] []] (Win) or ⌘[Shift] []] (Mac)	to top of stack*
	*Excluding the Background layer

Add a layer using the Layer menu

1. Click the **Lighthouse balloon layer** on the Layers panel.

2. Click **Layer** on the Application bar, point to **New**, then click **Layer** to open the New Layer dialog box, as shown in Figure 8.

   A new layer will be added above the active layer.

   TIP You can change the layer name in the New Layer dialog box before it appears on the Layers panel.

3. Click **OK**.

   The New Layer dialog box closes and the new layer appears above the Lighthouse balloon layer on the Layers panel. The New Layer state is added to the History panel. See Figure 9.

   You created a new layer above the Lighthouse balloon layer using the New command on the Layer menu. The layer does not yet contain any content.

FIGURE 8
New Layer dialog box

FIGURE 9
New layer in Layers panel

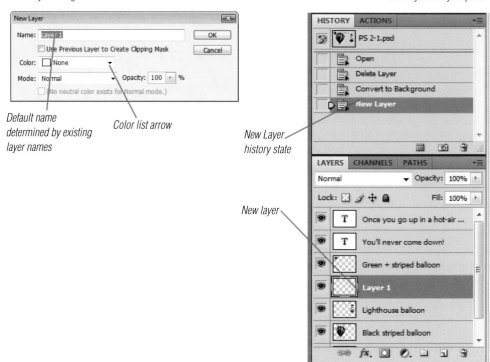

Default name determined by existing layer names

Color list arrow

New Layer history state

New layer

Inserting a layer beneath the active layer

When you add a layer to an image either by using the Layer menu or clicking the Create a new layer button on the Layers panel, the new layer is inserted above the active layer. But there might be times when you want to insert the new layer beneath, or in back of, the active layer. You can do so easily, by pressing [Ctrl] (Win) or ⌘ (Mac) while clicking the Create a new layer button on the Layers panel.

FIGURE 10
New layer with default settings

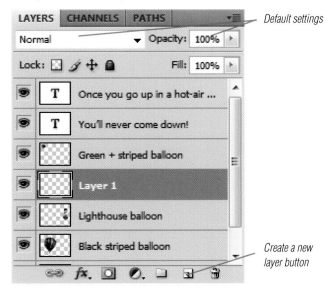

Default settings

Create a new layer button

Delete a layer

1. Position the **Layer selection pointer** 🖑 over Layer 1 on the Layers panel.

2. Drag **Layer 1** to the **Delete layer button** 🗑 on the Layers panel.

   TIP   You can also delete the layer by dragging the New Layer state on the History panel to the Delete current state button.

3. If the Delete the layer "Layer 1" dialog box opens, click the **Don't show again check box**, then click **Yes**.

   TIP   Many dialog boxes let you turn off this reminder feature by selecting the Don't show again check box. Selecting these check boxes can improve your efficiency.

You used the Delete layer button on the Layers panel to delete a layer.

Add a layer using the Layers panel

1. Click the **Lightouse balloon layer** on the Layers panel, if it is not already selected.

2. Click the **Create a new layer button** 🔲 on the Layers panel, then compare your Layers panel to Figure 10.

3. Save your work.

You used the Create a new layer button on the Layers panel to add a new layer.

ADD A SELECTION FROM ONE
IMAGE TO ANOTHER

What You'll Do

In this lesson, you'll use the Invert check box in the Color Range dialog box to make a selection, drag the selection to another image, and remove the fringe from a selection using the Defringe command.

Understanding Selections

Often the Photoshop file you want to create involves using an image or part of an image from another file. To use an image or part of an image, you must first select it. Photoshop refers to this as "making a selection." A selection is an area of an image surrounded by a **marquee**, a dashed line that encloses the area you want to edit or move to another image, as shown in Figure 11. You can drag a marquee around a selection using four marquee tools: Rectangular Marquee, Elliptical Marquee, Single Row Marquee, and Single Column Marquee. Table 2 displays the four marquee tools and other selection tools. You can set options for each tool on the options bar when the tool you want to use is active.

Understanding the Extract and Color Range Commands

In addition to using selection tools, Photoshop provides other methods for incorporating imagery from other files. The **Extract command**, located on the Filter menu, separates an image from a background or surrounding imagery. You can use the **Color Range command**, located on the Select menu, to select a particular color contained in an existing image. Depending on the area you want, you can use the Color Range dialog box to extract a portion of an image.

Cropping an image

You might find an image that you really like, except that it contains a particular portion that you don't need. You can exclude, or **crop**, certain parts of an image by using the Crop tool on the Tools panel. Cropping hides areas of an image from view *without* decreasing resolution quality. To crop an image, click the Crop tool on the Tools panel, drag the pointer around the area you *want to keep*, then press [Enter] (Win) or [return] (Mac).

For example, you can select the Invert check box to choose one color and then select the portion of the image that is every color *except* that one. After you select all the imagery you want from another image, you can drag it into your open file.

Making a Selection and Moving a Selection

You can use a variety of methods and tools to make a selection, which can then be used as a specific part of a layer or as the entire layer. You use selections to isolate an area you want to alter. For example, you can use the Magnetic Lasso tool to select complex shapes by clicking the starting point, tracing an approximate outline, then clicking the ending point. Later, you can use the Crop tool to trim areas from a selection. When you use the Move tool to drag a selection to the destination image, Photoshop places the selection in a new layer above the previously active layer.

Defringing Layer Contents

Sometimes when you make a selection, then move it into another image, the newly selected image can contain unwanted pixels that give the appearance of a fringe, or halo. You can remove this effect using a Matting command called Defringe. This command is available on the Layer menu and allows you to replace fringe pixels with the colors of other nearby pixels. You can determine a width for replacement pixels between 1 and 200. It's magic!

FIGURE 11
Marquee selections

Area selected using the Rectangular Marquee tool

Specific element selected using the Magnetic Lasso tool

TABLE 2: Selection Tools

tool	tool name	tool	tool name
	Rectangular Marquee tool		Lasso tool
	Elliptical Marquee tool		Polygonal Lasso tool
	Single Row Marquee tool		Magnetic Lasso tool
	Single Column Marquee tool		Eraser tool
	Crop tool		Background Eraser tool
	Magic Wand tool		Magic Eraser tool

Make a color range selection

1. Open PS 2-2.psd from the drive and folder where you store your Data Files, save it as **Yellow striped balloon**, click the **title bar**, then drag the **window** to an empty area of the workspace so that you can see both images.

   TIP When more than one file is open, each has its own set of rulers. The ruler on the inactive file appears dimmed.

2. With the Yellow striped balloon image selected, click **Select** on the Application bar, then click **Color Range**.

   TIP If the background color is solid, you can select the Invert check box to pick only the pixels in the image area.

3. Click the **Image option button**, then type **150** in the Fuzziness text box (or drag the **slider** all the way to the right until you see **150**).

4. Position the **Eyedropper pointer** 🖋 in the **blue background** of the image in the Color Range dialog box, then click the **background**.

5. Select the **Invert check box**. Compare the settings in your dialog box to Figure 12.

6. Click **OK**, then compare your Yellow striped balloon.psd image to Figure 13.

You opened a file and used the Color Range dialog box to select the image pixels by selecting the image's inverted colors. Selecting the inverse is an important skill in making selections.

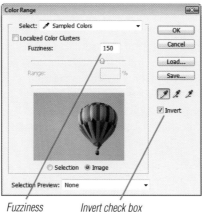

Fuzziness
text box

Invert check box

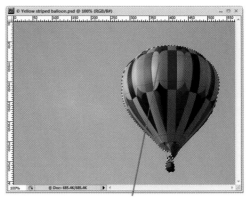

Marquee surrounds
everything that is the
inverse of the blue
background

Using the Place command

You can add an image from another image to a layer using the Place command. Place an image in a Photoshop layer by clicking File on the Application bar, then clicking Place. The placed artwork appears *flattened* inside a bounding box at the center of the Photoshop image. The artwork maintains its original aspect ratio; however, if the artwork is larger than the Photoshop image, it is resized to fit. The Place command works well if you want to insert a multi-layered image in another image. (If all you want is a specific layer from an image, you should just drag the layer you want into an image and not use the Place command.)

FIGURE 14

Yellow striped balloon image dragged to Balloons in flight image

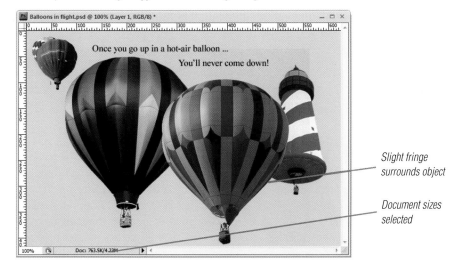

Slight fringe surrounds object

Document sizes selected

FIGURE 15

New layer defringed

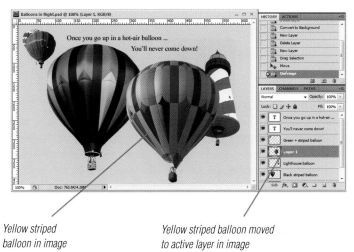

Yellow striped balloon in image

Yellow striped balloon moved to active layer in image

Move a selection to another image

1. Click the **Move tool** on the Tools panel.

2. Position the **Move tool pointer** anywhere over the selection in the Yellow striped balloon image.

3. Drag the **selection** to the Balloons in flight image, then release the mouse button.

   The Yellow striped balloon image moves to the Balloons in flight file appearing on Layer 1.

4. If necessary, use the **Move tool pointer** to drag the yellow-striped balloon to the approximate location shown in Figure 14.

5. Click the **triangle** in the document window status bar, point to **Show**, then verify that Document Sizes is selected.

You dragged a selection from one image to another. You verified that the document size is displayed in the window.

Defringe the selection

1. With Layer 1 selected, click **Layer** on the Application bar, point to **Matting** then click **Defringe**. Defringing a selection gets rid of the halo effect that sometimes occurs when objects are dragged from one image to another.

2. Type **2** in the Width text box, then click **OK**.

3. Save your work.

4. Close **Yellow striped ballon.psd**, then compare the Balloons in flight image to Figure 15.

You removed the fringe from a selection.

ORGANIZE LAYERS WITH
LAYER GROUPS AND COLORS

What You'll Do

In this lesson, you'll use the Layers panel menu to create, name, and color a layer group, and then add layers to it. You'll add finishing touches to the image, save it as a copy, then flatten it.

Understanding Layer Groups

A **layer group** is a Photoshop feature that allows you to organize your layers on the Layers panel. A layer group contains individual layers. For example, you can create a layer group that contains all the type layers in your image. To create a layer group, you click the Layers panel list arrow, then click New Group. As with layers, it is helpful to choose a descriptive name for a layer group.

QUICKTIP
You can press [Ctrl][G] (Win) or ⌘ [G] (Mac) to place the selected layer in a layer group.

Organizing Layers into Groups

After you create a layer group, you simply drag layers on the Layers panel directly on top of the layer group. You can remove layers from a layer group by dragging them out of the layer group to a new location on the Layers panel or by deleting them. Some changes made to a layer group, such as blending mode or opacity changes, affect every layer in the layer group. You can choose to expand or collapse layer groups, depending on the amount of information you need to see. Expanding a layer group

Duplicating a layer
When you add a new layer by clicking the Create a new layer button on the Layers panel, the new layer contains default settings. However, you might want to create a new layer that has the same settings as an existing layer. You can do so by duplicating an existing layer to create a copy of that layer and its settings. Duplicating a layer is also a good way to preserve your modifications, because you can modify the duplicate layer and not worry about losing your original work. To create a duplicate layer, select the layer you want to copy, click the Layers panel list arrow, click Duplicate Layer, then click OK. The new layer will appear above the original.

shows all of the layers in the layer group, and collapsing a layer group hides all of the layers in a layer group. You can expand or collapse a layer group by clicking the triangle to the left of the layer group icon. Figure 16 shows one expanded layer group and one collapsed layer group.

Adding Color to a Layer

If your image has relatively few layers, it's easy to locate the layers. However, if your image contains many layers, you might need some help in organizing them. You can organize layers by color-coding them, which makes it easy to find the layer or the group

you want, regardless of its location on the Layers panel. For example, you can put all type layers in red or put the layers associated with a particular portion of an image in blue. To color the Background layer, you must first convert it to a regular layer.

QUICKTIP

You can also color-code a layer group without losing the color-coding you applied to individual layers.

Flattening an Image

After you make all the necessary modifications to your image, you can greatly reduce

the file size by flattening the image.

Flattening merges all visible layers into a single Background layer and discards all hidden layers. Make sure that all layers that you want to display are visible before you flatten the image. Because flattening removes an image's individual layers, it's a good idea to make a copy of the original image *before* it is flattened. The status bar displays the file's current size and the size it will be when flattened. If you work on a Macintosh, you'll find this information in the lower-left corner of the document window.

FIGURE 16
Layer groups

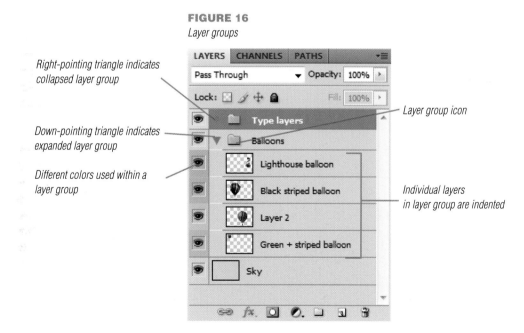

Right-pointing triangle indicates collapsed layer group

Down-pointing triangle indicates expanded layer group

Different colors used within a layer group

Layer group icon

Individual layers in layer group are indented

Understanding Layer Comps

The ability to create a **layer comp**, a variation on the arrangement and visibility of existing layers, is a powerful tool that can make your work more organized. You can create a layer comp by clicking the Layer Comps button on the vertical dock (if it's visible), or by clicking Window on the Application bar, then clicking Layer Comps. Clicking the Create New Layer Comp button on the panel opens the New Layer Comp dialog box, shown in Figure 17, which allows you to name the layer comp and set parameters.

Using Layer Comps

Multiple layer comps, shown in Figure 18, make it easy to switch back and forth between variations on an image theme. Say, for example, that you want to show a client multiple arrangements of layers. The layer comp is an ideal tool for this.

FIGURE 17
New Layer Comp dialog box

Type new comp name

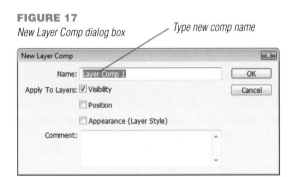

FIGURE 18
Multiple Layer Comps in image

Active layer comp

Create New Layer Comp button

Layer Comps button

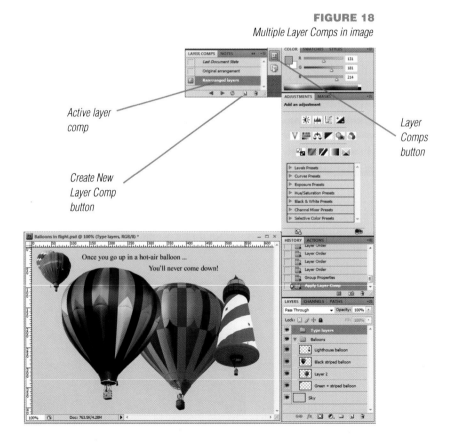

Working with Layers

FIGURE 19

New Group dialog box

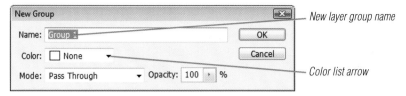
New layer group name

Color list arrow

FIGURE 20

New layer group in Layers panel

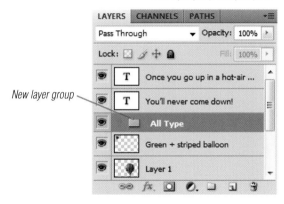
New layer group

FIGURE 21

Layers added to the All Type layer group

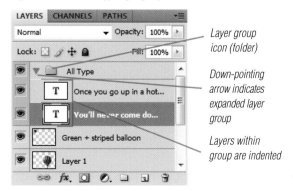

Layer group icon (folder)

Down-pointing arrow indicates expanded layer group

Layers within group are indented

Create a layer group

1. Click the **Green + striped balloon layer**, click the **Layers panel list arrow** ▾≣ , then click **New Group**.

   The New Group dialog box opens, as shown in Figure 19.

   > TIP Photoshop automatically places a new layer group above the active layer.

2. Type **All Type** in the Name text box.

3. Click the **Color list arrow**, click **Green**, then click **OK.**

   The New Group dialog box closes. Compare your Layers panel to Figure 20.

You used the Layers panel menu to create a layer group, then named and applied a color to it. This new group will contain all the type layers in the image.

Move layers to the layer group

1. Click the **Once you go up in a hot-air balloon layer** on the Layers panel, then drag it on to the **All Type layer group**.

2. Click the **You'll never come down! layer**, drag it on to the **All Type layer group**, then compare your Layers panel to Figure 21.

   > TIP If the You'll never come down! layer is not below the Once you go up in a hot-air balloon layer, move the layers to match Figure 21.

3. Click the **triangle** ▽ to the left of the layer group icon (folder) to collapse the layer group.

You created a layer group, then moved two layers into that layer group. Creating layer groups is a great organization tool, especially in complex images with many layers.

Rename a layer and adjust opacity

1. Double-click **Layer 1**, type **Yellow striped balloon**, then press **[Enter]** (Win) or **[return]** (Mac).

2. Double-click the **Opacity text box** on the Layers panel, type **85**, then press **[Enter]** (Win) or **[return]** (Mac).

3. Drag the **Yellow striped balloon layer** beneath the Lighthouse balloon layer, then compare your image to Figure 22.

4. Save your work.

You renamed the new layer, adjusted opacity, and rearranged layers.

Create layer comps

1. Click **Window** on the Application bar, then click **Layer Comps**.

2. Click the **Create New Layer Comp button** 🔲 on the Layer Comps panel.

3. Type **Green off/Yellow off** in the Name text box, as shown in Figure 23, then click **OK**.

4. Click the **Indicates layer visibility button** 👁 on the Green + striped balloon layer and the Yellow striped balloon layer.

5. Click the **Update Layer Comp button** 🔄 on the Layer Comps panel. Compare your Layer Comps panel to Figure 24.

6. Save your work, then click the **Layer Comps button** on the vertical dock to close the Layer Comps panel.

You created a Layer Comp in an existing image.

FIGURE 22
Finished image

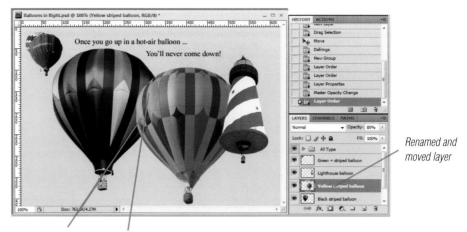

Overlapping balloon layers

Lower opacity allows pixels on lower layers to show through

Renamed and moved layer

FIGURE 23
New Layer Comp dialog box

New Layer Comp name

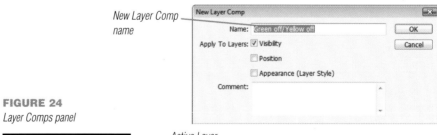

FIGURE 24
Layer Comps panel

Active Layer Comp

Create New Layer Comp

Delete Layer Comp

Apply Previous Selected Layer Comp

Apply Next Selected Layer Comp

Update Layer Comp

FIGURE 25

Save As dialog box

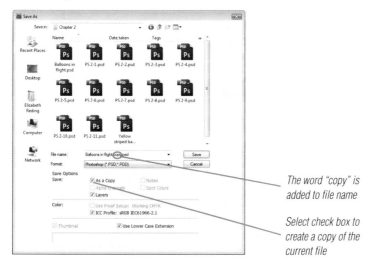

The word "copy" is
added to file name

Select check box to
create a copy of the
current file

FIGURE 26

Flattened image layer

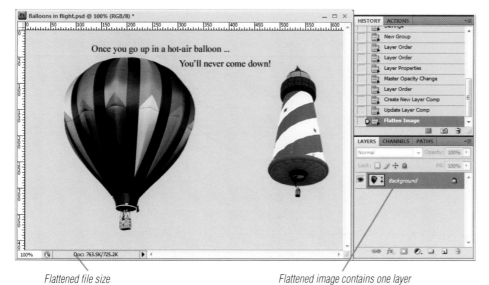

Flattened file size

Flattened image contains one layer

Flatten an image

1. Click **File** on the Application bar, then click **Save As**.

2. Click the **As a Copy check box** to add a check mark, then compare your dialog box to Figure 25.

   > TIP If "copy" does not display in the File name text box, click this text box and type copy to add it to the name.

3. Click **Save**.

   Photoshop saves and closes a copy of the file containing all the layers and effects.

4. Click **Layer** on the Application bar, then click **Flatten Image**.

5. Click **OK** in the warning box, if necessary, then save your work.

6. Compare your Layers panel to Figure 26.

7. Click the **workspace switcher** on the Application bar, then click **Essentials**.

8. Close all open images, then exit Photoshop.

You saved the file as a copy, and then flattened the image. The image now has a single layer.

Power User Shortcuts

to do this:	use this method:
Adjust layer opacity	Click Opacity list arrow on Layers panel, drag opacity slider or Double-click Opacity text box, type a percentage
Change measurements	Right-click (Win) or [Ctrl]-click (Mac) ruler
Color a layer	Click Layers panel list arrow, Layer Properties, Color list arrow
Create a layer comp	Click Create New Layer Comps button on the Layer Comps panel 🔲
Create a layer group	▾≣ , New Group
Delete a layer	🗑
Defringe a selection	Layer ➢ Matting ➢ Defringe

to do this:	use this method:
Flatten an image	Layer ➢ Flatten Image
Use the Move tool	▶⊹ or **V**
Make a New Background layer from existing layer	Layer ➢ New ➢ Background From Layer
Make a New layer	Layer ➢ New ➢ Layer or 🔲
Rename a layer	Double-click layer name, type new name
Select color range	Select ➢ Color Range
Show/Hide Rulers	View ➢ Rulers [Ctrl][R] (Win) ⌘[R] (Mac)
Update a layer comp	↻

Key: Menu items are indicated by ➢ between the menu name and its command. Blue bold letters are shortcuts for selecting tools on the Tools panel.

Examine and convert layers.

1. Start Photoshop.
2. Open PS 2-3.psd from the drive and folder where you store your Data Files, update any text layers if necessary, then save it as **Music Store**.
3. Make sure the rulers appear and that pixels are the unit of measurement.
4. Delete the Background layer.
5. Verify that the Rainbow blend layer is active, then convert the image layer to a Background layer.
6. Save your work.

Add and delete layers.

1. Make Layer 2 active.
2. Create a new layer above this layer using the Layer menu.
3. Accept the default name (Layer 4), and change the color of the layer to Red.
4. Delete Layer 4.
5. Make Layer 2 active (if it is not already the active layer), then create a new layer using the Create a new layer button on the Layers panel.
6. Save your work.

Add a selection from one image to another.

1. Open PS 2-4.psd.
2. Reposition this image of a horn by dragging the window to the right of the Music Store image.
3. Open the Color Range dialog box. (*Hint*: Use the Select menu.)
4. Verify that the Image option button is selected, the Invert check box is selected, then set the Fuzziness to 0.
5. Sample the white background in the preview window in the dialog box, then close the dialog box.
6. Use the Move tool to drag the selection into the Music Store image.
7. Position the selection so that the upper-left edge of the instrument matches the sample shown in Figure 27.
8. Defringe the horn selection (in the Music Store image) using a 3 pixel width.
9. Close PS 2-4.psd.
10. Drag Layer 4 above Layer 3.
11. Rename Layer 4 **Horn**.
12. Change the opacity for the Horn layer to 55%.
13. Drag the Horn layer so it is beneath Layer 2.
14. Hide Layer 1.
15. Hide the rulers.
16. Save your work.

Organize layers with layer groups and colors.

1. Create a Layer Group called **Type Layers** and assign the color yellow to the group.
2. Drag the following layers into the Type Layers folder: Allegro, Music Store, Layer 2.
3. Delete Layer 2, then collapse the Layer Group folder.
4. Move the Notes layer beneath the Horn layer.
5. Create a layer comp called **Notes layer on**.
6. Update the layer comp.
7. Hide the Notes layer.
8. Create a new layer comp called **Notes layer off**, then update the layer comp.
9. Display the previous layer comp, save your work, then close the tab group. (*Hint:* Click the Layer Comps list arrow, then click Close Tab Group.)
10. Save a copy of the Music Store file using the default naming scheme (add 'copy' to the end of the existing filename).
11. Flatten the original image. (*Hint*: Be sure to discard hidden layers.)
12. Save your work, then compare your image to Figure 27.

FIGURE 27
Completed Skills Review

A credit union is developing a hotline for members to use to help abate credit card fraud as soon as it occurs. They're going to distribute ten thousand refrigerator magnets over the next three weeks. As part of their effort to build community awareness of the project, they've sponsored a contest for the magnet design. You decide to enter the contest.

1. Open PS 2-5.psd, then save it as **Combat Fraud**. The Palatino Linotype font is used in this file. Please make a substitution if this font is not available on your computer.
2. Open PS 2-6.psd, use the Color Range dialog box or any selection tool on the Tools panel to select the cell phone image, then drag it to the Outlaw Fraud image.
3. Rename the newly created layer **Cell Phone** if necessary, then apply a color to the layer on the Layers panel. Make sure the Cell Phone layer is beneath the type layers.
4. Convert the Background layer to an image layer, then rename it **Banner**.
5. Change the opacity of the Banner layer to any setting you like.
6. Defringe the Cell Phone layer using the pixel width of your choice.
7. Save your work, close PS 2-6.psd, then compare your image to the sample shown in Figure 28.

FIGURE 28
Completed Project Builder 1

Working with Layers

Your local 4-H chapter wants to promote its upcoming fair and has hired you to create a promotional billboard commemorating this event. The Board of Directors decides that the billboard should be humorous.

1. Open PS 2-7.psd, then save it as **4H Billboard**. Substitute any missing fonts.
2. Open PS 2-8.psd, use the Color Range dialog box or any selection tool on the Tools panel to create a marquee around the llama, then drag the selection to the 4-H Billboard image.
3. Name the new layer **Llama**.
4. Change the opacity of the Llama layer to 90% and defringe the layer containing the llama.
5. Save your work, then compare your image to the sample shown in Figure 29.

FIGURE 29
Completed Project Builder 2

Working with Layers

A friend of yours has designed a new heat-absorbing coffee cup for take-out orders. She is going to present the prototype to a prospective vendor, but first needs to print a brochure. She's asked you to design an eye-catching cover.

1. Open PS 2-9.psd, update the text layers if necessary, then save it as **Coffee Cover**. The Garamond font is used in this file. Please make a substitution if this font is not available on your computer.
2. Open PS 2-10.psd, then drag the entire image to Coffee Cover.
3. Close PS 2-10.psd.
4. Rename Layer 1 with the name **Mocha**.
5. Delete the Background layer and convert the Mocha layer into a new Background layer.
6. Reposition the layer objects so they look like the sample. (*Hint*: You might have to reorganize the layers in the stack so all layers are visible.)
7. Create a layer group above Layer 2, name it **Hot Shot Text**, apply a color of your choice to the layer group, then drag the type layers to it.
8. Save your work, then compare your image to Figure 30.

FIGURE 30
Completed Design Project

Harvest Market, a line of natural food stores, and the trucking associations in your state have formed a coalition to deliver fresh fruit and vegetables to food banks and other food distribution programs. The truckers want to promote the project by displaying a sign on their trucks. Your task is to create a design that will become the Harvest Market logo. Keep in mind that the design will be seen from a distance.

1. Open PS 2-11.psd, then save it as **Harvest Market**. Update the text layers as necessary.

2. Obtain at least two images of different-sized produce. You can obtain images by using what is available on your computer, scanning print media, or connecting to the Internet and downloading images.

3. Open one of the produce files, select it, then drag or copy it to the Harvest Market image. (*Hint*: Experiment with some of the other selection tools. Note that some tools require you to copy and paste the image after you select it.)

4. Repeat step 3, then close the two produce image files.

5. Set the opacity of the Market layer to 80%.

6. Arrange the layers so that smaller images appear on top of the larger ones. (You can move layers to any location in the image you choose.)

7. Create a layer group for the type layers, and apply a color to it.

8. You can delete any layers you feel do not add to the image. (In the sample image, the Veggies layer has been deleted.)
9. Save your work, then compare your image to Figure 31.
10. What are the advantages and disadvantages of using multiple images? How would you assess the ease and efficiency of the selection techniques you've learned? Which styles did you apply to the type layers, and why?

FIGURE 31
Completed Portfolio Project

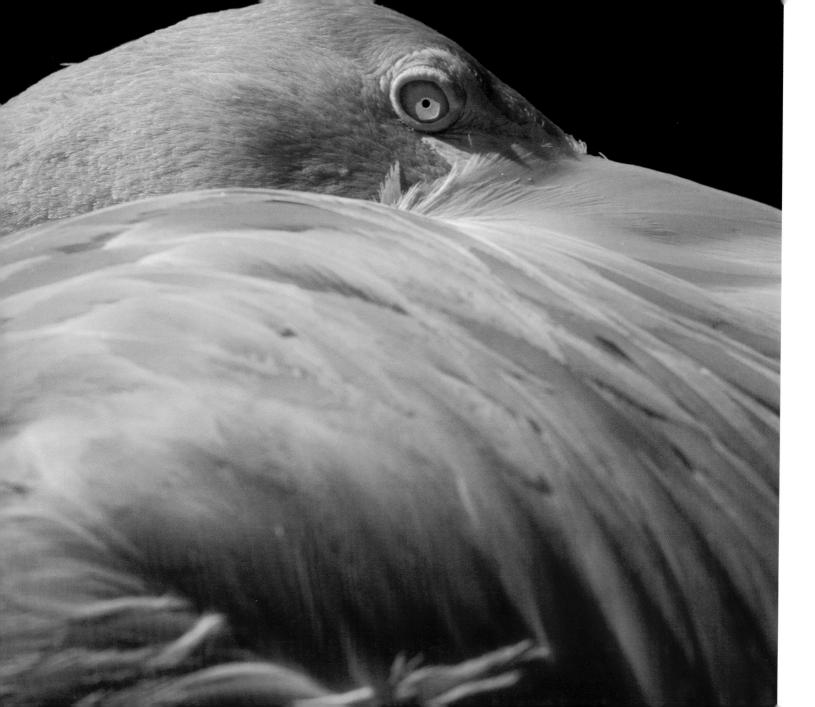

chapter

3

MAKING SELECTIONS

1. Make a selection using shapes

2. Modify a marquee

3. Select using color and modify a selection

4. Add a vignette effect to a selection

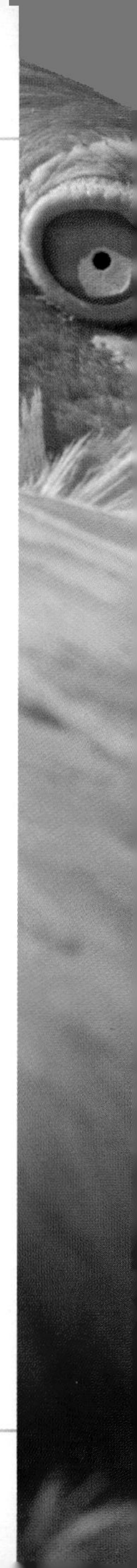

3 MAKING SELECTIONS

Combining Images

Most Photoshop images are created using a technique called **compositing**—combining images from different sources. These sources include other Photoshop images, royalty-free images, pictures taken with digital cameras, and scanned artwork. How you get all those images into your Photoshop images is an art unto itself. You can include additional images by using tools on the Tools panel and menu commands. And to work with all these images, you need to know how to select them—or exactly the parts you want to work with.

Understanding Selection Tools

The two basic methods you can use to make selections are using a tool or using color. You can use three free-form tools to create your own unique selections, four fixed area tools to create circular or rectangular selections, and a wand tool to make selections using color. In addition, you can use menu commands to increase or decrease selections that you made with these tools, or make selections based on color.

Understanding Which Selection Tool to Use

With so many tools available, how do you know which one to use? After you become familiar with the different selection options, you'll learn how to look at images and evaluate selection opportunities. With experience, you'll learn how to identify edges that can be used to isolate imagery, and how to spot colors that can be used to isolate a specific object.

Combining Imagery

After you decide on an object that you want to place in a Photoshop image, you can add the object to another image by cutting, copying, and pasting, dragging and dropping objects using the Move tool, or using the **Clipboard**, the temporary storage area provided by your operating system.

Tools You'll Use

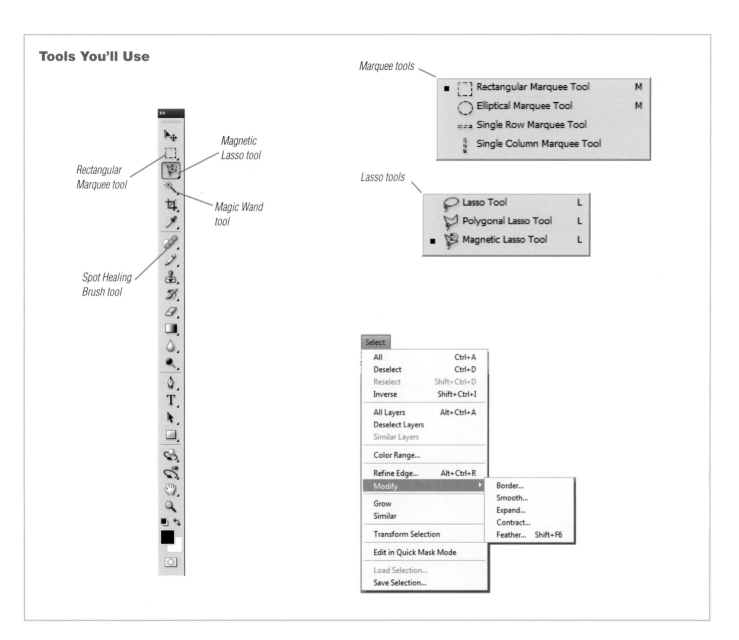

Rectangular
Marquee tool

Magnetic
Lasso tool

Magic Wand
tool

Spot Healing
Brush tool

Marquee tools

- Rectangular Marquee Tool   M
- Elliptical Marquee Tool   M
- Single Row Marquee Tool
- Single Column Marquee Tool

Lasso tools

- Lasso Tool   L
- Polygonal Lasso Tool   L
- Magnetic Lasso Tool   L

Select

All	Ctrl+A
Deselect	Ctrl+D
Reselect	Shift+Ctrl+D
Inverse	Shift+Ctrl+I
All Layers	Alt+Ctrl+A
Deselect Layers	
Similar Layers	
Color Range...	
Refine Edge...	Alt+Ctrl+R
Modify ▶	
Grow	
Similar	
Transform Selection	
Edit in Quick Mask Mode	
Load Selection...	
Save Selection...	

Border...	
Smooth...	
Expand...	
Contract...	
Feather...	Shift+F6

MAKE A SELECTION
USING SHAPES

What You'll Do

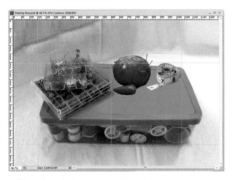

In this lesson, you'll make selections using a marquee tool and a lasso tool, position a selection with the Move tool, deselect a selection, and drag a complex selection into another image.

Selecting by Shape

The Photoshop selection tools make it easy to select objects that are rectangular or elliptical in nature. It would be a boring world if every image we wanted fell into one of those categories, so fortunately, they don't. While some objects are round or square, most are unusual in shape. Making selections can sometimes be a painstaking process because many objects don't have clearly defined edges. To select an object by shape, you need to click the appropriate tool on the Tools panel, then drag the pointer around the object. The selected area is defined by a **marquee**, or series of dotted lines, as shown in Figure 1.

Creating a Selection

Drawing a rectangular marquee is easier than drawing an elliptical marquee, but with practice, you'll be able to create both types of marquees easily. Table 1 lists the tools you can use to make selections using

shapes. Figure 2 shows a marquee surrounding an irregular shape.

> QUICKTIP
>
> A marquee is sometimes referred to as *marching ants* because the dots within the marquee appear to be moving.

Using Fastening Points

Each time you click one of the marquee tools, a fastening point is added to the image. A **fastening point** is an anchor within the marquee. When the marquee pointer reaches the initial fastening point (after making its way around the image), a very small circle appears on the pointer, indicating that you have reached the starting point. Clicking the pointer when this circle appears closes the marquee. Some fastening points, such as those in a circular marquee, are not visible, while others, such as those created by the Polygonal or Magnetic Lasso tools, are visible.

Selecting, Deselecting, and Reselecting

After a selection is made, you can move, copy, transform, or make adjustments to it. A selection stays selected until you unselect, or **deselect**, it. You can deselect a selection by clicking Select on the Application bar, then clicking Deselect. You can reselect a deselected object by clicking Select on the Application bar, then clicking Reselect.

QUICKTIP

You can select the entire image by clicking Select on the Application bar, then clicking All.

FIGURE 1
Elliptical Marquee tool used to create marquee

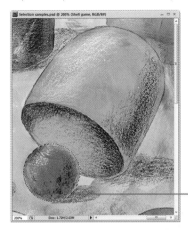

Elliptical Marquee tool surrounds object

QUICKTIP

Correcting a Selection Error

At some point, you'll spend a lot of time making a complex selection only to realize that the wrong layer was active. Remember the History panel? Every action you do is automatically recorded, and you can use the selection state to retrace your steps and recoup the time spent. Your fix may be as simple as selecting the proper History state and changing the active layer in the Layers panel.

TABLE 1: Selection Tools by Shape

tool	button	effect
Rectangular Marquee tool		Creates a rectangular selection. Press [Shift] while dragging to create a square.
Elliptical Marquee tool		Creates an elliptical selection. Press [Shift] while dragging to create a circle.
Single Row Marquee tool		Creates a 1-pixel-wide row selection.
Single Column Marquee tool		Creates a 1-pixel-wide column selection.
Lasso tool		Creates a freehand selection.
Polygonal Lasso tool		Creates straight line selections. Press [Alt] (Win) or [option] (Mac) to create freehand segments.
Magnetic Lasso tool		Creates selections that snap to an edge of an object. Press [Alt] (Win) or [option] (Mac) to alternate between freehand and magnetic line segments.

FIGURE 2
Marquee surrounding irregular shape

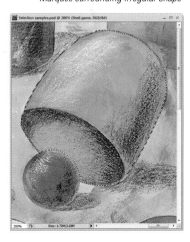

Placing a Selection

You can place a selection in a Photoshop image in many ways. You can copy or cut a selection, then paste it to a different location in the same image or to a different image. You can also use the Move tool to drag a selection to a new location.

QUICKTIP

You can temporarily change *any selected tool* into the Move tool by pressing and holding [Ctrl] (Win) or ⌘ (Mac). When you're finished dragging the selection, release [Ctrl] (Win) or ⌘ (Mac), and the functionality of the originally selected tool returns.

Using Guides

Guides are non-printing horizontal and vertical lines that you can display on top of an image to help you position a selection. You can create an unlimited number of horizontal and vertical guides. You create a guide by displaying the rulers, positioning the pointer on either ruler, then clicking and dragging the guide into position. Figure 3 shows the creation of a horizontal guide in a file that contains two existing guides. You delete a guide by selecting the Move tool on the Tools panel, positioning the pointer over the guide, then clicking and dragging it back to its ruler. If the Snap feature is enabled, as you drag an object toward a guide, the object will be pulled toward the guide. To turn on the Snap feature, click View on the Application bar, then click Snap. A check mark appears to the left of the command if the feature is enabled.

QUICKTIP

Double-click a guide to open the Preferences dialog box to change guide colors, width, and other features.

FIGURE 3
Creating guides in image

Dragging a guide to a new location

FIGURE 4
Rectangular Marquee tool selection

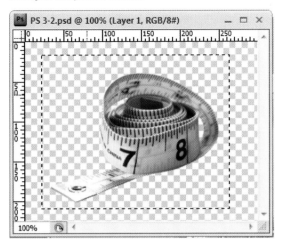

TABLE 2: Working with a Selection

if you want to:	then do this:
Move a selection (an image) using the mouse	Position the ⊹ over the selection, then drag the marquee and its contents
Copy a selection to the Clipboard	Activate image containing the selection, click Edit ➤ Copy
Cut a selection to the Clipboard	Activate image containing the selection, click Edit ➤ Cut
Paste a selection from the Clipboard	Activate image where you want the selection, click Edit ➤ Paste
Delete a selection	Make selection, then press [Delete] (Win) or [delete] (Mac)
Deselect a selection	Press [Ctrl][D] (Win) or ⌘[D] (Mac)

Create a selection with the Rectangular Marquee tool

1. Start Photoshop, open PS 3-1.psd from the drive and folder where you store your Data Files, save it as **Sewing Box**, then click **OK** if the Maximize compatibility dialog box displays.
2. Click the **workspace switcher** on the Application bar, click **Analysis**, click the **Layers tab**, then display the rulers (if necessary) in pixels.
3. Open PS 3-2.psd, then display the rulers in pixels for this image (if necessary).
4. Click the **Rectangular Marquee tool** ⬚ on the Tools panel.
5. Make sure the value in the Feather text box on the options bar is **0 px**.

   Feathering determines the amount of blur between the selection and the pixels surrounding it.
6. Drag the **Marquee pointer** ┼ to select the tape measure from approximately **20 H/20 V** to **260 H/210 V**. See Figure 4.

   The first measurement refers to the horizontal ruler (H); the second measurement refers to the vertical ruler (V).

   TIP You can also use the X/Y coordinates displayed in the Info panel.
7. Click the **Move tool** ⊹ on the Tools panel, then drag the selection to any location in the Sewing Box image.

   The selection now appears in the Sewing Box image on a new layer (Layer 1).

   TIP Table 2 describes methods you can use to work with selections in an image.

Using the Rectangular Marquee tool, you created a selection in an image, then you dragged that selection into another image. This left the original image intact, and created a copy of the selection in the destination image.

Position a selection with the Move tool

1. Verify that the **Move tool** ⊹ is selected on the Tools panel, and display the rulers (if necessary).

2. If you do not see guides in the Sewing Box image, click **View** on the Application bar, point to **Show**, then click **Guides**.

3. Drag the **tape measure** so that the top-right corner snaps to the ruler guides at approximately **1030 H/250 V**. Compare your image to Figure 5.

   Did you feel the snap to effect as you positioned the selection within the guides? This feature makes it easy to properly position objects within an image.

   TIP If you didn't feel the image snap to the guides, click View on the Application bar, point to Snap To, then click Guides.

4. Rename Layer 1 **Tape Measure**.

You used the Move tool to reposition a selection in an existing image, then you renamed the layer.

FIGURE 5
Rectangular selection in image

Tape measure

Using Smart Guides

Wouldn't it be great to be able to see a vertical or horizontal guide as you move an object? Using Smart Guides, you can do just that. Smart Guides are turned on by clicking View on the Application bar, pointing to Show, then clicking Smart Guides. Once this feature is turned on, horizontal and vertical purple guidelines appear automatically when you draw a shape or move an object. This feature allows you to align layer content as you move it.

Making Selections

FIGURE 6
Deselect command

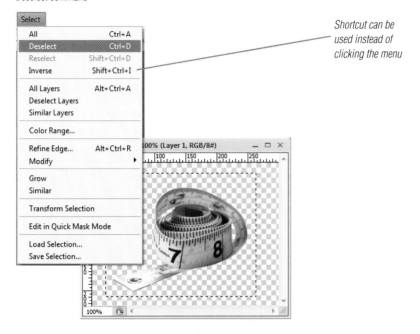

Shortcut can be
used instead of
clicking the menu

Deselect a selection

1. Click **Window** on the Application bar, then
   click **PS 3-2.psd**.

   TIP If you can see the window of the
   image you want anywhere on the screen,
   you can just click it to make it active instead
   of using the Window menu.

2. Click **Select** on the Application bar, then
   click **Deselect**, as shown in Figure 6.

*You hid the active layer, then used the Deselect
command on the Select menu to deselect the
object you had moved into this image. When you
deselect a selection, the marquee no longer
surrounds it.*

FIGURE 7
Save Selection dialog box

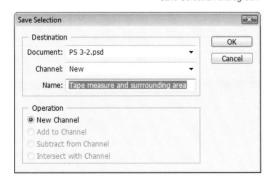

Saving and loading a selection

Any selection can be saved independently of the surrounding image, so that if you want
to use it again in the image, you can do so without having to retrace it using one of the
marquee tools. Once a selection is made, you can save it in the image by clicking Select
on the Application bar, then clicking Save Selection. The Save Selection dialog box
opens, as shown in Figure 7; be sure to give the selection a meaningful name. When
you want to load a saved selection, click Select on the Application bar, then click Load
Selection. Click the Channel list arrow, click the named selection, then click OK.

Create a selection with the Magnetic Lasso tool

1. Click the **Magnetic Lasso tool** on the Tools panel, then change the settings on the options bar so that they are the same as those shown in Figure 8. Table 3 describes Magnetic Lasso tool settings.

2. Open PS 3-3.psd from the drive and folder where you store your Data Files.

3. Click the **Magnetic Lasso tool pointer** once anywhere on the edge of the pin cushion, to create your first fastening point.

   TIP   If you click a spot that is not at the edge of the pin cushion, press [Esc] (Win) or ⌘ [Z] (Mac) to undo the action, then start again.

4. Drag the **Magnetic Lasso tool pointer** slowly around the pin cushion (clicking at the top of each pin may be helpful) until it is almost entirely selected, then click directly over the initial fastening point. See Figure 9.

   Don't worry about all the nooks and crannies surrounding the pin cushion: the Magnetic Lasso tool will select those automatically. You will see a small circle next to the pointer when it is directly over the initial fastening point, indicating that you are closing the selection. The individual segments turn into a marquee.

   TIP   If you feel that the Magnetic Lasso tool is missing some major details while you're tracing, you can insert additional fastening points by clicking the pointer while dragging. For example, click the mouse button at a location where you want to change the selection shape.

You created a selection with the Magnetic Lasso tool.

FIGURE 8
Options for the Magnetic Lasso tool

Feather: 0 px   ☑ Anti-alias   Width: 20 px   Contrast: 10%   Frequency: 57   Refine Edge...

FIGURE 9
Creating a selection with the Magnetic Lasso tool

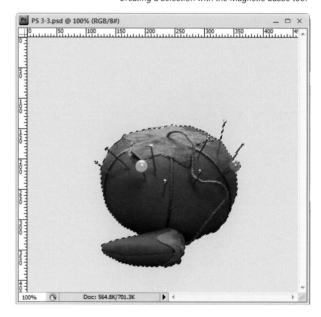

Mastering the art of selections

You might feel that it is difficult when you first start making selections. Making selections is a skill, and like most skills, it takes a lot of practice to become proficient. In addition to practice, make sure that you're comfortable in your work area, that your hands are steady, and that your mouse is working well. A non-optical mouse that is dirty will make selecting an onerous task, so make sure your mouse is well cared for and is functioning correctly.

FIGURE 10

Selection copied into image

Defringing the layer reduces the amount of the original background that appears; your results will vary

Complex selection includes only object, no background

TABLE 3: Magnetic Lasso Tool Settings

setting	description
Feather	The amount of blur between the selection and the pixels surrounding it. This setting is measured in pixels and can be a value between 0 and 250.
Anti-alias	The smoothness of the selection, achieved by softening the color transition between edge and background pixels.
Width	The interior width by detecting an edge from the pointer. This setting is measured in pixels and can have a value from 1 to 40.
Contrast	The tool's sensitivity. This setting can be a value between 1 percent and 100 percent: higher values detect high-contrast edges.
Frequency	The rate at which fastening points are applied. This setting can be a value between 0 and 100: higher values insert more fastening points.

Move a complex selection to an existing image

1. Click the **Move tool** ⊕ on the Tools panel.

    TIP   You can also click the Click to open the Tool Preset picker list arrow on the options bar, then double-click the Move tool.

2. Use the **Move tool pointer** ⊁ to drag the pin cushion selection to the Sewing Box image.

    The selection appears on a new layer (Layer 1).

3. Drag the object so that the left edge of the pin cushion snaps to the guide at approximately **600 Y** and the top of the pin cushion snaps to the guide at **200 X** using the coordinates on the info panel.

4. Use the Layer menu to defringe the new Layer 1 at a width of **1** pixel.

5. Close the PS 3-3.psd image without saving your changes.

6. Rename the new layer **Pin Cushion** in the Sewing Box image.

7. Save your work, then compare your image to Figure 10.

8. Click **Window** on the Application bar, then click **PS 3-2.psd**.

9. Close the PS 3-2.psd image without saving your changes.

You dragged a complex selection into an existing Photoshop image. You positioned the object using ruler guides and renamed a layer. You also defringed a selection to eliminate its white border.

MODIFY A
MARQUEE

What You'll Do

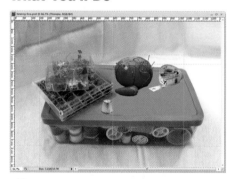

In this lesson, you'll move and enlarge
a marquee, drag a selection into a
Photoshop image, then position a selection using ruler guides.

Changing the Size of a Marquee

Not all objects are easy to select.
Sometimes, when you make a selection,
you might need to change the size or
shape of the marquee.

The options bar contains selection buttons
that help you add to and subtract from a
marquee, or intersect with a selection. The
marquee in Figure 11 was modified into
the one shown in Figure 12 by clicking the
Add to selection button. After the Add to
selection button is active, you can draw an
additional marquee (directly adjacent to
the selection), and it will be added to the
current marquee.

One method you can use to increase the
size of a marquee is the Grow command.
After you make a selection, you can
increase the marquee size by clicking Select
on the Application bar, then by clicking
Grow. The Grow command selects pixels
adjacent to the marquee that have colors

similar to those specified by the Magic
Wand tool. The Similar command selects
both adjacent and non-adjacent pixels.

> **QUICK**TIP
>
> While the Grow command selects adjacent pixels that have
> similar colors, the Expand command increases a selection
> by a specific number of pixels.

Modifying a Marquee

While a selection is active, you can
modify the marquee by expanding or
contracting it, smoothing out its edges, or
enlarging it to add a border around the
selection. These four commands, Expand,
Contract, Smooth, and Border, are sub-
menus of the Modify command, which is
found on the Select menu. For example,
you might want to enlarge your selection.
Using the Expand command, you can
increase the size of the selection, as shown
in Figure 13.

Moving a Marquee

After you create a marquee, you can move the marquee to another location in the same image or to another image entirely. You might want to move a marquee if you've drawn it in the wrong image or the wrong location. Sometimes it's easier to draw a marquee elsewhere on the page, and then move it to the desired location.

QUICKTIP

You can always hide and display layers as necessary to facilitate making a selection.

FIGURE 12
Selection with additions

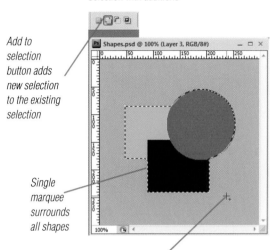

Add to selection button adds new selection to the existing selection

Single marquee surrounds all shapes

Add to selection pointer

FIGURE 11
New selection

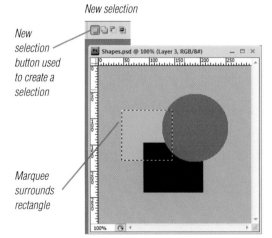

New selection button used to create a selection

Marquee surrounds rectangle

Using the Quick Selection Tool

The Quick Selection tool lets you paint-to-select an object from the interior using a resizeable brush. As you paint the object, the selection grows. Using the Auto-Enhance check box, rough edges and blockiness are automatically reduced to give you a perfect selection. As with other selection tools, the Quick Selection tool has options to add and subtract from your selection.

FIGURE 13
Expanded selection

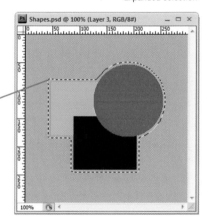

Marquee expanded by 5 pixels

Adding and subtracting from a selection

Of course knowing how to make a selection is important, but it's just as important to know how to make alterations in an existing selection. Sometimes it's almost impossible to create that perfect marquee on the first try. Perhaps your hand moved while you were tracing, or you just got distracted. Using the Add to selection, Subtract from selection, and Intersect with selection buttons (which appear with all selection tools), you can alter an existing marquee without having to start from scratch.

Lesson 2 Modify a Marquee

PHOTOSHOP 3-13

Move and enlarge a marquee

1. Open PS 3-4.psd from the drive and folder where you store your Data Files. Change the zoom factor to **200%**.

2. Click the **Elliptical Marquee tool** ⬭ on the Tools panel.

   TIP The Elliptical Marquee tool might be hidden under the Rectangular Marquee tool.

3. Click the **New selection button** ⬜ on the options bar (if it is not already selected).

4. Drag the **Marquee pointer** ╀ to select the area from approximately **150 X/50 Y** to **200 X/130 Y**. Compare your image to Figure 14.

5. Position the **pointer** ▷: in the center of the selection.

6. Drag the **Move pointer** ▶ so the marquee covers the thimble, at approximately **100 X/100 Y**, as shown in Figure 15.

   TIP You can also nudge a selection to move it, by pressing the arrow keys. Each time you press an arrow key, the selection moves one pixel in the direction of the arrow.

7. Click the **Magic Wand tool** ⤳ on the Tools panel, then enter a Tolerance of **16,** and select the **Anti-alias** and **Contiguous checkboxes**.

8. Click **Select** on the Application bar, then click **Similar**.

9. Click **Select** on the Application bar, point to **Modify**, then click **Expand**.

10. Type **1** in the Expand By text box of the Expand Selection dialog box, then click **OK**.

11. Deselect the selection.

You created a marquee, then dragged the marquee to reposition it. You then enlarged a selection marquee by using the Similar and Expand commands.

PHOTOSHOP 3-14

FIGURE 14
Selection in image

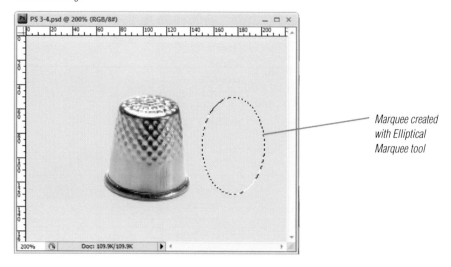

Marquee created
with Elliptical
Marquee tool

FIGURE 15
Moved selection

New marquee
location

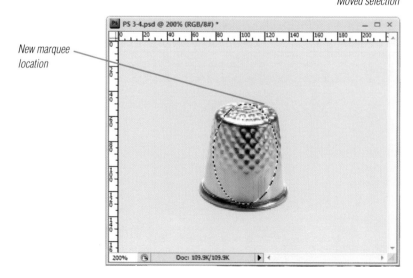

Making Selections

FIGURE 16
Quick Selection tool settings

FIGURE 17
Selection in file

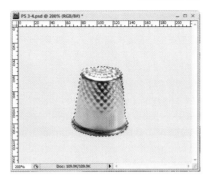

FIGURE 18
Selection moved to the Sewing Box image

Use the Quick Selection tool

1. Click the **Quick Selection tool** on the Tools panel, then adjust your settings using Figure 16.

    TIP If you need to change the Brush settings, click Brush list arrow on the options bar, then drag the sliders so the settings are 10 px diameter, 0% hardness, 1% spacing, 0° angle, 100% roundness, and Pen Pressure size.

2. Position the pointer in the **center of the thimble,** then slowly drag the pointer to the outer edges until the object is selected. See Figure 17.

    TIP Sometimes making a selection is easy, sometimes . . . not so much. Time and practice will hone your selection skills. It will get easier.

3. Click the **Move tool** on the Tools panel.

4. Position the **Move pointer** over the selection, then drag the **thimble** to the Sewing Box image.

5. Drag the **thimble** so that it is to the left of the pin cushion and snaps to the vertical guide at approximately **600 X/550Y**.

6. Defringe the thimble using a setting of **1** pixel.

7. Rename the new layer **Thimble**.

8. Save your work on the sewing box image, then compare your image to Figure 18.

9. Make **PS 3-4.psd** active.

10. Close PS 3-4.psd without saving your changes.

You selected an object using the Quick Selection tool, then you dragged the selection into an existing image.

SELECT USING COLOR AND
MODIFY A SELECTION

What You'll Do

 In this lesson, you'll make selections using both the Color Range command and the Magic Wand tool. You'll also flip a selection, then fix an image using the Healing Brush tool.

Selecting with Color

Selections based on color can be easy to make, especially when the background of an image is different from the image itself. High contrast between colors is an ideal condition for making selections based on color. You can make selections using color with the Color Range command on the Select menu, or you can use the Magic Wand tool on the Tools panel.

Using the Magic Wand Tool

When you select the Magic Wand tool, the following options are available on the options bar, as shown in Figure 19:

- The four selection buttons.
- The Tolerance setting, which allows you to specify whether similar pixels will be selected. This setting has a value from 0 to 255, and the lower the value, the closer in color the selected pixels will be.
- The Anti-alias check box, which softens the selection's appearance.
- The Contiguous check box, which lets you select pixels that are next to one another.
- The Sample All Layers check box, which lets you select pixels from multiple layers at once.

Knowing which selection tool to use

The hardest part of making a selection might be determining which selection tool to use. How are you supposed to know if you should use a marquee tool or a lasso tool? The first question you need to ask yourself is, "What do I want to select?" Becoming proficient in making selections means that you need to assess the qualities of the object you want to select, and then decide which method to use. Ask yourself: Does the object have a definable shape? Does it have an identifiable edge? Are there common colors that can be used to create a selection?

Using the Color Range Command

You can use the Color Range command to make the same selections as with the Magic Wand tool. When you use the Color Range command, the Color Range dialog box opens. This dialog box lets you use the pointer to identify which colors you want to use to make a selection. You can also select the Invert check box to *exclude* the chosen color from the selection. The **fuzziness** setting is similar to tolerance, in that the lower the value, the closer in color pixels must be to be selected.

QUICKTIP

Unlike the Magic Wand tool, the Color Range command does not give you the option of excluding contiguous pixels.

Transforming a Selection

After you place a selection in a Photoshop image, you can change its size and other qualities by clicking Edit on the Application bar, pointing to Transform, then clicking any of the commands on the submenu. After you select certain commands, small squares called **handles** surround the selection. To complete the command, you drag a handle until the image has the look you want, then press [Enter] (Win) or [return] (Mac). You can also use the Transform submenu to flip a selection horizontally or vertically.

Understanding the Healing Brush Tool

If you place a selection then notice that the image has a few imperfections, you can fix the image. You can fix imperfections such as dirt, scratches, bulging veins on skin, or wrinkles on a face using the Healing Brush tool on the Tools panel.

QUICKTIP

When correcting someone's portrait, make sure your subject looks the way he or she *thinks* they look. That's not always possible, but strive to get as close as you can to their ideal!

Using the Healing Brush Tool

This tool lets you sample an area, then paint over the imperfections. What is the result? The less-than-desirable pixels seem to disappear into the surrounding image. In addition to matching the sampled pixels, the Healing Brush tool also matches the texture, lighting, and shading of the sample. This is why the painted pixels blend so effortlessly into the existing image. Corrections can be painted using broad strokes, or using clicks of the mouse.

QUICKTIP

To take a sample, press and hold [Alt] (Win) or [option] (Mac) while dragging the pointer over the area you want to duplicate.

FIGURE 19
Options for the Magic Wand tool

Select using color range

1. Open PS 3-5.psd from the drive and folder where you store your Data Files.

2. Click **Select** on the Application bar, then click **Color Range**.

3. Click the **Image option button** (if it is not already selected).

4. Click the **Invert check box** to add a check mark (if necessary).

5. Verify that your settings match those shown in Figure 20, click anywhere in the background area surrounding the sample image, then click **OK**.

   The Color Range dialog box closes and the spool of thread in the image is selected.

6. Click the **Move tool** ▶✛ on the Tools panel.

7. Drag the selection into Sewing Box.psd, then position the selection as shown in Figure 21.

8. Rename the new layer **Thread**.

9. Defringe the spool of thread using a setting of **1** pixel.

10. Activate **PS 3-5.psd**, then close this file without saving any changes.

You made a selection within an image using the Color Range command on the Select menu, and dragged the selection to an existing image.

FIGURE 20
Completed Color Range dialog box

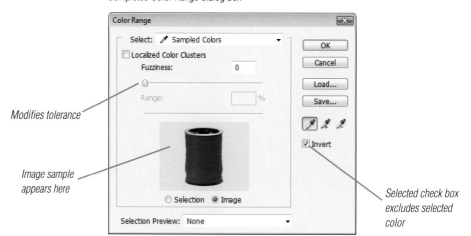

Modifies tolerance

Image sample appears here

Selected check box excludes selected color

FIGURE 21
Selection in image

FIGURE 22
Magic Wand tool settings

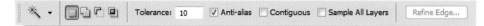

FIGURE 23
Selected area

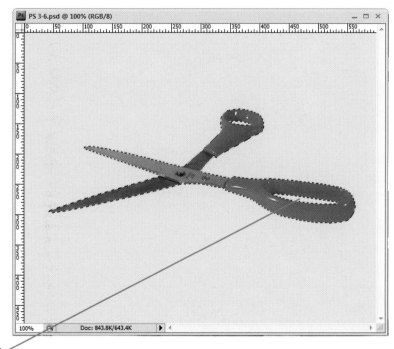

Selection excludes background color

Select using the Magic Wand tool

1. Open PS 3-6.psd from the drive and folder where you store your Data Files.
2. Click the **Magic Wand tool** on the Tools panel.
3. Change the settings on the options bar to match those shown in Figure 22.
4. Click anywhere in the background area of the image (such as **50 X/50 Y**).

   TIP Had you selected the Contiguous check box, the pixels within the handles *would not* have been selected. The Contiguous check box is a powerful feature of the Magic Wand tool.

5. Click **Select** on the Application bar, then click **Inverse**. Compare your selection to Figure 23.
6. Click the **Move tool** on the Tools panel, then drag the selection into Sewing Box.psd.

You made a selection using the Magic Wand tool, then dragged it into an existing image. The Magic Wand tool is just one more way you can make a selection. One advantage of using the Magic Wand tool (versus the Color Range tool) is the Contiguous check box, which lets you choose pixels that are next to one another.

Flip a selection

1. Click **Edit** on the Application bar, point to **Transform**, then click **Flip Horizontal**.

2. Rename Layer 1 as **Scissors**.

3. Defringe **Scissors** using a **1** pixel setting.

4. Drag the flipped selection with the **Move tool pointer** ▶⊹ so it is positioned as shown in Figure 24.

5. Make **PS 3-6.psd** the active file, then close PS 3-6.psd without saving your changes.

6. Save your work.

You flipped and repositioned a selection. Sometimes it's helpful to flip an object to help direct the viewer's eye to a desired focal point.

FIGURE 24
Flipped and positioned selection

Getting rid of red eye

When digital photos of your favorite people have that annoying red eye, what do you do? You use the Red Eye tool to eliminate this effect. To do this, select the Red Eye tool (which is grouped on the Tools panel with the Spot Healing Brush tool, the Healing Brush tool, and the Patch tool), then either click a red area of an eye or draw a selection over a red eye. When you release the mouse button, the red eye effect is removed.

FIGURE 25

Healing Brush tool options

FIGURE 26

Healed area

Crack removed
from image

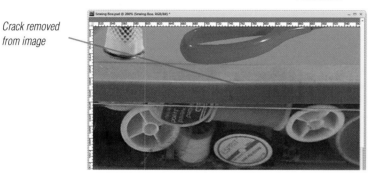

FIGURE 27

Image after using the Healing Brush

Lesson 3   Select Using Color and Modify a Selection

1. Click the **Sewing Box layer** on the Layers panel, then click the **Zoom tool** 🔍 on the Tools panel.

2. Click the image with the **Zoom tool pointer** ⊕ above the pink spool of thread (in the box) at **750 X/600 Y** until the zoom factor is **200%** and you can see the crack in the lid of the box.

3. Click the **Healing Brush tool** 🖌 on the Tools panel. Change the settings on the options bar to match those shown in Figure 25.

   TIP   If you need to change the Brush settings, click the Brush list arrow on the options bar, then drag the sliders so the settings are 10 px diameter, 0% hardness, 1% spacing, 0° angle, 100% roundness, and Pen Pressure size.

4. Press and hold **[Alt]** (Win) or **[option]** (Mac), click next to the crack at any location on the green lid, such as **700 X/580 Y**, then release **[Alt]** (Win) or **[option]** (Mac).

   You sampled an area of the box that is not cracked so that you can use the Healing Brush tool to paint a damaged area with the sample.

5. Click the crack (at approximately **720 X/580 Y**).

6. Repeat steps 4 and 5, each time choosing a new source location, then clicking at a parallel location on the crack.

   Compare the repaired area to Figure 26.

7. Click the **Zoom tool** 🔍 on the Tools panel press and hold **[Alt]** (Win) or **[option]** (Mac), click the center of the image with the **Zoom tool pointer** ⊖ until the zoom factor is **66.67%**, then release **[Alt]** (Win) or **[option]** (Mac).

8. Save your work, then compare your image to Figure 27.

You used the Healing Brush tool to fix an imperfection in an image.

ADD A VIGNETTE EFFECT
TO A SELECTION

What You'll Do

In this lesson, you'll create a vignette effect, using a layer mask and feathering.

Understanding Vignettes

Traditionally, a **vignette** is a picture or portrait whose border fades into the surrounding color at its edges. You can use a vignette effect to give an image an old-world appearance. You can also use a vignette effect to tone down an overwhelming background. You can create a vignette effect in Photoshop by creating a mask with a blurred edge. A **mask** lets you protect or modify a particular area and is created using a marquee.

Creating a Vignette

A **vignette effect** uses feathering to fade a marquee shape. The **feather** setting blurs the area between the selection and the surrounding pixels, which creates a distinctive fade at the edge of the selection. You can create a vignette effect by using a marquee or lasso tool to create a marquee in an image layer. After the selection is created, you can modify the feather setting (a 10- or 20-pixel setting creates a nice fade) to increase the blur effect on the outside edge of the selection.

Getting that Healing feeling

The Spot Healing Brush tool works in much the same way as the Healing Brush tool in that it removes blemishes and other imperfections. Unlike the Healing Brush tool, the Spot Healing Brush tool does not require you to take a sample. When using the Spot Healing Brush tool, you must choose whether you want to use a proximity match type (which uses pixels around the edge of the selection as a patch) or a create texture type (which uses all the pixels in the selection to create a texture that is used to fix the area). You also have the option of sampling all the visible layers or only the active layer.

FIGURE 28
Marquee in image

FIGURE 29
Layers panel

Feathered mask creates
vignette effect

FIGURE 30
Vignette in image

Vignette effect
fades border

Create a vignette

1. Verify that the **Sewing Box layer** is selected.
2. Click the **Rectangular Marquee tool** ▢, on the Tools panel.
3. Change the **Feather setting** on the options bar to **20px**.
4. Create a selection with the **Marquee pointer** ╋ from **50 X/50 Y** to **1200 X/800 Y**, as shown in Figure 28.
5. Click **Layer** on the Application bar, point to **Layer Mask**, then click **Reveal Selection**.

    The vignette effect is added to the layer.

    Compare your Layers panel to Figure 29.
6. Click **View** on the Application bar, then click **Rulers** to hide them.
7. Click **View** on the Application bar, then click **Clear Guides**.
8. Save your work, then compare your image to Figure 30.
9. Close the Sewing Box image, select **Essentials** from the workspace switcher, then exit Photoshop.

You created a vignette effect by adding a feathered layer mask. You also rearranged layers and defringed a selection. Once the image was finished, you hid the rulers and cleared the guides.

Power User Shortcuts

to do this:	use this method:
Copy selection	Click Edit ➤ Copy or [Ctrl][C] (Win) or ⌘[C] (Mac)
Create vignette effect	Marquee or Lasso tool, create selection, click Layer ➤ Layer Mask ➤ Reveal Selection
Cut selection	Click Edit ➤ Cut or [Ctrl][X] (Win) or ⌘[X] (Mac)
Deselect object	Select ➤ Deselect or [Ctrl][D] (Win) or ⌘[D] (Mac)
Elliptical Marquee tool	◯ or [Shift] **M**
Flip image	Edit ➤ Transform ➤ Flip Horizontal
Grow selection	Select ➤ Grow
Increase selection	Select ➤ Similar
Lasso tool	◯ or [Shift] **L**
Magnetic Lasso tool	🖉 or [Shift] **L**
Move tool	⊹ or **V**

to do this:	use this method:
Move selection marquee	Position pointer in selection, drag ⊹ to new location
Paste selection	Edit ➤ Paste or [Ctrl][V] (Win) or ⌘[V] (Mac)
Polygonal Lasso tool	⊠ or [Shift] **L**
Rectangular Marquee tool	⬚ or [Shift] **M**
Reselect a deselected object	Select ➤ Reselect, or [Shift][Ctrl][D] (Win) or [Shift]⌘[D] (Mac)
Select all objects	Select ➤ All, or [Ctrl][A] (Win) or ⌘[A] (Mac)
Select using color range	Select ➤ Color Range, click sample area
Select using Magic Wand tool	✳ or **W**, then click image
Select using Quick Selection tool	🖎 or [Shift] **W**, then drag pointer over image
Single Column Marquee tool	▮
Single Row Marquee tool	▭

Key: Menu items are indicated by ➤ between the menu name and its command. Blue bold letters are shortcuts for selecting tools on the Tools panel.

Make a selection using shapes.

1. Open PS 3-7.psd from the drive and folder where you store your Data Files, substitute any missing fonts, then save it as **Cool cats**.
2. Open PS 3-8.tif.
3. Display the rulers in each image window (if necessary), switch to the Analysis workspace, then display the Layers panel.
4. Use the Rectangular Marquee tool to select the entire image in PS 3-8.tif. (*Hint*: Reset the Feather setting to 0 pixels, if necessary.)
5. Deselect the selection.
6. Use the Magnetic Lasso tool to create a selection surrounding only the Block cat in the image. (*Hint*: You can use the Zoom tool to make the image larger.)
7. Drag the selection into the Cool cats image, positioning it so the right side of the cat is at 490 X, and the bottom of the right paw is at 450 Y.
8. Save your work.
9. Close PS 3-8.tif without saving any changes.

Modify a marquee.

1. Open PS 3-9.tif.
2. Change the settings on the Magic Wand tool to Tolerance = 5, and make sure that the Contiguous check box is selected.
3. Use the Elliptical Marquee tool to create a marquee from 100 X/50 Y to 200 X/100 Y, using a setting of 0 in the Feather text box.
4. Use the Grow command on the Select menu.
5. Use the Inverse command on the Select menu.

6. Drag the selection into the Cool cats image, positioning it so the upper-left corner of the selection is near 0 X/0 Y.
7. Defringe the new layer using a width of 2 pixels.
8. Save your work.
9. Close PS 3-9.tif without saving any changes.

Select using color and modify a selection.

1. Open PS 3-10.tif.
2. Use the Color Range dialog box to select only the kitten.
3. Drag the selection into the Cool cats image.
4. Flip the kitten image (in the Cool cats image) horizontally.

FIGURE 31
Completed Skills Review project

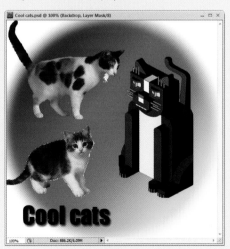

5. Position the kitten image so the bottom right snaps to the ruler guides at 230 X/450 Y.
6. Defringe the kitten using a width of 2 pixels.
7. Save your work.
8. Close PS 3-10.tif without saving any changes.

Add a vignette effect to a selection.

1. Use a 15-pixel feather setting and the Backdrop layer to create an elliptical selection surrounding the contents of the Cool cats image.
2. Add a layer mask that reveals the selection.
3. Hide the rulers and guides, then switch to the Essentials workspace.
4. Save your work.
5. Compare your image to Figure 31.

Making Selections

As a professional photographer, you often take photos of people for use in various publications. You recently took a photograph of a woman that will be used in a marketing brochure. The client is happy with the overall picture, but wants the facial lines smoothed out. You decide to use the Healing Brush tool to ensure that the client is happy with the final product.

1. Open PS 3-11.psd, then save it as **Portrait**.
2. Make a copy of the Original layer using the default name, or the name of your choice.
3. Use the Original copy layer and the Healing Brush tool to smooth the appearance of facial lines in this image. (*Hint*: You may have greater success if you use short strokes with the Healing Brush tool than if you paint long strokes.)
4. Create a vignette effect on the Original copy layer that reveals the selection using an elliptical marquee.
5. Reorder the layers (if necessary), so that the vignette effect is visible.
6. Save your work, then compare your image to the sample shown in Figure 32.

FIGURE 32
Completed Project Builder 1

The St. Louis Athletic Association, which sponsors the St. Louis Marathon, is holding a contest for artwork to announce the upcoming race. Submissions can be created on paper or computer-generated. You feel you have a good chance at winning this contest, using Photoshop as your tool.

1. Open PS 3-12.psd, then save it as **Marathon Contest**.
2. Locate at least two pieces of appropriate artwork—either on your hard disk, in a royalty-free collection, or from scanned images—that you can use in this file.
3. Use any appropriate methods to select imagery from the artwork.
4. After the selections have been made, copy each selection into Marathon Contest.
5. Arrange the images into a design that you think will be eye-catching and attractive.
6. Deselect the selections in the files you are no longer using, and close them without saving the changes.
7. Add a vignette effect to the Backdrop layer.
8. Display the type layers if they are hidden.
9. Defringe any layers, as necessary.
10. Save your work, then compare your screen to the sample shown in Figure 33.

FIGURE 33
Completed Project Builder 2

Making Selections

You are aware that there will be an opening in your firm's design department. Before you can be considered for the job, you need to increase your Photoshop compositing knowledge and experience. You have decided to teach yourself, using informational sources on the Internet and images that can be scanned or purchased.

1. Connect to the Internet and use your browser and favorite search engine to find information on image compositing. (Make a record of the site you found so you can use it for future reference, if necessary.)
2. Create a new Photoshop image, using the dimensions of your choice, then save it as **Sample Compositing**.
3. Locate at least two pieces of artwork—either on your hard disk, in a royalty-free collection, or from scanned images—that you can use. (The images can contain people, plants, animals, or inanimate objects.)
4. Select the images in the artwork, then copy each into the Sample Compositing image, using the method of your choice.
5. Rename each of the layers using meaningful names.
6. Apply a color to each new layer.
7. Arrange the images in a pleasing design. (*Hint*: Remember that you can flip any image, if necessary.)

8. Deselect the selections in the artwork, then close the files without saving the changes.
9. If desired, create a background layer for the image.
10. If necessary, add a vignette effect to a layer.

11. Defringe any images as you see necessary.
12. Save your work, then compare your screen to the sample shown in Figure 34.

FIGURE 34
Completed Design Project

At your design firm, a Fortune 500 client plans to start a 24-hour cable sports network called Total Sportz that will cover any nonprofessional sporting event. You have been asked to create some preliminary designs for the network, using images from multiple sources.

1. Open PS 3-13.psd, then save it as **Total Sportz**. (*Hint*: Click Update to close the warning box regarding missing fonts, if necessary.)
2. Locate several pieces of sports-related art-work—either on your hard disk, in a royalty-free collection, or from scanned images. Remember that the images should not show professional sports figures, if possible.
3. Select imagery from the artwork and move it into the Total Sportz image.
4. Arrange the images in an interesting design. (*Hint*: Remember that you can flip any image, if necessary.)
5. Change each layer name to describe the sport in the layer image.
6. Deselect the selections in the files that you used, then close the files without saving the changes.

7. If necessary, add a vignette effect to a layer and/or adjust opacity.
8. Defringe any images (if necessary).

9. Save your work, then compare your image to the sample shown in Figure 35.

FIGURE 35
Completed Portfolio Project

chapter

4

INCORPORATING COLOR
TECHNIQUES

1. Work with color to transform an image

2. Use the Color Picker and the Swatches panel

3. Place a border around an image

4. Blend colors using the Gradient tool

5. Add color to a grayscale image

6. Use filters, opacity, and blending modes

7. Match colors

Using Color

Color can make or break an image. Sometimes colors can draw us into an image; other times they can repel us. We all know which colors we like, but when it comes to creating an image, it is helpful to have some knowledge of color theory and be familiar with color terminology.

Understanding how Photoshop measures, displays, and prints color can be valuable when you create new images or modify existing images. Some colors you choose might be difficult for a professional printer to reproduce or might look muddy when printed. As you become more experienced using color, you will learn which colors reproduce well and which ones do not.

Understanding Color Modes and Color Models

Photoshop displays and prints images using specific color modes. A **mode** is the amount of color data that can be stored in a given file format, based on an established model. A **model** determines how pigments combine to produce resulting colors. This is the way your computer or printer associates a name or number with colors. Photoshop uses standard color models as the basis for its color modes.

Displaying and Printing Images

An image displayed on your monitor, such as an icon on your desktop, is a **bitmap**, a geometric arrangement of different color dots on a rectangular grid. Each dot, called a **pixel**, represents a color or shade. Bitmapped images are *resolution-dependent* and can lose detail—often demonstrated by a jagged appearance—when highly magnified. When printed, images with high resolutions tend to show more detail and subtler color transitions than low-resolution images.

Tools You'll Use

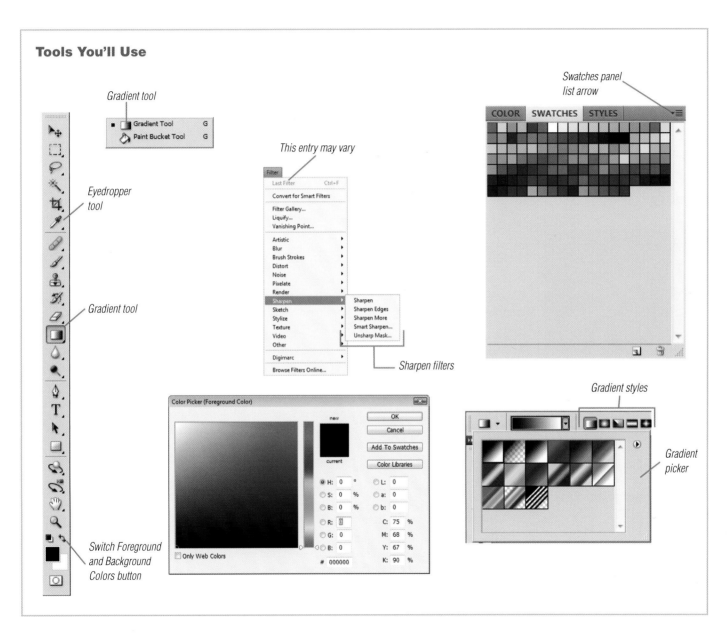

Gradient tool

Eyedropper tool

Gradient tool

Switch Foreground and Background Colors button

This entry may vary

Sharpen filters

Swatches panel list arrow

Gradient styles

Gradient picker

WORK WITH COLOR TO
TRANSFORM AN IMAGE

What You'll Do

In this lesson, you'll use the Color panel, the Paint Bucket tool, and the Eyedropper tool to change the background color of an image.

Learning About Color Models

Photoshop reproduces colors using models of color modes. The range of displayed colors, or **gamut**, for each model available in Photoshop is shown in Figure 1. The shape of each color gamut indicates the range of colors it can display. If a color is out of gamut, it is beyond the color space that your monitor can display or that your printer can print. You select the color mode from the Mode command on the Image menu. The available Photoshop color models include Lab, HSB, RGB, CMYK, Bitmap, and Grayscale.

QUICKTIP

A color mode is used to determine which color model will be used to display and print an image.

DESIGNTIP **Understanding the psychology of color**

Have you ever wondered why some colors make you react a certain way? You might have noticed that some colors affect you differently than others. Color is such an important part of our lives, and in Photoshop, it's key. Specific colors are often used in print and web pages to evoke the following responses:

- Blue tends to instill a feeling of safety and stability and is often used by financial services.
- Certain shades of green can generate a soft, calming feeling, while others suggest youthfulness and growth.
- Red commands attention and can be used as a call to action; it can also distract a reader's attention from other content.
- White evokes the feeling of purity and innocence, looks cool and fresh, and is often used to suggest luxury.
- Black conveys feelings of power and strength, but can also suggest darkness and negativity.

Lab Model

The Lab model is based on one luminance (lightness) component and two chromatic components (from green to red, and from blue to yellow). Using the Lab model has distinct advantages: you have the largest number of colors available to you and the greatest precision with which to create them. You can also create all the colors contained by other color models, which are limited in their respective color ranges. The Lab model is device-independent—the colors will not vary, regardless of the hardware. Use this model when working with photo CD images so that you can independently edit the luminance and color values.

HSB Model

Based on the human perception of color, the HSB (Hue, Saturation, Brightness) model has three fundamental characteristics: hue, saturation, and brightness. The color reflected from or transmitted through an object is called **hue**. Expressed as a degree (between 0° and 360°), each hue is identified by a color name (such as red or green). **Saturation** (or *chroma*) is the strength or purity of the color, representing the amount of gray in proportion to hue. Saturation is measured as a percentage from 0% (gray) to 100% (fully saturated). **Brightness** is the measurement of relative lightness or darkness of a color and is measured as a percentage from 0% (black) to 100% (white). Although you can use the HSB model to define a color on the Color panel or in the Color Picker dialog box, Photoshop *does not* offer HSB mode as a choice for creating or editing images.

RGB Mode

Photoshop uses color modes to determine how to display and print an image. Each mode is based on established models used in color reproduction. Most colors in the visible spectrum can be represented by mixing various proportions and intensities of red, green, and blue (RGB) colored light. RGB colors are additive colors. **Additive colors** are used for lighting, video, and computer monitors; color is created by light passing through red, green, and blue phosphors. When the values of red, green, and blue are zero, the result is black; when the values are all 255, the result is white. Photoshop assigns each component of the RGB mode an intensity value. Your colors can vary from monitor to monitor even if you are using the exact RGB values on different computers.

FIGURE 1
Photoshop color gamuts

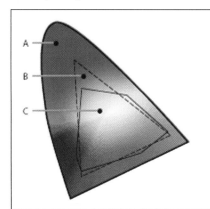

The gamuts of different color spaces
a. Lab color space encompasses all visible colors
b. RGB color space
c. CMYK color space

CMYK Mode

The light-absorbing quality of ink printed on paper is the basis of the CMYK (Cyan, Magenta, Yellow, Black) mode. Unlike the RGB mode—in which components are *combined* to create new colors—the CMYK mode is based on colors being partially *absorbed* as the ink hits the paper and being partially *reflected* back to your eyes. CMYK colors are **subtractive colors**—the *absence* of cyan, magenta, yellow, and black creates white. Subtractive (CMYK) and additive (RGB) colors are complementary colors; a pair from one model creates a color in the other. When combined, cyan, magenta, and yellow absorb all color and produce black. The CMYK mode—in which the lightest colors are assigned the highest percentages of ink colors—is used in four-color process printing. Converting an RGB image into a CMYK image produces a **color separation** (the commercial printing process of separating colors for use with

different inks). Note, however, that because your monitor uses RGB mode, you will not see the exact colors until you print the image, and even then the colors can vary depending on the printer and offset press.

Understanding the Bitmap and Grayscale Modes

In addition to the RGB and CMYK modes, Photoshop provides two specialized color modes: bitmap and grayscale. The **bitmap mode** uses black or white color values to represent image pixels, and is a good choice for images with subtle color gradations, such as photographs or painted images. The **grayscale mode** uses up to 256 shades of gray, assigning a brightness value from 0 (black) to 255 (white) to each pixel. Displayed colors can vary from monitor to monitor even if you use identical color settings on different computers.

Changing Foreground and Background Colors

In Photoshop, the **foreground color** is black by default and is used to paint, fill, and apply a border to a selection. The **background color** is white by default and is used to make **gradient fills** (gradual blends of multiple colors) and fill in areas of an image that have been erased. You can change foreground and background colors

using the Color panel, the Swatches panel, the Color Picker, or the Eyedropper tool. One method of changing foreground and background colors is **sampling**, in which an existing color is used. You can restore the default colors by clicking the Default Foreground and Background Colors button on the Tools panel, shown in Figure 2. You can apply a color to the background of a layer using the Paint Bucket tool. When you click an image with the Paint Bucket Tool, the current foreground color on the Tools panel fills the active layer.

FIGURE 2
Foreground and background color buttons

Default Foreground and Background Colors button

Set Foreground Color button

Switch Foreground and Background Colors button

Set Background Color button

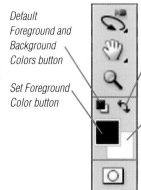

FIGURE 3
Image with rulers displayed

FIGURE 4

Color Settings dialog box

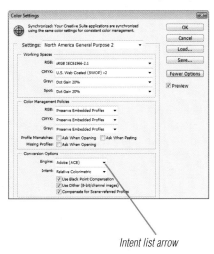

Intent list arrow

Creating a rendering intent

The use of a **rendering intent** determines how colors are converted by a color management system. A **color management system** is used to keep colors looking consistent as they move between devices. Colors are defined and interpreted using a **profile**. You can create a rendering intent by clicking Edit on the Application bar, then clicking Color Settings. Click the More Options button in the Color Settings dialog box, click the Intent list arrow shown in Figure 4, then click one of the four options. Since a gamut is the range of color that a color system can display or print, the rendering intent is constantly evaluating the color gamut and deciding whether or not the colors need adjusting. So, colors that fall inside the destination gamut may not be changed, or they may be adjusted when translated to a smaller color gamut.

Set the default foreground and background colors

1. Start Photoshop, open PS 4-1.psd from the drive and folder where you save your Data Files, then save it as **Rooster**.

   TIP   Whenever the Photoshop Format Options dialog box appears, click OK to maximize compatibility.

2. Click the **Default Foreground and Background Colors button** ▪ on the Tools panel.

   TIP   If you accidently click the Set foreground color button, the Color Picker (Foreground Color) dialog box opens.

3. Change the status bar so the document sizes display (if necessary).

   TIP   Document sizes will not display in the status bar if the image window is too small. Drag the lower-right corner of the image window to expand the window and display the menu button and document sizes.

4. Display the rulers in pixels (if necessary), show the guides (if necessary), then compare your screen to Figure 3.

   TIP   You can right-click (Win) or [control]-click (Mac) one of the rulers to choose Pixels, Inches, Centimeters, Millimeters, Points, Picas, or Percent as a unit of measurement, instead of using the Rulers and Units Preferences dialog box.

You set the default foreground and background colors and displayed rulers in pixels.

Change the background color using the Color panel

1. Click the **Background layer** on the Layers panel.

2. Display the History and Layers workspace.

3. Click the **Color panel tab** COLOR (if necessary).

4. Drag each color slider on the Color panel until you reach the values shown in Figure 5.

   The active color changes to the new color. Did you notice that this image is using the RGB mode?

   > TIP You can also double-click each component's text box on the Color panel and type the color values.

5. Click the **Paint Bucket tool** ⬦ on the Tools panel.

   > TIP If the Paint Bucket tool is not visible on the Tools panel, click the Gradient tool on the Tools panel, press and hold the mouse button until the list of hidden tools opens, then click the Paint Bucket tool.

6. Click the image with the **Paint Bucket pointer** ⬦.

7. Drag the **Paint Bucket state** on the History panel onto the **Delete current state button** ▦.

   > TIP You can also undo the last action by clicking Edit on the menu bar, then clicking Undo Paint Bucket.

You set new values in the Color panel, used the Paint Bucket tool to change the background to that color, then undid the change. You can change colors on the Color panel by dragging the sliders or by typing values in the color text boxes.

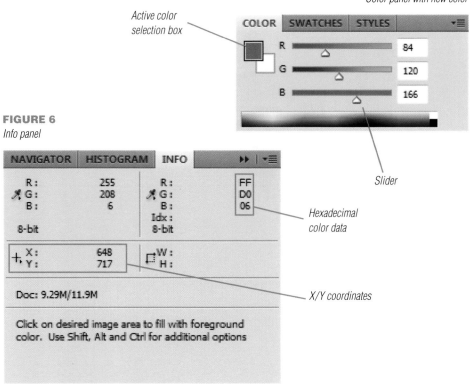

FIGURE 5
Color panel with new color

Active color selection box

Slider

FIGURE 6
Info panel

Hexadecimal color data

X/Y coordinates

Using ruler coordinates

Photoshop rulers run along the top and left sides of the document window. Each point on an image has a horizontal and vertical location. These two numbers, called X and Y coordinates, appear on the Info panel (which is located in the tab group with the Navigator and Histogram panels) as shown in Figure 6. The X coordinate refers to the horizontal location, and the Y coordinate refers to the vertical location. You can use one or both sets of guides to identify coordinates of a location, such as a color you want to sample. If you have difficulty seeing the ruler markings, you can increase the size of the image; the greater the zoom factor, the more detailed the measurement hashes.

FIGURE 7
New foreground color applied to Background layer

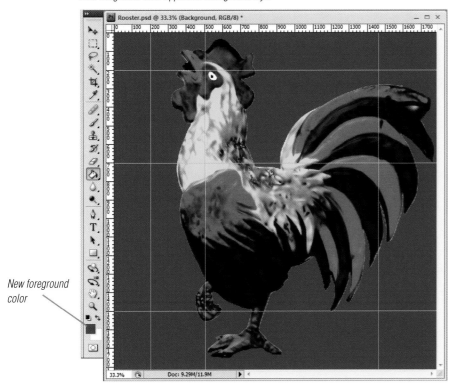

New foreground
color

Change the background color using the Eyedropper tool

1. Click the **Background layer** on the Layers panel.
2. Click the **Eyedropper tool** 🖊 on the Tools panel.
3. Click the **red part of the rooster's crown** in the image with the **Eyedropper pointer** 🖊, using the Info panel and the blue guides to help ensure accuracy.

   The Set foreground color button displays the red color that you clicked (or sampled).

   TIP Don't worry if you see a warning sign on the Color panel.

4. Click the **Paint Bucket tool** ◇ on the Tools panel.
5. Click the image, then compare your screen to Figure 7.

   You might have noticed that in this instance, it doesn't matter where on the layer you click, as long as the correct layer is selected.

6. Save your work.

You used the Eyedropper tool to sample a color as the foreground color, then used the Paint Bucket tool to change the background color to the color you sampled. Using the Eyedropper tool is a convenient way of sampling a color in any Photoshop image.

Using hexadecimal values in the Info panel

Colors can be expressed in a **hexadecimal value**, three pairs of letters or numbers that define the R, G, and B components of a color. The three pairs of letters/numbers are expressed in values from 00 (minimum luminance) to ff (maximum luminance). 000000 represents the value of black, ffffff is white, and ff0000 is red. To view hexadecimal values in the Info panel, click the Info panel list arrow, then click Panel Options. Click Web Color from either the First Color Readout or Second Color Readout Mode list arrow, then click OK. This is just one more way you can exactly determine a specific color in an image.

USE THE COLOR PICKER AND
THE SWATCHES PANEL

What You'll Do

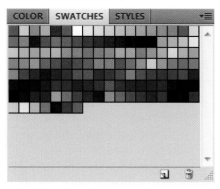

In this lesson, you'll use the Color Picker and the Swatches panel to select new colors, then you'll add a new color to the background and to the Swatches panel. You'll also learn how to access and download color themes from kuler.

Making Selections from the Color Picker

Depending on the color model you are using, you can select colors using the **Color Picker**, a feature that lets you choose a color from a color spectrum or numerically define a custom color. You can change colors in the Color Picker dialog box by using the following methods:

- Drag the sliders along the vertical color bar.
- Click inside the vertical color bar.
- Click a color in the Color field.
- Enter a value in any of the text boxes.

Figure 8 shows a color in the Color Picker dialog box. A circular marker indicates the active color. The color slider displays the range of color levels available for the active color component. The adjustments you make by dragging or clicking a new color are reflected in the text boxes; when you choose a new color, the previous color appears below the new color in the preview area.

Using kuler to coordinate colors

Kuler, by Adobe Labs, is a web-hosted application from which you can download pre-coordinated color themes or design your own. These collections can be saved in your own Mykuler space or shared with others. Use kuler as a fast, effective way of ensuring that your use of color is consistent and harmonious. If you decide to select an existing kuler theme, you'll find that there are thousands from which to choose. Kuler themes can be seen by clicking the Window menu, pointing to Extensions, then clicking Kuler. You can also access kuler through your browser at *kuler.adobe.com*, using the kuler desktop (which requires the installation of Adobe AIR), or from Adobe Illustrator (CS4 or higher). When you pass the mouse over any paint chip in the kuler website, the colors in the theme expand. Click the theme name, and the colors display in the paint chips at the top of the window.

Using the Swatches Panel

You can also change colors using the Swatches panel. The **Swatches panel** is a visual display of colors you can choose from, as shown in Figure 9. You can add your own colors to the panel by sampling a color from an image, and you can also delete colors. When you add a swatch to the Swatches panel, Photoshop assigns a default name that has a sequential number, or you can name the swatch whatever you like. Photoshop places new swatches in the first available space at the end of the panel. You can view swatch names by clicking the Swatches panel list arrow, then clicking Small List. You can restore the default Swatches panel by clicking the Swatches panel list arrow, clicking Reset Swatches, then clicking OK.

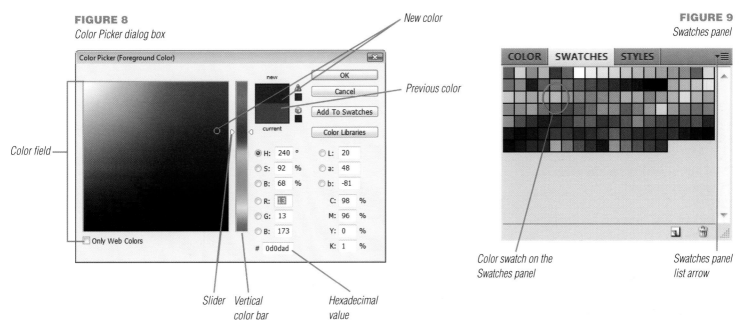

FIGURE 8
Color Picker dialog box

New color

Previous color

Color field

Slider   *Vertical color bar*

Hexadecimal value

FIGURE 9
Swatches panel

Color swatch on the Swatches panel

Swatches panel list arrow

Downloading a kuler theme

Once you've logged into kuler, you can download a theme as an Adobe Swatch Exchange (ASE) file. Click the download button, select a name and location for the downloaded file, then click Save. You can add a kuler theme to your color panel by clicking the Swatches panel option button, then clicking Load Swatches. The new colors will display at the end of the Swatches panel.

Select a color using the Color Picker dialog box

1. Click the **Set foreground color button** on the Tools panel, then verify that the H: option button is selected in the Color Picker dialog box.

2. Click the **R: option button**.

3. Click the **bottom-right corner** of the Color field (purple), as shown in Figure 10.

   TIP   If the Warning: out-of-gamut for print- ing indicator appears next to the color, then this color exceeds the printable range.

4. Click **OK**.

You opened the Color Picker dialog box, selected a different color mode, and then selected a new color.

Select a color using the Swatches panel

1. Click the **Swatches panel tab** SWATCHES .

2. Click the **second swatch from the left in the first row** (RGB Yellow), as shown in Figure 11.

   Did you notice that the foreground color on the Tools panel changed to a light, bright yellow?

3. Click the **Paint Bucket tool** ◇ on the Tools panel (if it is not already selected).

4. Click the image with the **Paint Bucket pointer** ◇, then compare your screen to Figure 12.

You opened the Swatches panel, selected a color, and then used the Paint Bucket tool to change the background to that color.

FIGURE 10
Color Picker dialog box

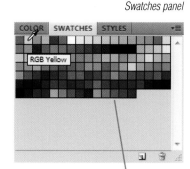

New color

Out-of-gamut indicator

Click to add a color to the Swatches panel

Your values might vary

Click here for new color   Previous color

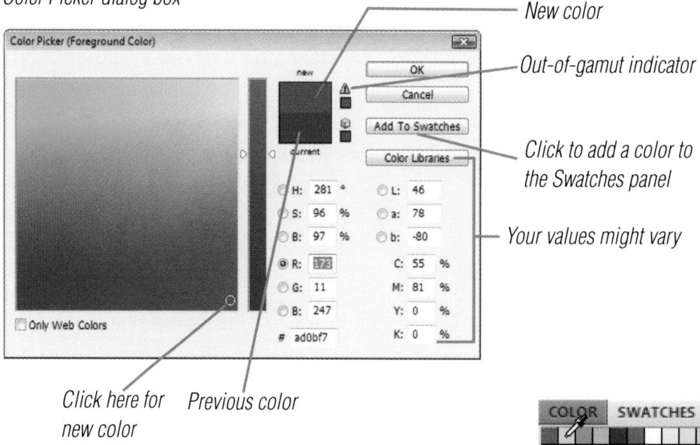

FIGURE 11
Swatches panel

Your swatches on the last row might vary

FIGURE 12
New foreground color applied to Background layer

Add a new color to the Swatches panel

1. Click the **Eyedropper tool** 🖋️ on the Tools panel.

2. Click **above and to the left of the rooster's eye** at coordinates **500 X/200 Y**.

   > TIP Use the Zoom tool whenever necessary to enlarge/decrease your workspace so you can better see what you're working on.

3. Click the **empty area to the right of the last swatch** in the bottom row of the Swatches panel with the **Paint Bucket pointer** 🪣.

4. Type **Rooster eye surround** in the Name text box.

5. Click **OK** in the Color Swatch Name dialog box.

   > TIP To delete a color from the Swatches panel, press [Alt] (Win) or [option] (Mac), position the pointer over a swatch, then click the swatch.

6. Save your work, then compare the new swatch on your Swatches panel to Figure 13.

You used the Eyedropper tool to sample a color, and then added the color to the Swatches panel, and gave it a descriptive name. Adding swatches to the Swatches panel makes it easy to reuse frequently used colors.

FIGURE 13
Swatch added to Swatches panel

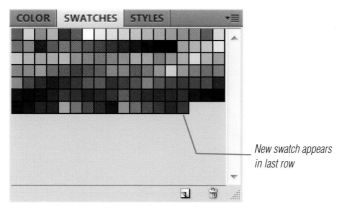

New swatch appears in last row

Maintaining your focus

Adobe Photoshop is probably unlike any other program you've used before. In other programs, there's a central area on the screen where you focus your attention. In Photoshop, there's the workspace containing your document, but you've probably already figured out that if you don't have the correct layer selected in the Layer's panel, things won't quite work out as you expected. In addition, you have to make sure you've got the right tool selected in the Tools panel. You also need to keep an eye on the History panel. As you work on your image, it might feel a lot like negotiating a shopping mall parking lot on the day before a holiday: you've got to be looking in a lot of places at once.

Use kuler from a web browser

1. Open your favorite browser, then type **kuler.adobe.com** in the URL text box.

2. Click the **Sign In link**, then type your **Adobe ID** and **password**. (If you don't have an Adobe ID, click the Register link and follow the instructions.)

3. Click the **Newest link**, then compare your results with Figure 14. (Your color results will be different.)

4. Type **wine olives** in the Search text box, press **[Enter]** (Win) or **[return]** (Mac). The swatch shown in Figure 15 will display.

5. Click the **Download this theme as an Adobe Swatch Exchange file button** , find the location where you save your Data Files in the Select location for download by kuler.adobe.com dialog box, then click **Save**.

6. Sign Out from kuler, then activate Photoshop.

7. Click the **Swatches list arrow**, then click **Load Swatches**.

8. Find the location where you save your Data Files, click the **Files of type list arrow** (Win), click **Swatch Exchange (*.ASE)**, click **Wine, Olives and Cheese**, then click **Load**.

You searched the kuler website and downloaded a color theme to your Photoshop Swatches panel.

FIGURE 14
Kuler website

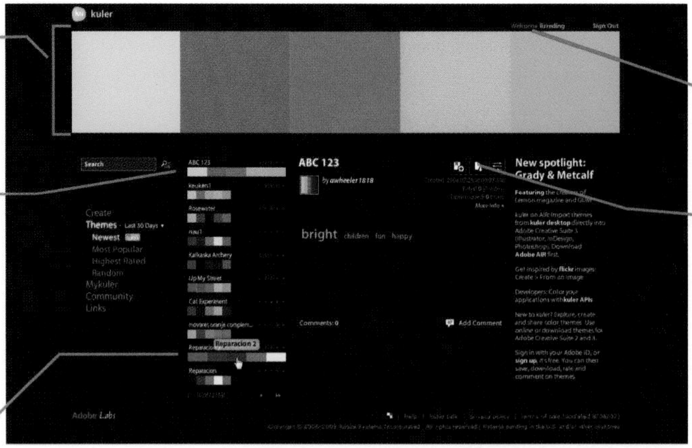

Color chip for active theme: the displayed theme will vary

Active color theme is expanded

Hover pointer over a theme to expand it

Indicates the current user

Click to download the active theme

FIGURE 15
Theme in kuler

FIGURE 16
Kuler panel

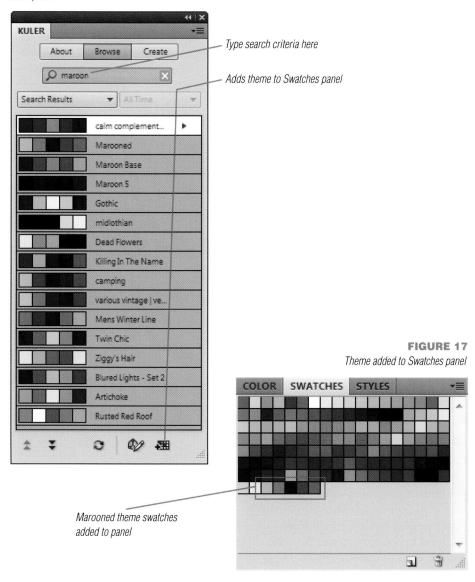

Type search criteria here

Adds theme to Swatches panel

Use kuler from Photoshop

1. Click **Window** on the Application bar, point to **Extensions**, then click **Kuler**.

2. Click the **Search text box**, type **maroon**, then press **[Enter]** (Win) or **[return]** (Mac). Compare your kuler panel to Figure 16.

   TIP Your kuler panel may differ as themes change frequently.

3. Click the **Marooned** theme, then click the **Add selected theme to swatches button**. Compare your Swatches panel to Figure 17.

4. Close the kuler panel.

You opened kuler in Photoshop, then added a color theme to the Swatches panel.

FIGURE 17
Theme added to Swatches panel

Marooned theme swatches
added to panel

PLACE A BORDER AROUND
AN IMAGE

What You'll Do

In this lesson, you'll apply a downloaded color and add a border to an image.

Emphasizing an Image

You can emphasize an image by placing a border around its edges. This process is called **stroking the edges**. The default color of the border is the current foreground color on the Tools panel. You can change the width, color, location, and blending mode of a border using the Stroke dialog box. The default stroke width is the setting last applied; you can apply a width from 1 to 16 pixels. The location option buttons in the dialog box determine where the border will be placed. If you want to change the location of the stroke, you must first delete the previously applied stroke, or Photoshop will apply the new border over the existing one.

Locking Transparent Pixels

As you modify layers, you can lock some properties to protect their contents. The ability to lock—or protect—elements within a layer is controlled from within the Layers panel, as shown in Figure 18. It's a good idea to lock transparent pixels when you add borders so that stray marks will not be included in the stroke. You can lock the following layer properties:

- Transparency: Limits editing capabilities to areas in a layer that are opaque.
- Image: Makes it impossible to modify layer pixels using painting tools.
- Position: Prevents pixels within a layer from being moved.

> **QUICK**TIP
>
> You can lock transparency or image pixels only in a layer containing an image, not in one containing type.

FIGURE 18
Layers panel locking options

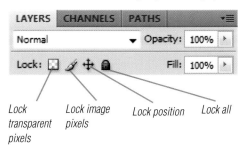

Lock transparent pixels   Lock image pixels   Lock position   Lock all

FIGURE 19
Locking transparent pixels

Lock transparent pixels button

Lock icon

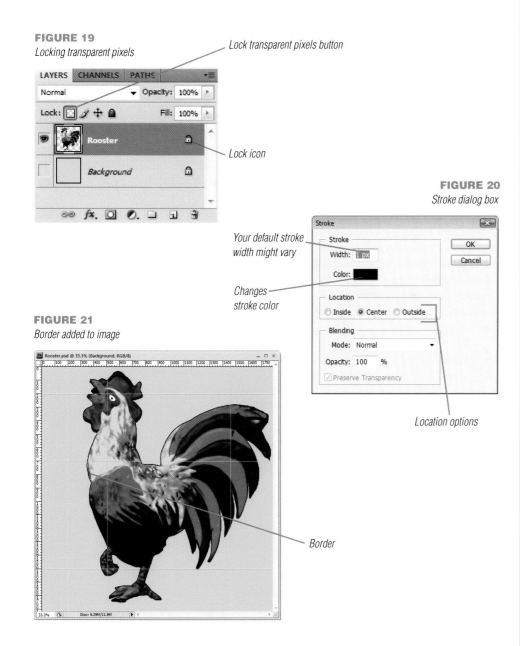

FIGURE 20
Stroke dialog box

Your default stroke width might vary

Changes stroke color

FIGURE 21
Border added to image

Location options

Border

Create a border

1. Click the **Indicates layer visibility button** 👁 on the Background layer on the Layers panel.

   TIP You can click the Indicates layer visibility button to hide distracting layers.

2. Click the **Default Foreground and Background Colors button** ▣.

   The foreground color will become the default border color.

3. Click the **Rooster layer** on the Layers panel.

4. Click the **Lock transparent pixels button** ⊡ on the Layers panel. See Figure 19.

   The border will be applied only to the pixels on the edge of the rooster.

5. Click **Edit** on the menu bar, then click **Stroke** to open the Stroke dialog box. See Figure 20.

6. Type **5** in the Width text box, click the **Inside option button**, then click **OK**.

   TIP Determining the correct border location can be confusing. Try different settings until you achieve the look you want.

7. Click the **Indicates layer visibility button** ▭ on the Background layer on the Layers panel.

8. Activate the Background layer on the Layers panel, click the newly-added tan-colored box in the Swatches panel (255 R, 211 G, 114 B), click the **Paint Bucket tool** ◇ on the Tools panel, then click the image.

9. Save your work, then compare your image to Figure 21.

You hid a layer, changed the foreground color to black, locked transparent pixels, then used the Stroke dialog box to apply a border to the image.

Lesson 3 Place a Border Around an Image

BLEND COLORS USING THE
GRADIENT TOOL

What You'll Do

In this lesson, you'll create a gradient fill from a sampled color and a swatch, then apply it to the background.

Understanding Gradients

A **gradient fill**, or simply **gradient**, is a blend of colors used to fill a selection of a layer or an entire layer. A gradient's appearance is determined by its beginning and ending points, and its length, direction, and angle. Gradients allow you to create dramatic effects, using existing color combinations or your own colors. The Gradient picker, as shown in Figure 22, offers multi-color gradient fills and a few that use the current foreground or background colors on the Tools panel.

FIGURE 22
Gradient picker

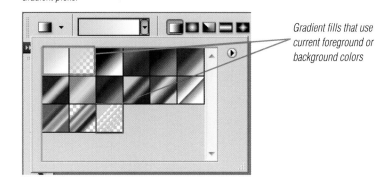

Gradient fills that use current foreground or background colors

Incorporating Color Techniques

Using the Gradient Tool

You use the Gradient tool to create gradients in images. When you choose the Gradient tool, five gradient styles become available on the options bar. These styles—Linear, Radial, Angle, Reflected, and Diamond—are shown in Figure 23. In each example, the gradient was drawn from 50 X/50 Y to 100 X/100 Y.

Customizing Gradients

Using the **gradient presets**—predesigned gradient fills that are displayed in the Gradient picker—is a great way to learn how to use gradients. But as you become more familiar with Photoshop, you might want to venture into the world of the unknown and create your own gradient designs. You can create your own designs by modifying an existing gradient using the Gradient Editor. You can open the Gradient Editor, shown in Figure 24, by clicking the selected gradient pattern that appears on the options bar. After it's open, you can use it to make the following modifications:

- Create a new gradient from an existing gradient.
- Modify an existing gradient.
- Add intermediate colors to a gradient.
- Create a blend between more than two colors.
- Adjust the opacity values.
- Determine the placement of the midpoint.

FIGURE 23
Sample gradients

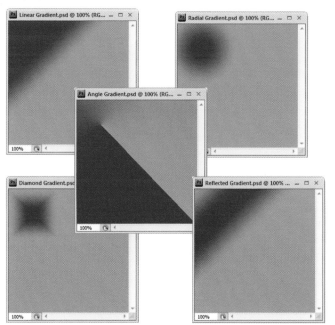

FIGURE 24
Gradient Editor dialog box

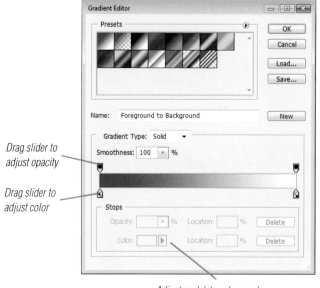

Drag slider to adjust opacity

Drag slider to adjust color

Adjust or delete colors and opacity values

Create a gradient from a sample color

1. Verify that the **Eyedropper tool** 🖋 is selected.

2. Click the **yellow neck** in the image at coordinates **500 X/600 Y**.

   | TIP To accurately select the coordinates, adjust the zoom factor as necessary.

3. Click the **Switch Foreground and Background Colors button** ↕ on the Tools panel.

4. Click the **Maroon swatch** (R=180 G=25 B=29) on the Swatches panel (one of the new swatches you added) with the **Eyedropper pointer** 🖋.

5. Click the **Indicates layer visibility button** 👁 on the Rooster layer, as shown in Figure 25.

6. Click the **Paint Bucket tool** 🪣 on the Tools panel, then press and hold the mouse button until the list of hidden tools opens.

7. Click the **Gradient tool** 🟦 on the Tools panel, then click the **Angle Gradient button** 🔷 on the options bar (if it is not already selected).

8. Click the **Click to open Gradient picker list arrow** on the options bar, then click **Foreground to Background** (the first gradient fill in the first row), as shown in Figure 26.

You sampled a color on the image to set the background color, changed the foreground color using an existing swatch, selected the Gradient tool, and then chose a gradient fill and style.

FIGURE 25
Rooster layer hidden

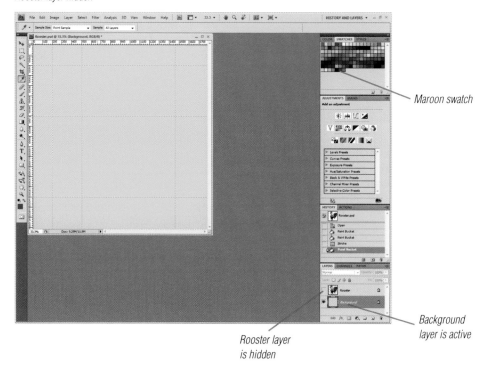

Maroon swatch

Rooster layer is hidden

Background layer is active

Click to open Gradient picker list arrow

FIGURE 26
Gradient picker

Foreground to Background (Current foreground and background colors)

Gradient styles

Gradient picker

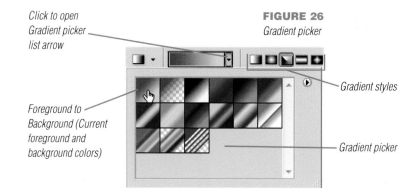

FIGURE 27
Gradient fill applied to Background layer

Apply a gradient fill

1. Click the **Click to open Gradient picker list arrow** to close the Gradient picker.

   TIP You can also close the Gradient picker by pressing [Esc] (Win) or [esc] (Mac).

2. Drag the **Gradient pointer** -+- from **1430 X/200 Y** to **200 X/1500 Y** using the Info panel and the guides to help you create the gradient in the work area.

3. Click the **Indicates layer visibility button** on the Rooster layer.

   The Rooster layer appears against the new background, as shown in Figure 27.

   TIP It is a good practice to save your work early and often in the creation process, especially before making significant changes or printing.

4. Save your work.

You applied the gradient fill to the background. You can create dramatic effects using the gradient fill in combination with foreground and background colors.

Collaborating with ConnectNow

Adobe has created a tool to help you collaborate with others: ConnectNow. This online tool lets you share information and collaborate with others. Using screen sharing, chat, shared notes, audio, and video, you can more effectively manage your workflow and get your work done. Open ConnectNow from within Photoshop by clicking File on the Application bar, then clicking Share My Screen or type *www.adobe.com/acom/connect-now* in your favorite browser. Once you have logged into Adobe ConnectNow, you can invite participants, share your computer screen, and upload files. ConnectNow uses the metaphor of a meeting, into which you invite participants and use pod tools to interact. When you are finished, you click the End Meeting command from the Meeting menu. You can use the Connections panel in Photoshop by clicking Window on the Application bar, pointing to Extensions, then clicking Connections to log in and check for updates.

ADD COLOR TO A
GRAYSCALE IMAGE

What You'll Do

In this lesson, you'll convert an image to grayscale, change the color mode, then colorize a grayscale image using the Hue/Saturation dialog box.

Colorizing Options

Grayscale images can contain up to 256 shades of gray, assigning a brightness value from 0 (black) to 255 (white) to each pixel. Since the earliest days of photography, people have been tinting grayscale images with color to create a certain mood or emphasize an image in a way that purely realistic colors could not. To capture this effect in Photoshop, you convert an image to the Grayscale mode, then choose the color mode you want to work in before you continue. When you apply a color to a grayscale image, each pixel becomes a shade of that particular color instead of gray.

Converting Grayscale and Color Modes

When you convert a color image to grayscale, the light and dark values—called the **luminosity**—remain, while the color information is deleted. When you change from grayscale to a color mode, the foreground and background colors on the Tools panel change from black and white to the previously selected colors.

Converting a color image to black and white

Using the Black & White command, you can easily convert a color image to black and white. This feature lets you quickly make the color to black and white conversion while maintaining full control over how individual colors are converted. Tones can also be applied to the grayscale by applying color tones (the numeric values for each color). To use this feature, click Image on the menu bar, point to Adjustments, then click Black & White. The Black & White command can also be applied as an Adjustment layer.

Tweaking Adjustments

Once you have made your color mode conversion to grayscale, you may want to make some adjustments. You can fine-tune the Brightness/Contrast, filters, and blending modes in a grayscale image.

Colorizing a Grayscale Image

In order for a grayscale image to be colorized, you must change the color mode to one that accommodates color. After you change the color mode, and then adjust settings in the Hue/Saturation dialog box, Photoshop determines the colorization range based on the hue of the currently selected foreground color. If you want a different colorization range, you need to change the foreground color.

FIGURE 28
Gradient Map dialog box

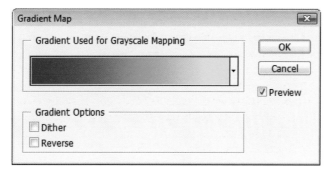

Applying a gradient effect

You can also use the Gradient Map to apply a colored gradient effect to a grayscale image. The Gradient Map uses gradient fills (the same ones displayed in the Gradient picker) to colorize the image, which can produce some stunning effects. You use the Gradient Map dialog box, shown in Figure 28, to apply a gradient effect to a grayscale image. You can access the Gradient Map dialog box using the Adjustments command on the Image menu.

Change the color mode

1. Open PS 4-2.psd from the drive and folder where you store your Data Files, save it as **Rooster Colorized**, then turn off the rulers if they are displayed.

2. Click **Image** on the Application bar, point to **Mode**, then click **Grayscale**.

3. Click **Flatten** in the warning box, then click **Discard**.

   The color mode of the image is changed to grayscale, and the image is flattened so there is only a single layer. All the color information in the image has been discarded.

4. Click **Image** on the Application bar, point to **Mode**, then click **RGB Color**.

   The color mode is changed back to RGB color, although there is still no color in the image. Compare your screen to Figure 29.

You converted the image to Grayscale, which discarded the existing color information. Then you changed the color mode to RGB color.

FIGURE 29
Image with RGB mode

Mode changed to RGB

Converting color images to grayscale
Like everything else in Photoshop, there is more than one way of converting a color image into one that is black and white. Changing the color mode to grayscale is the quickest method. You can also make this conversion through desaturation by clicking Image on the menu bar, pointing to Adjustments, then clicking Black & White, or Desaturate. Converting to Grayscale mode generally results in losing contrast, as does the desaturation method, while using the Black & White method retains the contrast of the original image.

FIGURE 30
Hue/Saturation dialog box

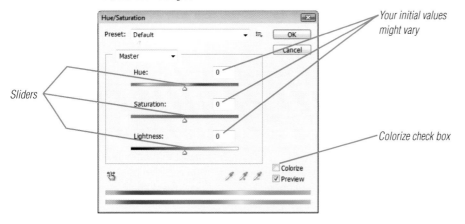

Your initial values might vary

Sliders

Colorize check box

FIGURE 31
Colorized image

Colorize a grayscale image

1. Click **Image** on the Application bar, point to **Adjustments**, then click **Hue/Saturation** to open the Hue/Saturation dialog box, as shown in Figure 30.

2. Click the **Colorize check box** in the Hue/Saturation dialog box to add a check mark.

3. Drag the **Hue slider** until the text box displays **240**.

   TIP You can also type values in the text boxes in the Hue/Saturation dialog box. Negative numbers must be preceded by a minus sign or a hyphen. Positive numbers can be preceded by an optional plus sign (+).

4. Drag the **Saturation slider** until the text box displays **55**.

5. Drag the **Lightness slider** until the text box displays **-15**.

6. Click **OK**.

7. Save your work, then compare your screen to Figure 31.

You colorized a grayscale image by adjusting settings in the Hue/Saturation dialog box.

Understanding the Hue/Saturation dialog box
The Hue/Saturation dialog box is an important tool in the world of color enhancement. Useful for both color and grayscale images, the saturation slider can be used to boost a range of colors. By clicking the Edit list arrow, you can isolate which colors (all, cyan, blue, magenta, red, yellow, or green) you want to modify. Using this tool requires patience and experimentation, but gives you great control over the colors in your image.

USE FILTERS, OPACITY, AND BLENDING MODES

What You'll Do

 In this lesson, you'll adjust the brightness and contrast in the Rooster colorized image, apply a Sharpen filter, and adjust the opacity of the lines applied by the filter. You'll also adjust the color balance of the Rooster image.

Manipulating an Image

As you work in Photoshop, you might realize that some images have fundamental problems that need correcting, while others just need to be further enhanced. For example, you might need to adjust an image's contrast and sharpness, or you might want to colorize an otherwise dull image. You can use a variety of techniques to change the way an image looks. For example, you have learned how to use the Adjustments command on the Image menu to modify hue and saturation, but you can also use this command to adjust brightness and contrast, color balance, and a host of other visual effects.

Understanding Filters

Filters are Photoshop commands that can significantly alter an image's appearance. Experimenting with Photoshop's filters is a fun way to completely change the look of an image. For example, the Watercolor filter gives the illusion that your image was

Fixing blurry scanned images

An unfortunate result of scanning a picture is that the image can become blurry. You can fix this, however, using the Unsharp Mask filter. This filter both sharpens and smoothes the image by increasing the contrast along element edges. Here's how it works: the smoothing effect removes stray marks, and the sharpening effect emphasizes contrasting neighboring pixels. Most scanners come with their own Unsharp Masks built into the TWAIN driver, but using Photoshop, you have access to a more powerful version of this filter. You can use Photoshop's Unsharp Mask to control the sharpening process by adjusting key settings. In most cases, your scanner's Unsharp Mask might not give you this flexibility. Regardless of the technical aspects, the result is a sharper image. You can apply the Unsharp Mask by clicking Filter on the menu bar, pointing to Sharpen, then clicking Unsharp Mask.

painted using traditional watercolors. Sharpen filters can appear to add definition to the entire image, or just the edges. Compare the different Sharpen filters applied in Figure 32. The **Sharpen More filter** increases the contrast of adjacent pixels and can focus a blurry image. Be careful not to overuse sharpening tools (or any filter), because you can create high-contrast lines or add graininess in color or brightness.

Choosing Blending Modes

A **blending mode** controls how pixels are made either darker or lighter based on underlying colors. Photoshop provides a variety of blending modes, listed in Table 1, to combine the color of the pixels in the current layer with those in layer(s) beneath it. You can see a list of blending modes by clicking the Add a layer style button on the Layers panel.

Understanding Blending Mode Components

You should consider the following underlying colors when planning a blending mode: **base color**, which is the original color of the image; **blend color**, which is the color you apply with a paint or edit tool; and **resulting color**, which is the color that is created as a result of applying the blend color.

Softening Filter Effects

Opacity can soften the line that the filter creates, but it doesn't affect the opacity of the entire layer. After a filter has been applied, you can modify the opacity and apply a blending mode using the Layers panel or the Fade dialog box. You can open the Fade dialog box by clicking Edit on the menu bar, then clicking the Fade command.

Balancing Colors

As you adjust settings, such as hue and saturation, you might create unwanted imbalances in your image. You can adjust colors to correct or improve an image's appearance. For example, you can decrease a color by increasing the amount of its opposite color. You use the Color Balance dialog box to balance the color in an image.

FIGURE 32
Sharpen filters

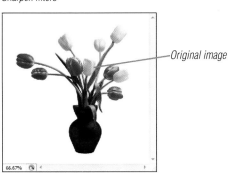

Original image

Sharpen filter applied

Sharpen More filter applied excessively

TABLE 1: Blending Modes

blending mode	description
Dissolve, Behind, and Clear modes	Dissolve mode creates a grainy, mottled appearance. The Behind mode paints on the transparent part of the layer—the lower the opacity, the grainier the image. The Clear mode paints individual pixels. All modes are available only when the Lock transparent pixels check box is *not* selected.
Multiply and Screen modes	Multiply mode creates semitransparent shadow effects. This mode assesses the information in each channel, then multiplies the value of the base color by the blend color. The resulting color is always *darker* than the base color. The Screen mode multiplies the value of the inverse of the blend and base colors. After it is applied, the resulting color is always *lighter* than the base color.
Overlay mode	Dark and light values (luminosity) are preserved, dark base colors are multiplied (darkened), and light areas are screened (lightened).
Soft Light and Hard Light modes	Soft Light lightens a light base color and darkens a dark base color. The Hard Light blending mode creates a similar effect, but provides greater contrast between the base and blend colors.
Color Dodge and Color Burn modes	Color Dodge mode brightens the base color to reflect the blend color. The Color Burn mode darkens the base color to reflect the blend color.
Darken and Lighten modes	Darken mode selects a new resulting color based on whichever color is darker—the base color or the blend color. The Lighten mode selects a new resulting color based on the lighter of the two colors.
Difference and Exclusion modes	The Difference mode subtracts the value of the blend color from the value of the base color, or vice versa, depending on which color has the greater brightness value. The Exclusion mode creates an effect similar to that of the Difference mode, but with less contrast between the blend and base colors.
Color and Luminosity modes	The Color mode creates a resulting color with the luminance of the base color, and the hue and saturation of the blend color. The Luminosity mode creates a resulting color with the hue and saturation of the base color, and the luminance of the blend color.
Hue and Saturation modes	The Hue mode creates a resulting color with the luminance of the base color and the hue of the blend color. The Saturation mode creates a resulting color with the luminance of the base color and the saturation of the blend color.

FIGURE 33
Brightness/Contrast dialog box

FIGURE 34
Shadows/Highlights dialog box

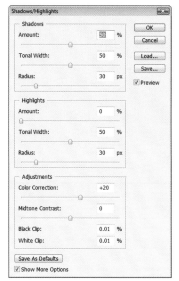

Adjust brightness and contrast

1. Click **Image** on the Application bar, point to **Adjustments**, then click **Brightness/Contrast** to open the Brightness/Contrast dialog box.

2. Drag the **Brightness slider** until **15** appears in the Brightness text box.

3. Drag the **Contrast slider** until **25** appears in the Contrast text box. Compare your screen to Figure 33.

4. Click **OK**.

You adjusted settings in the Brightness/Contrast dialog box. The image now looks much brighter, with a higher degree of contrast, which obscures some of the finer detail in the image.

Correcting shadows and highlights

The ability to correct shadows and highlights will delight photographers everywhere. This image correction feature (opened by clicking Image on the Application bar, pointing to Adjustments, then clicking Shadows/Highlights) lets you modify overall lighting and make subtle adjustments. Figure 34 shows the Shadows/Highlights dialog box with the Show More Options check box selected. Check out this one-stop shopping for shadow and highlight adjustments!

Lesson 6   Use Filters, Opacity, and Blending Modes

Work with a filter, a blending mode, and an opacity setting

1. Click **Filter** on the Application bar, point to **Sharpen**, then click **Sharpen More**.

   The border and other features of the image are intensified.

2. Click **Edit** on the Application bar, then click **Fade Sharpen More** to open the Fade dialog box, as shown in Figure 35.

3. Drag the **Opacity slider** until **45** appears in the Opacity text box.

   The opacity setting softened the lines applied by the Sharpen More filter.

4. Click the **Mode list arrow**, then click **Dissolve**.

   The Dissolve setting blends the surrounding pixels.

5. Click **OK**.

6. Save your work, then compare your image to Figure 36.

You applied the Sharpen More filter, then adjusted the opacity and changed the color mode in the Fade dialog box. The border in the image looks crisper than before, with a greater level of detail.

FIGURE 35
Fade dialog box

FIGURE 36
Image settings adjusted

FIGURE 37

Color Balance dialog box

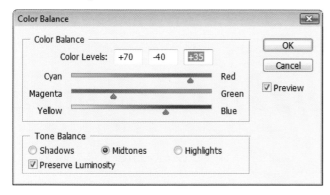

FIGURE 38

Image with colors balanced

Adjust color balance

1. Switch to the Rooster image, with the Background layer active.

   The image you worked with earlier in this chapter becomes active.

2. Click **Image** on the Application bar, point to **Adjustments**, then click **Color Balance**.

3. Drag the **Cyan-Red slider** until **+70** appears in the first text box.

4. Drag the **Magenta-Green slider** until **–40** appears in the middle text box.

5. Drag the **Yellow-Blue slider** until **+35** appears in the last text box, as shown in Figure 37.

   Subtle changes were made in the color balance in the image.

6. Click **OK**.

7. Save your work, then compare your image to Figure 38.

You balanced the colors in the Rooster image by adjusting settings in the Color Balance dialog box.

MATCH COLORS

What You'll Do

In this lesson, you'll make selections in source and target images, then use the Match Color command to replace the target color.

Finding the Right Color

If it hasn't happened already, at some point you'll be working on an image and wish you could grab a color from another image to use in this one. Just as you can use the Eyedropper tool to sample any color in the current image for the foreground and background, you can sample a color from any other image to use in the current one. Perhaps the skin tones in one image look washed out: you can use the Match Color command to replace those tones with skin tone colors from another image. Or maybe the jacket color in one image would look better using a color in another image.

Using Selections to Match Colors

Remember that this is Photoshop, where everything is about layers and selections.

To replace a color in one image with one you've matched from another, you work with—you guessed it—layers and selections.

Suppose you've located the perfect color in another image. The image you are working with is the **target**, and the image that contains your perfect color is the **source**. By activating the layer on which the color lies in the source image, and making a selection around the color, you can have Photoshop match the color in the source and replace a color in the target. To accomplish this, you use the Match Color command, which is available by pointing to Adjustments on the Image menu.

FIGURE 39
Selection in source image

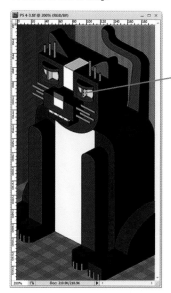

Selected area

FIGURE 40
Match Color dialog box

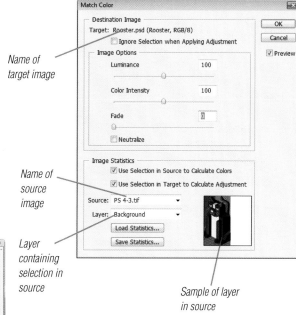

Name of
target image

Name of
source
image

FIGURE 41
Image with matched colors

Layer
containing
selection in
source

Sample of layer
in source

Modified selection

Match a color

1. Click the **Rooster layer** on the Layers panel, then zoom (once) into the eye of the rooster.

2. Click the **Magic Wand tool** ✳ on the Tools panel.

3. Verify that the **Anti-alias** and **Contiguous check boxes** on the options bar are selected, then set the **Tolerance** to **10**.

4. Click the image with the **Magic Wand pointer** ✳ on the white of the eye at approximately **550 X/210 Y**.

5. Open PS 4-3.tif from the drive and folder where you store your Data Files, zoom into the image (if necessary), change the tolerance to **40**, then click the **light green part of the cat's eye** (at **100 X/95 Y**) with the **Magic Wand pointer** ✳. Compare your selection to Figure 39.

6. Activate the **Rooster image**, click **Image** on the Application bar, point to **Adjustments**, then click **Match Color**.

7. Click the **Source list arrow**, then click **PS 4-3.tif**. Compare your settings to Figure 40.

8. Click **OK**.

9. Deselect the selection, turn off the rulers and the guides, save your work, then compare your image to Figure 41.

10. Close all open images, display the Essentials workspace then exit Photoshop.

You used the Match Color dialog box to replace a color in one image with a color from another image. The Match Color dialog box makes it easy to sample colors from other images, giving you even more options for incorporating color into an image.

Power User Shortcuts

to do this:	use this method:
Apply a sharpen filter	Filter ➢ Sharpen
Balance colors	Image ➢ Adjustments ➢ Color Balance
Change color mode	Image ➢ Mode
Choose a background color from the Swatches panel	[Ctrl]Color swatch (Win) ⌘Color swatch (Mac)
Delete a swatch from the Swatches panel	[Alt], click swatch (Win) [option], click swatch (Mac)
Eyedropper tool	🖊 or I
Fill with background color	[Shift][Backspace] (Win) ⌘[delete] (Mac)
Fill with foreground color	[Alt][Backspace] (Win) option [delete] (Mac)
Gradient tool	▮
Guide pointer	◀╫▶ or ⬍
Hide a layer	👁

to do this:	use this method:
Hide or show rulers	[Ctrl][R] (Win) ⌘[R] (Mac)
Hide or show the Color panel	[F6] (Win) COLOR
Lock transparent pixels check box on/off	[/]
Make Swatches panel active	SWATCHES
Paint Bucket tool	◊ or G
Return background and foreground colors to default	▮ or D
Show a layer	☐
Show hidden Paint Bucket/ Gradient tools	[Shift] G
Switch between open files	[Ctrl][Tab] (Win) [control][tab] (Mac)
Switch foreground and background colors	↺ or X

Key: Menu items are indicated by ➢ between the menu name and its command. Blue bold letters are shortcuts for selecting tools on the Tools panel.

Work with color to transform an image.

1. Start Photoshop.
2. Open PS 4-4.psd from the drive and folder where you store your Data Files, then save it as **Firetruck**.
3. Make sure the rulers display in pixels, and that the default foreground and background colors display.
4. Use the Eyedropper tool to sample the red color at 90 X/165 Y using the guides to help.
5. Use the Paint Bucket tool to apply the new foreground color to the Background layer.
6. Undo your last step using either the Edit menu or the History panel. (*Hint:* You can switch to another workspace that displays the necessary panels.)
7. Switch the foreground and background colors.
8. Save your work.

Use the Color Picker and the Swatches panel.

1. Use the Set foreground color button to open the Color Picker dialog box.
2. Click the R:, G:, and B: option buttons, one at a time. Note how the color panel changes.
3. With the B: option button selected, click the panel in the upper-left corner, then click OK.
4. Switch the foreground and background colors.
5. Add the foreground color (red) to the Swatches panel using a meaningful name of your choice.

Place a border around an image.

1. Make Layer 1 active (if it is not already active).
2. Revert to the default foreground and background colors.
3. Create a border by applying a 2-pixel outside stroke to the firetruck.
4. Save your work.

Blend colors using the Gradient tool.

1. Change the foreground color to the sixth swatch from the right in the top row of the Swatches panel (35% Gray). (Your swatch location may vary.)
2. Switch foreground and background colors.
3. Use the new red swatch that you added previously as the foreground color.
4. Make the Background layer active.
5. Use the Gradient tool, apply the Angle Gradient with its default settings, then using the guides to help, drag the pointer from 145 X/70 Y to 35 X/165 Y.
6. Save your work, and turn off the rulers display.

Add color to a grayscale image.

1. Open PS 4-5.psd, then save it as **Firetruck Colorized**.
2. Change the color mode to RGB Color.
3. Open the Hue/Saturation dialog box, then select the Colorize check box.
4. Drag the sliders so the text boxes show the following values: 155, 56, and –30, then click OK.
5. Save your work.

Use filters, opacity, and blending modes.

1. Use the Sharpen filter to sharpen the image.
2. Open the Fade Sharpen dialog box by using the Edit menu, change the opacity to 40%, change the mode to Hard Light, then save your work.
3. Open the Color Balance dialog box.
4. Change the color level settings so the text boxes show the following values: +61, –15, and +20.
5. Turn off the rulers display (if necessary).
6. Save your work.

Match colors.

1. Open PS 4-6.tif, then use the Magic Wand tool to select the light yellow in the cat's eye.
2. Select the white areas of the firetruck cab in Firetruck.psd. (*Hint:* You can press [Shift] and click on multiple areas using the Magic Wand tool.)
3. Use the Match Color dialog box to change the white in Layer 1 of the firetruck image to yellow (in the cat's eye). Compare your images to Figure 42. (The brightness of your colors may vary.)
4. Save your work.
5. Exit Photoshop.

FIGURE 42
Completed Skills Review

You are finally able to leave your current job and pursue your lifelong dream of opening a furniture repair and restoration business. While you're waiting for the laser stripper and refinisher to arrive, you start to work on a sign design.

1. Open PS 4-7.psd, substitute any missing fonts, then save it as **Furniture Fixer**.
2. Move the objects to any location to achieve a layout you think looks attractive and eye-catching.
3. Sample the blue pliers in the tool belt, then switch the foreground and background colors.
4. Sample the red tape measure in the tool belt.
5. Use any Gradient tool to create an interesting effect on the Background layer.
6. Save the image, then compare your screen to the sample shown in Figure 43.

FIGURE 43
Completed Project Builder 1

You're painting the swing set at the PB&J Preschool, when you notice a staff member struggling to create a flyer for the school. Although the basic flyer is complete, it doesn't convey the high energy of the school. You offer to help, and soon find yourself in charge of creating an exciting background for the image.

1. Open PS 4-8.psd, update layers as needed, then save it as **Preschool**.
2. Apply a foreground color of your choice to the Background layer.
3. Add a new layer above the Background layer, then select a background color and apply a gradient you have not used before to the layer. (*Hint*: Remember that you can immediately undo a gradient that you don't want.)
4. Add the foreground and background colors to the Swatches panel.
5. Apply a Sharpen filter to the Boy at blackboard layer and adjust the opacity of the filter.
6. Save your work.
7. Compare your screen to the sample shown in Figure 44.

FIGURE 44
Completed Project Builder 2

A local Top 40 morning radio show recently conducted a survey about chocolate, and discovered that only one in seven people knew about its health benefits. Now everyone is talking about chocolate. An interior designer wants to incorporate chocolates into her fall decorating theme, and has asked you to create a poster. You decide to highlight as many varieties as possible.

1. Open PS 4-9.psd, then save it as **Chocolate**.
2. If you choose, you can add any appropriate images that have been scanned or captured using a digital camera.
3. Activate the Background layer, then sample colors from the image for foreground and background colors. (*Hint*: Try to sample unusual colors, to widen your design horizons.)
4. Add the sampled colors to the Swatches panel.
5. Display the rulers, then move the existing guides to indicate the coordinates of the colors you sampled.
6. Create a gradient fill by using both the foreground and background colors and the gradient style of your choice.
7. Defringe the Chocolate layer, if necessary.
8. Hide the rulers, save your work, then compare your image to the sample shown in Figure 45.

FIGURE 45
Completed Design Project

An educational toy and game store has hired you to design a poster announcing this year's Most Unusual Hobby contest. After reviewing the photos from last year's awards ceremony, you decide to build a poster using the winner of the Handicrafts Award. You'll use your knowledge of Photoshop color modes to convert the color mode, adjust color in the image, and add an interesting background.

1. Open PS 4-10.psd, then save it as **Rubberband**.
2. Convert the image to Grayscale mode. (*Hint*: When Photoshop prompts you to flatten the layers, click Don't Flatten.)
3. Convert the image to RGB Color mode. (*Hint*: When Photoshop prompts you to flatten the layers, click Don't Flatten.)
4. Colorize the image and adjust the Hue, Saturation, and Lightness settings as desired.
5. Adjust Brightness/Contrast settings as desired.
6. Adjust Color Balance settings as desired.
7. Sample the image to create a new foreground color, then add a color of your choice as the background color.
8. Apply any two Sharpen filters and adjust the opacity for one of them.
9. Add a reflected gradient to the Background layer that follows the path of one of the main bands on the ball.

10. Save your work, then compare your image to the sample shown in Figure 46.
11. Be prepared to discuss the color-correcting methods you used and why you chose them.

FIGURE 46
Completed Portfolio Project

Incorporating Color Techniques

chapter

5

PLACING TYPE IN
AN IMAGE

1. Learn about type and how it is created

2. Change spacing and adjust baseline shift

3. Use the Drop Shadow style

4. Apply anti-aliasing to type

5. Modify type with the Bevel and Emboss style

6. Apply special effects to type using filters

7. Create text on a path

Learning About Type

Text plays an important design role when combined with images for posters, magazine and newspaper advertisements, and other graphics materials that need to communicate detailed information. In Photoshop, text is referred to as **type**. You can use type to express the ideas conveyed in a file's imagery or to deliver an additional message. You can manipulate type in many ways to reflect or reinforce the meaning behind an image. As in other programs, type has its own unique characteristics in Photoshop. For example, you can change its appearance by using different fonts (also called typefaces) and colors.

Understanding the Purpose of Type

Type is typically used along with imagery to deliver a message quickly and with flare. Because type is used sparingly (often there's not a lot of room for it), its appearance is very important; color and imagery are frequently used to *complement* or *reinforce* the message within the text. Type should be limited, direct, and to the point. It should be large enough for easy reading, but should not overwhelm or distract from the central image. For example, a vibrant and daring advertisement should contain just enough type to interest the reader, without demanding too much reading.

Getting the Most Out of Type

Words can express an idea, but the appearance of the type is what drives the point home. After you decide on the content you want to use and create the type, you can experiment with its appearance by changing its **font** (characters with a similar appearance), size, and color. You can also apply special effects that make it stand out, or appear to pop off the page.

Tools You'll Use

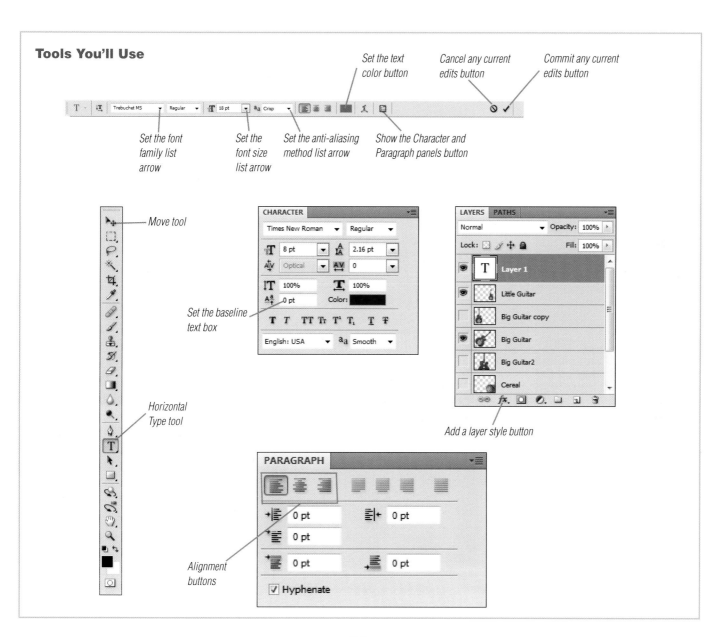

Set the text color button

Cancel any current edits button

Commit any current edits button

Set the font family list arrow

Set the font size list arrow

Set the anti-aliasing method list arrow

Show the Character and Paragraph panels button

Move tool

Set the baseline text box

Horizontal Type tool

Add a layer style button

Alignment buttons

LEARN ABOUT TYPE AND
HOW IT IS CREATED

What You'll Do

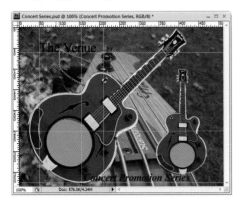

In this lesson, you'll create a type layer, then change the alignment, font family, size, and color of the type.

Introducing Type Types

Outline type is mathematically defined, which means that it can be scaled to any size without losing its sharp, smooth edges. Some programs, such as Adobe Illustrator, create outline type, also known as **vector fonts**. **Bitmap type** is composed of pixels, and, like images, can develop jagged edges when enlarged. The type you create in Photoshop is initially outline type, but it is converted into bitmap type when you apply special filters. Using the type tools and the options bar, you can create horizontal or vertical type and modify font size and alignment. You use the Color Picker dialog box to change type color. When you create type in Photoshop, it is automatically placed on a new type layer on the Layers panel.

QUICKTIP
Keeping type on separate layers makes it much easier to modify and change positions within the image.

Getting to Know Font Families

Each **font family** represents a complete set of characters, letters, and symbols for a particular typeface. Font families are generally divided into three categories: serif, sans serif, and symbol. Characters in **serif fonts** have a tail, or stroke, at the end of some characters. These tails make it easier for the eye to recognize words. For this reason, serif fonts are generally used in text passages. **Sans serif fonts** do not have tails and are commonly used in headlines.

TIP The Verdana typeface was designed primarily for use on a computer screen.

Symbol fonts are used to display unique characters (such as $, ÷, or ™). Table 1 lists some commonly used serif and sans serif fonts. After you select the Horizontal Type tool, you can change font families using the options bar.

Measuring Type Size

The size of each character within a font is measured in **points**. **PostScript**, a programming language that optimizes printed text and graphics, was introduced by Adobe in 1985. In PostScript measurement, one inch is equivalent to 72 points or six picas. Therefore, one pica is equivalent to 12 points. In traditional measurement, one inch is equivalent to 72.27 points. The default Photoshop type size is 12 points. In Photoshop, you have the option of using PostScript or traditional character measurement.

Acquiring Fonts

Your computer has many fonts installed on it, but no matter how many fonts you have, you probably can use more. Fonts can be purchased from private companies, individual designers, computer stores, or catalog companies. Fonts are delivered on CD, DVD, or over the Internet. Using your browser and your favorite search engine, you can locate websites where you can purchase or download fonts. Many websites offer specialty fonts, such as the website shown in Figure 1. Other websites offer these fonts free of charge or for a nominal fee.

TABLE 1: Commonly Used Serif and Sans Serif Fonts

serif fonts	sample	sans serif fonts	sample
Lucida Handwriting	*Adobe Photoshop*	Arial	Adobe Photoshop
Rockwell	Adobe Photoshop	Bauhaus	Adobe Photoshop
Times New Roman	Adobe Photoshop	Century Gothic	Adobe Photoshop

FIGURE 1
Font website

Courtesy of Fonts.com - http://fonts.com/

Create and modify type

1. Start Photoshop, open PS 5-1.psd from the drive and folder where you store your Data Files, update the layers (if necessary), then save the file as **Concert Series**.

2. Display the document size in the status bar, the rulers in pixels (if they are not already displayed), and change the workspace to **Typography**.

   TIP   You can quickly toggle the rulers on and off by pressing [Ctrl][R] (Win) or ⌘[R] (Mac).

3. Click the **Default Foreground and Background Colors button** ◼ on the Tools panel.

4. Click the **Horizontal Type tool** T on the Tools panel.

5. Click the **Set the font family list arrow** on the options bar, click **Arial** (a sans serif font), click the **Set the font style list arrow**, then click **Italic**.

   TIP   If Arial is not available, make a reasonable substitution.

6. Click the **Set the font size list arrow** on the options bar, then click **6 pt** (if it is not already selected).

7. Click the image with the **Horizontal Type pointer** ⌶ at approximately **155 X/375 Y**, then type **Concert Promotion Series** as shown in Figure 2.

You created a type layer by using the Horizontal Type tool on the Tools panel and modified the font family and font size.

FIGURE 2
New type in image

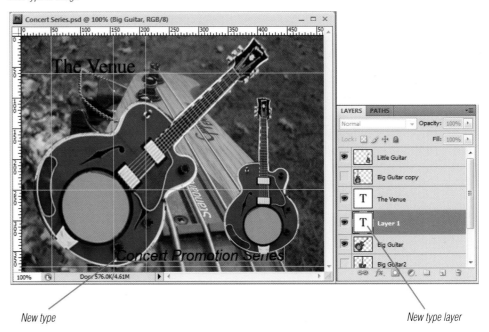

New type

New type layer

Using the active layer panel background (Macintosh)

Icons used in Macintosh to identify type layers are similar to those found in Windows. In Macintosh, the active layer has the same Type and Layer style buttons. The active layer's background color is the same color as the color used to highlight a selected item. (In Windows, the active layer's background color is a dark cyan blue.)

FIGURE 3
Type with new color

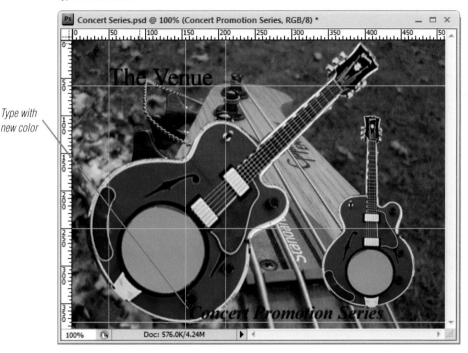

Type with new color

1. Press **[Ctrl][A]** (Win) or ⌘**[A]** (Mac) to select all the text.

2. Click the **Set the font family list arrow** on the options bar, scroll down, then click **Times New Roman**.

   TIP Click in the Set the font family text box and you can select a different font by typing the first few characters of the font name. Scroll through the fonts by clicking in the Set the font family text box, then pressing the [UpArrow] or [DownArrow].

3. Click the **Set the font style list arrow**, then click **Bold Italic**.

4. Click the **Set the text color button** ▬ on the options bar.

   TIP Drag the Set text color dialog box out of the way if it blocks your view of the image.

   As you position the pointer over the image, the pointer automatically becomes an Eyedropper pointer.

5. Click the image with the **Eyedropper pointer** 🖊 anywhere in the blue area at the top of the large guitar at approximately **155 X/175 Y**.

   The new color is now the active color in the Set text color dialog box.

6. Click **OK** in the Select text color dialog box.

7. Click the **Commit any current edits button** ✔ on the options bar.

   Clicking the Commit any current edits button accepts your changes and makes them permanent in the image.

8. Save your work, then compare your image to Figure 3.

You changed the font family, modified the color of the type by using an existing image color, and committed the current edits.

Using the Swatches panel to change type color

You can also use the Swatches panel to change type color. Select the type, then click a color on the Swatches panel. The new color that you click will appear in the Set foreground color button on the Tools panel and will be applied to type that is currently selected.

CHANGE SPACING AND
ADJUST BASELINE SHIFT

What You'll Do

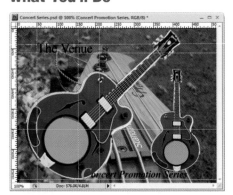

 In this lesson, you'll adjust the spacing between characters and change the baseline of type.

Adjusting Spacing

Competition for readers on the visual landscape is fierce. To get and maintain an edge over other designers, Photoshop provides tools that let you make adjustments to your type, offering you the opportunity to make your type more distinctive. These adjustments might not be very dramatic, but they can influence readers in subtle ways. For example, type that is too small and difficult to read might make the reader impatient (at the very least), and he or she might not even look at the image (at the very worst). You can make finite adjustments, called **type spacing**, to the space between characters and between lines of type. Adjusting type spacing affects the ease with which words are read.

Understanding Character and Line Spacing

Fonts in desktop publishing and word processing programs use proportional spacing, whereas typewriters use monotype spacing. In **monotype spacing**, each character occupies the same amount of space. This means that wide characters such as "o" and "w" take up the same real estate on the page as narrow ones such as "i" and "l". In **proportional spacing**, each character can take up a different amount of space, depending on its width. **Kerning** controls the amount of space between characters and can affect several characters, a word, or an entire paragraph. **Tracking** inserts a *uniform* amount of space between selected characters. Figure 4 shows an example of type before and after it has been kerned.

The second line of text takes up less room and has less space between its characters, making it easier to read. You can also change the amount of space, called **leading**, between lines of type, to add or decrease the distance between lines of text.

Using the Character Panel

The **Character panel**, shown in Figure 5, helps you manually or automatically control type properties such as kerning, tracking, and leading. You open the Character panel from the options bar and the Dock.

Adjusting the Baseline Shift

Type rests on an invisible line called a **baseline**. Using the Character panel, you can adjust the **baseline shift**, the vertical distance that type moves from its baseline. You can add interest to type by changing the baseline shift. Negative adjustments to the baseline move characters *below* the baseline, while positive adjustments move characters *above* the baseline.

QUICKTIP

Clicking the Set the text color button on either the options bar or the Character panel opens the Select text color dialog box.

FIGURE 4
Kerned characters

FIGURE 5
Character panel

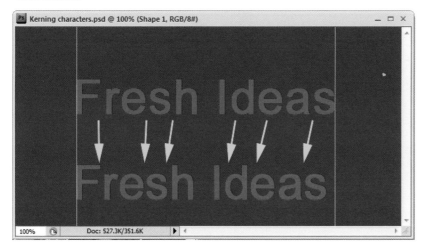

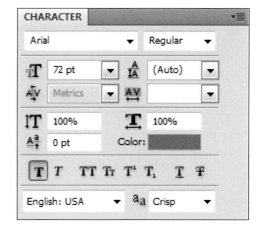

Kern characters

1. Click the **Concert Promotion Series type layer** on the Layers panel (if it is not already selected).

2. Click the **Horizontal Type tool** T. on the Tools panel.

3. Click between "r" and "i" in the word "Series."

4. Click the **Set the kerning between two characters list arrow** ᴬⱽ on the Character panel, then click **−25**.

   The spacing between the two characters decreases.

   TIP You can close the Character panel by clicking the list arrow in the upper-right corner of its title bar then clicking the Close command. You can also open and close the Character panel by clicking the Character button on the vertical dock.

5. Click between "i" and "o" in the word "Promotion."

6. Click ᴬⱽ, then click **−25**, as shown in Figure 6.

7. Click the **Commit any current edits button** ✓ on the options bar.

You modified the kerning between characters by using the Character panel.

FIGURE 6
Kerned type

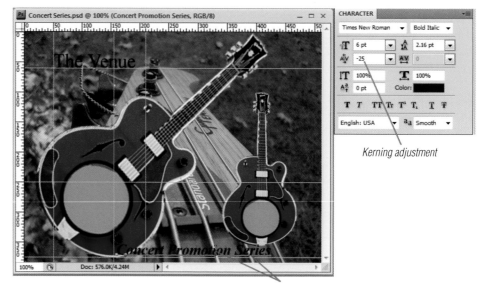

Kerning adjustment

Kerned type

Correcting spelling errors

Are you concerned that your gorgeous image will be ruined by misspelled words? Photoshop understands your pain and has included a spelling checker to make sure you are never plagued by incorrect spellings. If you want, the spelling checker will check the type on the current layer, or all the layers in the image. First, make sure the correct dictionary for your language is selected. English: USA is the default, but you can choose another language by clicking the Set the language on selected characters for hyphenation and spelling list arrow at the bottom of the Character panel. To check spelling, click Edit on the Application bar, then click Check Spelling. The spelling checker will automatically stop at each word not already appearing in the dictionary. One or more suggestions might be offered, which you can either accept or reject.

FIGURE 7
Select text color dialog box

Your color field may differ (Mac)

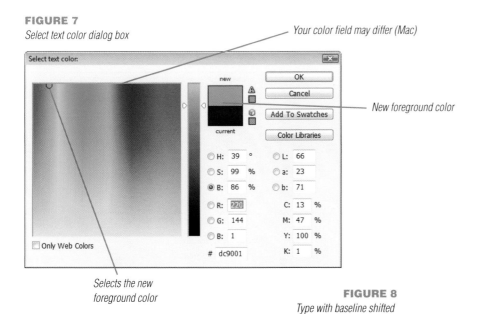

New foreground color

*Selects the new
foreground color*

FIGURE 8
Type with baseline shifted

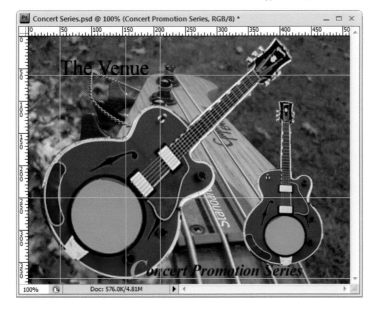

Shift the baseline

1. Use the **Horizontal Type pointer** to select the "C" in "Concert".

2. Click the **Set the text color button** on the options bar.

3. Click anywhere in the gold area in the center of either guitar, such as **100 X/250 Y**, compare your Select text color dialog box to Figure 7, then click **OK**.

4. Double-click **6** in the Set the font size text box on the Character panel, type **10**, double-click **0** in the Set the baseline shift text box on the Character panel, then type **–1**.

5. Click the **Commit any current edits button** ✓ on the options bar.

6. Save your work, then compare your screen to Figure 8.

You changed the type color, then adjusted the baseline of the first character in a word, to make the first character stand out.

USE THE DROP
SHADOW STYLE

What You'll Do

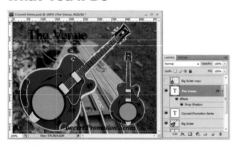

In this lesson, you'll apply the drop shadow style to a type layer, then modify drop shadow settings.

Adding Effects to Type

Layer styles (effects which can be applied to a type or image layer) can greatly enhance the appearance of type and improve its effectiveness. A type layer is indicated by the appearance of the T icon in the layer's thumbnail box. When a layer style is applied to any layer, the Indicates layer effects icon (*fx*) appears in that layer when it is active. The Layers panel is a great source of information. You can see which effects have been applied to a layer by clicking the arrow to the left of the Indicates layer effects icon on the Layers panel if the layer is active or inactive. Figure 9 shows a layer that has two type layer styles applied to it. Layer styles are linked to the contents of a layer, which means that if a type layer is moved or modified, the layer's style will still be applied to the type.

Using the Drop Shadow

One method of placing emphasis on type is to add a drop shadow to it. A **drop shadow** creates an illusion that another colored layer of identical text is behind the selected type. The drop shadow default color is black, but it can be changed to another color using the Color Picker dialog box, or any of the other methods for changing color.

Applying a Style

You can apply a style, such as a drop shadow, to the active layer, by clicking Layer on the Application bar, pointing to Layer Style, then clicking a style.

The settings in the Layer Style dialog box are "sticky," meaning that they display the settings that you last used. An alternative method to using the Application bar is to select the layer that you want to apply the style to, click the Add a layer style button on the Layers panel, then click a style. Regardless of which method you use, the Layer Style dialog box opens. You use this dialog box to add all kinds of effects to type. Depending on which style you've chosen, the Layer Style dialog box displays options appropriate to that style.

QUICKTIP
You can apply styles to objects as well as to type.

Controlling a Drop Shadow

You can control many aspects of a drop shadow's appearance, including its angle, its distance behind the type, and the amount of blur it contains. The **angle** determines where the shadow falls relative to the text, and the **distance** determines how far the shadow falls from the text. The **spread** determines the width of the shadow text,

and the **size** determines the clarity of the shadow. Figure 10 shows samples of two different drop shadow effects. The first line of type uses the default background color (black), has an angle of 160 degrees, a distance of 10 pixels, a spread of 0%, and a size of five pixels. The second line of type uses a purple background color, has an angle of 120 degrees, a distance of 20 pixels, a spread of 10%, and a size of five pixels. As you modify the drop shadow, the preview window displays the changes.

FIGURE 9
Effects in a type layer

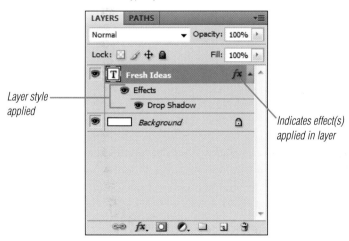

Layer style applied

Indicates effect(s) applied in layer

FIGURE 10
Sample drop shadows

Add a drop shadow

1. Click the **layer thumbnail** on The Venue type layer.

2. Double-click **8** in the Set the font size text box in the Character panel, type **12**, then press **[Enter]** (Win) or **[return]** (Mac).

3. Click the **Add a layer style button** *fx.* on the Layers panel.

   TIP   You can make your life easier by creating your own styles. Do you apply the stroke effect often? You can create your own stroke style by clicking the Add a layer style button on the Layers panel, clicking Stroke, entering your settings, then clicking New Style.

4. Click **Drop Shadow**.

5. Compare your Layer Style dialog box to Figure 11.

   The default drop shadow settings are applied to the type. Table 2 describes the drop shadow settings.

   TIP   You can also open the Layer Style dialog box by double-clicking a layer on the Layers panel.

You created a drop shadow by using the Add a layer style button on the Layers panel and the Layer Style dialog box.

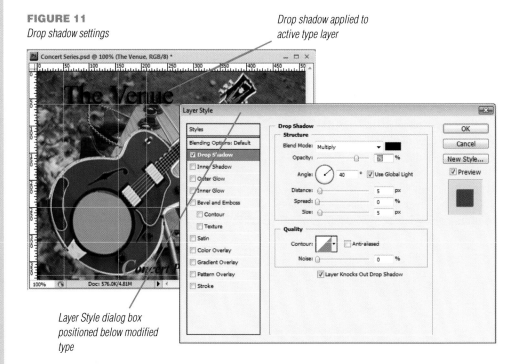

FIGURE 11
Drop shadow settings

Drop shadow applied to active type layer

Layer Style dialog box positioned below modified type

TABLE 2: Drop Shadow Settings

setting	scale	explanation
Angle	0–360 degrees	At 0 degrees, the shadow appears on the baseline of the original text. At 90 degrees, the shadow appears directly below the original text.
Distance	0–30,000 pixels	A larger pixel size increases the distance from which the shadow text falls relative to the original text.
Spread	0–100%	A larger percentage increases the width of the shadow text.
Size	0–250 pixels	A larger pixel size increases the blur of the shadow text.

FIGURE 12

Layer Style dialog box

Angle text box

Distance text box

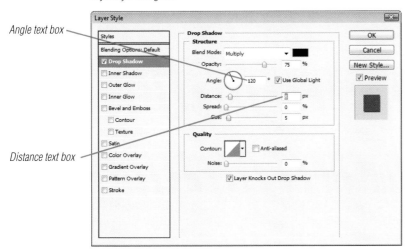

FIGURE 13

Drop shadow added to type layer

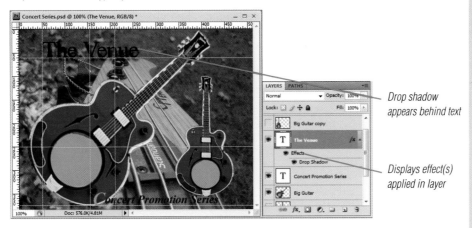

Drop shadow appears behind text

Displays effect(s) applied in layer

Modify drop shadow settings

1. Double-click the number in the Angle text box, then type **120**.

   Each style in the Layer Style dialog box shows different options in the center section. These options are displayed as you click each style (in the Styles pane).

   TIP You can also set the angle by dragging the dial slider in the Layer Style dialog box.

2. Double-click the number in the Distance text box, then type **8**. See Figure 12.

   TIP You can create your own layer style in the Layer Style dialog box, by selecting style settings, clicking New Style, typing a new name or accepting the default, then clicking OK. The new style appears as a preset in the Styles list of the Layer Style dialog box.

3. Click **OK**, then compare your screen to Figure 13.

4. Click the **list arrow to the right of the Indicates layer effects icon** on The Venue layer to collapse the list.

5. Save your work.

You used the Layer Style dialog box to modify the settings for the drop shadow.

APPLY ANTI-ALIASING
TO TYPE

What You'll Do

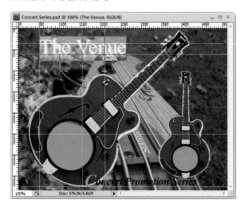

In this lesson, you'll view the effects of the anti-aliasing feature, then use the History panel to return the type to its original state.

Eliminating the "Jaggies"

In the good old days of dot-matrix printers, jagged edges were obvious in many print ads. You can still see these jagged edges in designs produced on less sophisticated printers. To prevent the jagged edges (sometimes called "jaggies") that often accompany bitmap type, Photoshop offers an anti-aliasing feature. **Anti-aliasing** partially fills in pixel edges with additional colors, resulting in smooth-edge type and an increased number of colors in the image. Anti-aliasing is useful for improving the display of large type in print media; however, this can cause a file to become large.

Knowing When to Apply Anti-Aliasing

As a rule, type that has a point size greater than 12 should have some anti-aliasing method applied. Sometimes, smaller type sizes can become blurry or muddy when anti-aliasing is used. As part of the process, anti-aliasing adds intermediate colors to your image in an effort to reduce the jagged edges. As a designer, you need to weigh these three factors (type size, file size, and image quality) when determining if you should apply anti-aliasing.

Understanding Anti-Aliasing

Anti-aliasing improves the display of type against the background. You can use five anti-aliasing methods: None, Sharp, Crisp, Strong, and Smooth. An example of each method is shown in Figure 14. The **None** setting applies no anti-aliasing, and can result in type that has jagged edges.

The **Sharp** setting displays type with the best possible resolution. The **Crisp** setting gives type more definition and makes type appear sharper. The **Strong** setting makes type appear heavier, much like the bold attribute. The **Smooth** setting gives type more rounded edges.

QUICKTIP

Generally, the type used in your image should be the messenger, not the message. As you work with type, keep in mind that using more than two fonts in one image might be distracting or make the overall appearance unprofessional.

FIGURE 14
Anti-aliasing effects

Anti-aliasing method: None

Anti-aliasing method: Sharp

Anti-aliasing method: Crisp

Anti-aliasing method: Strong

Anti-aliasing method: Smooth

Apply anti-aliasing

1. Double-click the **layer thumbnail** on The Venue layer.

2. Click the **Set the anti-aliasing method list arrow** ªª Sharp ▼ on the options bar.

   TIP You've probably noticed that some items, such as the Set the anti-aliasing method list arrow, the Set the text color button, and the Set the kerning between two characters list arrow are duplicated on the options bar and the Character panel. So which should you use? Whichever one you feel most comfortable using. These tasks are performed identically regardless of the feature's origin.

3. Click **Strong**, then compare your work to Figure 15.

4. Click the **Commit any current edits button** ✓ on the options bar.

You applied the Strong anti-aliasing setting to see how the setting affected the appearance of type.

FIGURE 15
Effect of Strong anti-aliasing

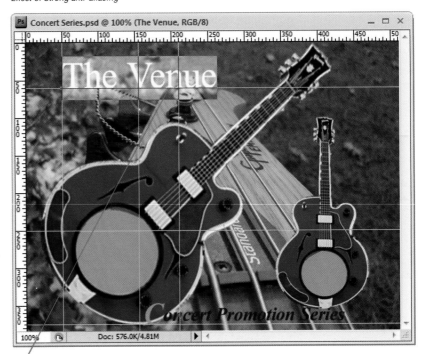

Type appearance altered

Different strokes for different folks

You're probably already aware that you can use different methods to achieve the same goals in Photoshop. For instance, if you want to see the type options bar, you can either double-click a type layer thumbnail or single-click it, then click the Horizontal Type tool. The method you use determines what you'll see in the History panel. Using the double-clicking method, a change in the anti-aliasing method will result in the following history state 'Edit Type Layer'. Using the single-clicking method to change to the anti-alias method to Crisp results in an 'Anti Alias Crisp' history state.

Placing Type in an Image

FIGURE 16

Deleting a state from the History panel

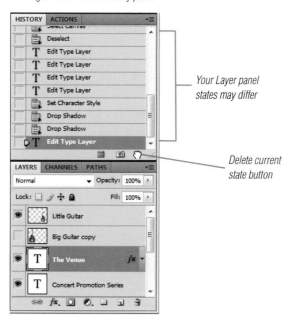

Your Layer panel states may differ

Delete current state button

Undo anti-aliasing

1. Click the **workspace switcher** on the Application bar, then click **History and Layers**.

    The History panel is now visible.

2. Click the **Edit Type Layer state** listed at the bottom of the History panel, then drag it to the **Delete current state button** 🗑 , as shown in Figure 16.

    > TIP Various methods of undoing actions are reviewed in Table 3.

3. Return the display to the **Typography** workspace.

4. Save your work.

You deleted a state in the History panel to return the type to its original appearance. The History panel offers an easy way of undoing previous steps.

TABLE 3: Undoing Actions

method	description	keyboard shortcut
Undo	Edit ➢ Undo	[Ctrl][Z] (Win) ⌘[Z] (Mac)
Step Backward	Click Edit on the Application bar, then click Step Backward	[Alt][Ctrl][Z] (Win) [option] ⌘[Z] (Mac)
History panel	Drag state to the Delete current state button on the History panel, or click the Delete current state button on the History panel	[Alt] 🗑 (Win) [option] 🗑 (Mac) 🗑

MODIFY TYPE WITH THE
BEVEL AND EMBOSS STYLE

What You'll Do

 In this lesson, you'll apply the Bevel and Emboss style, then modify the Bevel and Emboss settings.

Using the Bevel and Emboss Style

You use the Bevel and Emboss style to add combinations of shadows and highlights to a layer and make type appear to have dimension and shine. You can use the Layer menu or the Layers panel to apply the Bevel and Emboss style to the active layer. Like all Layer styles, the Bevel and Emboss style is linked to the type layer to which it is applied.

Understanding Bevel and Emboss Settings

You can use two categories of Bevel and Emboss settings: structure and shading. **Structure** determines the size and physical properties of the object, and **shading** determines the lighting effects. Figure 17 contains several variations of Bevel and Emboss structure settings, while additional Bevel and Emboss structure settings are listed in Table 4. The shading

Filling type with imagery

You can use the imagery from a layer in one file as the fill pattern for another image's type layer. To create this effect, open a multi-layer file that contains the imagery you want to use (the source), then open the file that contains the type you want to fill (the target). In the source file, activate the layer containing the imagery you want to use, use the Select menu to select all, then use the Edit menu to copy the selection. In the target file, press [Ctrl] (Win) or ⌘ (Mac) while clicking the type layer to which the imagery will be applied, then click Paste Into on the Edit menu. The imagery will appear within the type.

used in the Bevel and Emboss style determines how and where light is projected on the type. You can control a variety of settings, including the angle, altitude, and gloss contour, to create a unique appearance. The **Angle** setting determines where the shadow falls relative to the text, and the **Altitude** setting affects the amount of visible dimension. For example, an altitude of 0 degrees looks flat, while a setting of 90 degrees has a more three-dimensional appearance. The **Gloss Contour** setting determines the pattern with which light is reflected, and the **Highlight Mode** and **Shadow Mode** settings determine how pigments are combined. When the Use Global Light check box is selected, *all the type* in the image will be affected by your changes.

FIGURE 17
Bevel and Emboss style samples

TABLE 4: Bevel and Emboss Structure Settings

sample	style	technique	direction	size	soften
1	Inner Bevel	Smooth	Up	5	1
2	Outer Bevel	Chisel Hard	Up	5	8
3	Emboss	Smooth	Down	10	3
4	Pillow Emboss	Chisel Soft	Up	10	3

Add the Bevel and Emboss style with the Layer menu

1. Verify that **The Venue layer** is the active layer, then use any Zoom tool so the image is viewed at a zoom level of 200%.

2. Click the **Set the text color button** ▬ on the options bar, click the silver area in the large guitar (at approximately **70 X/330 Y**), then click **OK**.

3. Click **Layer** on the Application bar, point to **Layer Style**, click **Bevel and Emboss**, then click **Bevel and Emboss** in the Styles column (if it is not already selected).

4. Review the Layer Style dialog box shown in Figure 18, then move the Layer Style dialog box (if necessary), so you can see "The Venue" type.

You applied the Bevel and Emboss style by using the Layer menu. This gave the text a more three-dimensional look.

FIGURE 18
Layer Style dialog box

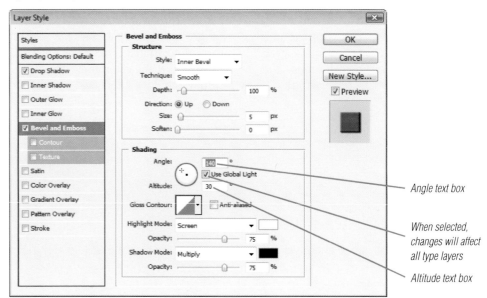

Angle text box

When selected, changes will affect all type layers

Altitude text box

Warping type

You can add dimension and style to your type by using the Warp Text feature. After you select the type layer you want to warp, click the Horizontal Type tool on the Tools panel. Click the Create warped text button on the options bar to open the Warp Text dialog box. If a warning box opens telling you that your request cannot be completed because the type layer uses a faux bold style, click the Toggle the Character and Paragraph panels button on the options bar, click the Character panel list arrow, click Faux Bold to deselect it, then click the Create warped text button again. You can click the Style list arrow to select from 15 available styles. After you select a style, you can modify its appearance by dragging the Bend, Horizontal Distortion, and Vertical Distortion sliders.

Placing Type in an Image

FIGURE 19
Bevel and Emboss style applied to type

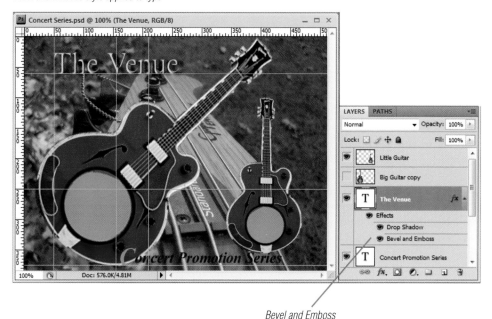

Bevel and Emboss
style applied to layer

1. Double-click the number in the Angle text box, then type **165**.

   You can use the Layer Style dialog box to change the structure by adjusting style, technique, direction, size, and soften settings.

2. Double-click the **Altitude text box**, then type **20**.

3. Click **OK**, reduce the zoom level to 100%, expand The Venue layer in the Layers panel, then compare your type to Figure 19.

4. Save your work.

You modified the default settings for the Bevel and Emboss style. Experimenting with different settings is crucial to achieve the effect you want.

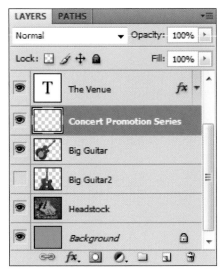

APPLY SPECIAL EFFECTS TO
TYPE USING FILTERS

What You'll Do

In this lesson, you'll rasterize a type layer, then apply a filter to it to change its appearance.

Understanding Filters

Like an image layer, a type layer can have one or more filters applied to it to achieve special effects and make your text look unique. Some filter dialog boxes have preview windows that let you see the results of the particular filter before it is applied to the layer. Other filters must be applied to the layer before you can see the results. Before a filter can be applied to a type layer, the type layer must first be **rasterized**, or converted to an image layer. After it is rasterized, the type characters *can no longer be edited* because it is composed of pixels, just like artwork. When a type layer is rasterized, the T icon in the layer thumbnail becomes an image thumbnail while the Effects icons remain on the type layer.

Creating Special Effects

Filters enable you to apply a variety of special effects to type, as shown in Figure 20. Notice that none of the original type layers on the Layers panel in Figure 20 display the T icon in the layer thumbnail because the layers have all been rasterized.

QUICKTIP

Because you cannot edit type after it has been rasterized, you should save your original type by making a copy of the layer *before* you rasterize it, then hide it from view.

Producing Distortions

Distort filters let you create waves or curves in type. Some of the types of distortions you can produce include Glass, Pinch, Ripple, Shear, Spherize, Twirl, Wave, and Zigzag. These effects are sometimes used as the basis of a corporate logo. The Twirl dialog box, shown in Figure 21, lets you determine the amount of twirl effect you want to apply. By dragging the Angle slider, you control how much twirl effect is added to a layer. Most filter dialog boxes have Zoom In and Zoom Out buttons that make it easy to see the effects of the filter.

Using Textures and Relief

Many filters let you create the appearance of textures and **relief** (the height of ridges within an object). One of the Stylize filters, Wind, applies lines throughout the type, making it appear shredded. The Wind dialog box, shown in Figure 22, lets you determine the kind of wind and its direction. The Texture filter lets you choose the type of texture you want to apply to a layer: Brick, Burlap, Canvas, or Sandstone.

Blurring Imagery

The Gaussian Blur filter softens the appearance of type by blurring its edge pixels. You can control the amount of blur applied to the type by entering high or low values in the Gaussian Blur dialog box. The higher the blur value, the blurrier the effect.

QUICKTIP

Be careful: too much blur applied to type can make it unreadable.

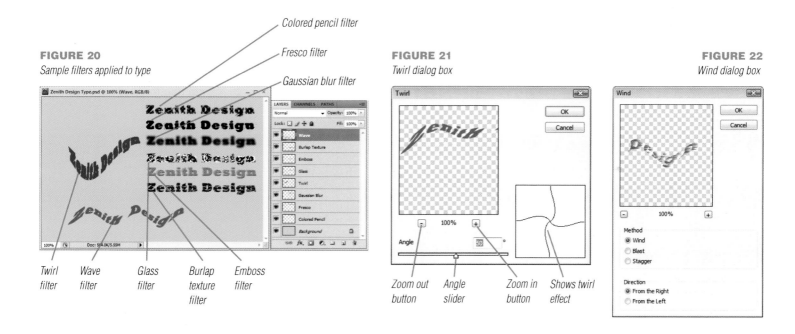

FIGURE 20
Sample filters applied to type

Colored pencil filter
Fresco filter
Gaussian blur filter

Twirl filter   Wave filter   Glass filter   Burlap texture filter   Emboss filter

FIGURE 21
Twirl dialog box

Zoom out button   Angle slider   Zoom in button   Shows twirl effect

FIGURE 22
Wind dialog box

Rasterize a type layer

1. Click the **Concert Promotion Series** layer on the Layers panel.

2. Click **Filter** on the Application bar, point to **Noise**, then click **Dust & Scratches**.

3. Click **OK** to rasterize the type and close the warning box shown in Figure 23.

   TIP   You can also rasterize a type layer by clicking Layer on the Application bar, pointing to Rasterize, then clicking Type.

   The Dust & Scratches dialog box opens.

You rasterized a type layer in preparation for filter application.

FIGURE 23
Warning box

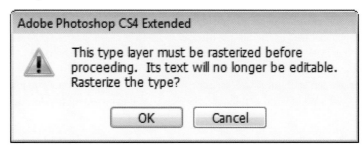

DESIGNTIP   Using multiple filters

Sometimes, adding one filter doesn't achieve the effect you had in mind. You can use multiple filters to create a unique effect. Before you try your hand at filters, though, it's a good idea to make a copy of the original layer. That way, if things don't turn out as you planned, you can always start over. You don't even have to write down which filters you used, because you can always look at the History panel to review which filters you applied.

FIGURE 24

Dust & Scratches dialog box

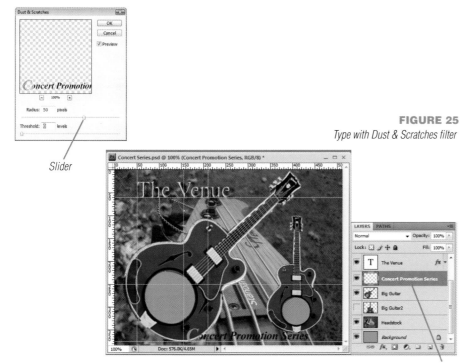

Slider

FIGURE 25

Type with Dust & Scratches filter

No longer a type layer

Modify filter settings

1. Drag the default background patterns in the preview window of the dialog box to position the type so at least part of the type is visible.

2. Drag the sliders in the Dust & Scratches dialog box until **50** appears in the Radius pixels text box, and **0** appears in the Threshold levels text box, as shown in Figure 24.

3. Click **OK**.

4. Save your work. Compare your modified type to Figure 25.

You modified the Dust & Scratches filter settings to modify the appearance of the layer.

Creating a neon glow

Want to create a really cool effect that takes absolutely no time at all, and works on both type and objects? You can create a neon glow that appears to surround an object. You can apply the Neon Glow filter (one of the Artistic filters) to any flattened image. This effect works best by starting with any imagery—either type or objects—that has a solid color background. Flatten the image so there's only a Background layer. Click the Magic Wand tool on the Tools panel, then click the solid color (in the background). Click Filter on the Application bar, point to Artistic, then click Neon Glow. Adjust the glow size, the glow brightness, and color, if you wish, then click OK. (An example of this technique is used in the Design Project at the end of this chapter.)

CREATE TEXT
ON A PATH

What You'll Do

In this lesson, you'll create a shape, then add type to it.

Understanding Text on a Path

Although it is possible to create some cool type effects by adding layer styles such as bevel, emboss, and drop shadow, you can also create some awesome warped text. Suppose you want type to conform to a shape, such as an oval or a free-form you've drawn? No problem—just create the shape and add the text!

Creating Text on a Path

You start by creating a shape using one of the Photoshop shape tools on the Tools panel, and then adding type to that shape (which is called a path). Add type to a shape by clicking the Horizontal Type tool. When the pointer nears the path, you'll see that it changes to the Type tool pointer. Click the path when the Type tool pointer displays and begin typing. You can change fonts, font sizes, add styles, and any other interesting effects you've learned to apply with type. As you will see, the type is on a path!

QUICKTIP

Don't worry when you see the outline of the path on the screen. The path won't print, only the type will.

FIGURE 26
Type on a path

Path does not display when image is printed

1. Click the **Rectangle tool** on the Tools panel.

2. Click the **Ellipse tool** on the options bar.

3. Click the **Paths button** on the options bar.

4. Drag the **Paths pointer** to create a circular path within the gold circle on the large guitar from **100 X/250 Y** while holding [Shift].

5. Click the **Horizontal Type tool** T on the Tools panel.

6. Change the font to **Arial**, use the Bold font style, set the font size to **8** pt, then verify that the **Left align text button** is selected.

   > TIP You can change to any point size by typing the number in the Set the font size text box.

7. Click the **Horizontal Type pointer** at approximately **90 X/270 Y** on the left edge of the ellipse.

8. Change the font color by sampling the blue at the top of the large guitar then type **The Venue**.

9. Commit any current edits.

10. Hide the rulers and guides, return to the **Essentials** workspace, and save your work. Compare your image to Figure 26.

11. Close the Concert Series.psd file and exit Photoshop.

You created a path using a shape tool, then added type to it.

Power User Shortcuts

to do this:	use this method:
Apply anti-alias method	aa Sharp ▼
Apply Bevel and Emboss style	fx. , Bevel and Emboss
Apply blur filter to type	Filter ➤ Blur ➤ Gaussian Blur
Apply Drop Shadow style	fx. , Drop Shadow
Cancel any current edits	⊘
Change font family	Times New Roman ▼
Change font size	T 6 pt ▼
Change type color	▬
Close type effects	▽
Commit current edits	✓
Display/hide rulers	[Ctrl][R] (Win) or ⌘ [R] (Mac)
Erase a History state	Select state, drag to 🗑

to do this:	use this method:
Horizontal Type tool	T. or T
Kern characters	AV Metrics ▼
Move tool	▶+ or V
Open Character panel	🗐
Save image changes	[Ctrl][S] (Win) or ⌘ [S] (Mac)
See type effects (active layer)	▼
See type effects (inactive layer)	▼
Select all text	[Ctrl][A] (Win) or ⌘ [A] (Mac)
Shift baseline of type	IT 100%
Warp type	工

Key: Menu items are indicated by ➤ between the menu name and its command. Blue bold letters are shortcuts for selecting tools on the Tools panel.

Learn about type and how it is created.

1. Open PS 5-2.psd from the drive and folder where you store your Data Files, then save it as **ZD-Logo**.
2. Display the rulers with pixels.
3. Use the Horizontal Type tool to create a type layer that starts at 45 X/95 Y.
4. Use a black 35 pt Lucida Sans font or substitute another font.
5. Type **Zenith**.
6. Use the Horizontal Type tool and a 16 pt type size to create a type layer at 70 X/180 Y, then type **Always the best**.
7. Save your work.

Change spacing and adjust baseline shift.

1. Use the Horizontal Type tool to create a new type layer at 205 X/95 Y.
2. Use a 35 pt Myriad font.
3. Type **Design**.
4. Select the Design type.
5. Change the type color to the color used in the lower-left background.
6. Change the type size of the Z and D to 50 pts.
7. Adjust the baseline shift of the Z and D to –5.
8. Save your work.

Use the Drop Shadow style.

1. Activate the Zenith type layer.
2. Apply the Drop Shadow style.
3. In the Layer Style dialog box, set the angle to 150°, then close the Layer Style dialog box.
4. Save your work.

Apply anti-aliasing to type.

1. Activate the Zenith type layer.
2. Change the Anti-Alias method to Smooth (if necessary).
3. Save your work.

Modify type with the Bevel and Emboss style.

1. Activate the Design type layer.
2. Apply the Bevel and Emboss style.
3. In the Layer Style dialog box, set the style to Inner Bevel.
4. Set the angle to 150° and the altitude to 30°.
5. Close the Layer Style dialog box.
6. Activate the Zenith type layer.
7. Apply the Bevel and Emboss style.
8. Set the style to Inner Bevel.
9. Verify that the angle is set to 150° and the altitude is set to 30°.
10. Close the Layer Style dialog box.
11. Save your work.

Apply special effects to type using filters.

1. Apply a 1.0 pixel Gaussian Blur effect to the "Always the best" layer.
2. Save your work.

Create text on a path.

1. Use the Ellipse tool to draw an ellipse from approximately 200 X/120 Y to 370 X/185 Y.
2. Click the line with the Horizontal Type tool at 210 X/130 Y.
3. Type **Founded in 1957** using the second color swatch in the first row of the Swatches panel (RGB Yellow), in a 16 pt Arial font.
4. Change the anti-aliasing method to Crisp.
5. Change the opacity of the type (using the Opacity slider in the Layers panel) on the path to 45%.
6. Turn off the ruler display.
7. Save your work, then compare your image to Figure 27.

FIGURE 27
Completed Skills Review Project

A local flower shop, Beautiful Blooms, asks you to design its color advertisement for the trade magazine, *Florists United*. You have already started on the image, and need to add some type.

1. Open PS 5-3.psd, then save it as **Beautiful Blooms Ad**.
2. Click the Horizontal Type tool, then type **Beautiful Blooms** using a 55 pt Impact font in black.
3. Create a catchy phrase of your choice, using a 24 pt Verdana font.
4. Apply a drop shadow style to the name of the flower shop using the following settings: Multiply blend mode, 75% Opacity, 30%, 5 pixel distance, 0° spread, and 5 pixel size.
5. Apply a Bevel and Emboss style to the catch phrase using the following settings: Inner Bevel style, Smooth technique, 100% depth, Up direction, 5 pixel size, 0 pixel soften, 30° angle, 30° altitude, and using global light.
6. Compare your image to the sample in Figure 28.
7. Save your work.

FIGURE 28
Sample Project Builder 1

Placing Type in an Image

You are a junior art director for an advertising agency. You have been working on an ad that promotes milk and milk products. You have started the project, but still have a few details to finish up before it is complete.

1. Open PS 5-4.psd, then save it as **Milk Promotion**.
2. Create a shape using any shape tool, then use the shape as a text path and type a snappy phrase of your choosing on the shape.
3. Use a 24 pt Arial font in the style and color of your choice for the catch phrase type layer. (If necessary, substitute another font.)
4. Create a Bevel and Emboss style on the type layer, setting the angle to 100° and the altitude to 30°.
5. Compare your image to the sample in Figure 29.
6. Save your work.

FIGURE 29
Sample Project Builder 2

Milk Promotion.psd @ 100% (Are you thirsty?, RGB/8) *

Are you thirsty?

100%   Doc: 830.8K/1.29M

You are a freelance designer. A local clothing store, Attitude, is expanding and has hired you to work on an advertisement. You have already created the file, and inserted the necessary type layers. Before you proceed, you decide to explore the Internet to find information on using type to create an effective design.

1. Connect to the Internet and use your browser to find information about typography. (Make a record of the site you found so you can use it for future reference, if necessary.)
2. Find information about using type as an effective design element.
3. Open PS 5-5.psd, update the layers (if necessary), then save the file as **Attitude**.
4. Modify the existing type by changing fonts, font colors, and font sizes.
5. Edit the type, if necessary, to make it shorter and clearer.
6. Rearrange the position of the type to create an effective design.
7. Add a Bevel and Emboss style using your choice of settings, then compare your image to the sample in Figure 30. (The fonts Mistral and Trebuchet MS are used in this image. Make substitutions if you don't have these fonts on your computer.)
8. Save your work.

FIGURE 30
Sample Design Project

You have been hired by your community to create an advertising campaign that promotes tourism. Decide what aspect of the community you want to emphasize. Locate appropriate imagery (already existing on your hard drive, on the web, your own creation, or using a scanner), then add type to create a meaningful Photoshop image.

1. Create an image with the dimensions 550 pixels × 550 pixels.
2. Save this file as **Community Promotion**.
3. Locate appropriate imagery of your community on your hard drive, from a digital camera, or a scanner.
4. Add at least two layers of type in the image, using multiple font sizes. (Use any fonts available on your computer. You can use multiple fonts if you want.)
5. Add a Bevel and Emboss style to at least one type layer, and add a drop shadow to at least one layer. (*Hint*: You can add both effects to the same layer.)
6. Position type layers to create an effective design.
7. Compare your image to the sample in Figure 31.
8. Save your work.

FIGURE 31
Sample Portfolio Project

Placing Type in an Image

6

USING PAINTING
TOOLS

1. Paint and patch an image

2. Create and modify a brush tip

3. Use the Smudge tool

4. Use a library and an airbrush effect

Painting Pixels

In addition to the color-enhancing techniques you've already learned, Photoshop has a variety of painting tools that allow you to modify colors. Unlike the tools an oil painter might use to *apply* pigment to a canvas, such as a brush or a palette knife, these virtual painting tools let you *change* existing colors and pixels.

Understanding Painting Tools

In most cases, you use a painting tool by selecting it, then choosing a brush tip. Just like a real brush, the brush size and shape determines how colors are affected. You paint the image by applying the brush tip to an image, which is similar to the way pigment is applied to a real brush and then painted on a canvas. In Photoshop, the results of the painting process can be deeper, richer colors, bleached or blurred colors, or filter-like effects in specific areas. You can select the size and shape of a brush tip, and control the point at which the brush stroke fades.

Learning About Brush Libraries

Brushes that are used with painting tools are stored within a brush library. Each **brush library** contains a variety of brush tips that you can use, rename, delete, or customize. After you select a tool, you can select a brush tip from the default brush library, which is automatically available from the Brush Preset picker list arrow. Photoshop comes with the following additional brush libraries:

- Assorted Brushes
- Basic Brushes
- Calligraphic Brushes
- Drop Shadow Brushes
- Dry Media Brushes
- Faux Finish Brushes
- Natural Brushes
- Natural Brushes 2
- Special Effect Brushes
- Square Brushes
- Thick Heavy Brushes
- Wet Media Brushes

Tools You'll Use

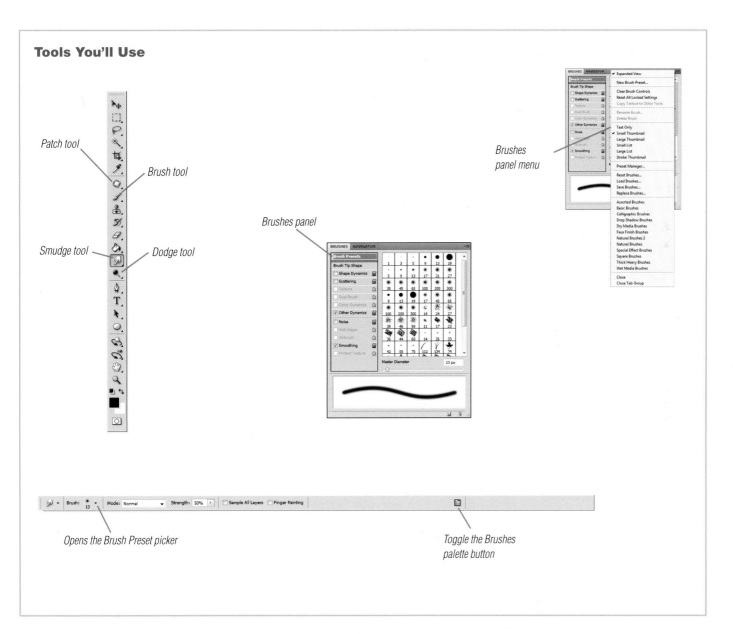

Patch tool

Brush tool

Smudge tool

Dodge tool

Brushes panel

Brushes panel menu

Opens the Brush Preset picker

Toggle the Brushes palette button

PAINT AND
PATCH AN IMAGE

What You'll Do

 In this lesson, you'll use the Sharpen tool to give pixels more definition, the Burn tool to darken specific areas, then use fade settings to paint an area. You'll also use the Patch tool to hide unnecessary imagery.

Using Painting Tools

As you've probably realized, you can use many different methods to achieve similar effects in Photoshop. No one method is necessarily better than another. Like a mask that hides a specific area, Photoshop painting tools can be used to enhance specific areas of a layer. You can use the painting tools, shown in Table 1, to create the effects shown in Figure 1. Unlike a mask that is applied to a defined area within a layer, or a filter that is applied to an entire layer, the effects of painting tools are applied to whatever areas the pointer contacts. In some ways, Photoshop painting tools function very similarly to real painting brushes; in others, they go far beyond traditional tools to let you achieve some incredible effects.

Understanding Fade Options

When you dip a real brush in paint and then stroke the brush across canvas, the brush stroke begins to fade as more of the pigment is left on the canvas than on the brush. This effect can be duplicated in Photoshop using fade options. Fade options are brush settings that determine how and when colors fade toward the end of brush strokes. Fade option settings are measured in steps. A **step** is equivalent to one mark of the brush tip and can be any value from 1–9999. The larger the step value, the longer the fade. You can set fade options for most of the painting tools using the Size Jitter Control option on several of the Brush Tip Shape options within the Brushes panel.

QUICKTIP

To picture a brush fade, imagine a skid mark left by a tire. The mark starts out strong and bold, then fades out gradually or quickly, depending on conditions. This effect is analogous to a brush fade.

Learning About the Patch Tool

Photoshop offers many tools to work with damaged or unwanted imagery. One such tool is the Patch tool. Although this is not a painting tool, you might find as you work in Photoshop, you have to combine a variety of tool strategies to achieve the effect you want. The Patch tool is located on the

Tools panel and is grouped with the Healing Brush tool and Spot Healing Brush tool. You can use this tool to cover a selected area with pixels from another area, or a pattern. Both the Patch tool and the Healing Brush tool match the texture, lighting, and shading of the sampled pixels so your repaired area will look seamless. The Healing Brush tool, however, also matches the transparency of the pixels.

QUICKTIP

As you drag a selection made with the Patch tool, look at the selection and you'll see what the pixels will be replaced with.

Using the Patch Tool

The Patch tool provides a quick and easy way to repair or remove an area within an image. You can use the Patch tool in the following ways:

- Select the area you want to fix, click the Source option button on the options bar, then drag the selection over the area you want to replicate.
- Select the area you want replicated, click the Destination option button on the options bar, then drag the selection over the area you want to fix.

QUICKTIP

There's not necessarily one "right tool" for any given job; there might be several methods of completing a task.

Eliminating Red Eye

The red eye effect is the appearance of red eyes in photos due to the use of a flash. It is more evident in people, and animals, with light-colored eyes. The effect can be eliminated using the Red Eye tool. Select the tool (grouped on the Tools panel with the Patch tool, the Healing Brush tool, and the Spot Healing Brush tool), then click in the red eye area. The Pupil Size list arrow lets you increase or decrease the area affected, and the Darken Amount list arrow sets the darkness of the correction.

FIGURE 1
Painting samples

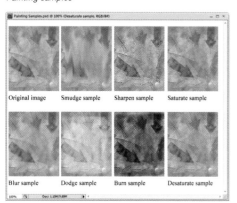

TABLE 1: Painting Tools

tool	button	effect
Smudge tool		Smears colors across an image as if you dragged your finger across wet ink. (Grouped with the Blur tool.)
Sharpen tool		Increases contrast between pixels, giving a sharp, crisp look. (Grouped with the Blur tool.)
Blur tool		Decreases contrast between pixels, giving a soft, blurred look.
Dodge tool		Lightens underlying pixels, giving a lighter, underexposed appearance.
Burn tool		Darkens underlying pixels, giving a richer, overexposed appearance. (Grouped with the Dodge tool.)
Sponge tool		Increases or decreases the purity of a color by saturating or desaturating the color. (Grouped with the Dodge tool.)

Use the Sharpen tool

1. Start Photoshop, open PS 6-1.psd from the drive and folder where you store your Data Files, then save it as **CyberArt**.
2. Display the guides, the rulers in pixels (if they are not already displayed), and make sure the document size displays in the status bar.
3. Use the workspace switcher to display the **Painting workspace**.
4. Click the **Sharpen tool** △ on the Tools panel.

   TIP Look under the Blur tool if the Sharpen tool is hidden.

5. Click **Brush Presets** in the Brushes panel (if necessary), scroll up the list, then click **19 (Hard Round 19 pixels)**.

   TIP You can also click the Click to open the Brush Preset picker list arrow on the options bar to select brushes.

6. Drag the **Brush pointer** ⬭ from **20 X/20 Y** to **530 X/20 Y**, to sharpen across the top area of the image.
7. Press and hold **[Shift]**, click the image in the lower-right corner at **530 X/530 Y**, then release **[Shift]**.

   TIP Instead of dragging to create a line from point to point, you can click a starting point, press and hold [Shift], click an ending point, then release [Shift] to create a perfectly straight line.

8. Press and hold **[Shift]**, click the image in the lower-left corner at **20 X/530 Y**, then release **[Shift]**.
9. Press and hold **[Shift]**, click the image in the upper-left corner at **20 X/20 Y**, then release **[Shift]**. Compare your image to Figure 2.

You used the Sharpen tool to focus on the pixels around the perimeter of the image. The affected pixels now appear sharper and crisper.

FIGURE 2
Results of Sharpen tool

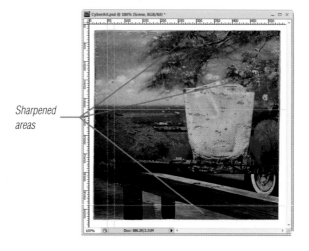

Sharpened areas

FIGURE 3
Red eyes – before and after

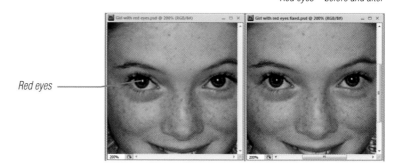

Red eyes

Getting rid of red eye

What do you do with that picture of your niece's doggie that looks so cute but has annoying red eye? You use the Red Eye tool, that's what! Hidden in with the Patch tool and the Healing Brush tool, you can select the Red Eye tool and drag it over any red eye in an image and the eye will be magically corrected. If necessary, you can adjust the pupil size in the Options bar. Figure 3 shows an image before (on the left) and after red eye correction.

FIGURE 4

Results of Burn tool

Burned areas

1. Click the **Burn tool** 🖎 on the Tools panel.

   TIP Look under the Dodge tool if the Burn tool is hidden.

2. Click **Brush:** 🖌 **27 (Soft Round 27 pixels)** on the Brushes panel.

   TIP You can change any brush tip size at any time. Press []] to increase the brush tip or [[] to decrease the brush tip in increments of 5.

3. Drag the **Brush pointer** ⭕ from **20 X/25 Y** to **550 X/25 Y**.

   Did you notice that the area you painted became darker? It looks as though the edges are burned.

4. Drag the **Brush pointer** ⭕ back and forth throughout the upper-right corner from **400 X/25 Y** to **530 X/120 Y**. Compare your image to Figure 4.

You used the Burn tool to tone down the pixels in the upper-right corner of the image. This technique increases the darker tones, changing the mood of the image.

Painting with a pattern

Suppose you have an area within an image that you want to replicate on a new or existing layer. You can paint an existing pattern using the desired area and the Pattern Stamp tool. To create this effect, select the Rectangular Marquee tool using a 0 pixel feather setting, then drag the outline around an area in your image. With this area outlined, click Edit on the Application bar, click Define Pattern, type a name in the Name text box, then click OK. Deselect the marquee, click the Pattern Stamp tool on the Tools panel (hidden under the Clone Stamp tool), click the Click to open Pattern picker list arrow on the options bar, then click the new pattern. Each time you click the pointer on a layer, the new pattern will be applied. You can delete a custom pattern by right-clicking the pattern swatch in the Pattern picker, then clicking Delete Pattern.

Set fade options and paint an area

1. Click the **Eyedropper tool** 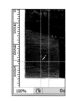 on the Tools panel.

2. Use the **Eyedropper pointer** ✎ to click the image at **50 X/490 Y**, as shown in Figure 5.

3. Click the **Brush tool** ✎. on the Tools panel.

4. Click **19 (Hard Round 19 pixels)** on the Brushes panel.

   TIP   You can also open the Brushes panel by clicking the Brushes button 📷 on the dock, if it is displayed.

5. Click **Shape Dynamics** on the Brushes panel, then adjust your settings using Figure 6 as a guide.

   Available fade options and their locations on the Brushes panel are described in Table 2.

   TIP   Click the option Brush Tip Shape on the Brushes panel to see the option settings. Selecting an option's check box turns the option on, but doesn't display the settings.

6. Press and hold **[Shift]**, drag the **Brush pointer** ○ from **25 X/25 Y** to **525 X/25 Y**, then release **[Shift]**.

7. Use the **Brush pointer** ○ to click the image at **25 X/40 Y**, press and hold **[Shift]**, click the image at **25 X/520 Y**, then release **[Shift]**, as shown in Figure 7.

You modified the fade options, then painted areas using the Brush tool.

FIGURE 5
Location to sample

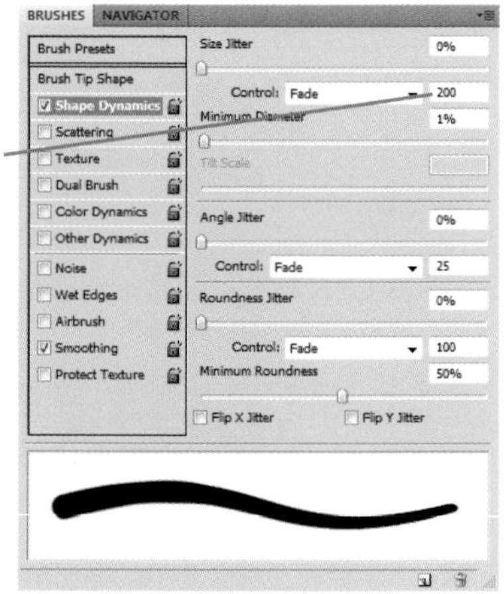

FIGURE 7
Areas painted with fade

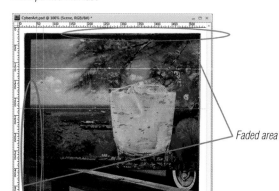

Faded area

FIGURE 6
Brushes panel

Indicates how many steps it takes for fade to occur

TABLE 2: Fade Options

option	on Brushes panel	description
Size Jitter	Shape Dynamics	Decreases the brush stroke size toward the end of the stroke.
Opacity Jitter	Other Dynamics	Decreases the brush stroke opacity toward the end of the stroke.
Foreground/ Background Jitter	Color Dynamics	Causes the foreground color to shift to the background color toward the end of the stroke. Available in the following tools: Brush ✎ and Pencil ✎.

FIGURE 8
Marquee surrounding source area

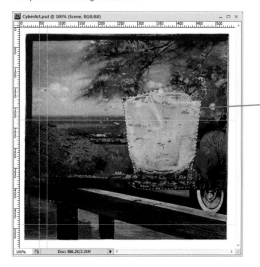

Selection to be patched

FIGURE 9
Results of Patch tool

The location of your
young girl may vary

Patch an area

1. Click the **Patch tool** ⊘ on the Tools panel.

    TIP   Look under the Healing Brush tool if the Patch tool is hidden.

2. Drag the **Patch tool pointer** ✿ around the periphery of the glass, being sure to complete the loop so you create the selection as shown in Figure 8.

3. Click the **Source option button** on the options bar, if it is not already selected.

4. Drag the selection so that the outline of the left edge of the glass (the outline source) is at approximately **60 X/170 Y**.

    The selection is replaced with imagery from the location that you defined with the selection. As you drag, you'll see the pixels that will be replacing the selection. When finished, the horizon should be aligned.

    TIP   You can reverse steps using the History panel, then retry until you're satisfied with the results.

5. Click **Select** on the Application bar, then click **Deselect**.

6. Click the **Young girl** on the Layers panel and display the layer.

7. Click the **Move tool** ▸⊹ on the Tools panel, then press the arrow keys as needed until the right side of the young girl covers any remnants of the glass. Compare your image to Figure 9.

    Selecting and patching are difficult skills to master. Your results might differ.

8. Click the **Scene layer** on the Layers panel.

9. Save your work.

You used the Patch tool to cover an area within an image. The tool makes it possible to correct flaws within an image using existing imagery.

CREATE AND MODIFY
A BRUSH TIP

What You'll Do

 In this lesson, you'll create a brush tip and modify its settings, then you'll use it to paint a border. This new brush tip will be wide and have a distinctive shape that adds an element of mystery to the image.

Understanding Brush Tips

You use brush tips to change the size and pattern of the brush used to apply color. Brushes are stored within libraries. In addition to the default brushes that are available from the Brush Preset picker list, you can also select a brush tip from one of 12 brush libraries. You can access these additional libraries, shown in Figure 10, by clicking the Brush Preset picker list arrow on the options bar, then clicking the menu list arrow.

Learning About Brush Tip Modifications

You can adjust the many brush tip settings that help determine the shape of a brush. One factor that influences the shape of a brush stroke is jitter. **Jitter** is the randomness of dynamic elements such as size, angle, roundness, hue, saturation, brightness, opacity, and flow. The number beneath the brush tip indicates the diameter, and the image of the tip changes as its values are modified. Figure 11 shows

some of the types of modifications that you can make to a brush tip using the Brushes palette. The shape of the brush tip pointer reflects the shape of the brush tip. As you change the brush tip, its pointer also changes.

FIGURE 10
Brush tip libraries

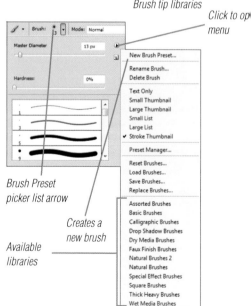

Click to op[en] menu

Brush Preset picker list arrow

Creates a new brush

Available libraries

Creating a Brush Tip

You can create your own brush tip by clicking the Brushes panel list arrow, then clicking New Brush Preset to open the Brush Name dialog box, where you can type a descriptive name in the Name text box. All the options on the Brushes panel are available to you as you adjust the settings. As you select settings, a sample appears at the bottom of the panel. You can delete the current brush tip by clicking the Brush Preset picker list arrow, clicking Delete Brush, then clicking OK in the warning box. You can also right-click (Win) or [Ctrl]-click (Mac) a brush tip on the Brushes panel, then click Delete Brush.

FIGURE 11

Brush Presets in the Brushes panel

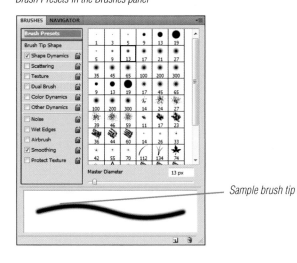

Sample brush tip

FIGURE 12

Tinted image

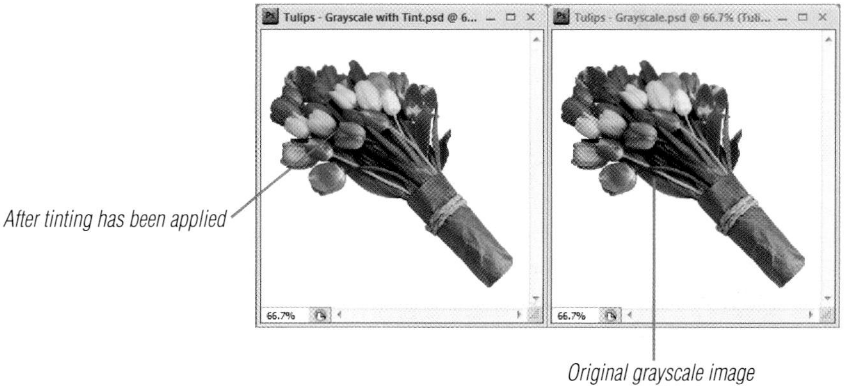

After tinting has been applied

Original grayscale image

Applying a tint

You can use brush tips to apply a tint to a grayscale image. By changing the mode of a grayscale image to RGB color, you can use painting tools to tint an image. After you change the image mode, create a new layer, click the Mode list arrow in the New Layer dialog box, click Color, select colors from the Swatches panel, then apply tints to the new layer. See Figure 12 for an example.

Create a brush tip

1. Click the **Brush tool** on the Tools panel.

2. Click the **list arrow** ▾≡ to the right of the Brushes panel, then click **Clear Brush Controls**.

3. Click the **Brushes panel list arrow** ▾≡ again, then click **New Brush Preset**.

4. Type **Custom oval brush tip** to replace the current name, then click **OK**.

   TIP A newly added brush tip generally is added in brush tip size order in the Brushes panel.

   The new brush tip appears on the options bar or by opening the Brushes panel and scrolling to the bottom.

5. Click **Brush Tip Shape** on the Brushes panel, then adjust your settings using Figure 13 as a guide.

   TIP If you have a pen tablet installed on your computer, you may periodically see a floating icon indicating that your tablet can be used to make entries.

You cleared the current brush settings, and then created a brush tip using the Brushes panel. You modified its settings to create a custom brush tip for painting a border.

FIGURE 13

Brush Tip Shape settings

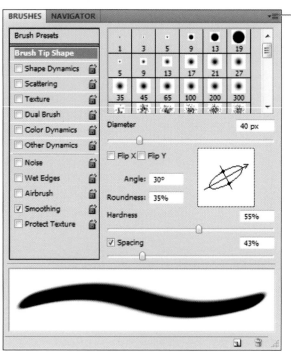

Brushes panel list arrow

FIGURE 14
Painted image

Effects of the custom
brush tip

Paint a border

1. Click the **Mode list arrow** on the options bar, then click **Multiply**.

   TIP The Multiply blend mode creates semi-transparent shadow effects and multiplies the value of the base color by the blend color.

2. Double-click the **Opacity text box**, then type **75**.

3. Click **Shape Dynamics** on the Brushes panel.

4. Click the **Control list arrow** under the Size Jitter section, then click **Fade**.

5. Type **400** in the text box to the right of the Control list arrow.

6. Use the **Brush pointer** to click the image near the upper-right corner at **515 X/25 Y**, press and hold **[Shift]**, click the image near the lower-right corner at **515 X/515 Y**, then release **[Shift]**.

7. Save your work, then compare your image to Figure 14.

Using the newly created brush tip, you painted an area of the image. You also made adjustments to the opacity and fade settings to make the brush stroke more dramatic.

USE THE SMUDGE TOOL

What You'll Do

In this lesson, you'll smudge pixels to create a surreal effect in an image.

Blurring Colors

You can create the same finger-painted look in your Photoshop image that you did as a kid using paints in a pot. Using the Smudge tool, you can create the effect of dragging your finger through wet paint. Like the Brush tool, the Smudge tool has many brush tips that you can select from the Brushes panel, or you can create a brush tip of your own.

> QUICKTIP
>
> You can use the Smudge tool to minimize defects in an image.

Smudging Options

Figure 15 shows an original image and three examples of Smudge tool effects. In each example, the same brush tip is used with different options on the options bar. If you select the Smudge tool with the default settings, your smudge effect will be similar to the image shown in the upper-right corner of Figure 15.

Using Finger Painting

The image in the lower-right corner of Figure 15 shows the effect with the Finger Painting check box selected *prior* to the smudge stroke. The image in the upper-right corner did not have the Finger Painting check box selected. The image in the lower-left corner had the Finger Painting option off, but had the Use All Layers check box selected. The Use All Layers check box enables your smudge stroke to affect all the layers beneath the current layer.

QUICKTIP

The Finger Painting option uses the foreground color at the beginning of each stroke. Without the Finger Painting option, the color under the pointer is used at the beginning of each stroke.

FIGURE 15
Smudge samples

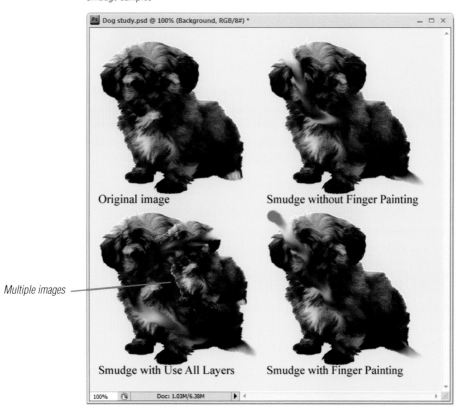

Multiple images

Modify smudge settings

1. Click the **Smudge tool**  on the Tools panel.

   | TIP Look for the Smudge tool under the Sharpen tool.

2. Click **Brush Presets** on the Brushes panel.

3. Click **46 (Spatter 46 pixels)**.

   | TIP This brush tip is located in the middle of the list.

4. Select the **Finger Painting check box** on the options bar (if it is not already selected).

5. Make sure your settings match those shown in Figure 16.

You modified the existing smudge settings to prepare to smudge the image.

FIGURE 16
Smudge tool options bar

FIGURE 17
Pen tablet

Using a graphics tablet

If you really want to see Photoshop take off when you use brush tools, try using a graphics tablet. Although you can find a pen tablet for as little as $50, this nifty high-end item might set you back several thousand dollars, but you'll love what you get in return.

Figure 17 shows the Wacom Cintiq 21UX graphics tablet, with a cordless, battery-free pen and a 21.3" high-resolution display. The dynamically adjustable stand makes it possible to rotate, incline, or use the display on your lap. (You can learn more about the product at *www.wacom.com.*) The benefits of using a graphics tablet include the following:

- Multiple levels of pressure sensitivity
- Use of pressure-sensitive tools already included in Photoshop
- Programmable menu buttons, touch strips, and a contoured grip pen
- The ability to move even faster than when you use shortcut keys

And as an added bonus, you'll probably experience fewer problems with repetitive stress injuries.

FIGURE 18
Smudged area

Unchanged imagery

Smudge an image

1. Verify that the **Scene layer** is active.
2. Drag the **Smudge tool pointer** (zigzagging from right to left) from **0 X/400 Y** to **530 X/530 Y**.

   Dragging the pointer back and forth as you move from left to right creates an interesting smudge effect. The degree and effect of your smudging will vary.

   An area on the current layer is smudged. Did you notice that the young girl layer is unchanged?
3. Save your work, then compare your image to Figure 18.

   You used the Smudge tool to smear the pixels in the bottom third of the image. That area now has a dreamy quality.

FIGURE 19A
Original image

FIGURE 19B
Painted image

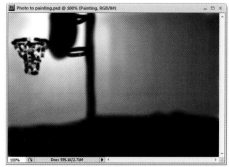

Turning a photo into a "painting"

You can create a painting-like appearance using a photographic image and a few simple Photoshop brush tools. Take an image, like the one shown in Figure 19A, and make any necessary color adjustments. Define the entire image as a pattern by clicking Edit on the Application bar, clicking Define Pattern, typing a name, then clicking OK. Click the Pattern Stamp tool, click the Create new fill or adjustment layer button on the Layers panel, then click Solid Color. Choose white from the Color Picker, then lower the opacity so you can see the image. Create another new layer, then use the Pattern Stamp tool and the new pattern you created to paint over the existing image. Figure 19B shows the same image after the painting treatment.

USE A LIBRARY AND AN
AIRBRUSH EFFECT

What You'll Do

 In this lesson, you'll sample an area of the image, then use brush tips from a library to create additional effects. You'll also use an airbrush effect to apply gradual tones.

Learning About the Airbrush Effect

You might have heard of professional photographers using an airbrush to minimize or eliminate flaws in faces or objects. In Photoshop, the effect simulates the photographer's technique by applying gradual tones to an image. Airbrushing creates a diffused effect on the edges of pixels. The airbrush effect is located on the options bar and on the Brushes panel. You can apply the airbrush effect with any brush tip size, using the Brush tool, History Brush tool, Dodge tool, Burn tool, and Sponge tool. The **flow** setting determines how much paint is sprayed while the mouse button is held.

> **QUICK**TIP
>
> When using the airbrush effect, you can accumulate color by holding the mouse button without dragging.

Restoring pixel data

You can use the History Brush tool to restore painted pixels. The History Brush tool makes a copy of previous pixel data, and then lets you paint with that data, making this tool another good source for undoing painting errors. The Art History Brush tool also lets you re-create imagery using pixel data, but with more stylized effects. This tool has many more options than the History Brush tool, including Style, Area, and Tolerance. Style controls the shape of the paint stroke. Area controls the area covered by the brush tip (a higher area value covers a larger area). Tolerance controls the region where the paint stroke is applied, based on color tolerance. A greater spacing value causes paint strokes to occur in areas that differ in color from the original area. Some of the Art History Brush tool options are shown in Figure 20.

Using Brush Tip Libraries

Photoshop comes with 12 brush libraries that can replace or be appended to the current list of brushes. All the libraries are stored in a folder called Brushes. Each of the libraries is stored in its own file (having the extension .abr). The Load dialog box, from which additional libraries are loaded, is shown in Figure 21. When you use the Load Brushes command (found by clicking the Brushes panel list arrow), the brush tips are added to the end of the brushes list. When you click the name of a brush tip library from the Brush Preset picker list, you are given the option of replacing the existing brush tips with the contents of the library, or appending the brush tips to the existing list.

QUICKTIP

You can restore the default brush tip settings by clicking the list arrow on the Brushes panel, clicking Reset Brushes, then clicking OK.

Managing the Preset Manager

The **Preset Manager** is a Photoshop feature that allows you to manage libraries of preset brushes, swatches, gradients, styles, patterns, contours, custom shapes, and tools. You can display the Preset Manager by clicking Edit on the Application bar, and then clicking Preset Manager. Options for the Preset Manager are shown in Figure 22. You can delete or rename individual elements for each type of library. Changes that you make in the Preset Manager dialog box are reflected on the corresponding panels.

FIGURE 21
Load dialog box

FIGURE 20
Art History Brush tool options

FIGURE 22
Preset Manager dialog box

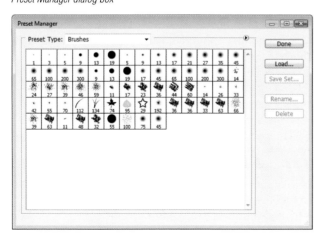

Load a brush library

1. Click the **Eyedropper tool**  on the Tools panel.

2. Use the **Eyedropper pointer** to click the image at **50 X/230 Y** (at the intersection of the guides).

3. Click the **Brush tool** on the Tools panel.

4. Click the **Brushes list arrow** ▾≣ , then click **Faux Finish Brushes**, as shown in Figure 23.

   TIP   This brush library is located in the Brushes folder. The Brushes folder is located in /Program Files/Adobe/Adobe Photoshop CS4/Presets/Brushes (Win) and the Presets folder in the Adobe Photoshop CS4 folder in Applications (Mac).

5. Click **Append**.

6. Scroll to the bottom of the list of brush tips, then click **75 (Veining Feather 1)** near the bottom of the list.

   The active brush tip is from the Faux Finish Brushes library.

You sampled a specific location in the image, then loaded the Faux Finish Brushes library. You selected a brush tip from this new library, which you will use to paint an area.

FIGURE 23
Load Brushes command

Added benefits of using a pen tablet in Photoshop CS4

If you are using a pen tablet in Photoshop CS4, you'll find that you have more options than ever for image fine-tuning. Using your pen and tablet in conjunction with Photoshop CS4, you'll find that:

- A pressure-sensitive pen and tablet can be used to selectively apply adjustments to a layer mask using the presets in the Adjustments panel.
- By adjusting the intensity setting of your pen, you can use the Dodge, Burn, and Sponge tools with a higher degree of accuracy.
- You'll be able to get into hard-to-reach places by changing the Shape Dynamics setting to Pen Pressure.
- In OpenGL-enabled documents, you can use your pen in combination with the Rotate View tool (grouped with the Hand tool in the Tools panel or on the Application bar) to spin your image canvas.
- You can easily pan your image using your pen.

FIGURE 24
Brush tool options

Click to enable airbrush
capabilities

FIGURE 25
Results of Airbrush option and style

Airbrushed effect; your
results may differ

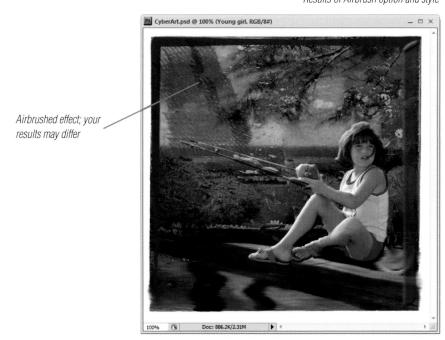

Create an airbrush effect

1. Click the **Set to enable airbrush capabilities button** on the options bar.

2. Change the settings on the options bar so they match those shown in Figure 24.

3. Drag the **Brush pointer** back and forth over the areas of the image containing the sky (from approximately **30 X/50 Y** to **150 X/200 Y**).

4. Hide the rulers.

5. Clear the guides.

6. Click the **Young girl layer** on the Layers panel.

7. Click the **Add a layer style button** *fx.* on the Layers panel.

8. Click **Bevel and Emboss,** then click **OK** to accept the existing settings.

9. Save your work, restore the **Essentials** work-space, then compare your image to Figure 25.

10. Close the image and exit Photoshop.

You used an airbrush effect to paint the sky in the image. You applied the Bevel and Emboss style to a layer to add finishing touches.

Power User Shortcuts

to do this:	use this method:
Apply tint to grayscale image	Image ➤ Mode ➤ RGB Color, choose paint tool, then apply color from Swatches panel
Blur an image	⬩.
Burn an image	⬤ or [Shift] O
Create a brush tip	⬩, ▾≣, click New Brush Preset
Define a pattern	Edit ➤ Define Pattern, type name, click OK
Delete brush tip	▾≣, then click Delete Brush
Dodge an image	⬤. or [Shift] O
Load brush library	Click painting tool ▾≣, in Brushes panel, click Load Brushes in Brushes panel, choose a library, then click Load

to do this:	use this method:
Paint a straight line	Press and hold [Shift] while dragging pointer
Paint an image	⬩ or [Shift] B
Patch a selection	⬤ or [Shift] J
Restore default brushes	▾≣, click Reset Brushes in Brushes panel
Select Fade options	⬩, then click Shape Dynamics
Sharpen an image	◬
Smudge an image	⬤

Key: Menu items are indicated by ➤ between the menu name and its command. Bold blue letters are shortcuts for selecting tools on the Tools panel.

Paint and patch an image.

1. Open PS 6-2.psd from the drive and folder where you store your Data Files, then save it as **The Maze**.
2. Display the rulers in pixels.
3. Select the Sharpen tool.
4. Select brush tip 27 (Soft Round 27 pixels).
5. Drag the pointer back and forth over the maze walls along the right edge of the image, as shown in Figure 26; start at 740 X/20 Y and finish at 840 X/540 Y.
6. Select the Burn tool.
7. Select brush tip 19 (Hard Round 19 pixels).
8. Drag the pointer back and forth over the two (middle) dark red arrows.
9. Sample the image at the ball's shadow (located at 50 X/100 Y) with the Eyedropper tool.
10. Select the Brush tool, then use brush tip 17 (Soft Round 17 pixels).
11. Toggle the Brushes panel (if necessary), choose Shape Dynamics, set the Control to Fade, adjust the Size Jitter Fade to 700 steps, then drag the pointer over the inside perimeter of the entire image. (You can perform this action several times.)
12. Select the Patch tool.
13. Select the far-left red arrow (located at 150 X/350 Y) by outlining it with the Patch tool.
14. Select the Destination option button.
15. Drag the selection up and to the right, to the cubicle located at approximately 500 X/140 Y.
16. Deselect the selection.
17. Save your work.

Create and modify a brush tip.

1. Create a brush called **25 Pixel Sample** using the Brush tool and Brushes panel.
2. Change the existing settings (using the Brush Tip Shape area on the Brushes panel) to the following: Diameter = 25 pixels, Hardness = 15%, Spacing = 65%, Angle = 15 degrees, and Roundness = 80%.
3. Use the new brush and the current foreground color to fill in the remaining white space surrounding the perimeter of the image.
4. Save your work.

Use the Smudge tool.

1. Select the Smudge tool.
2. Select brush tip 24 (Spatter 24 pixels).
3. Verify that the Finger Painting check box is selected.
4. Use the Normal mode and 70% strength settings.
5. Drag the pointer in a jagged line from the top left to the bottom right of the image.
6. Save your work.

Use a library and an airbrush effect.

1. Use the Eyedropper tool to sample the aqua arrow in the lower-right corner of the image.
2. Select the Brush tool and apply the airbrush effect.
3. Replace the existing brushes with the Calligraphic Brushes library.
4. Select brush tip 45 (Soft Round 45) towards the end of the list.
5. Drag the pointer over the aqua arrow.
6. Hide the rulers.
7. Create three type layers, using the text shown in Figure 26. The type layers were created using a black 35 pt Poor Richard font; use a different font if this one is not available on your computer. The first layer should read "Help Me," the second should read "Find," and the third should read "My Way Home."
8. Save your work.
9. Compare your image to Figure 26. The appearance of your image might differ.

FIGURE 26
Completed Skills Review project

A national bank has hired you to create artwork for its new home loan division. The bank wants this artwork to be original. They have instructed you to go wild, and make this ad look like a work of art. You have created a suitable image, but want to add some artistic touches.

1. Open PS 6-3.psd, then save it as **Bank Artwork**.
2. Use the Burn tool and any brush tip you think is appropriate to accentuate the money and the hand that is holding it.
3. Sample a dark brown area within the image (an area on the coat sleeve of the outstretched arm, located at 420 X/180 Y, was used in the sample).
4. Use a painting tool and brush tip of your choice (brush tip 27 is used in the sample) to paint areas within the suits. (*Hint*: In the sample, the suit lapels are painted.)
5. Create a brush tip using a size and shape of your choice, and give the brush tip a descriptive name.
6. Use any painting tool and any color to create a border that surrounds the image. Use the Fade options of your choice.
7. Use the Smudge tool and the settings of your choice to create an interesting effect in the image. (In the sample, the Smudge tool is used on the shaking hands.)
8. Add a library of your choice, and apply an effect using the Burn tool and the airbrush effect. (Brush tip 43 from the Drop Shadow library is used in the sample.)
9. Make any color adjustments you want. (*Hint*: The Brightness was changed to –26, and the Contrast was changed to +15 in the sample.)

FIGURE 27
Sample Project Builder 1

10. Add a type layer using the wording of your choice and any desired effects. (A 75 pt Perpetua font is used on an elliptical path in the sample.)
11. Save your work, then compare your image to the sample in Figure 27.

The Robotics Department of a major chip manufacturer is conducting an art contest in the hopes of creating a new image for itself. The contest winner will be used in their upcoming advertising campaign, and they want the ad to be lighthearted and humorous. You have decided to enter the contest and have created a preliminary image. You still need to add the finishing touches.

1. Open PS 6-4.psd, then save it as **Robotics Contest Entry**.
2. Use the Sharpen tool to sharpen the pixels in an area of your choice.
3. Burn any area within the image, using any size brush tip.
4. Use any additional painting tools, libraries, and settings to enhance colors and imagery within the image.
5. Add descriptive type to the image, using the font and wording of your choice. (In the sample, a 36 pt Perpetua font is used. A bevel and emboss effect was added to the type.)
6. Make any color adjustments you want. (In the sample, the Hue is modified to –15, the Saturation is modified to +34, and the Lightness is modified to –20.)
7. Save your work, then compare your image to the sample in Figure 28.

FIGURE 28
Sample Project Builder 2

You have been hired by a local art gallery, Expressions, to teach a course that describes how Photoshop can be used to create impressionistic artwork. This gallery specializes in offbeat, avant-garde art, and wants you to inspire the attendees to see the possibilities of this important software program. They hired you because you have a reputation for creating daring artwork. As you prepare your lecture, you decide to explore the Internet to see what information already exists.

1. Connect to the Internet and use your browser and favorite search engine to find information about digital artwork. (Make a record of the site you found so you can use it for future reference, if necessary.)

2. Identify and print a page containing an interesting piece of artwork that you feel could be created in Photoshop.

3. Using your word processor, create a document called **Art Course**. A sample document is shown in Figure 29. (*Tip*: You can capture your image, then paste it in your document by pressing [Print Scrn], then [Ctrl][V] in your word processor (Win) or pressing [Ctrl] [shift][4] , then ⌘[V] (Mac).)

FIGURE 29
Sample Design Project

4. In the document, analyze the image, pointing out which effects could be created in Photoshop, and which Photoshop tools and features you would use to achieve these effects.

5. Save your work.

Courtesy of Fred Casselman - http://www.earthecho.com/sun/ni13.html

A local car dealer has hired you to create a poster that can be used in magazine ads and highway billboards. The dealership's only requirement is that an automobile be featured within the artwork. You can use any appropriate imagery (already existing on your hard drive, from the web, or your own creation, using a scanner or a digital camera), then compile the artwork and use Photoshop's painting tools to create daring effects. You should create a tag line for the image. You do not need to add a name for the dealership; it will be added at a later date.

1. Start Photoshop and create an image with any dimensions.
2. Save this file as **Dealership Ad**.
3. Make selections and create a composite image.
4. Use any painting tools and settings to create interesting effects.
5. Add at least one layer of type and an effect in the image. Use any fonts available on your computer. (The font shown in the sample is 136 pt Informal Roman.)
6. Make color adjustments.
7. Save your work, then compare your image to the sample in Figure 30.

FIGURE 30
Sample Portfolio Project

Using Painting Tools

7

WORKING WITH SPECIAL
LAYER FUNCTIONS

1. Use a layer mask with a selection

2. Work with layer masks and layer content

3. Control pixels to blend colors

4. Eliminate a layer mask

5. Use an adjustment layer

6. Create a clipping mask

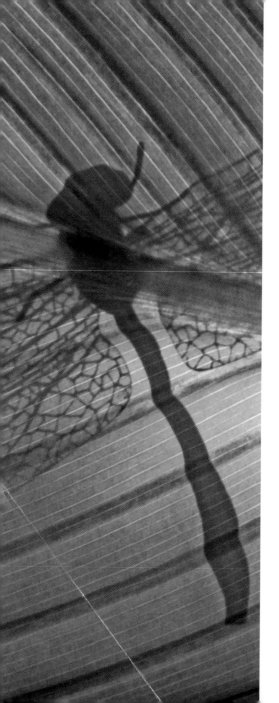

Designing with Layers

Photoshop is rich with tools and techniques for creating and enhancing images. After the imagery is in place, you can hide and modify objects to create special effects. When used in conjunction with other relatively simple techniques, such as merging layers or duplicating layers, the results can be dramatic.

Making Non-destructive Changes to a Layer

If you want to alter a layer, the easiest thing to do is to select the layer and then make the changes. But if you do that, the layer is changed forever, and once you end the current Photoshop session, there is no going back. Adjustment layers make it possible to alter a layer non-destructively, so you *can* go back and revise (or reverse) your changes.

Modifying Specific Areas Within a Layer

You can use special layer features to modify the entire image or a single layer of an image. For example, suppose that you have an image with objects in multiple layers. Perhaps you want to include certain elements from each layer, but you also want to hide some imagery in the finished image. You can *define* the precise area you want to manipulate in each layer, and then accurately adjust its appearance to exactly what you want, without permanently altering the original image. You can turn your changes on or off, align images, blend and adjust color, and combine elements to enhance your image.

Tools You'll Use

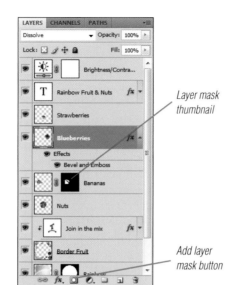

Layer mask thumbnail

Add layer mask button

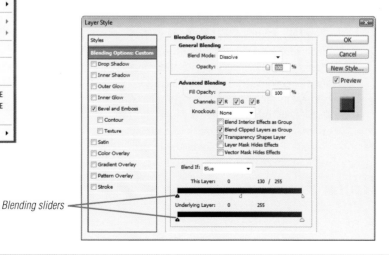

Blending sliders

USE A LAYER MASK WITH
A SELECTION

What You'll Do

 In this lesson, you'll use the Elliptical Marquee tool to make a selection and create a layer mask on the Market layer and on the Bananas layer. You'll select the Brush tool and a brush tip, and then paint on the layer mask to hide pixels.

About Layer Masks

You can hide or reveal a selection within a layer by using a layer mask. A **layer mask** can cover an entire layer or specific areas within a layer. When a layer contains a mask, a layer mask thumbnail appears on the Layers panel to the left of the layer name. As you hide or reveal portions of a layer, the layer mask thumbnail mirrors the changes you make to the object. Some Photoshop features are permanent after you implement them. Masks, however, are extremely flexible—you can hide their effect when you view the image, or change them at will. Because you alter the mask and not the image, no actual pixels are harmed in the creation of your image. You can add an unlimited number of masks to an image, but only one mask to each layer. You can also continue to edit the layer without affecting the layer mask.

Creating a Layer Mask

You can use tools on the Tools panel to create the area you want to mask. You can apply a mask to the selection, or you can apply the mask to everything except the selection. You can also feather a selection (control the softness of its edges) by typing pixel values in the Feather text box on the options bar.

Using the Masks Panel

Once you have created an area to be masked, you can create and refine the masked area using the Masks panel. This panel can be found in both the Essentials and Color and Tone workspaces, and is grouped with the Adjustments panel. It provides a central area where you can create and control a mask. Using the Masks panel, you can adjust the mask density and feathering *non-destructively*. (Non-destructive changes are those that can be reversed even after the image has been closed.)

Painting a Layer Mask

After you add a layer mask to a layer, you can reshape it with the Brush tool and a specific brush size, or tip. Photoshop offers dozens of brush tips, so you can paint just the area you want. For example, you can create a smooth transition between the hidden and visible areas using a soft-edged brush. Here are some important facts about painting a layer mask:

- When you paint the image with a black foreground, the size of the mask *increases*, and each brush stroke hides pixels on the image layer. *Paint with black to hide pixels.*
- When you paint an object using white as the foreground color, the size of the mask *decreases*, and each brush stroke restores pixels of the layer object. *Paint with white to reveal pixels.*

In Figure 1, the School Bus layer contains a layer mask. The area where the bus intersects with the camera has been painted in black so that the bus appears to be driving through the lens of the camera.

Correcting and Updating a Mask

If you need to make a slight correction to an area, you can just switch the foreground and background colors and paint over the mistake. The layer mask thumbnail on the Layers panel automatically updates itself to reflect changes you make to the mask.

FIGURE 1

Example of a layer mask

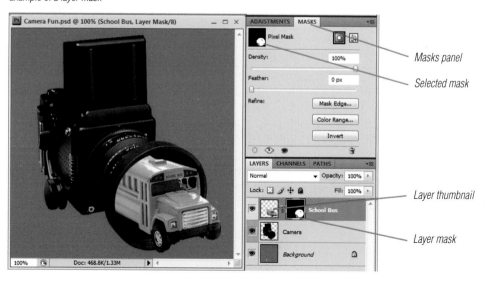

Create a layer mask using the Layer menu

1. Start Photoshop, open PS 7-1.psd from the drive and folder where you store your Data Files, then save it as **Produce Market**.

   TIP   If you see a message stating that some text layers need to be updated before they can be used for vector-based output, click Update (Mac).

2. Click the **Default Foreground and Background Colors button** ◼ on the Tools panel.

3. Display the guides, and the rulers in pixels (if necessary), and verify that the Essentials workspace is displayed.

4. Verify that the **Market layer** is the active layer.

5. Click the **Elliptical Marquee tool** ⬭ on the Tools panel.

   TIP   Look under the Rectangular Marquee tool if the Elliptical Marquee tool is hidden.

6. Change the Feather setting to **5 px** (if this is not the current setting).

7. Drag the **Marquee pointer** ╋ from **30 X/20 Y** to **550 X/540 Y**, to create a marquee that includes the text, bananas, and blueberries using the guides, then compare your image to Figure 2.

8. Click **Layer** on the Application bar, point to **Layer Mask**, then click **Reveal Selection**.

   TIP   You can deselect a marquee by clicking Select on the Application bar, then clicking Deselect; by clicking in another area of the image with the marquee tool that you are using; or by right-clicking the object, then clicking Deselect in the shortcut menu.

You used the Elliptical Marquee tool to create a selection, and created a layer mask on the Market layer using the Layer Mask command on the Layer menu.

FIGURE 2
Elliptical selection on the Market layer

Elliptical marquee selection

Creating a selection from a Quick Mask

Once you have created a selection, you can click the Edit in Quick Mask Mode button 🔲 on the Tools panel to create a mask that can be saved as a selection. When you click the Edit in Quick Mask Mode button, a red overlay displays. Use any painting tools to form a shape in and around the selection. When your mask is finished, click the Edit in Standard Mode button on the Tools panel, and the shape will be outlined by a marquee. You can then save the selection for future use, or use any other Photoshop tools and effects on it.

FIGURE 3
Elliptical selection on the Bananas layer

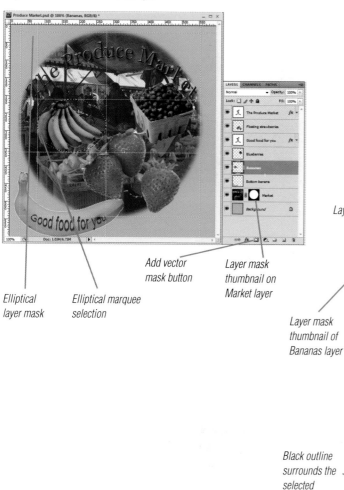

Add vector
mask button

Layer mask
thumbnail on
Market layer

Elliptical
layer mask

Elliptical marquee
selection

FIGURE 4
Layer mask icons on the Layers and Masks panels

Layer mask
thumbnail of
Bananas layer

Black outline
surrounds the
selected
thumbnail

Create a layer mask using the Masks panel

1. Click the **Bananas layer** on the Layers panel.

2. Drag the **Marquee pointer** ╋ from approximately **80 X/210 Y** to **280 X/360 Y** (to surround the bunch of bananas), as shown in Figure 3.

3. Click the **Masks tab** ▐ MASKS ▌ to make it active.

4. Click the **Add a pixel mask button** ▣ on the Masks panel.

   The lower-left edge of the Bananas layer is partially obscured by the layer mask. The layer mask thumbnail appears to the right of the layer thumbnail in the Layers panel and appears at the top of the Masks panel. Once the mask is created, the Masks panel options are available (and no longer dimmed).

   > TIP You can also create a layer mask by clicking the Add layer mask button in the Layers panel. If you use this method, you can press and hold [Alt] (Win) or [option] (Mac) while clicking the Add layer mask button to add a mask that *hides* the selection, rather than reveals it.

5. Verify that the **layer mask thumbnail** on the Bananas layer is active, then compare your Layers panel to Figure 4.

   > TIP You can tell whether the layer mask or the layer object is active by the outline surrounding the thumbnail and by its appearance in the Masks panel.

You used the Elliptical Marquee tool to create a selection, and then used the Select the pixel mask button on the Masks panel to create a layer mask on the Bananas layer.

Paint a layer mask

1. Click the **Zoom tool** 🔍 on the Application bar.

2. Select the **Resize Windows To Fit check box** on the options bar.

3. Click the **bananas** at approximately **150 X/300 Y** with the **Zoom pointer** 🔍 until the bananas are centered and the zoom factor is **200%**.

4. Click the **Brush tool** ✏️ on the Tools panel.

5. Click the **Click to open the Brush Preset picker list arrow** on the options bar, then double-click the **Hard Round 9 pixels brush tip**.

6. Change the Painting Mode on the options bar to **Normal** and the Opacity to **100%** (if necessary).

7. Verify that **Black** is the foreground color and **White** is the background color. (*Hint*: You may have to switch foreground and background colors.)

> TIP Learning to paint a layer mask can be challenging. It's important to make sure the correct layer (and thumbnail) is active before you start painting, to know whether you're adding to or subtracting from the mask, and to set your foreground and background colors correctly.

8. Drag the **Brush pointer** ⭕ along the far-left banana until it is completely hidden. Compare your screen to Figure 5.

As you painted, the shape of the mask thumbnail changed in both the Masks and Layers panels.

> TIP Select a different brush tip if the brush is too big or too small.

You used the Zoom tool to keep a specific portion of the image in view as you increased the zoom percentage, selected a brush tip, and painted pixels on the layer mask to hide a banana.

FIGURE 5
Layer mask painted

Painted area

FIGURE 6
Refine Mask dialog box

FIGURE 7
Modified layer mask

Modify the layer mask

1. Drag the **Brush pointer** ⬭ along the right edge of the object, until the far-right banana is no longer visible and you revealed more produce from the Market layer.

   TIP As you paint, a new History state is created each time you release the mouse button.

2. Click the **Mask Edge button** in the Masks panel.

   The Refine Mask dialog box opens with the On White box selected, as shown in Figure 6. You can use this feature to see if you missed any areas that need to be painted away.

3. Click **OK** to close Refine Mask dialog box, then use the brush pointer to paint away any omissions.

4. Click the **Zoom tool** 🔍 on the Application bar.

5. Press **[Alt]** (Win) or **[option]** (Mac), click at **150 X/300 Y** with the Zoom pointer 🔍 until the zoom factor is **100%**, then release **[Alt]** (Win) or **[option]** (Mac).

6. Save your work, then compare your screen to Figure 7.

You painted pixels to hide the far-right banana, then reset the zoom percentage to 100%.

Editing a layer mask versus editing a layer

Modifying a layer mask can be tricky because you have to make sure that you've selected the layer mask and not the layer thumbnail. Even though the active thumbnail is surrounded by an outline, it can be difficult to see. To make sure whether the layer mask or layer thumbnail is selected, click each one so you can see the difference, then make sure the one you want is selected. You'll know if you've selected the wrong item as soon as you start painting!

WORK WITH LAYER MASKS
AND LAYER CONTENT

What You'll Do

In this lesson, you'll select three layers simultaneously, align the images on three layers, and then deselect the layers. You'll also scale and horizontally flip the strawberries on the Floating strawberries layer.

Understanding Layers and Their Masks

The ability to repeatedly alter the appearance of an image without ever disturbing the actual pixels on the layer makes a layer mask a powerful editing tool. By default, Photoshop links the mask to the layer. This means that if you move the layer, the mask moves as well.

Understanding the Link Icon

The link icon automatically appears when you create a layer mask. When you create a layer mask, the link icon appears *between* the layer thumbnail and the layer mask thumbnail, indicating that the layer and the layer mask are linked together. To unlink the layer mask from its layer, you click the link icon. The Unlink Mask state displays in the History panel. You can re-link a mask to its layer by clicking the space between the layer and mask thumbnails. The Link Mask state displays in the History panel.

Selecting Multiple Layers

You can select more than one layer on the Layers panel to allow multiple layers to behave as one. Selecting multiple layers in

Photoshop is analogous to grouping objects in other programs. You select multiple layers or layer sets by clicking a layer on the Layers panel. To select contiguous layers (layers that are next to one another on the Layers panel), press and hold [Shift] while clicking additional layers on the Layers panel. To select non-contiguous layers, press and hold [Ctrl] (Win) or [⌘] (Mac) while clicking additional layers on the Layers panel. When selecting multiple layers make sure that you click the layer, *not the layer mask*. You can make multiple selections that include the active layer and any other layers on the Layers panel, even if they are in different layer sets. You can select entire layer sets along with a single layer or with other layer sets.

QUICKTIP

When you move multiple selections of layers, the relocation of layers affects the objects' appearance in your image, as well as the layers' position on the Layers panel. This means that you can link two layers and then align them in your image. You can also select two non-contiguous layers and then move them simultaneously as a unit to the top of the Layers panel where they will become contiguous.

Working with Layers

After you select multiple layers, you can perform actions that affect the selection such as moving their content as a single unit in your image. To deselect multiple layers, click any layer (within the selection) on the Layers panel with [Ctrl] for each layer you want to deselect. When you deselect each layer, each one returns to its independent state. You can also turn off a layer's display while it is part of a selection of layers by clicking the layer's Indicates layer visibility button.

QUICKTIP

To move a layer mask from one layer to another, make sure that the layer mask that you want to move is active, and that the destination layer doesn't already have a layer mask. Drag the layer mask thumbnail from the layer containing the layer mask onto the layer where you want to move the mask.

Aligning Selected Layers

Suppose you have several type layers in your image and need to align them by their left edges. Rather than individually moving and aligning numerous layers, you can precisely position selected layers in your image. You can align the content in the image by first selecting layers on the Layers panel, then choosing one of six subcommands from the Align command on the Layer menu. Photoshop aligns layers relative to each other or to a selection border. So, if you have four type layers and want to align them by their left edges, Photoshop will align them relative to the far-left pixels in those layers only, not to any other (nonselected) layers on the Layers panel or to other content in your image.

Distributing Selected Layers

To distribute (evenly space) the content on layers in your image, you must first select three or more layers, verify that their opacity settings are 50% or greater, and then select one of the six options from the Distribute command on the Layer menu. Photoshop spaces out the content in your image relative to pixels in the selected layers. For example, imagine an image that is 700 pixels wide and has four type layers that are 30 pixels wide each and span a range between 100 X and 400 Y. If you select the four type layers and click the Horizontal Centers command on the Distribute Layers menu, Photoshop will distribute them evenly, but only between 100 X and 400 Y. To distribute the type layers evenly across the width of your entire image, you must first move the left and right layers to the left and right edges of your image, respectively.

QUICKTIP

By activating the Move tool on the Tools panel you can use the 13 align and distribute buttons on the options bar to align and distribute layers.

Transforming Objects

You can **transform** (change the shape, size, perspective, or rotation) of an object or objects on a layer, using one of 11 transform commands on the Edit menu. When you use some of the transform commands, eight selection handles surround the contents of the active layer. When you choose any transform command, a transform box appears around the object you are transforming. A **transform box** is a rectangle that surrounds an image and contains handles that can be used to change dimensions. You can pull the handles with the pointer to start transforming the object. After you transform an object, you can apply the changes by clicking the Commit transform (Return) button on the options bar, or by pressing [Enter] (Win) or [return] (Mac). You can use transform commands individually or in a chain. After you choose your initial transform command, you can try out as many others as you like before you apply the changes by pressing [Enter] (Win) or [return] (Mac). If you attempt another command (something other than another transform command) before pressing [Enter] (Win) or [return] (Mac), a warning box will appear. Click Apply to accept the transformation you made to the layer.

QUICKTIP

You can transform selected layers using the same transform commands that you use to transform individual layers. For example, you might want to scale or rotate selected layers. Photoshop transforms selected layers when any of the selected layers are active.

Select and align layers

1. Verify that the **Bananas layer** on the Layers panel is active.

2. Press and hold **[Ctrl]** (Win) or ⌘ (Mac), click the **Floating strawberries layer** on the Layers panel, then release **[Ctrl]** (Win) or ⌘ (Mac).

3. Press and hold **[Ctrl]** (Win) or ⌘ (Mac), click the **Blueberries layer** on the Layers panel, release **[Ctrl]** (Win) or ⌘ (Mac), then compare your Layers panel to Figure 8.

4. Click **Layer** on the Application bar, point to **Align**, then click **Vertical Centers**.

   The centers of the Blueberries and Floating strawberries layers are aligned with the center of the Bananas layer. Compare your image to Figure 9.

5. Press and hold **[Ctrl]** (Win) or ⌘ (Mac), click the **Floating strawberries layer** and the **Blueberries layer** on the Layers panel, then release **[Ctrl]** (Win) or ⌘ (Mac).

   The additional objects are no longer selected, yet all retain their new locations.

You selected three layers on the Layers panel, aligned the objects on those layers by their vertical centers using the Align Vertical Centers command on the Layer menu, then you deselected the layers.

FIGURE 8
Blueberries layer and Floating strawberries layer selected with Bananas layer

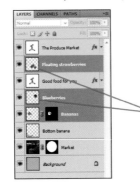

Layers selected with Bananas layer

FIGURE 9
Aligned layers

Center pixel of blueberries and floating strawberries layers aligned with center pixel of bananas layer

Grouping layers

You can quickly turn multiple selected layers into a group. Select as many layers as you'd like—even if they are not contiguous, click Layer on the Application bar, then click Group Layers. Each of the selected layers will be placed in a Group (which looks like a layer set) in the Layers panel. You can ungroup the layers by selecting the group in the Layers panel, clicking Layer on the Application bar, then clicking Ungroup Layers.

Working with Special Layer Functions

FIGURE 10
Floating strawberries layer scaled

Drag handle to resize

FIGURE 11
Floating strawberries layer transformed

Floating strawberries
layer flipped horizontally

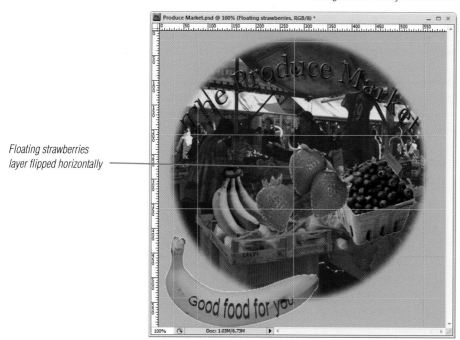

Transform a layer using Scale

1. Click the **Floating strawberries layer** on the Layers panel.

2. Click **Edit** on the Application bar, point to **Transform**, then click **Scale**.

3. Position the **Scaling pointer** ⤡ over the **bottom-right sizing handle** using the ruler pixel measurements at approximately **495 X/465 Y**, drag to **400 X/405 Y** up and to the left, as shown in Figure 10, then release the mouse button.

4. Click the **Commit transform (Return) button** ✔ on the options bar.

   The strawberries image is reduced.

You resized the Floating strawberries layer using the Scale command. This command makes it easy to resize an object while maintaining its proportions.

Transform a layer using Flip Horizontal

1. Verify that the **Floating strawberries layer** is the active layer.

2. Click **Edit** on the Application bar, point to **Transform**, then click **Flip Horizontal**.

3. View the transformation.

4. Save your work, then compare your image to Figure 11.

You horizontally flipped the Floating strawberries layer using the Flip Horizontal command. You can use this command to change the orientation of an object on a layer.

CONTROL PIXELS
TO BLEND COLORS

What You'll Do

 In this lesson, you'll apply styles to layers using the Layer Style dialog box. You'll also work with blending modes to blend pixels on various layers.

Blending Pixels

You can control the colors and form of your image by blending pixels on one layer with pixels on another layer. You can control *which* pixels from the active layer are blended with pixels from lower layers on the Layers panel. You can control how the pixels are blended by specifying which color pixels you want to change. If you set the Blend If color to Red, then all pixels on the layer that are red will be blended based on your new settings. Blending options are found in the Layer Style dialog box. You can control *how* these pixels are blended by choosing a color as the Blend If color, and using the This Layer and Underlying Layer sliders. The **Blend If** color determines the color range for the pixels you want to blend. You use the **This Layer** sliders to specify the range of pixels that will be blended on the active layer. You use the **Underlying Layer** sliders to specify the range of pixels that will be blended on all the lower—but still visible—layers. The color channels available depend on the color mode. For example, an RGB image will have Red, Green, and Blue color channels available.

QUICKTIP
Color channels contain information about the colors in an image.

Using duplicate layers to blend pixels

You can create interesting effects by duplicating layers. To duplicate a layer, click the layer you want to duplicate to activate it, click the Layers panel list arrow, click Duplicate Layer, then click OK. The duplicate layer is given the same name as the active layer with "copy" attached to it. (You can also create a duplicate layer by dragging the layer to the Create a new layer button on the Layers panel.) You can modify the duplicate layer by applying effects or masks to it. In addition, you can alter an image's appearance by moving the original and duplicate layers to different positions on the Layers panel.

Using Color Sliders

The colors that are outside the pixel range you set with the color sliders will not be visible, and the boundary between the visible and invisible pixels will be sharp and hard. You can soften the boundary by adjusting the slider position and creating a gradual transition between the visible and invisible pixels. Normally, you determine the last visible color pixel by adjusting its slider position, just as you can set opacity by dragging a slider on the Layers panel. Photoshop also allows you to split the color slider in two. When you move the slider halves apart, you create a span of pixels for the visible boundary. Figure 12 shows two objects before they are blended and Figure 13 shows the two objects after they are blended. Do you see how the blended pixels conform to the shape of the underlying pixels?

QUICKTIP

A slider that displays a hand when the pointer covers its label is sometimes referred to as a scrubby slider because it lets you change the value without actually having to drag the slider.

FIGURE 12
Pixels before they are blended

All red cap pixels are visible (unblended)

FIGURE 13
Pixels after they are blended

Red cap pixels blended using sliders in the Layer Style dialog box

Blend pixels with a color range

1. Double-click the **Floating strawberries thumbnail** on the Layers panel to open the Layer Style dialog box.

   TIP   Move the Layer Style dialog box if it obscures your view of the strawberries.

2. Click to highlight the **Blending Options: Default bar** at the top of the list (if it is not already selected).

3. Select the **Drop Shadow check box**.

4. Click the **Blend If list arrow**, then click **Red**.

5. Drag the right (white) **This Layer slider** to **240**, as shown in Figure 14.

   TIP   Slider position determines the number of visible pixels for the color channel you've selected.

6. Click **OK**, then view the fade-out effect on the Strawberries layer.

   TIP   If you want to really observe the fade-out effect, display the History panel, then delete the last state and redo steps 4 through 6.

You opened the Layer Style dialog box for the Floating strawberries layer, applied the Drop Shadow style, selected Red as the Blend If color, and then adjusted the This Layer slider to change the range of visible pixels. The result is that you blended pixels on the Floating strawberries layer so that red pixels outside a specific range will not be visible.

FIGURE 14
Layer Style dialog box

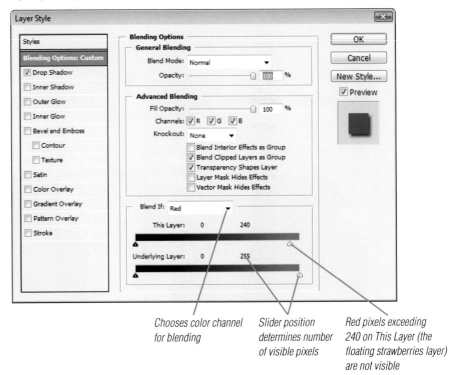

Chooses color channel for blending

Slider position determines number of visible pixels

Red pixels exceeding 240 on This Layer (the floating strawberries layer) are not visible

FIGURE 15
Transition range for visible pixels

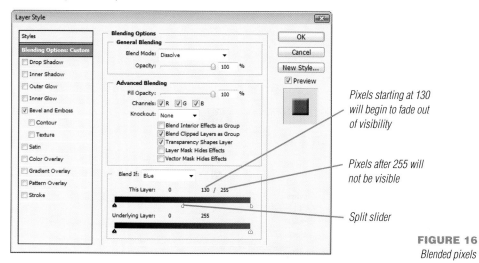

Pixels starting at 130 will begin to fade out of visibility

Pixels after 255 will not be visible

Split slider

FIGURE 16
Blended pixels

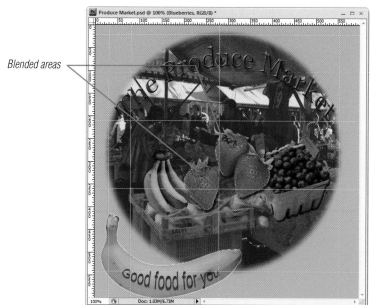

Blended areas

1. Double-click the **Blueberries thumbnail** on the Layers panel to open the Layer Style dialog box.

2. Click to highlight the **Blending Options: Default bar** at the top of the list (if necessary), then click the **Bevel and Emboss check box**.

3. Click the **Blend Mode list arrow**, then click **Dissolve**.

4. Click the **Blend If list arrow**, then click **Blue**.

5. Press and hold **[Alt]** (Win) or **[option]** (Mac), click the right **This Layer slider**, drag the left half of the **Right slider** to **130**, then release **[Alt]** (Win) or **[option]** (Mac).

   TIP Pressing [Alt] (Win) or [option] (Mac) splits the slider into two halves.

6. Compare your dialog box to Figure 15, then click **OK**.

7. Save your work, then compare your image to Figure 16.

You opened the Layer Style dialog box for the Blueberries layer, applied the Bevel and Emboss style to the layer and changed the blending mode to Dissolve, specifying the blue pixels as the color to blend. To fine-tune the blend, you split the right This Layer slider and set a range of pixels that smoothed the transition between visible and invisible pixels.

ELIMINATE
A LAYER MASK

What You'll Do

In this lesson, you'll use the Layer menu to temporarily disable a layer mask, and discard a layer mask using the Layers panel.

Disposing of Layer Masks

As you have seen, layer masks enable you to radically change an image's appearance. However, you might not want to keep every layer mask you create, or you might want to turn the layer mask on or off, or you might want to apply the layer mask to the layer and move on to another activity. You can enable or disable the layer mask (turn it on or off), or remove it from the Layers panel by deleting it from the layer entirely or by permanently applying it to the layer.

Disabling a Layer Mask

Photoshop allows you to temporarily disable a layer mask from a layer to view the layer without the mask. When you disable a layer mask, Photoshop indicates that the layer mask is still in place, but not currently visible, by displaying a red X over the layer mask thumbnail in both the Layers and Masks panels, as shown in Figure 17. Temporarily disabling a layer mask has many advantages. For example, you can create duplicate layers and layer masks, apply different styles and effects to them, and then enable and disable (show and hide) layer masks individually until you decide which mask gives you the look you want.

QUICKTIP

The command available for a layer mask changes depending on whether the layer is visible or not. If the layer mask is enabled, the Layer Mask Disable command is active on the Layer menu. If the layer mask is disabled, the Layer Mask Enable command is active.

Removing Layer Masks

If you are certain that you don't want a layer mask, you can permanently remove it. Before you do so, Photoshop gives you two options:

- You can apply the mask to the layer so that it becomes a permanent part of the layer.
- You can discard the mask and its effect completely.

QUICKTIP

Each layer mask increases the file size, so it's a good idea to perform some routine maintenance as you finalize your image. Remove any unnecessary, unwanted layer masks, and then apply the layer masks you want to keep.

If you apply the mask, the layer will retain the *appearance* of the mask effect, but it will no longer contain the actual layer mask. If you discard the mask entirely, you delete the effects you created with the layer mask, and return the layer to its original state.

QUICKTIP

You can select a layer mask by pressing [Ctrl][\] (Win) or ⌘[\] (Mac) and select the layer thumbnail by pressing [Ctrl][~] (Win) or ⌘[~] (Mac).

FIGURE 17
Layer mask disabled

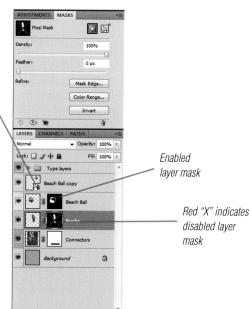

Smart Object thumbnail

Enabled layer mask

Red "X" indicates disabled layer mask

Working with Smart Objects

Just as multiple layers can be selected, you can combine multiple objects into a Smart Object. This combination, which has a visible indicator in the lower-right corner of the layer thumbnail, makes it possible to *non-destructively* scale, rotate, and warp layers without losing image quality. Once the layers you want to combine are selected, you can create a Smart Object by clicking Layer on the Application bar, pointing to Smart Objects, then clicking Group into New Smart Object; or by clicking the Layers panel list arrow, then clicking Convert to Smart Object.

Disable and enable a layer mask

1. Click **Window** on the Application bar, point to **Workspace**, then click **History and Layers**.

2. Click the **Bananas layer** on the Layers panel.

3. Click **Layer** on the Application bar, point to **Layer Mask,** then click **Disable**. See Figure 18.

   When you disable the mask, the bananas are fully displayed.

   > TIP   You can also disable a layer mask by pressing [Shift] and then clicking the layer mask thumbnail, and then enable it by pressing [Shift] and clicking the layer mask thumbnail again.

4. Drag the **Disable Layer Mask history state** to the **Delete current state button** 🗑 on the History panel.

   Deleting the Disable Layer Mask history state causes the remasking of the bananas.

   > TIP   Before you remove a layer mask, verify that the layer mask, not just the layer, is active. Otherwise, if you use the Delete layer button on the Layers panel to remove the mask, you will delete the layer, not the layer mask.

You disabled the layer mask on the Bananas layer, using commands on the Layer menu, and deleted the Disable Layer Mask history state using the History panel.

FIGURE 18
Layer mask disabled

Original view of bananas
without the layer mask

Disabled layer mask

Working with Special Layer Functions

FIGURE 19
Warning box

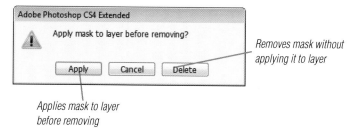

Removes mask without applying it to layer

Applies mask to layer before removing

FIGURE 20
Market layer with layer mask removed

Layer mask reverts to original appearance

Layer mask removed

1. Click the **layer mask thumbnail** on the Market layer on the Layers panel.

2. Click the **Masks tab** MASKS to activate the Masks panel.

3. Click the **Delete layer button** 🗑 on the Layers panel, then compare your warning box to Figure 19.

4. Click **Delete** to remove the mask without first applying it to the Market layer. Compare your screen to Figure 20.

   TIP You can use the Delete Mask button 🗑 in the Masks panel to delete the mask *without* seeing the warning box.

5. Click **Edit** on the Application bar, then click **Undo Delete Layer Mask**.

6. Save your work.

You used the Delete layer button on the Layers panel to delete a layer mask, chose the Delete option in the warning box to remove the mask without applying it to the Market layer, and then used the Edit menu to undo the action to restore the layer mask on the Market layer.

USE AN
ADJUSTMENT LAYER

What You'll Do

In this lesson, you'll create an adjustment layer, choose Brightness/Contrast as the type of adjustment layer, adjust brightness and contrast settings for the layer, and then use the Layers panel to change the blending mode of the adjustment layer.

Understanding Adjustment Layers

An **adjustment layer** is a special layer that acts as a color filter for a single layer or for all the layers beneath it. Just as you can use a layer mask to edit the layer content without permanently deleting pixels on the image, you can create an adjustment layer to adjust color and tone. If you were to make changes directly on the original layer, the changes would be irreversible. (You could use the Undo feature or the History panel to undo your changes, but only in the current Photoshop session.) However, the color changes you make to the adjustment layer exist only in the adjustment layer.

Creating an Adjustment Layer

You can create an adjustment layer by selecting the layer you want to adjust, then clicking the button for the preset in the Adjustments panel; by using the Layer menu to click a new adjustment layer command; or by clicking the Create new fill or adjustment layer button on the Layers panel. When you create an adjustment layer, it affects all the layers beneath it, by default, but you can change this setting so that it affects only the selected layer. When creating color adjustments, you must specify which one you want to use. Color adjustment presets that can be made directly on a layer or by using an adjustment layer are described in Table 1. (Also included in Table 1 are preset symbols used in the Adjustments panel.)

> **QUICK**TIP
>
> If you use the Create new fill or adjustment layer button on the Layers panel, you'll see three additional menu items: Solid Color, Gradient, and Pattern. You can use these commands to create fill layers, which fill a layer with a solid color.

Modifying an Adjustment Layer

You can change the adjustment layer settings by double-clicking the layer thumbnail on the adjustment layer. Photoshop identifies the type of adjustment layer on the Layers panel by including the type of adjustment layer in the layer name.

> **QUICK**TIP
>
> When you double-click an adjustment layer thumbnail, its settings display in the Adjustments panel.

TABLE 1: Color Adjustments

symbol	color adjustment	description	symbol	color adjustment	description
	Black & White	Converts a color image to grayscale while controlling how individual colors are converted, and applies color tones such as a sepia effect.		Match Color	Changes the brightness, color saturation, and color balance in an image.
	Brightness/Contrast	Makes simple adjustments to a tonal range.		Photo Filter	Similar to the practice of adding a color filter to a camera lens to adjust the color balance and color temperature.
	Channel Mixer	Modifies a color channel, using a mix of current color channels.		Posterize	Specifies the number of tonal levels for each channel.
	Color Balance	Changes the overall mixture of color.		Replace Color	Replaces specific colors using a mask.
	Curves	Makes adjustments to an entire tonal range, using three variables: highlights, shadows, and midtones.		Selective Color	Increases or decreases the number of process colors in each of the additive and subtractive primary color components.
	Equalize	Redistributes brightness values of pixels so that they evenly represent the entire range of brightness levels. (Available on the Image > Adjustments menu.)		Shadows/ Highlights	Corrects images with silhouetted images due to strong backlighting, as well as brightening up areas of shadow in an otherwise well-lit image. (Available on the Image > Adjustments menu.)
	Exposure	Controls the tone.		Threshold	Converts images to high contrast, black-and white images.
	Gradient Map	Maps the equivalent grayscale range of an image to colors of a specific gradient fill.		Variations	Adjusts the color balance, contrast, and saturation of an image, and shows alternative thumbnails. (Available on the Image > Adjustments menu.)
	Hue/Saturation	Changes position on the color wheel (hue) or purity of a color (saturation).		Vibrance	Controls the color.
	Invert	Converts an image's brightness values to the inverse values on the 256-step color-values scale.			
	Levels	Sets highlights and shadows by increasing the tonal range of pixels, while preserving the color balance.			

Create and set an adjustment layer

1. Click the **The Produce Market layer** on the Layers panel.

2. Display the **Essentials** workspace.

3. Click the **Brightness/ Contrast** button ☼ in the Adjustments panel. Compare your Adjustments panel to Figure 21.

   TIP You can also create a new adjustment layer by clicking the Create new fill or adjustment layer button on the Layers panel, then selecting a color adjustment or by clicking Layer on the Application bar, pointing to New Adjustment Layer, then clicking the type of adjustment you want.

4. Type **–15** in the Brightness text box.

5. Type **30** in the Contrast text box. Compare your Layers panel to Figure 22.

   Did you notice that the new adjustment layer appears on the Layers panel above the The Produce Market layer? The new layer is named Brightness/Contrast 1 because you chose Brightness/Contrast as the type of color adjustment.

You used the Adjustments panel to create a Brightness/Contrast adjustment layer on the The Produce Market layer, then adjusted the brightness and contrast settings.

Understanding Adjustment panel controls

The Adjustments panel, in Figure 23, is grouped with the Masks panel, and allows you to apply 15 preset adjustment levels. Presets are grouped by theme. The top four presets (Brightness/Contrast, Levels, Curves, and Exposure) are tonal controls; the next six presets (Vibrance, Hue/Saturation, Color Balance, Black & White, Photo Filter, and Channel Mixer) are color controls, and the remaining five presets are creative/advanced controls (Invert, Posterize, Threshold, Gradient Map, and Selective Color).

FIGURE 21
New adjustment layer

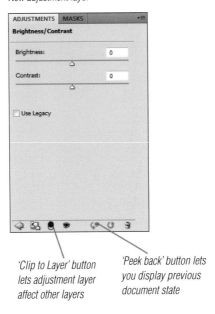

'Clip to Layer' button lets adjustment layer affect other layers

'Peek back' button lets you display previous document state

FIGURE 22
Adjustment layer in Layers panel

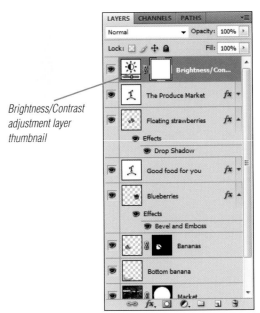

Brightness/Contrast adjustment layer thumbnail

FIGURE 23
Adjustments panel

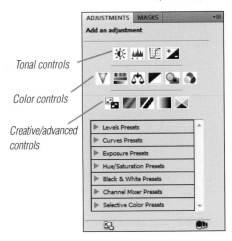

Tonal controls

Color controls

Creative/advanced controls

Working with Special Layer Functions

FIGURE 24
Result of adjustment layer

*Set the blending
mode for the layer
list arrow*

*Layer thumbnail for
adjustment layer*

Modifying an adjustment layer

What if you've created an adjustment layer that affects all the layers beneath it, and then you decide you want it to only affect the previous layer? Do you have to delete this adjustment layer and start over? Certainly not. To toggle an adjustment layer between applying to all the layers beneath it and only the layer immediately beneath it, position the pointer between the adjustment layer and the layer beneath it. Press [Alt] (Win) and [option] (Mac), then click between the two layers. So, when you see an adjustment layer that is *inset* (not aligned with all the other layers) it applies only to the layer immediately beneath it.

Set the blending mode

1. Make sure that the **Brightness/Contrast 1** layer is the active layer.

    TIP   If you choose, you can rename an adjustment layer by double-clicking its name in the Layers panel, typing the new name, then pressing [Enter] (Win) or [return] (Mac).

2. Click the **Set the blending mode for the layer list arrow** on the Layers panel, then click **Soft Light**.

    TIP   You can use as many adjustment layers as you want, but you must create them one at a time. At first glance, this might strike you as a disadvantage, but when you're working on an image, you'll find it to be very helpful. By adding one or more adjustment layers, you can experiment with a variety of colors and tones, then hide and show each one to determine the one that best suits your needs. Adjustment layers can also contain layer masks, which allow you to fine-tune your alterations by painting just the adjust- ment layer mask. When you are positive that the changes in your adjustment layers should be permanent, you can merge them with any *visible* layers in the image, including linked layers. You cannot, however, merge one adjustment layer with another adjust- ment layer. Merging adjustment layers reduces file size and ensures that your adjustments will be permanent.

3. Save your work, then compare your image to Figure 24.

*You changed the blending mode for the adjust-
ment layer to Soft Light, using the Layers panel.*

CREATE A
CLIPPING MASK

What You'll Do

In this lesson, you'll create a clipping mask, adjust the opacity of the base layer, remove and restore the clipping mask, then flatten the image.

Understanding Clipping Masks

A **clipping mask** (sometimes called a *clipping group*) is a group of two or more contiguous layers that are linked for the purpose of masking. Clipping masks are useful when you want one layer to act as the mask for other layers, or if you want an adjustment layer to affect only the layer directly beneath it. The bottom layer in a clipping mask is called the **base layer**, and it serves as the group's mask. For example, you can use a type layer as the base of a clipping mask so that a pattern appears through the text on the base layer, as shown in Figure 25. (On the left side of the figure is the imagery used as the pattern in the type.) The properties of the base layer determine the opacity and visible imagery of a clipping mask. You can, however, adjust the opacity of the individual layers in a clipping mask.

> **QUICK**TIP
>
> You can merge layers in a clipping mask with an adjustment layer, as long as the layers are visible.

Creating a Clipping Mask

To create a clipping mask, you need at least two layers: one to create the shape of the mask, and the other to supply the content for the mask. You can use a type or an image layer to create the clipping mask shape, and when the shape

Working with Special Layer Functions

is the way you want it, you can position the pointer between the two layers, then press [Alt] (Win) or [option] (Mac). The pointer changes to two circles with a left-pointing arrowhead. Simply click the line between the layers to create the clipping mask. You can tell if a clipping mask exists by looking at the Layers panel. A clipping mask is indicated when one or more layers are indented and appear with a down arrow icon, and the base layer is underlined.

QUICKTIP

Not all clipping mask effects are so dramatic. You can use a clipping mask to add depth and texture to imagery.

Removing a Clipping Mask

When you create a clipping mask, the layers in the clipping mask are grouped together. To remove a clipping mask, press and hold [Alt] (Win) or [option] (Mac), position the clipping mask pointer over the line separating the grouped layers on the Layers panel, then click the mouse. You can also select the mask layer, click Layer on the Application bar, and then click Release Clipping Mask.

FIGURE 25
Result of clipping group

Imagery used in the clipping mask

Clipped texture appears in layer

Create a clipping mask

1. Click the **Good food for you layer** on the Layers panel to make it the active layer.

2. Drag the **active layer** below the **Bananas layer** on the Layers panel.

3. Press and hold **[Alt]** (Win) or **[option]** (Mac), then point with the **Clipping mask pointer** 🔻 to the line between the Bottom Banana and the Good food for you layers. Compare your Layers panel to Figure 26.

4. Click the line between the two layers with the **Clipping mask pointer** 🔻, then release **[Alt]** (Win) or **[option]** (Mac).

   The Good food for you (member) is filled with the image from the Bottom banana layer (base).

5. Verify that the clipping icon (a small down-ward pointing arrow) appears in the Good food for you layer, then compare your Layers panel to Figure 27.

6. Make sure the **Good food for you layer** is active, click the **Opacity list arrow** on the Layers panel, drag the slider to **100%**, then press **[Enter]** (Win) or **[return]** (Mac).

You created a clipping mask, using the Bottom banana layer as the base and the Good food for you layer as a member of the clipping mask to make the banana peel appear as the fill of the Good food for you layer, and then you adjusted the opacity of the Good food for you layer.

FIGURE 26
Creating a clipping group

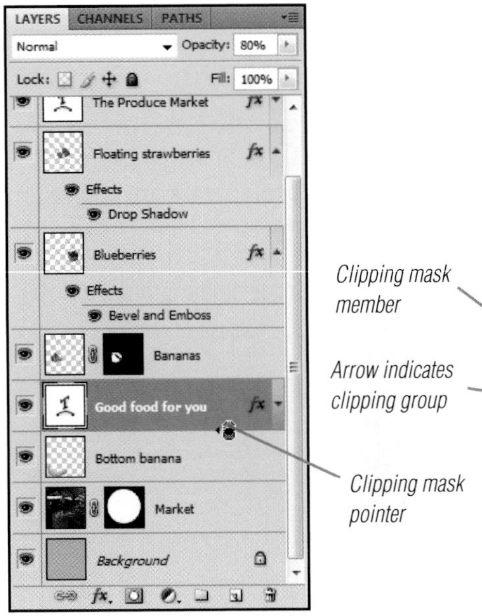

FIGURE 27
Clipping group on Layers panel

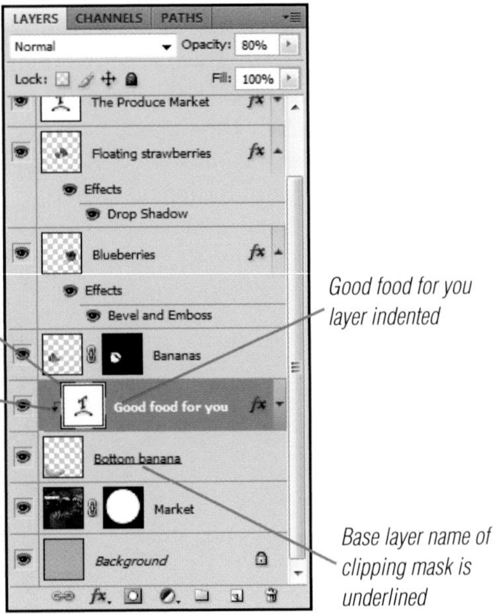

Clipping mask member

Arrow indicates clipping group

Clipping mask pointer

Good food for you layer indented

Base layer name of clipping mask is underlined

Creating 3D files in Photoshop

The Photoshop Extended version of Photoshop CS4 allows you to open and work with 3D files created in programs like Adobe Acrobat 3D Version 8, 3d Studio Max, Alias, Maya, and Google Earth. Photoshop puts 3D models on a separate layer that you can move or scale, change the lighting, or change rendering modes. Although you must have a 3D authoring program to actually edit the 3D model, you can add multiple 3D layers to an image, combine a 3D layer with a 2D layer, or convert a 3D layer into a 2D layer or Smart Object. Textures within a 3D file appear as separate layers in Photoshop and can be edited using any painting or adjustment tools. With Photoshop CS4 Extended you can paint directly on 3D models, and edit, enhance, and manipulate 3D images without using dialog boxes. 2D images can be wrapped around common 3D geometric shapes (such as cylinders and spheres) and you can convert gradient maps to 3D objects.

FIGURE 28
Finished product

*Good food for you
layer text filled in
with banana texture*

1. Click the **Good food for you layer** on the Layers panel (if necessary).

2. Hide the rulers and guides.

3. Defringe the Bottom banana layer using two pixels.

4. Click the **Good food for you layer** in the Layers panel, click **Layer** on the Application bar, then click **Release Clipping Mask**.

5. Click **Edit** on the Application bar, then click **Undo Release Clipping Mask**. Compare your screen to Figure 28.

6. Click **File** on the Application bar, click **Save As**, using the name given, select the **As a Copy check box**, then click **Save**.

   The text **copy** is inserted after the original filename.

7. Click **Layer** on the Application bar, then click **Flatten Image**.

8. Save your work, then close the file and exit Photoshop.

You removed the clipping mask by using the Release Clipping Mask command on the Layer menu, restored the clipping mask by using the Undo command on the Edit menu, saved a copy of the image, and then flattened the file.

Power User Shortcuts

to do this:	use this method:
Activate layer mask	Press and hold [Ctrl][\] (Win) or ⌘ [\] (Mac)
Add an adjustment layer	⬤.
Align linked layers by vertical centers	Layer ➤ Align ➤ Vertical Centers
Blend pixels on a layer	Double-click a layer thumbnail, click Blend; If list arrow, choose color, drag This Layer and Underlying Layer sliders
Brush tool	✎. or B
Change brush tip	Select Brush tool, right-click, then select brush tip
Create a clipping mask	Press and hold [Alt] (Win) or option –click (Mac), move the pointer to the line between two layers, then click
Create a layer/vector mask	▣
Create a layer mask that hides the selection	Press and hold [Alt] (Win) or option -click (Mac) ➤ ▣

to do this:	use this method:
Create a layer mask that reveals the selection	Layer ➤ Layer Mask ➤ Reveal Selection
Delete layer	🗑
Disable layer mask	Layer ➤ Layer Mask ➤ Disable
Previous or Next brush tip in Brushes panel	[,] or [.]
Remove a clipping mask	Click a layer in the group ➤ Layer ➤ Release Clipping Mask
Remove a link	Click 🔗
Scale a layer	Edit ➤ Transform ➤ Scale
Rotate a layer 90° to the left	Edit ➤ Transform ➤ Rotate 90° CCW
Select first or last brush tip in Brushes panel	[Shift][,] or [Shift][.]

Key: Menu items are indicated by ➤ between the menu name and its command. Blue bold letters are shortcuts for selecting tools on the Tools panel.

Working with Special Layer Functions

Use a layer mask with a selection.

1. Start Photoshop, open PS 7-2.psd from the drive and folder where you store your Data Files, then save it as **Stripes**.
2. Make sure the rulers are displayed in pixels.
3. Change the zoom factor to 150% or 200%, to enlarge your view of the image.
4. Create a type layer title in black with the text "See Stripes?" above the Zebra layer and add the drop shadow layer style (using default settings). (*Hint*: A 30 pt Segoe Print font is shown in the sample. Use any other font on your computer if this font is not available.)
5. Make the Zebra layer active, then select the Elliptical Marquee tool.
6. Change the Feather setting on the options bar to 5 pixels.
7. Create a marquee selection from 35 X/35 Y to 235 X/360 Y. (*Hint*: Feel free to add guides, if necessary.)
8. Use the Masks panel to add a layer mask.
9. Save your work.

Work with layer masks and layer content.

1. Select the Brush tool.
2. Hide the type layer.
3. Change the existing brush tip to Soft Round 9 pixels.
4. Change the Painting mode to Normal, and the flow and opacity to 100% (if those are not the current settings).
5. Use the default foreground and background colors to paint the area from 20 X/70 Y to

65 X/290 Y. (*Hint*: Make sure the layer mask thumbnail is selected and that white is the foreground color and black is the background color.)
6. Display the type layer.
7. Make the Fern layer active.
8. Unlink the Background layer.
9. Rotate the fern so that its left edge barely touches the zebra's nose.
10. Save your work.

Control pixels to blend colors.

1. Double-click the Fern layer thumbnail.
2. Using green as the Blend If color, drag the right This Layer slider to 200.
3. Split the right This Layer slider, drag the right half to 240, then click OK. (*Hint*: Click OK to close the Layer Style dialog box after step 2, *before* splitting the slider. You may have to reopen the dialog box.)
4. Save your work.

Eliminate a layer mask.

1. Click the layer mask thumbnail on the Zebra layer.
2. Use the Layer menu to disable the layer mask.
3. Use the Layer menu to enable the layer mask.
4. Save your work.

Use an adjustment layer.

1. Make the Fern layer active.
2. Using the Layer menu, create a Color Balance adjustment layer called **Modifications**.
3. Make sure the Midtones option button is selected, drag the Cyan/Red, Magenta/Green,

and Yellow/Blue sliders to +36, +12, and −19, respectively.
4. Create a Brightness/Contrast adjustment layer, above the Modifications layer.
5. Change the Brightness to −25 and the Contrast to +20.
6. Hide the Modifications layer.
7. Hide the Brightness/Contrast layer.
8. Display both adjustment layers.
9. Save your work.

Create a clipping mask.

1. Make the Background layer active.
2. Create a clipping mask (with the Background layer as the base layer) that includes the type layer. (*Hint*: Move the type layer to a new location, if necessary.)
3. Include the Zebra layer in the clipping mask.
4. Save your work, then compare your image to Figure 29.

FIGURE 29
Completed Skills Review

Your cousin has recently purchased a beauty shop and wants to increase the number of manicure customers. She's hired you to create an eye-catching image that can be used in print ads. You decided to take an ordinary image and use your knowledge of masks and adjustment layers to make the image look striking.

1. Open PS 7-3.psd, then save it as **Manicure**.
2. Duplicate the Polishes layer, then name the new layer Red Polish.
3. On the Red Polish layer, select the red nail polish bottle and cap, then delete everything else in the layer. (*Hint*: You can do this by deleting a selection.)
4. Hide the Red Polish layer, then make the Polishes layer active.
5. Create a layer mask that hides the red polish, then brush in the remaining items on the Polishes layer.
6. Use any tools at your disposal to fix the area where the red polish (on the Polishes layer) has been masked.
7. Display the Red Polish layer.
8. Move the Red Polish layer below the Polishes layer in the Layers panel (if necessary).
9. Use the existing layer mask to hide the white polish (with the blue cap).
10. Position the red polish bottle so it appears where the white polish bottle was visible.
11. Use any tools necessary to fix areas you want to improve, such as the Blur tool to soften the edges of polish bottles.
12. Add an adjustment layer to the Red Polish layer that makes the polish color violet. (*Hint*: In the sample, a Hue/Saturation adjustment layer was used with the following settings: Hue: –45, Saturation: +35, and Lightness: –5.)
13. Add one or two brief type layers, and apply layer styles to at least one of them. (*Hint*: In the sample, the type used is a 60 pt Edwardian Script ITC and a 50 pt Perpetua font.)
14. Save a copy of the file as **Manicure copy,** then flatten the original image.
15. Save your work, then compare your image to the sample in Figure 30.

FIGURE 30
Sample Project Builder 1

Working with Special Layer Functions

In exchange for free concert tickets, you have volunteered to work on the cleanup crew for an outdoor concert facility. After the second concert, the promoter asks you to design a poster to inspire concert-goers to throw trash in the trash barrels. You decide to create a Photoshop image that contains several unique illusions. Using any city or locale other than your own as a theme, you'll use your Photoshop skills to create and paint layer masks in an image that conveys a cleanup message.

1. Obtain the following images: a landscape, a sign, one large inanimate object, and two or more smaller objects that evoke a city or locale of your choice. You can use images that are available on your computer, scan print media, or use a digital camera. (*Hint*: Try to obtain images that fit your theme.)

2. Open the images you obtained, then create a new Photoshop image and save it as **Cleanup**.

3. Drag the landscape to the Cleanup image above the Background layer, then delete the Background layer.

4. Drag the large object image to the Cleanup image above the landscape layer.

5. Transform the large object as necessary to prepare it to be partially buried in the land-scape. (*Hint*: The tower layer in the sample has been rotated and resized.)

6. Apply a layer mask to the large object, then paint the layer mask to reshape the mask and partially obscure the object.

7. Drag the sign image to the Cleanup image, and then place it below the large object layer.

8. Create a type layer for the sign layer with a message (humor optional), link the layers, then transform the layers as needed to fit in the image. (*Hint*: The sign layer and type layer in the sample have been skewed.)

9. Drag other images as desired to the Cleanup image, and add styles to them or transform them as necessary.

10. Create other type layers (humor optional) as desired, and apply a style to at least one layer. (*Hint*: The title layer in the sample has drop shadow and outer glow styles applied to it. A 14 pt, Arial Narrow font is used in the sign, and a 35 and 24 pt Arial Black is used in the title.)

11. Add an adjustment layer to the landscape layer, and to any other layer that would benefit from it.

12. Save a copy of your file as **Cleanup copy**, then flatten the original image.

13. Save your work, then compare your image to the sample in Figure 31.

FIGURE 31
Sample Project Builder 2

As the publishing director for a large accounting firm, you've been asked to design a banner for the new International Monetary Division website. They've asked that you include a flag, paper currency, and coinage of a country of your choice. You decide to use techniques to create an interesting collage of those three items.

1. Obtain several images of paper currency and coins, and a flag from a country (or countries) of your choice. You can use the images that are available on your computer, scan print media, or connect to the Internet and download images. (*Hint*: Try to obtain at least two denominations of both paper and coin.)

2. Create a new image in Photoshop and save it as **Currency**.

3. Open the paper money image files, then drag the paper money images to the currency image above the Background layer.

4. Transform the paper money layers as desired. (*Hint*: The paper money layers in the sample have been rotated and skewed.)

5. Add layer masks as desired.

6. Add an adjustment layer to the paper money layer, and apply at least one color adjustment. (*Hint*: The paper money layers in the sample have a Brightness/Contrast adjustment applied to them.)

7. Open the flag file, then drag the flag image to the Currency image, and position it to appear on top of the paper money layers, then resize it and adjust opacity, as necessary.

8. Apply a Curves adjustment to the flag.

9. Open the coin image files, drag the coin images to the Currency image, duplicate the coin layers as desired, position them above the flag layer, then apply at least one transformation and one layer style to them.

(*Hint*: The coins in the sample have a Drop Shadow style and have been rotated.)

10. Blend the pixels for two of the coin layers.

11. Save a copy of the file as **Currency copy**, flatten the original image, then close the other files.

12. Save your work, then compare your image to the sample in Figure 32.

FIGURE 32
Sample Design Project

Working with Special Layer Functions

Lost Horizons, a tragically hip coffee-house, is hosting a regional multimedia Poetry Slam contest. You have teamed up with the Surreal Poetry Enclave, an eclectic poetry group. The contest consists of the poetry group reading poetry while you create a visual interpretation using two preselected images and as many elective images as you want. First, though, you must submit an entry design. Find a poem for inspiration, design the interpretation, obtain images, and write some creative copy (tag line or slogan) to be used in the design.

1. Obtain images for your interpretative design. The images you must include are a picture frame and a background image; the other pieces are up to you. You can use the images that are available on your computer, scan print media, or connect to the Internet and download images.

2. Create a new Photoshop image, then save it as **Poetry Poster**.

3. Open the background image file, drag the background image to the Poetry Poster image above the Background layer.

4. Open the picture frame image file, drag it to the Poetry Poster image above the Background layer, transform it as necessary, then apply styles to it if desired. (*Hint*: The frame in the sample has been skewed.)

5. Open the image files that will go in or on the picture frame, drag them to the Poetry Poster image, then transform them as necessary.

6. Arrange the image layers on the Layers panel in the configuration you want, and apply styles to them if you think they will enhance the image.

7. Apply a layer mask to two or more of the image layers.

8. Create a clipping mask using two or more of the image layers. (*Hint*: The clipping mask in the sample consists of the frame layer as the base and the Lantern and Alarm clock layers as members.)

9. Create type layers as desired and apply styles to them. (*Hint*: The type layer in the sample has an Outer Glow style applied to it.)

10. Close the image files, save your work, then compare your image to the sample in Figure 33.

11. Be prepared to discuss the creative ways you can use clipping masks.

FIGURE 33
Sample Portfolio Project

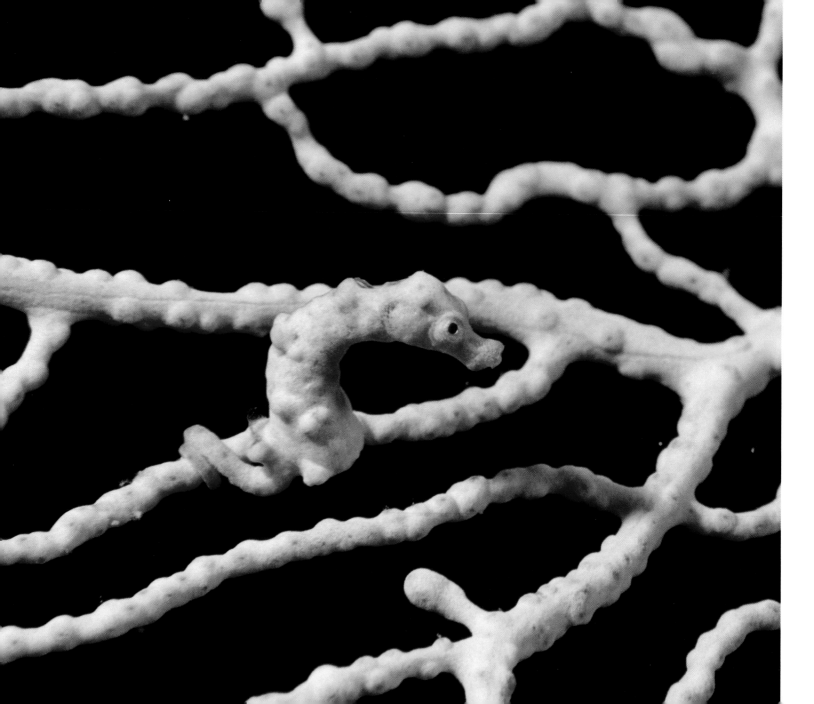

8

CREATING SPECIAL
EFFECTS WITH
FILTERS

8 CREATING SPECIAL
EFFECTS WITH
FILTERS

Understanding Filters

You've already seen some of the filters that Photoshop offers. Filters modify the look of an image by altering pixels in a particular pattern or format, across a layer or a selection. This results in a unique, customized appearance. You use filters to apply special effects, such as realistic textures, distortions, changes in lighting, and blurring. Although you can use several types of filters and options, and can apply them to multiple layers in an image, the most important thing to remember when using filters is subtlety.

Applying Filters

You can apply filters to any layer (except the Background layer) using commands on the Filter menu. Most filters have their own dialog box, where you can adjust filter settings and preview the effect before applying it. The preview window in the dialog box allows you to evaluate the precise effect of the filter on your selection. You can zoom in and out, and pan the image in the dialog box to get a good look before making a final decision. Other filters—those whose menu command is not followed by an ellipsis (...)—apply their effects instantly as soon as you click the command.

> **QUICK**TIP
>
> Does your computer have enough RAM? You'll know for sure when you start using filters because they are very memory-intensive.

Tools You'll Use

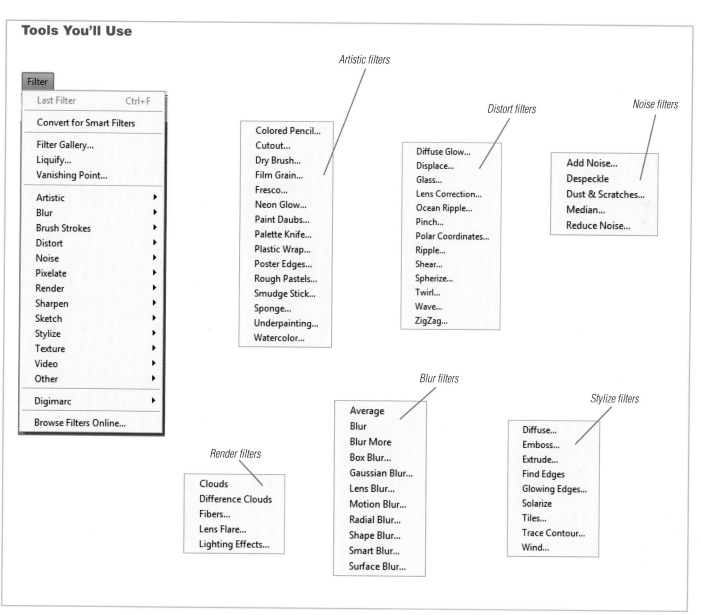

Filter

Last Filter	Ctrl+F
Convert for Smart Filters	
Filter Gallery...	
Liquify...	
Vanishing Point...	
Artistic	▶
Blur	▶
Brush Strokes	▶
Distort	▶
Noise	▶
Pixelate	▶
Render	▶
Sharpen	▶
Sketch	▶
Stylize	▶
Texture	▶
Video	▶
Other	▶
Digimarc	▶
Browse Filters Online...	

Artistic filters

Colored Pencil...
Cutout...
Dry Brush...
Film Grain...
Fresco...
Neon Glow...
Paint Daubs...
Palette Knife...
Plastic Wrap...
Poster Edges...
Rough Pastels...
Smudge Stick...
Sponge...
Underpainting...
Watercolor...

Distort filters

Diffuse Glow...
Displace...
Glass...
Lens Correction...
Ocean Ripple...
Pinch...
Polar Coordinates...
Ripple...
Shear...
Spherize...
Twirl...
Wave...
ZigZag...

Noise filters

Add Noise...
Despeckle
Dust & Scratches...
Median...
Reduce Noise...

Blur filters

Average
Blur
Blur More
Box Blur...
Gaussian Blur...
Lens Blur...
Motion Blur...
Radial Blur...
Shape Blur...
Smart Blur...
Surface Blur...

Stylize filters

Diffuse...
Emboss...
Extrude...
Find Edges
Glowing Edges...
Solarize
Tiles...
Trace Contour...
Wind...

Render filters

Clouds
Difference Clouds
Fibers...
Lens Flare...
Lighting Effects...

LEARN ABOUT FILTERS AND
HOW TO APPLY THEM

What You'll Do

In this lesson, you'll apply the Motion Blur filter to the Red bar layer and convert a layer into a Smart Object.

Understanding the Filter Menu

The Filter menu sorts filters into categories and subcategories. Many filters are memory-intensive, so depending on the capabilities of your computer, you might need to wait several seconds while Photoshop applies the effect. Using filters might slow down your computer's performance. Figure 1 shows samples of several filters.

Learning About Filters

You can read about filters all day long, but until you apply one yourself, it's all academic. When you do, here are a few tips to keep in mind.

- Distort filters can completely reshape an image; they are highly resource-demanding.
- Photoshop applies most of the Pixelate filters as soon as you click the command, without opening a dialog box.

- Digimarc filters notify users that the image is copyright-protected.

QUICKTIP

Some imported files may require rasterizing before they can be used in Photoshop. These files have vector artwork. During rasterization, the mathematically defined lines and curves of vector art are converted into pixels or bits of a bitmap image.

Applying a Filter

You can apply a filter by clicking its category and name under the Filter menu. When you click a Filter menu name, a dialog box opens displaying a sample of each filter in the category. You can also apply one or more filters using the Filter Gallery.

FIGURE 1

Examples of filters

You will be amazed by how many filters there are, how much they can do for an image, and just how much fun they can be. Table 1 describes each filter category.

Understanding the Filter Gallery

The **Filter Gallery** is a feature that lets you see the effects of each filter *before* its application. You can also use the Filter Gallery to apply filters (either individually, or in groups), rearrange filters, and change individual filter settings. The Filter Gallery is opened by clicking Filter on the Application bar, then clicking Filter Gallery. In Figure 2, the Mosaic Tiles filter (in the Texture category) is applied to the active layer, which has been enlarged for easier viewing in the preview window.

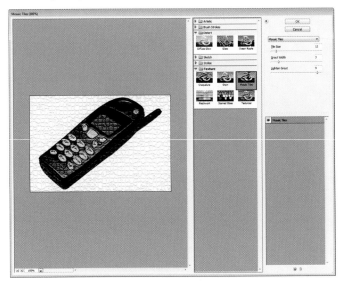

FIGURE 2
Filter Gallery dialog box

TABLE 1: Filter Categories			
category	**use**	**category**	**use**
Artistic	Replicates traditional fine arts effects.	Sharpen	Refocuses blurry objects by increasing contrast in adjacent pixels.
Blur	Simulates an object in motion; can use to retouch photographs.	Sketch	Applies a texture, or simulates a fine arts hard-drawn effect.
Brush Strokes	Mimics fine arts brushwork and ink effects.	Stylize	Produces a painted or impressionistic effect.
Distort	Reshapes an image.	Texture	Gives the appearance of depth or substance.
Noise	Gives an aged look; can use to retouch photographs.	Video	Restricts color use to those that are acceptable for television reproduction and smooth video images.
Pixelate	Adds small honeycomb shapes based on similar colors.	Other	Creates unique filters, modifies masks, or makes quick color adjustments.
Render	Transforms three-dimensional shapes; simulates light reflections.	Digimarc	Embeds a digital watermark that stores copyright information.

FIGURE 3

Current Layers panel

Learning about Motion filters

When you apply a Blur filter, keep in mind how you want your object to appear—as if it's moving. Blur filters smooth the transitions between different colors. The effect of the Blur More filter is four times stronger than the Blur filter. The Gaussian Blur filter produces more of a hazy effect. The direction of the blur is determined by the Angle setting—a straight horizontal path has an angle set to zero. The Motion Blur filter simulates taking a picture of an object in motion, and the Radial Blur filter simulates zooming or rotation. You can use the Smart Blur filter to set exactly how the filter will blur the image.

Open a Blur filter

1. Start Photoshop, display the **Essentials** workspace (if necessary), open PS 8-1.psd from the drive and folder where you store your Data Files, then save it as **Sunflowers**.

2. Click the **Default Foreground and Background Colors button** on the Tools panel to display the default settings (if necessary).

   TIP   It's a good habit to check Photoshop settings and display the rulers before you begin your work if you'll need these features.

3. Click the **Indicates layer visibility button** on the Sunflower LEFT layer on the Layers panel.

4. Click the **Indicates layer visibility button** on the Sunflower RIGHT layer on the Layers panel.

5. Click the **Indicates layer visibility button** on the Sunflower CENTER layer on the Layers panel.

6. Click the **Red bar layer** on the Layers panel to make it active. Compare your Layers panel to Figure 3.

7. Use the **Zoom tool** on the Application bar to increase the magnification to 200%.

8. Click **Filter** on the Application bar, point to **Blur**, then click **Motion Blur**.

   TIP   The last filter applied to a layer appears at the top of the Filter menu.

You set default foreground and background colors, hid three layers, then opened the Motion Blur dialog box.

Apply a Blur filter

1. Position the **red bar** in the preview window with the **Hand pointer** 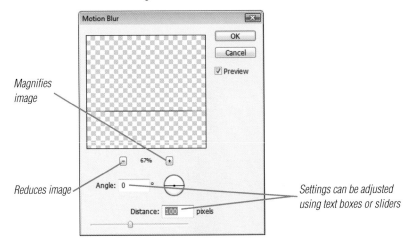, reduce or enlarge the image with the buttons beneath the preview window so it displays in the center.

   The red bar image is repositioned from the lower area to the center of the preview window.

2. Verify that **0** is in the Angle text box.

   > TIP   In this case, increasing the angle results in a thicker bar.

3. Type **100** in the Distance text box, then compare your dialog box to Figure 4.

   > TIP   You can also adjust the settings in the Motion Blur dialog box by dragging the Angle radius slider and Distance slider.

4. Click **OK**.

   The Motion Blur filter is applied to the Red bar layer.

You repositioned the Red bar layer in the preview window and then applied a Motion Blur filter to the layer.

FIGURE 4
Motion Blur dialog box

Magnifies image

Reduces image

Settings can be adjusted using text boxes or sliders

Destructive vs. nondestructive editing

In the early days of Photoshop (i.e., a few years ago), any editing change you made was *destructive*, in that it permanently altered the pixels in your image. There was no going back, except of course if you made duplicate layers of everything you ever did. *Nondestructive* editing, as the name implies, means that you can go back and re-edit what used to be a permanent change to pixels. An example of nondestructive editing is the application of adjustment layers versus applying an adjustment to a layer and hoping that you never have to remove or change it.

Reducing blur with the Smart Sharpen Filter

You can use the Smart Sharpen Filter to remove or reduce blurriness. This filter can be used to remove blur effects in images created by Gaussian Blur, Lens Blur, or Motion Blur filters. The Smart Sharpen Filter is available by clicking Filter on the Application bar, pointing to Sharpen, then clicking Smart Sharpen. Using the Smart Sharpen dialog box, you can change the amount as a percentage and the radius in pixels of the settings. You can choose the type of blur to be removed from the image.

FIGURE 5
Motion Blur filter applied to layer

Effect of Motion
Blur filter

Smart Object
in layer

Using Smart Filters

Smart Objects, one or more objects on one or more layers that have been modified so that they can be scaled, rotated, or warped without losing image quality, can have filters applied to them. These filters are called Smart Filters. **Smart Filters** can be adjusted, removed, or hidden, and are nondestructive. Any filter, with the exception of Extract, Liquify, Pattern Maker, and Vanishing Point, can be applied as a Smart Filter. You won't find the Smart Filter command on the Filter menu; simply apply a filter to a Smart Object and it will be applied as a Smart Filter. Once the filter is applied, the Smart Filter appears in the Layers panel. Double-clicking the filter on the Layers panel opens the Filter Gallery, enabling you to modify or change the existing filter.

Create a Smart Object

1. Click the **Indicates layer visibility button** on the Sunflower RIGHT layer on the Layers panel.

2. Click the **Indicates layer visibility button** on the Sunflower CENTER layer on the Layers panel.

3. Click the **Indicates layer visibility button** on the Sunflower LEFT layer on the Layers panel.

4. Click the **Sunflower RIGHT layer** on the Layers panel.

   TIP   Any layer can be turned into a Smart Object. Before you apply any filters to a layer, convert it to a Smart Object to give you full editing capabilities over your filter selections.

5. Click **Layer** on the Application bar, point to **Smart Objects**, then click **Convert to Smart Object**.

6. Save your work, then compare your image and Layers panel to Figure 5.

You restored the visibility of three layers and converted one of the layers into a Smart Object. The ability to turn layers on and off while working on an image means you can decrease distracting elements and concentrate on specific objects.

CREATE AN EFFECT WITH
AN ARTISTIC FILTER

What You'll Do

In this lesson, you'll apply the Poster Edges filter from the Artistic category to the Sunflower RIGHT layer and adjust the contrast and brightness of the layer.

Learning About Artistic Filters

You can dramatically alter an image by using Artistic filters. **Artistic filters** are often used for special effects in television commercials and other multimedia venues.

Taking Advantage of Smart Filters

Just as you can convert an object on a layer into a Smart Object to make your edits nondestructive, you can perform a similar operation to give the application of filters the same power. So, while you can apply a filter directly to a layer, you can just as easily apply a Smart Filter. If the active layer is not already a Smart Object, you can apply a Smart Filter on-the-fly

using the Convert for Smart Filters command on the Filter menu.

> **QUICK**TIP A Smart Filter is nothing more than a filter that is applied to a Smart Object.

Using Artistic Filters

There are 15 Artistic filters. Figure 6 shows examples of some of the Artistic filters. The following list contains the names of each of the Artistic filters and their effects.

- Colored Pencil has a colored pencil effect and retains important edges.
- Cutout allows high-contrast images to appear in silhouette and has the effect of using several layers of colored paper.

Learning about third-party plug-ins

A **plug-in** is any external program that adds features and functionality to another program while working from within that program. Plug-ins enable you to obtain and work in additional file types and formats, add dazzling special effects, or provide efficient shortcut modules. You can purchase Photoshop plug-ins from third-party companies, or download them from freeware sites. To locate Photoshop plug-ins, you can use your favorite Internet search engine, or search for plug-ins on Adobe's website: *www.adobe.com.*

- Dry Brush simplifies an image by reducing its range of colors.
- Film Grain applies even color variations throughout an object.
- Fresco paints an image with short, rounded dabs of color.
- Neon Glow adds a glow effect to selected objects.
- Paint Daubs gives an image a painterly effect.
- Palette Knife reduces the level of detail in an image, revealing underlying texture.

- Plastic Wrap accentuates surface details and makes the contents of a layer appear to be covered in plastic.
- Poster Edges reduces the number of colors in an image.
- Rough Pastels makes an image look as if it is stroked with colored pastel chalk on a textured background.
- Smudge Stick softens an image by smudging or smearing darker areas.
- Sponge creates highly textured areas, making an object look like it was painted with a sponge.

- Underpainting paints the image on a textured background.
- Watercolor simplifies the appearance of an object, making it look like it was painted with watercolors.

Adjusting Filter Effects

You can change the appearance of a filter by using any of the functions listed under the Adjustments command on the Image menu. For example, you can modify the color balance or the brightness/contrast of a layer before or after you apply a filter to it.

FIGURE 6
Examples of Artistic filters

Lesson 2   Create an Effect with an Artistic Filter

Apply a Smart Filter (Artistic filter) with the Filter Gallery

1. Click **Filter** on the Application bar, click **Filter Gallery**, then move and enlarge the image so that it is visible in the preview window (if necessary).

   The Filter Gallery displays thumbnails of each filter as you expand each category, so you can see a quick overview of what effects are available.

   TIP The settings available for a filter in the Filter Gallery are the same as those in the individual dialog box that opens when you click the category name in the menu.

2. Click the **triangle to the left of the Artistic folder** ▷, then click **Poster Edges**.

3. Type **5** in the Edge Thickness text box.

   The Edge Thickness determines the settings of the edges within the image.

4. Type **5** in the Edge Intensity text box.

   The Edge Intensity setting gives the edges more definition.

5. Type **3** in the Posterization text box, then compare your dialog box to Figure 7.

   The Posterization setting controls the number of unique colors the filter will reproduce in the image.

6. Click **OK**, then compare your image and Layers panel to Figure 8.

Using the Filter Gallery, you applied the Poster Edges filter to the Sunflower RIGHT layer. The far right sunflower now looks less realistic than the flowers next to it, and has poster effects.

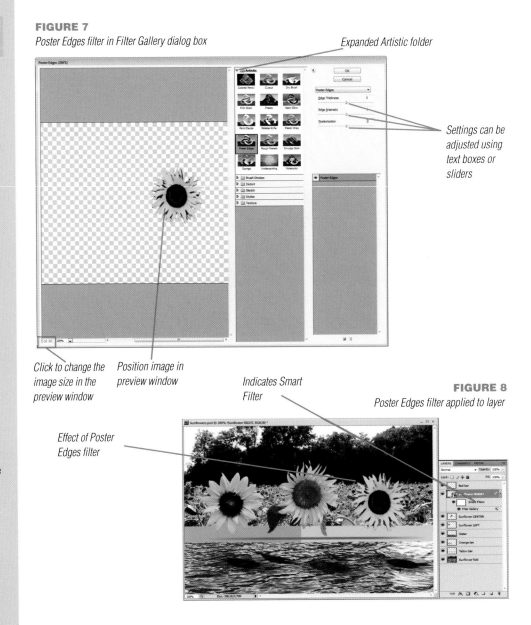

FIGURE 7
Poster Edges filter in Filter Gallery dialog box

Expanded Artistic folder

Settings can be adjusted using text boxes or sliders

Click to change the image size in the preview window

Position image in preview window

Indicates Smart Filter

Effect of Poster Edges filter

FIGURE 8
Poster Edges filter applied to layer

FIGURE 9
Image adjusted

Brightness and contrast
adjusted on layer

Adjust the filter effect and modify the Smart Filter

1. Click the **Brightness/Contrast button** on the Adjustments panel.

   The effects of the adjustment layer will be limited to the active layer.

2. Type **20** in the Brightness text box.

3. Type **15** in the Contrast text box.

4. Double-click the **Filter Gallery effect** under the Sunflower RIGHT layer on the Layers panel.

5. Click **OK** if a warning box opens.

   This warning box indicates that Smart Filters stacked on top of this filter will not preview while this filter is being edited and will be applied after committing the filter parameters.

6. Click **Watercolor** in the Artistic category, then click **OK**.

7. Save your work, then compare your image to Figure 9.

You adjusted the brightness and contrast of the Sunflower RIGHT layer and changed the existing filter type.

ADD UNIQUE EFFECTS
WITH STYLIZE FILTERS

What You'll Do

▶ In this lesson, you'll apply a solarize filter to the Sunflower field layer and a Wind filter to the Orange bar layer. You'll also apply the Poster Edges filter to two layers using the Filter Gallery.

Learning About Stylize Filters

Stylize filters produce a painted or impressionistic effect by displacing pixels and heightening the contrast within an image. Figure 10 shows several Stylize filters. Several commonly used Stylize filters and their effects are listed below:

- The Diffuse filter breaks up the image so that it looks less focused. The Darken Only option replaces light pixels with dark pixels, and the Lighten Only option replaces dark pixels with light pixels.

- The Wind filter conveys directed motion.
- The Extrude filter converts the image into pyramids or blocks.

Applying a Filter to a Selection

Instead of applying a filter to an entire layer, you can specify a particular area of a layer to which you want to apply a filter. You need to first define the area by using a marquee tool, and then apply the desired filter. If you want to apply a filter to a layer that contains a mask, be sure to select the layer name, not the layer mask thumbnail.

Detecting a watermark

Before you can embed a watermark, you must first register with Digimarc Corporation. When Photoshop detects a watermark in an image, it displays the copyright image © in the image file's title bar. To check if an image has a watermark, make the layer active, click Filter on the Application bar, point to Digimarc, then click Read Watermark.

FIGURE 10
Examples of Stylize filters

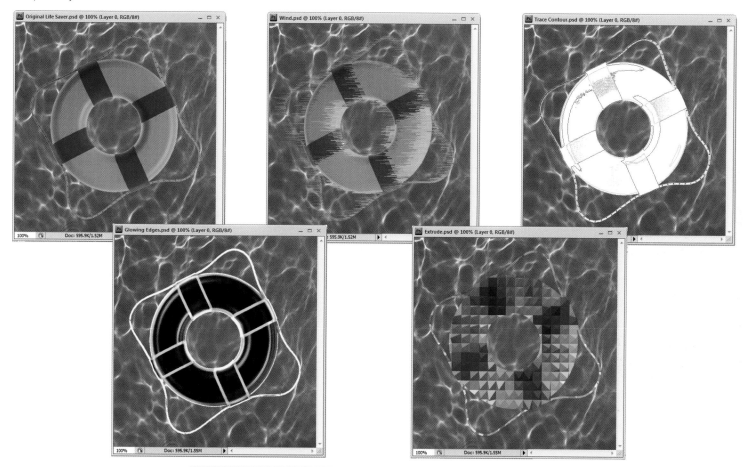

Browsing filters online

You might notice that at the bottom of the Filter menu is the option to Browse Filters Online. When you click this option, your browser will open and go to an Adobe website that contains links for filter downloads. You can also use your favorite browser to locate sites that offer Photoshop filters that are either available for free or for a small fee. (Some filters are available as plug-ins.)

Apply a Stylize filter

1. Click the **Sunflower field layer** on the Layers panel.

2. Click **Filter** on the Application bar, point to **Stylize** as shown in Figure 11, then click **Solarize**.

   TIP   In addition to just looking interesting, the Solarize filter can be used to reduce shadows and make an image more equalized. In this effect, dark areas appear lighter and light areas appear darker.

3. Compare your image to Figure 12.

You applied the Solarize filter to the Sunflower field layer.

FIGURE 11
Stylize options on the Filter menu

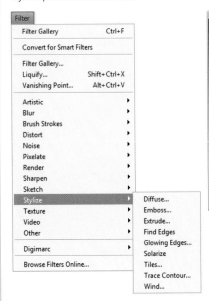

FIGURE 12
Effect of Solarize filter

Pixels appear darker

Using filters to reduce file size

If you apply a filter to a small area, you can view the effect while conserving your computer's resources. For example, you can test several filters on a small area and then decide which one you want to apply to one or more layers. Alternatively, you can apply a filter to a large portion of a layer, such as applying a slight Motion Blur filter to a grassy background. Your viewers will not notice an appreciable difference when they look at the grass, but by applying the filter, you reduce the number of green colors Photoshop must save in the image, which reduces the size of the file.

Creating Special Effects with Filters

FIGURE 13
Elliptical Marquee selection

Marquee surrounds
the box

FIGURE 14
Wind dialog box

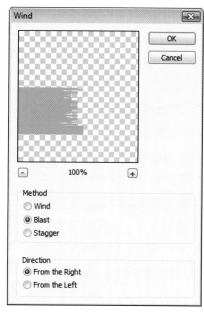

FIGURE 15
Effect of Wind filter

Wind filter applied
to orange bar

Apply a filter to a selection

1. Click the **Orange bar layer** on the Layers panel.

2. Click the **Rectangular Marquee tool** ⬚, on the Tools panel.

3. Change the Feather setting to **0 px** (if it is not already set to 0).

4. Draw a rectangle around an area that includes the right side of the bar (from approximately **140 X/140 Y** to **250 X/225 Y**) using the **Marquee pointer** ┼, as shown in Figure 13.

5. Click **Filter** on the Application bar, point to **Stylize**, then click **Wind**.

6. Click the **Blast option button** in the Method section of the Wind dialog box.

7. Click the **From the Right option button** in the Direction section of the Wind dialog box (if it is not already selected), then compare your dialog box to Figure 14.

8. Click **OK**.

9. Deselect the marquee, then compare your image to Figure 15.

You used the Rectangular Marquee tool to select a specific area on the Orange bar layer, then applied the Wind filter to the selection.

Use the Filter Gallery to apply a previously used filter

1. Click the **Sunflower CENTER layer** on the Layers panel.

2. Click **Filter** on the Application bar, then click **Filter Gallery**. Compare your Filter Gallery dialog box to Figure 16.

   TIP When the Filter Gallery opens, the filter that was last applied using the Filter Gallery is selected by default.

3. Click **OK**.

   The filter last applied using the Filter Gallery is applied to the active layer.

You applied the Poster Edges filter to a layer using the Filter Gallery.

FIGURE 16
Last filter applied on Filter Gallery

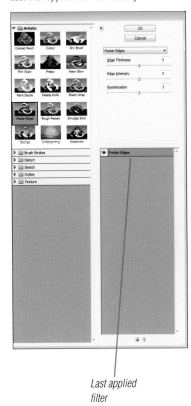

Last applied
filter

FIGURE 17
Combining filters

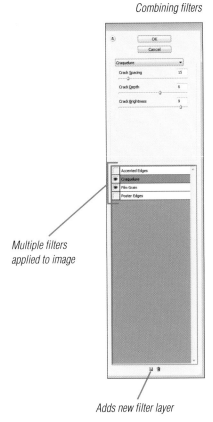

Multiple filters
applied to image

Adds new filter layer

Using the Filter Gallery to combine effects

The Filter Gallery offers more than just another way of applying a single filter. Using this feature, you can apply multiple filters. And using the same principles as on the Layers panel, you can rearrange the filter layers and control their visibility. Figure 17 shows an image to which four different filters have been applied, but only the effects of two are visible. Each time you apply, reorder, or turn off one of the filters, the preview image is updated, so you'll always know how your image is being modified.

Creating Special Effects with Filters

FIGURE 18
Solarize filter applied to multiple layers

Solarize filter
applied to all
Sunflowers layers

1. Click the **Sunflower LEFT layer** on the Layers panel.

2. Click **Filter** on the Application bar, then click the first instance of **Filter Gallery**.

   The Sunflower LEFT and Sunflower CENTER layers have the same filter applied.

3. Save your work, then compare your image to Figure 18.

You used the last filter applied on the Filter Gallery to apply the Poster Edges filter to the Sunflower LEFT layer and the Sunflower CENTER layer.

Getting some perspective with Vanishing Point

In the real world, perspective changes as you move towards and away from objects. If you use Photoshop to stretch the top of a skyscraper, to maintain proper perspective the modified shape should change so it appears to get taller and narrower. Using a grid, the Vanishing Point filter lets you do this by defining the area of any angle you want to modify so you can wrap objects around corners having multiple planes and into the distance while maintaining the correct perspective. The sky's the limit! The Vanishing Point feature is opened by clicking Filter on the Application bar, then clicking Vanishing Point.

Lesson 3   Add Unique Effects with Stylize Filters

ALTER IMAGES WITH DISTORT
AND NOISE FILTERS

What You'll Do

In this lesson, you'll apply the Twirl filter to the Water layer and the Noise filter to the Yellow bar layer.

Understanding Distort and Noise Filters

Distort filters use the most memory, yet even a minimal setting can produce dramatic results. They can create a 3D effect or reshape an object. The Diffuse Glow filter mutes an image, similar to how classic film cinematographers layered cheesecloth or smeared Vaseline on the lens of a movie camera when filming leading ladies. Others, such as the Ocean Ripple, Glass, Wave, and Ripple filters make an object appear as if it is under or in water. The Twirl filter applies a circular effect to a layer. By adjusting the angle of the twirl, you can make images look as if they are moving or spinning. Figure 19 shows the diversity of the Distort filters.

Noise filters give an image an appearance of texture. You can apply them to an image layer or to the Background layer. If you want to apply a Noise filter to a type layer, you must rasterize the type layer to convert it to an image layer. You can apply effects to the rasterized type layer; however, you can no longer edit the text.

Optimizing Memory in Photoshop

Many of the dynamic features in Photoshop are memory-intensive, particularly layer masks and filters. In addition to significantly increasing file size, they require a significant quantity of your computer memory to take effect. Part of the fun of working in Photoshop is experimenting with different styles and effects; however, doing so can quickly consume enough memory to diminish Photoshop's performance, or can cause you to not be able to work in other programs while Photoshop is running. You can offset some of the resource loss by freeing up memory as you work in Photoshop, and by adjusting settings in the Preferences dialog box.

Understanding Memory Usage

Every time you change your image, Photoshop stores the previous state in its buffer, which requires memory. You can control some of the memory that Photoshop uses by reducing the number of states available on the History panel.

To change the number of states, point to Preferences on the Edit menu (Win) or Photoshop menu (Mac), select Performance, then enter a number in the History States text box. You can also liberate the memory used to store Undo commands, History states, and items on the clipboard by clicking Edit on the Application bar, pointing to Purge, then clicking the area you want to purge. It's a good idea to use the Purge command after you've tried out several effects during a session, but be aware that you cannot undo the Purge command. For example, if you purge the History states, they will no longer appear on the History panel.

Controlling Memory Usage

Factors such as how much memory your computer has, the average size file you work with, and your need to multitask (have other programs open) can determine how Photoshop uses the memory currently allotted to it. To change your memory settings, click Edit (Win) or Photoshop (Mac) on the Application bar, point to Preferences, then click Performance. Make the desired change in the Let Photoshop Use text box (in the Memory Usage section), then click OK. You should carefully consider your program needs before changing the default settings. For additional tips on managing resources, visit Adobe's Photoshop Help and Support website: *www.adobe.com/support/photoshop*.

FIGURE 19
Examples of Distort filters

Apply a Twirl filter

1. Click the **Water layer** on the Layers panel.

2. Click **Filter** on the Application bar, point to **Distort**, then click **Twirl**.

3. Drag the **Angle slider** to **225**, as shown in Figure 20.

   TIP The selection is rotated more sharply in the center of the selection than at the edges.

4. Click **OK**.

5. Click the **Red bar layer** on the Layers panel, drag it beneath the Water layer, then compare your image to Figure 21.

You applied a Twirl filter to the Water layer. You moved the Red bar layer beneath the water to complete the effect.

FIGURE 20
Twirl dialog box

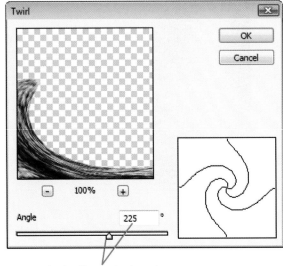

Angle setting can be changed using text box or slider

FIGURE 21
Twirl filter applied to Water layer

Effect of Twirl filter

Correction lens distortion

Some distortions occur as a result of the camera lens. You can use the Lens Correction filter to counteract barrel (convex appearance), pincushion (concave appearance), and perspective distortions. You can also correct for chromatic aberrations and lens vignetting. These distortions can occur as a result of the focal length or f-stop in use. The Lens Correction filter can also be used to rotate an image or fix perspectives caused by camera tilt. Click Filter on the Application bar, point to Distort, and then click Lens Correction.

Creating Special Effects with Filters

FIGURE 22
Add Noise dialog box

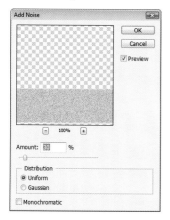

FIGURE 23
Add Noise filter applied to Yellow bar layer

*Effect of Add
Noise filter*

FIGURE 24
Reduce Noise dialog box

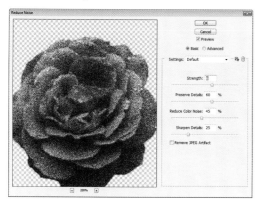

Apply a Noise filter

1. Click the **Yellow bar layer** on the Layers panel.

2. Click **Filter** on the Application bar, point to **Noise**, then click **Add Noise**.

3. Drag the **Amount slider** to **30** (or type the value in the text box), then compare your dialog box to Figure 22.

   TIP The Uniform setting distributes color values using random numbers between 0 and a specified value, while the Gaussian setting distributes color values along a bell-shaped curve for a speckled effect.

4. Click **OK**.

   Flecks of noise are visible in the layer.

5. Save your work, then compare your image to Figure 23.

You applied a Noise filter to the active layer.

Reducing noise
While some images look better when you've added some noise, others can benefit from a little noise reduction. You can quiet things down using the Reduce Noise dialog box shown in Figure 24. Here you can adjust the strength, details, and color noise, and can also sharpen the image.

ALTER LIGHTING WITH
A RENDER FILTER

What You'll Do

In this lesson, you'll add a lighting effect to the Sunflower LEFT layer, add text, save a copy of the file, then flatten the original image.

Understanding Lighting Effects

The Lighting Effects filter in the **Render** category of the Filter menu allows you to set an atmosphere or highlight elements in your image. You can select the style and type of light, adjust its properties, and texturize it. The preview window displays an ellipse that shows the light settings and allows you to position the light relative to your image, so that it looks like the light in the image is coming from a specific source. You can drag the handles on each circle, ellipse, or bar to change the direction and distance of the light sources. Figure 25 shows how you can position the light using the Soft Spotlight style.

Adjusting Light by Setting the Style and Light Type

You can choose from over a dozen lighting styles, including spotlights, floodlights, and full lighting, as shown in Figure 25. After you select a style, you choose the type of light—Directional, Omni, or Spotlight—and set its intensity and focus. Directional lighting washes the surface with a constant light source, Omni casts light from the center, and Spotlight directs light outward from a single point. As shown in Figure 26, you can adjust the brightness of the light by using the Intensity slider. You can use the Focus slider to adjust the size of the beam of light filling the ellipse. The light source begins where the radius touches the edge of the ellipse. The Light type color swatch lets you modify the color of the light. You can also create custom lighting schemes and save them for use in other images. Custom lighting schemes will appear in the Style list.

Adjusting Surrounding Light Conditions

You can adjust the surrounding light conditions using the Gloss, Material, Exposure, or Ambience properties, as shown in Figure 26. The Gloss property controls the amount of surface reflection on the lighted surfaces. The Material

Creating Special Effects with Filters

property controls the parts of an image that reflect the light source color. The Exposure property lightens or darkens the ellipse (the area displaying the light source). The Ambience property controls the balance between the light source and the overall light in an image. The Properties color swatch changes the ambient light around the spotlight.

FIGURE 25

Lighting Effects dialog box

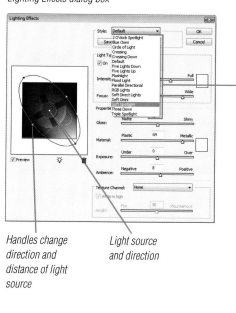

Handles change direction and distance of light source

Light source and direction

Adding Texture to Light

The Texture Channel allows you to add 3D effects to the lighting filter. The Texture Channel controls how light reflects off an image. If a channel is selected and the 'White is High' check box is also selected, white parts of the channel will be raised. To use this option, you select one of the three RGB color channels, then drag the Height slider to the relief setting you want. You

FIGURE 26

Settings in the Lighting Effects dialog box

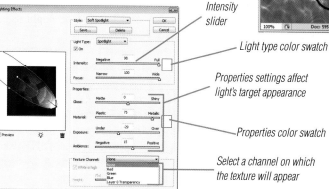

Intensity slider

Light type color swatch

Properties settings affect light's target appearance

Properties color swatch

Select a channel on which the texture will appear

can also choose whether the black or white areas appear highest in the relief. Figure 27 shows a lighting effect texture with black colors highest.

QUICKTIP

You can add additional light sources by dragging the light bulb icon onto the preview window, and then adjusting each new light source that you add.

FIGURE 27

Texture added to lighting effect

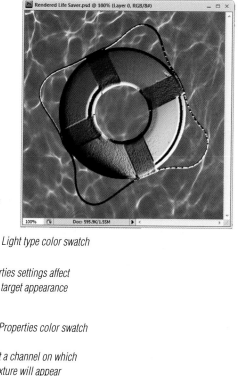

Light styles

Select lighting settings

1. Click the **Sunflower LEFT layer** on the Layers panel.

2. Click **Filter** on the Application bar, point to **Render**, then click **Lighting Effects**.

3. Click the **Style list arrow**, then click **Flashlight**.

   The preview window displays the newly selected style.

4. Click the **Light type list arrow**, then click **Omni** (if it is not already selected).

5. Verify that the **On check box** is selected.

   The preview window shows the settings for the Flashlight light source.

6. Drag the **center handle** of the flashlight so it is directly over the sunflower in the preview box.

   As you drag the ellipse handle, the preview window automatically displays the change in the lighting direction and distance.

7. Drag any **one of the handles** on the edge of the flashlight so the spotlight is larger than the sunflower (if necessary).

8. Adjust the **slider settings** as shown in Figure 28 in the Lighting Effects dialog box.

   TIP   Lighting effects must include at least one light source.

You selected a lighting style and type, then changed the direction and distance of the lighting.

FIGURE 28
Light direction and source repositioned

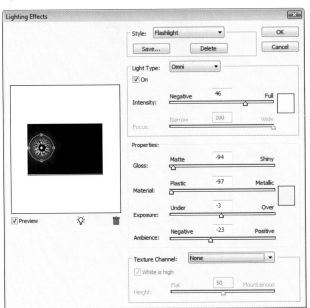

Using Analysis and Measurement Tools

One of the menus tucked between Filter and View on the Application bar is the Analysis menu. This group of commands lets you select many options, such as changing the measurement scale, selecting data points, selecting the Ruler Tool (which help you position images or elements, and calculates the distance between any two points). The Count Tool lets you manually count items. You can record measurements, and place a scale marker at the top or bottom of the image. Recorded measurements are displayed in the Measurement Log panel (which appears behind the Animation [Timeline] panel) and can be opened by clicking Window on the Application bar, then clicking Measurement Log.

Creating Special Effects with Filters

FIGURE 29

Lighting Effects filter applied to Sunflower LEFT

FIGURE 30

Type layer in flattened file

1. Click **OK**.

   The light appears brightest in the center of the flower.

   TIP   When there are multiple sources of light, you can delete a light source ellipse by dragging its center point over the Delete icon in the Lighting Effects dialog box.

2. Compare your image to Figure 29. Your results may vary, depending on your settings in the Lighting Effects dialog box.

You applied a lighting effect to the Sunflower LEFT layer.

Apply finishing touches

1. Use a 36-point black Impact font to create a type layer at approximately 210 H/ 220 V that says **Sunflower Grill**.

2. Save a copy of this file using the default naming scheme, flatten the file, then compare your image to Figure 30.

3. Save your work.

You added a type layer to the image, then saved a copy and flattened the file.

Creating custom lighting effects

As you modify a style in the Lighting Effects dialog box, you can save the settings as a new style with a unique name. To create a custom style, choose your settings, then click the Save button beneath the Style list arrow. Enter a new name in the Save As dialog box, then click OK. The new style name will appear in the Style list. You can delete an entry by selecting it from the Style list, then clicking the Delete button.

USE VANISHING POINT
TO ADD PERSPECTIVE

What You'll Do

In this lesson, you'll use Vanishing Point to apply a Photoshop image to the perspective created in another image.

Understanding Vanishing Point

Vanishing Point, which is found in the Filter menu, allows you to create planes which can visually adjust for perspective caused by width, height, and depth. With Vanishing Point, matching perspective is made easy. (Without this feature, you can fuss with the Transform commands to try to create the illusion of perspective. You'll work very hard and may not be very happy with the results.) From within Vanishing Point, you can create an unlimited number of planes from which you can copy and clone objects around corners.

Creating Planes

You may find it helpful to use this feature on a newly created empty layer. That way, if you make a mistake, your original image will still be intact. Once you've opened Vanishing Point, you create an initial plane from which others can be drawn.

Each plane is surrounded by a light blue line, and while any image can have multiple planes, only one plane can be active at a time in editing mode. The active plane is indicated by a displayed grid. Figure 31 shows the Vanishing Point window, and an object containing two drawn planes. As you draw each plane (using tools in the Vanishing Point window), the grid color lets you know if your perspective is realistic. A red grid indicates that the drawn perspective is not possible. A yellow grid indicates that the perspective is unlikely.

Pasting One Image into Another

Using the Clipboard, you can copy an image which can then be pasted and manipulated in Vanishing Point. When imagery is initially pasted into Vanishing Point, it floats at the top until you pull it within the planes you have created. Figure 32 shows imagery that has been pulled onto the planes of a gift box.

Getting that Healing Feeling

Vanishing Point tools are located in the upper-left corner of the dialog box. You can use the Transform tool to flip images and the Stamp tool and Brush tool to paint over pixels.

QUICKTIP

You can use Vanishing Point and create a grid even if you don't have an image in which to paste it. If you don't have an image in which to paste a graphic, create a new layer or open a new file, open Vanishing Point, create a grid, then paste your graphic.

FIGURE 31
Vanishing Point window   *Tools*

FIGURE 32
Image applied to multiple planes

Outline of inactive plane   *Handle of grid on active plane*

TABLE 2: Vanishing Point tools

tool	name	used to
	Edit Plane tool	Selects, edits, moves, and resizes planes.
	Create Plane tool	Defines a plane, adjusts its size and shape, and tears off a new plane.
	Marquee tool	Makes square or rectangular selections, and moves and clones selections.
	Stamp tool	Paints with a sample of the image.
	Brush tool	Paints with a selected color in a plane.
	Transform tool	Scales, rotates, and moves a floating selection using handles.
	Eyedropper tool	Selects a color for painting when you click in the preview image.
	Measure tool	Measures distances and angles of an item in a plane.
	Hand tool	Repositions the image in the preview window.
	Zoom tool	Magnifies/reduces the image in the preview window.

Lesson 6 Use Vanishing Point to Add Perspective

Prepare to use Vanishing Point

1. Select the entire flattened image.
2. Copy the selection to the Clipboard.
3. Open PS 8-2.psd from the drive and folder where you store your Data Files, then save it as **Sunflower Grill-VP**.
4. Create a new layer.
5. Click **Filter** on the Application bar, then click **Vanishing Point**.
6. If necessary, select the **Create Plane tool** 🔲 .
7. Click point 1 in the building, click point 2, click point 3, then click point 4 using Figure 33 as a guide.

You selected the contents of a flattened image, copied it to the Clipboard, opened Vanishing Point, then created an initial plane.

Create an additional plane

1. Click the **Create Plane tool** 🔲 .
2. Position the pointer over the right center handle, as shown in Figure 34.
3. Drag the grid along the long edge of the building, stopping at the extension towards the building's right edge.
4. With the **Edit Plane tool** 🔲 , **[Ctrl]-drag** (Win) or 🔲 -**drag** (Mac) the **right-most** handles so they cover the top four floors of the building, as shown in Figure 35.

You created an additional plane in Vanishing Point, then adjusted the points in the plane to include a specific area in an image.

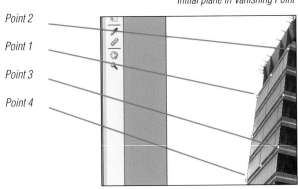

FIGURE 33
Initial plane in Vanishing Point

Point 2
Point 1
Point 3
Point 4

FIGURE 34
Preparing to create new plane

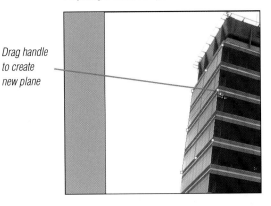

Drag handle to create new plane

FIGURE 35
Grid covering 4 top floors of building

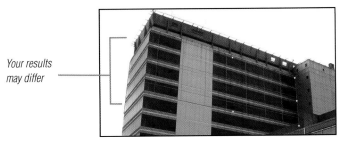

Your results may differ

Creating Special Effects with Filters

FIGURE 36

Pasted contents floating in Vanishing Point

Pasted
contents

FIGURE 37

Clipboard contents in grid

FIGURE 38

Repositioned Clipboard contents

Paste image in Vanishing Point

1. Paste the copied image.

   The contents of the Clipboard is copied into Vanishing Point, as shown in Figure 36.

2. Position the pointer over the pasted selection, then drag the pointer ▲ over the left side of the grid until you feel it pop into place, as shown in Figure 37.

3. Drag the pointer ▲ until the image fills the grid and the type displays. (*Hint*: If you need to reposition the pasted object, click it again with the pointer.)

4. Click **OK** to close Vanishing Point.

5. Save your work, then compare your image to Figure 38. (Your zoom factor and results may differ.)

6. Close the file, then exit Photoshop.

You pasted the contents of the Clipboard into Vanishing Point, then adjusted the image within the grid.

Power User Shortcuts

to do this:	use this method:
Apply a filter	Filter ➤ Filter category ➤ Filter name
Apply last filter	[Ctrl][F] (Win) or ⌘ [F] (Mac)
Apply last filter, but set new options	[Ctrl][Alt][F] (Win) or ⌘ option [F] (Mac)
Ascend one layer at a time on the Layers panel	[Alt][]] (Win) or option []] (Mac)

to do this:	use this method:
Descend one layer at a time on the Layers panel	[Alt][[] (Win) or option [[] (Mac)
Fades effect of previous filter	[Ctrl][Shift][F] (Win) or ⌘ [Shift][F] (Mac)
Open Filter Gallery	Filter ➤ Filter Gallery
Open Vanishing Point	Filter ➤ Vanishing Point

Key: Menu items are indicated by ➤ between the menu name and its command.

Creating Special Effects with Filters

Learn about filters and how to apply them.

1. Start Photoshop, open PS 8-3.psd from the drive and folder where you store your Data Files, then save it as **B&B Poster**.
2. Make the Dunes layer active.
3. Use the Elliptical Marquee tool to draw an ellipse around the bend in the driftwood limb.
4. Apply a Gaussian Blur filter (Blur category) with the following setting: Radius = 1.0 pixels. Remember to deselect the selection when you are finished.
5. Create four separate type layers with the text **Fish**, **Swim**, **Hike**, and **Relax**, and arrange them vertically starting from below the bend in the tree limb down over the tree trunk on the left side of the image. (*Hint*: A 36 pt Pure Yellow Copperplate Gothic Bold is used in the sample.)
6. Save your work.

Create an effect with an Artistic filter.

1. Make the B&B layer active, then convert the layer into a Smart Object.
2. Apply a Film Grain filter (Artistic category) with the following settings: Grain = 3, Highlight Area = 1, Intensity = 10.
3. Save your work.

Add unique effects with Stylize filters.

1. Make the Trout layer active.
2. Apply a Glowing Edges filter (Stylize category), with the following settings: Edge Width = 2,

Edge Brightness = 2, Smoothness = 3.
3. Transform the Trout layer by resizing and rotating the trout so that it appears to be jumping, then drag it behind the Fish type layer.
4. Save your work.

Alter images with Distort and Noise filters.

1. Make the Swim type layer active.
2. Apply a Ripple filter (Distort category) with the following settings: Amount = 55%, Size = Medium. (*Hint*: Click OK to rasterize the layer.)
3. Make the Relax type layer active.
4. Recolor the type to the following settings: R = 227, G = 4, B = 178.
5. Apply an Add Noise filter (Noise category) with the following settings: Amount = 25%, Distribution = Uniform, Monochromatic = Selected.
6. Save your work.

Alter lighting with a Render filter.

1. Make the Dunes layer active.
2. Apply Lighting Effects (Render category) with the following settings: Style = Crossing, type = Spotlight.
3. Use the following Lighting Effects settings: Intensity = 28, Focus = 100, Gloss = 0, Material = -100, Exposure = 0, Ambience = 11. (Your results may vary.)
4. Save your work as a copy using the default naming, flatten this file, then save your work.

Use Vanishing Point to add perspective.

1. Use the Image menu to change the image size to have a width of 3".
2. Select the contents of the flattened file, then copy it into the Clipboard.
3. Open PS 8-4.psd from the drive and folder where you store your Data Files, then save it as **Billboard**.
4. Create a new layer, then open Vanishing Point.
5. Create a realistic plane in the billboard, then paste the Clipboard contents into the image.
6. Center the B&B poster image in the sign, then return to Photoshop. (*Hint*: It's okay if Fish, Swim, Hike, Relax do not all display in the sign as the image and billboard have different dimensions.)
7. Save your work, close the flattened file *without saving the changes*, then compare your image to Figure 39.

FIGURE 39
Completed Skills Review

Theatre in the Park, an outdoor production company, is adding Shakespeare's comedies to their summer repertoire. The company has convinced several rollerbladers to wear sandwich boards promoting the event as they blade downtown during the noon hour. You've volunteered to design the board for the Bard. You can use the title from any Shakespearian comedy in the sign.

1. Obtain the following images that reflect the production: a park, an image related to Shakespeare, and any other images that reflect a summer theater production. You can use the images that are available on your computer, scanned images, or images from a digital camera.

2. Create a new Photoshop image with the dimensions 630 × 450 pixels, then save it as **Play**.

3. Drag or copy the Park image to the Play image above the Background layer, apply at least one filter to it, then rename the Background layer. (*Hint*: The Park layer in the sample has a Render category Lighting Effects filter applied to it.)

4. Drag the Shakespeare image to the Play image above the Park layer, and modify it as desired. (*Hint*: The face in the sample has an opacity setting of 64%, and has been rotated.)

5. Create a sign announcing the play, and apply at least one style and filter to it. (*Hint*: The sign in the sample was created using the Rectangle tool, and has the Drop Shadow, Satin, and Bevel and Emboss styles, and a Texture category Craquelure filter applied to it.)

6. Create type layers as desired, and apply at least one style or filter to them. (*Hint*: A 23 pt Myriad Pro font is used in the sample.)

7. Drag or copy the remaining images to the Play image, close the image files, then transform them or apply at least one style or filter to them.

8. Save your work, then compare your image to the sample in Figure 40.

FIGURE 40
Sample Project Builder 1

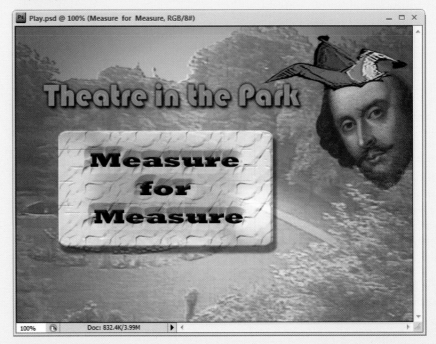

Creating Special Effects with Filters

Local musical instrument shops in your town are producing a classic jazz and blues event. Last year, the poster displayed sponsor logos and never conveyed the feel of the genre. This year, they've decided not to include sponsor logos, and have asked you to design a poster that focuses attention on the music itself. Use your Photoshop skills to express the sponsors' intent.

1. Obtain images for the design, including at least one with one or more instrument that will dominate the image. You can use the images that are available on your computer, scanned images, or images from a digital camera.
2. Create a new Photoshop image of any dimension, then save it as **Jazz and Blues**.
3. Open the main instrument file, drag it to the Jazz and Blues image above the Background layer, then remove the Background layer.
4. Open the remaining image files, drag or copy them to the Jazz and Blues image, then close the image files.

5. Apply filters and styles and transform the other image layers as desired. (*Hint*: The Keyboard layer was converted into a Smart Object and has a Color Overlay layer applied to it.)
6. Create type layers as desired and apply filters or styles to them. (*Hint*: The Jazz Title type layer has a 43.83 pt Times New Roman font with the Drop Shadow, Inner Shadow, Bevel and Emboss, and Gradient Overlay

styles applied to it. The text in the lower-left corner has a 9.98 pt Century Gothic font.)
7. Save your work, then compare your image to the sample in Figure 41.

FIGURE 41
Sample Project Builder 2

Destined Nations, a local travel agency, is looking to hire a freelance graphic artist to design their marketing pieces. Rather than peruse portfolios, they are holding a contest to select a poster design. Each entrant is given the same image to modify as they see fit. As an incentive to get the very best entries, they're offering an all-expense paid week vacation to the winner. You like vacations, so you decide to enter the contest.

1. Obtain at least one image for the vacation destination design. You can use the images that are available on your computer, scanned images, or images from a digital camera.
2. Open PS 8-5.psd, then save it as **Shield**.
3. Verify that the Shield layer is active, open the Lighting Effects dialog box, then choose a lighting style.
4. Continue working in the Lighting Effects dialog box. Change the Light type color swatch to yellow. (*Hint*: To change color, click the color swatch.)
5. Place at least two other spotlights around the preview window using different colored lights. (*Hint*: To add a spotlight, drag the light bulb icon to the preview window.) Close the Lighting Effects dialog box and view the image.
6. Apply a subtle texture to the Shield layer. (*Hint*: The Shield layer in the sample has the Smudge Stick Artistic filter applied to it.)
7. Delete the large center circle from the Shield layer. (*Hint*: To delete the circle quickly, select

the Elliptical Marquee tool, draw a selection around the circle, then press [Delete], or you can apply a layer mask and paint the circle.)
8. Delete the triangles from the Shield layer. (*Hint*: To delete the triangles quickly, select the Polygonal Lasso tool, draw a selection around the edges of the triangles, then press [Delete], or you can apply a layer mask and paint the triangles.)
9. Create a new layer at the bottom of the Layers panel, and then fill it in black.
10. Create a new layer above the black layer and name it **Blur**.
11. Use a Lasso tool or any other shape tool to create a shape that fills the left side of the layer, then apply a fill color to the selection.

FIGURE 42
Sample Design Project

12. Apply at least one Blur filter to the Blur layer.
13. Transform the shield so that it has dimension, then move it to the left side of the window. (*Hint*: The Shield layer in the sample has been distorted.)
14. Add type layers as desired and apply styles or filters to them. (*Hint*: The Acapulco layer in the sample has a border applied by clicking the Rasterize command on the Layer menu, and then using the Stroke command on the Edit menu. The your ultimate playground! layer in the sample is a 36 pt Monotype Corsiva.)
15. Open the image files, drag or copy them to the Shield image, close the image files, then apply filters or styles to them.
16. Save your work, then compare your image to the sample in Figure 42.

You have been asked to put together a presentation on traditional and modern dance styles from around the world. Choose a dance style and use your Photoshop skills to create a title slide that conveys the feel of that style.

1. Obtain at least three images that reflect the style of dance you've chosen. You can use the images that are available on your computer, scanned images, images from a digital camera, or images downloaded from the Internet. Try to select images that you can transform and to which you can add styles and apply filters. Make sure that one image can be used as a background.

2. Create a new Photoshop image, then save it as **Dance**.

3. Drag or copy the background to the Dance image above the Background layer, then rename the Background layer and apply a fill color as desired.

4. Drag an image to the Dance image, transform it as desired, then apply a filter to it. (*Hint*: The Swan layer [dancer in lower-left corner] in the sample has an Artistic category Plastic Wrap filter applied to it.)

5. Drag or copy the remaining images, transform as needed, and apply at least one style or filter to them. (*Hint*: The Large Ballerina layer has a layer mask applied to it, and the Shoes layer has the Distort category Diffuse Glow filter applied to it.)

6. Create type layers as desired, and apply at least one style or filter to them. (*Hint*: The Dancing type layer was created in a separate image using an image as a member of a clipping mask, then a variety of effects was applied to it. The Start when you're young type layer in the sample uses a 20 pt Kalinga font with Outer and Inner Glow layer styles applied.)

7. Be prepared to discuss the effects you generate when you add filters to styles and vice versa.

8. Save your work, then compare your image to the sample in Figure 43.

FIGURE 43
Sample Portfolio Project

Dance.psd @ 100% (Dancing, RGB/8#)

Start when you're young

100%   Doc: 788.8K/5.79M

Creating Special Effects with Filters

9

ENHANCING SPECIFIC
SELECTIONS

1. Create an alpha channel

2. Isolate an object

3. Erase areas in an image to enhance appearance

4. Use the Clone Stamp tool to make repairs

5. Use the Magic Wand tool to select objects

6. Learn how to create snapshots

7. Create multiple-image layouts

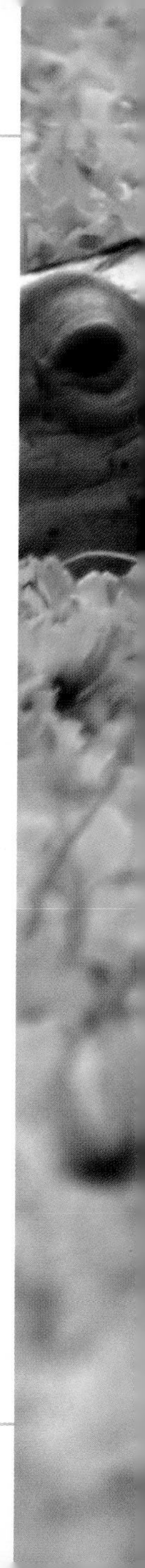

Modifying Objects

As you have most likely figured out by now, a great part of the power of Photoshop resides in its ability to isolate graphics and text objects and make changes to them. This chapter focuses on several of the techniques used to isolate graphics objects and then make changes that enhance their appearance.

Using Channels

Nearly every image you open or create in Photoshop is separated into **channels**. Photoshop uses channels to house the color information for each layer and layer mask in your image. The number of color information channels depends on the color mode of the image. You can also create specific channels for layer masks.

> QUICKTIP
>
> Photoshop creates default channels based on the image mode, but you can create additional channels to gain more control of an image.

Fixing Imperfections

From time to time, you'll probably work with flawed images. Flawed images are not necessarily "bad," they just might contain imagery that does not fit your needs. Photoshop offers several ways to repair an image's imperfections. You can use the following methods—or combinations of these methods—to fix areas within an image that are less than ideal:

- Isolate areas using the Extract feature.
- Erase areas using a variety of eraser tools.
- Take a sample and then paint that sample over an area using the Clone Stamp tool.

Creating Snapshots

The Snapshot command lets you make a temporary copy of any state of an image. The snapshot is added to the top of the History panel and lets you work on a new version of the image. Snapshots are like the states found on the History panel but offer a few more advantages:

- You can name a snapshot to make it easy to identify and manage.
- You can compare changes to images easily. For example, you can take a snapshot before and after changing the color of a selection.
- You can recover your work easily. If your experimentation with an image doesn't satisfy your needs, you can select the snapshot to undo all the steps from the experiment.

Using Automation Features

After you complete an image that you want to share, you can create an image that contains various sizes of the same image, or several different images. Using a multiple-image layout, for example, makes it possible to print images in a variety of sizes and shapes on a single sheet. Another example is a contact sheet, a file that displays thumbnail views of a selection of images, so that you can easily catalog and preview them without opening each individual file.

Tools You'll Use

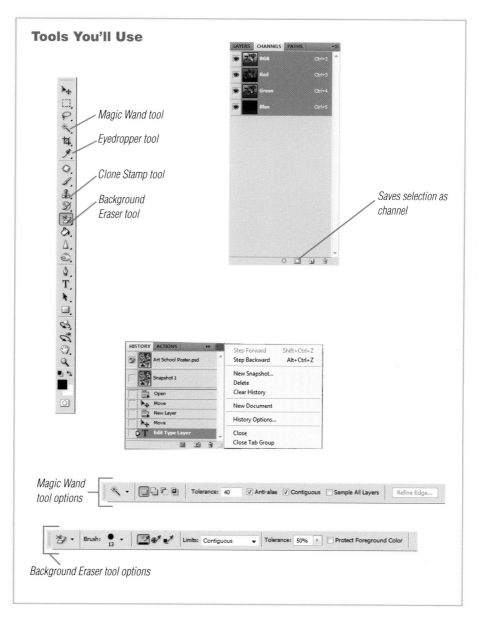

Magic Wand tool

Eyedropper tool

Clone Stamp tool

Background Eraser tool

Saves selection as channel

Magic Wand tool options

Background Eraser tool options

CREATE AN ALPHA CHANNEL

What You'll Do

In this lesson, you'll view the colors in the default color mode on the Channels panel. You'll also create a selection, save it as an alpha channel, and then change the color of the alpha channel.

Defining Channels

Photoshop automatically creates channel information in a new image and uses channels to store color information about images. Channels are created at the same time the image is created, and the number of channels is determined by the image mode. For example, a CMYK image has at least four channels (one each for cyan, magenta, yellow, and black), whereas an RGB image has three channels (one each for red, green, and blue). Every Photoshop image has at least one channel, and can have a maximum of 24 color channels. The color channels contained in an image are known as **default channels**, which Photoshop creates automatically. You can add specific color information by adding an **alpha channel** or a **spot channel**. You use an alpha channel to create and store masks, which let you manipulate, isolate, and protect parts of an image. A spot channel contains information about special pre-mixed inks used in CMYK color printing. The default number of channels is determined by the color mode you select in the New dialog box that opens when you create

a new file, as shown in Figure 1. You can add channels to images displayed in all color modes, except the bitmap modes.

Understanding Alpha Channels

You create alpha channels on the Channels panel. You can create an alpha channel that masks all or specific areas of a layer. For example, you can create a selection and then convert it into an alpha channel. Photoshop superimposes the color in an alpha channel onto the image; however, an alpha channel might appear in grayscale on the Channels panel thumbnail. You can use alpha channels to preserve a selection, to experiment with, to use later, to create special effects, such as screens or shadows, or to save and reuse in other images. Photoshop supports the following formats for saving an alpha channel: PSD, PDF, PICT, TIFF, and Raw. If you use other formats, you might lose some channel information. You can copy the alpha channel to other images and instantly apply the same information. Alpha channels do not print—they will not be visible in print media.

Understanding the Channels Panel

The Channels panel lists all the default channels contained in a layer and manages all the image's channels. To access this panel, click the Channels tab next to the Layers tab, as shown in Figure 2. The top channel is a **composite channel**—a combination of all the other default channels. The additional default channels, based on the existing color mode, are shown below the composite channel, followed by spot color channels, and finally by the alpha channels.

Channels have many of the same properties as layers. You can hide channels in the same way as you hide layers, by clicking a button in the column to the left of the thumbnail on the Channels panel. Each channel has a thumbnail that mirrors the changes you make to the image's layers. You can also change the order of channels by dragging them up or down on the Channels panel.

The thumbnails on the Channels panel might appear in grayscale. To view the channels in their actual color, click Edit (Win) or Photoshop (Mac) on the Application bar, point to Preferences, click Interface, select the Show Channels in Color check box, then click OK. The default channels will appear in the color mode colors; an alpha channel will appear in the color selected in the Channel Options dialog box. You open the Channel Options dialog box by double-clicking the alpha channel on the Channels panel.

FIGURE 1
New dialog box

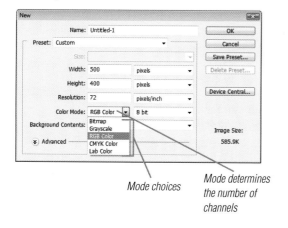

Mode choices
Mode determines the number of channels

FIGURE 2
Channels on the Channels panel

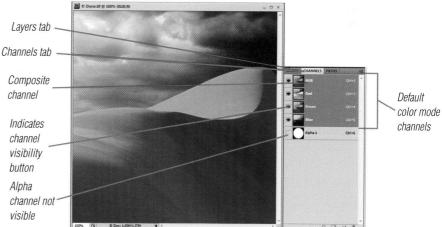

Layers tab
Channels tab
Composite channel
Indicates channel visibility button
Alpha channel not visible
Default color mode channels

View the Channels panel

1. Start Photoshop, open PS 9-1.psd from the drive and folder where you store your Data Files, update the text layer (if necessary), then save it as **Market Fresh**.

2. Click the **Default Foreground and Background Colors button** ■⌐ on the Tools panel to display the default settings (if necessary).

3. Verify that the **Essentials** workspace is displayed.

4. Display the rulers in pixels, change the zoom factor to **100%**, then make sure you can see the guide at 685V.

5. Click **Edit** (Win) or **Photoshop** (Mac) on the Application bar, point to **Preferences**, click **Interface**, verify that there is a check mark in the **Show Channels in Color check box**, then click **OK** to verify that the default color channels are displayed in color.

6. Click the **Channels tab** CHANNELS next to the Layers tab on the Layers panel, then compare your Channels panel to Figure 3.

   The Channels panel is active and displays the four channels for RGB color mode: RGB (composite), Red, Green, and Blue.

You opened the Channels panel, and verified that colors are displayed in the default color channels. This allows you to see the actual colors contained in each channel when working with images.

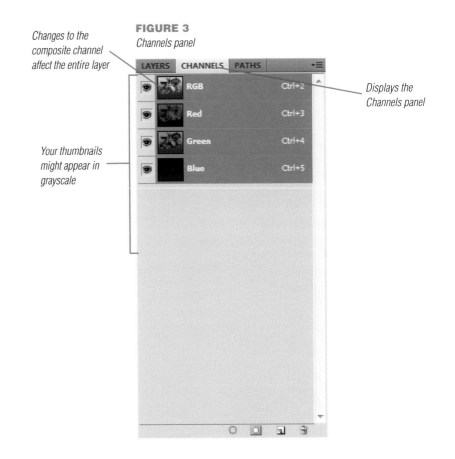

Changes to the composite channel affect the entire layer

FIGURE 3
Channels panel

Displays the Channels panel

Your thumbnails might appear in grayscale

Changing alpha channel colors

You can change the color that the alpha channel displays (to alter the appearance of the image) by picking a color in the Channel Options dialog box. To open the Channel Options dialog box, double-click the alpha channel (which appears at the bottom of the Channels panel once it is created), click the color box, select a color in the Select color channel dialog box, then click OK. Click an option button in the Channel Options dialog box to choose whether the color indicates masked areas, selected areas, or a spot color, then click OK.

FIGURE 4
Selection created

Elliptical marquee

Save selection as
a channel button

FIGURE 5
Alpha channel created

Alpha 1 channel

Create an alpha channel from a selection

1. Click the **Elliptical Marquee tool** ⬭ on the Tools panel, then set the Feather setting on the options bar to **0 px** (if it is not already set to 0).

2. Drag the **Marquee pointer** ✚ from approximately **10 X/10 Y** to **685 X/590 Y**, then compare your image to Figure 4.

3. Click the **Save selection as channel button** ▣ on the Channels panel.

4. Double-click the **Alpha 1 thumbnail** on the Channels panel, then click the **color box** in the Channel Options dialog box.

5. Verify that the **R option button** is selected in the Select channel color dialog box (R=255, G=0, B=0), then click **OK**.

6. Verify that the opacity setting is **50%** and that the **Masked Areas option button** is selected, then click **OK**.

7. On the Channels panel, click the **RGB channel**, then click the **Indicates channel visibility button** ▢ for the Alpha 1 channel to view the alpha channel.

   The combination of the red alpha channel color overlaying blue produces the rose color at the bottom of the image.

8. Click **Select** on the Application bar, click **Deselect**, then compare your image to Figure 5.

9. Save your work.

You used the Elliptical Marquee tool to create a selection and then saved the selection as an alpha channel. You also verified the alpha channel color and reviewed the results by viewing the alpha channel.

ISOLATE AN OBJECT

What You'll Do

In this lesson, you'll create a duplicate layer, and use tools to extract the kiwi from the Fruit and Vegetables layer so that you can adjust its color. You'll also adjust the color of the kiwi by applying a Gradient Map to it.

Using Your Photoshop Knowledge

The goal in isolating an object is to use your knowledge of Photoshop tools to pick the best tool to select an object, then place the selection on its own layer so you can perform any additional tasks on it. Easier said than done.

Isolating Objects

You can use a variety of Photoshop tools to isolate a foreground object from its background. Using any of the tools at your disposal, you can define the object you want to extract, even if its edge is vaguely defined. When you extract an object from a layer, Photoshop deletes the non-extracted

Using the Extract plug-in on a complex object

The Extract feature is an Adobe plug-in that is used not only to isolate objects, but to *filter out* background imagery. It's great for objects that you want to look blurry, in motion, or translucent. (You can find this plug-in on the web by using your favorite browser and search engine and searching for *Photoshop CS4 Extract plug-in*.) Let's say you want to extract a woman who has bushy hair—the kind with strands you can see through. Use a larger brush tip and trace on the outside edge of the object you want to extract. If your object has a well-defined edge (even in only a few places), turn on the Smart Highlighting feature. This feature highlights just the edge. It ignores the current brush size and applies a highlight wide enough to cover the edge. In our example, only the woman and her hair will be extracted, not the pieces of sky between individual strands of hair. If you are going to be working with images that involve complex selections, consider adding this plug-in to your tools repertoire.

portion of the image's background to underlying transparency. It's always a good idea to first copy the original layer and then extract an object from the duplicate layer. This preserves the original layer, which you can use as a reference, and helps you to avoid losing any of the original image information. After you extract an image, you can modify the extracted object layer as you wish.

QUICKTIP

To make sure you've correctly isolated content, add a layer filled with an ugly color (beneath the isolated content), then delete the color-filled layer.

FIGURE 6
Outlined content in the Extract dialog box

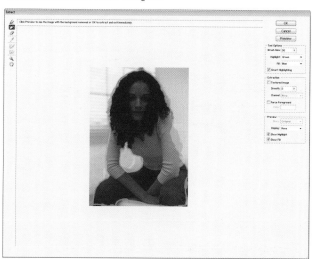

FIGURE 7
Results of complex extraction

Understanding the Extract plug-In

You isolate objects using tools in the Extract dialog box. You first trace the edge of the object you want to extract with the Edge Highlighter tool, then you select everything inside of the edge with the Fill tool. In the example shown in Figure 6, the woman and her hair will be extracted, not the pieces of background between individual strands of hair. Figure 7 shows the result. It takes practice to become proficient at using the Edge Highlighter tool. If you do not draw a continuous edge around the object, Photoshop might not fill in the area accurately. You can edit portions of the edge as often as necessary. Depending on the size of the brush tip you select, the dimensions of your extracted object will vary.

Isolate an object

1. Click the **Layers tab** LAYERS on the Layers panel.

2. Click the **Fruit and Vegetables layer** on the Layers panel, click the **Layers panel list arrow** ▾≡ , then click **Duplicate Layer**.

3. Type **Kiwi** in the As text box, then click **OK** to close the Duplicate Layer dialog box.

   The new layer appears above the Fruit and Vegetables layer on the Layers panel, and is now the active layer.

4. Click the **Channels tab** CHANNELS , click the **Indicates layer visibility button** ☐ for any channel that is not visible, then click the **Layers tab** LAYERS .

5. Click the **Indicates layer visibility button** 👁 for the Fruit and Vegetables layer, so the layer is not visible.

6. Click the **Zoom tool** 🔍 on the Application bar, then click the **center of the kiwi** three times.

7. Click the **Magnetic Lasso tool** 〽 on the Tools panel.

8. Verify that the feather setting is 0, drag the **pointer** 〽 around the inner edge of the kiwi, avoiding the celery leaf (if possible), then compare your screen to Figure 8.

   The kiwi is selected.

You created and named a duplicate layer of the Fruit and Vegetables layer, then used the Magnetic Lasso tool to outline the kiwi.

FIGURE 8
Selection in image

Selection

FIGURE 9
Layer containing the extracted object

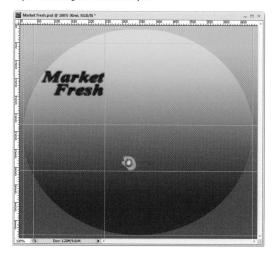

FIGURE 10
Sample gradients

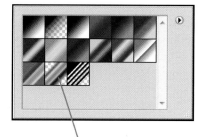

Transparent Rainbow gradient

FIGURE 11
Extracted object with a Gradient Map applied

Gradient Map adjustment
on the extracted object

Exclude pixels

1. Click the **Zoom tool** 🔍 on the Application bar, press and hold **[Alt]**, click the center of the kiwi three times, then release **[Alt]**.

2. Click **Select** on the Application bar, then click **Inverse**.

3. Press **[Del]**, deselect the selection, then click the **Indicates layer visibility button** 👁 on the Apples and Pineapple layers on the Layers panel. See Figure 9.

   The kiwi appears on the layer with a transparent background.

You inverted the pixel selection, then viewed the layer containing the extracted object.

Enhance an extracted object

1. Click the **Gradient Map button** ▮ on the Adjustments panel.

2. Click the **Reverse check box**, click the **Gradient list arrow**, click the **Transparent Rainbow gradient box**, as shown in Figure 10, then click anywhere outside the gradient picker to deselect the gradient box.

3. Click the **This adjustment affects all layers below (click to clip to layer) button** 👤 in the Adjustments panel, then click the **Return to adjustment list button** ◁ in the Adjustments panel.

4. Click the **Indicates layer visibility button** 👁 on the Fruit and Vegetables, Apples, and Pineapple layers on the Layers panel.

5. Save your work, then compare your image to Figure 11.

You adjusted the color for the extracted kiwi by applying a Gradient Map to the layer, then viewed the color-adjusted image.

ERASE AREAS IN AN IMAGE
TO ENHANCE APPEARANCE

What You'll Do

 In this lesson, you'll use the Background Eraser tool to delete pixels on the Fruit and Vegetables layer, then adjust the brightness and contrast of the isolated object.

Learning How to Erase Areas

As you have learned, you can discard pixels by selecting and then inverting the selection. But there may be times when you want to simply erase an area *without* making a selection. Photoshop provides three eraser tools that can accommodate all your expunging needs. Figure 12 shows samples of the effects of each eraser tool. The specific use for each eraser tool is reflected in its options bar, as shown in Figure 13.

Understanding Eraser Tools

The **Eraser tool** has the opposite function of a brush. Instead of brushing *on* pixel color, you drag it *off*. When you erase a layer that has a layer beneath it, and the Lock transparent pixels button is not selected, you'll expose the color on the underlying layer when you erase. If there is no underlying layer, you'll expose transparency. If the Lock transparent pixels button *is* selected, you'll expose the current background color on the Tools panel, regardless of the color of an underlying layer.

Setting options for eraser tools

Each eraser tool has its own options bar. You can select the brush mode for the Eraser tool, and the brush tip and size for both the Eraser tool and Background Eraser tool. Depending on the tool, you can also set the **tolerance**—how close a pixel color must be to another color to be erased with the tool. The lower the tolerance, the closer the color must be to the selection. You can also specify the opacity of the eraser strength. A 100% opacity erases pixels to complete transparency. To set options, click an eraser tool on the Tools panel, then change the tolerance and opacity settings using the text boxes and list arrows on the options bar.

Enhancing Specific Selections

The **Magic Eraser tool** grabs similarly colored pixels based on the tool settings, and then exposes background color in the same way as the Eraser tool. However, instead of dragging the eraser, you click the areas you want to change. The Magic Eraser tool erases all pixels on the current layer that are close in color value to where you first click or just those pixels that are contiguous to that area.

The **Background Eraser tool** contains small crosshairs in the brush tip. When you click, the tool selects a color in the crosshairs, then erases that particular color anywhere within the brush tip size. The Background Eraser tool exposes the color of the layer beneath it, or it exposes transparency if there is no layer beneath it. You can preserve objects in the foreground, while eliminating the background (it works best with a large brush tip size). The Background Eraser tool will sample the background colors of the current layer as you drag the tool in your image—you can watch the current background color change on the Tools panel.

FIGURE 12
Examples of eraser tools

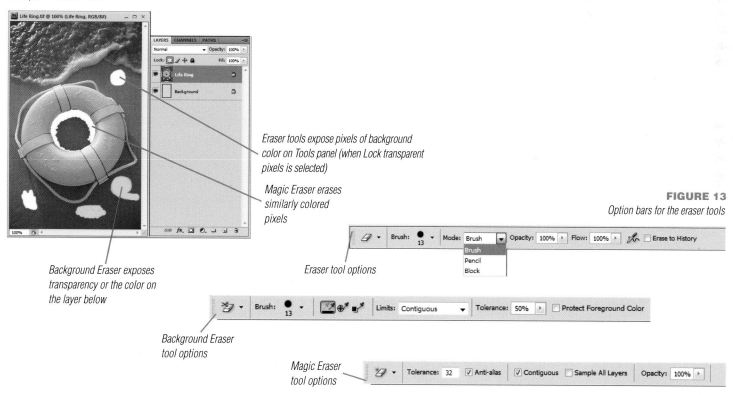

Eraser tools expose pixels of background color on Tools panel (when Lock transparent pixels is selected)

Magic Eraser erases similarly colored pixels

Background Eraser exposes transparency or the color on the layer below

FIGURE 13
Option bars for the eraser tools

Eraser tool options

Background Eraser tool options

Magic Eraser tool options

Use the Background Eraser tool

1. Click the **Indicates layer visibility button** 👁 on the Kiwi layer to hide the layer.

2. Click the **Fruit and Vegetables layer** to make it the active layer.

3. Click the **Zoom tool** 🔍 on the Application bar.

4. Click the **center of the kiwi** with the **Zoom pointer** 🔍 until the zoom factor is **300%**.

5. Click the **Background Eraser tool** 🧽 on the Tools panel.

   TIP   Look under the Eraser tool if the Background Eraser tool is hidden. To cycle through the eraser tools, press and hold [Shift], then press [E].

6. Click the **Click to open the Brush Preset picker list arrow** on the options bar, set the Diameter to **5 px**, the Hardness to **100%**, and the Spacing to **15%** as shown in Figure 14.

7. Press **[Enter]** (Win) or **[return]** (Mac).

8. Keeping the crosshairs of the **Brush tip pointer** ⊕ on the kiwi, drag the brush tip over the **kiwi** until it is completely erased, as shown in Figure 15.

You hid the Kiwi layer, zoomed in on the Fruit and Vegetables layer, selected a brush tip for the Background Eraser tool, and erased the kiwi on the Fruit and Vegetables layer.

FIGURE 14
Brush Preset picker

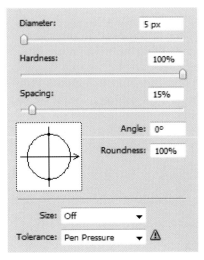

FIGURE 15
Selection erased on layer

Erased area exposes pixels
on Background layer

FIGURE 16
Object adjusted in image

Market Fresh.psd @ 100% (Kiwi, RGB/8)

Market Fresh

100%   Doc: 1.20M/9.61M

Equalize adjustment
applied to Kiwi layer

Equalize brightness and contrast

1. Click the **Kiwi layer** on the Layers panel, then make the Kiwi layer visible.

2. Click the **Zoom tool** 🔍 on the Application bar.

3. Press and hold **[Alt]** (Win) or **[option]** (Mac), click the center of the kiwi with the **Zoom pointer** 🔍 until the zoom factor is **100%**, then release **[Alt]** (Win) or **[option]** (Mac).

4. Click **Image** on the Application bar, point to **Adjustments**, then click **Equalize**.

   The Equalize command evens out the brightness and contrast values in the kiwi.

5. Save your work, then compare your image to Figure 16.

You adjusted the color of the kiwi by equalizing the colors, then viewed the color-adjusted image.

Redistributing brightness values

The Equalize command changes the brightness values of an image's pixels so they more evenly display the entire range of brightness levels. Photoshop changes the brightest and darkest values by remapping them so that the brightest values appear as white and the darkest values appear as black, then it redistributes the intermediate pixel values evenly throughout the grayscale. You can use this command to "tone down" an image that is too bright. Conversely, you could use it on a dark image that you want to make lighter.

USE THE CLONE STAMP TOOL
TO MAKE REPAIRS

What You'll Do

In this lesson, you'll use the Clone Stamp tool to sample an undamaged portion of an image and use it to cover up a flaw on the image.

Touching Up a Damaged Area

Let's face it, many of the images you'll want to work with will have a visual flaw of some kind, such as a scratch, or an object obscuring what would otherwise be a great shot. While you cannot go back in time and move something out of the way, you can often use the Clone Stamp tool to remove an object or cover up a flaw.

Using the Clone Stamp Tool

The Clone Stamp tool can copy a sample (a pixel selection) in an image, and then paste it over what you want to cover up. The size of the sample taken with the Clone Stamp tool depends on the brush tip size you choose on the Brushes panel. Figure 17 shows the Clone Stamp tool in action. In addition to using the Clone Stamp tool to touch up images, you can use it to copy one image onto another. Using the Clone Stamp tool to copy an image differs from copying an image because you have extensive control over how much of the cloned area you expose and at what opacity.

FIGURE 17
Clone Stamp tool in action

Object to be deleted

Sampled area

Sampled area applied twice to hide portions of the object

FIGURE 18
Comparing images

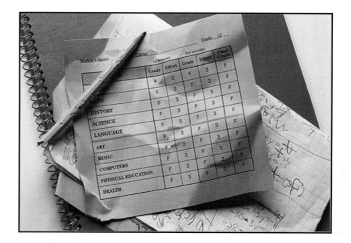

DESIGNTIP **Perfecting your analytical skills**

An important step in making an adjustment to any image is to examine it critically and figure out what is wrong. An area that you select for fixing does not necessarily have to look bad or appear wrong. An image might be "wrong" because it simply does not convey the right meaning or mood. Compare the two images in Figure 18. They contain basically the same elements but express entirely different ideas. The figure on the left conveys a more positive image than the one on the right; clearly the grades are better for the student on the left, however, this is also reflected in the lighter colored paper, which is in pristine condition. The elements that you choose for your content should depend on what you want to convey. For example, if you want to convey a positive mood, using the elements in the image on the right would be inappropriate for your image. Choosing the right content in the beginning can save you a lot of time in the end. It is much easier and quicker to reach a destination if you know where you are going before you begin the journey.

Sample an area to clone

1. Click the **Fruit and Vegetables layer** on the Layers panel.

2. Click the **Zoom tool** 🔍 on the Application bar.

3. Click the **center of the far-left tomato** with the **Zoom pointer** ⊕ until the zoom factor is **300%** so you can clearly see the fly.

4. Click the **Clone Stamp tool** 🖫 on the Tools panel.

5. Click the **Click to open the Brush Preset picker list arrow** on the options bar, then double-click the **Hard Round 13 pixels brush tip**.

6. Verify that the Opacity setting on the options bar is **100%**.

7. Position the **Brush pointer** ◯ at approximately **60 X/400 Y**, as shown in Figure 19.

8. Press **[Alt]** (Win) or **[option]** (Mac), click once, then release **[Alt]** (Win) or **[option]** (Mac).

   The sample is collected and is ready to be applied to the fly.

You selected the Fruit and Vegetables layer, set the zoom percentage, selected a brush tip for the Clone Stamp tool, and sampled an undamaged portion of the tomato.

FIGURE 19
Defining the area to be sampled

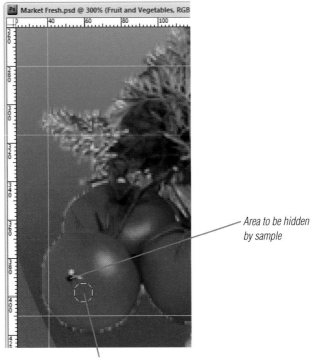

Area to be hidden by sample

Area to be sampled

Using the Clone Source panel

You can open the Clone Source panel using the Window command on the Application bar or a button on the options bar when the Clone Stamp tool is active. Use the Clone Source panel to set up to five sample sources for use with the Clone Stamp tools or Healing Brush tools. The sample source can be displayed as an overlay so you can clone the source at a specific location. You can also rotate or scale the sample source at a specific size and orientation.

FIGURE 20
Clone Stamp tool positioned over defect

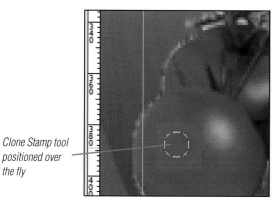

Clone Stamp tool
positioned over
the fly

1. Position the **Brush pointer** ○ *directly* over the fly, as shown in Figure 20.

2. Click the **fly.**

    > TIP   Select a different brush size if your brush is too small or too large, and then reapply the stamp.

3. Click the **Zoom tool** 🔍 on the Application bar.

4. Press and hold **[Alt]** (Win) or **[option]** (Mac), click the **center of the tomato** with the Zoom **pointer** 🔍 until the zoom factor is **100%**, then release **[Alt]** (Win) or **[option]** (Mac).

5. Save your work, then compare your image to Figure 21.

You fixed the damaged area of the tomato by covering up the fly.

FIGURE 21
Corrected image

Using pressure-sensitive tablets

For specialized painting that gives you maximum control when you create an image, you can purchase a pressure-sensitive stylus or tablet. A pressure-sensitive device mimics the force you'd use with an actual brush; you paint softer when you press lightly and paint darker when you press harder. You can set the stylus or tablet pressure for the Magnetic Lasso, Freeform Pen, Pencil, Brush, Eraser, Clone Stamp, Pattern Stamp, History Brush, Art History Brush, Smudge, Blur, Sharpen, Dodge, Burn, and Sponge tools. Also affected by pen pressure are the magnetic pen feature and the airbrush feature. To access the magnetic pen, select the Freeform Pen tool, then click the Magnetic checkbox. To use the Airbrush feature, click the Brush, Clone Stamp, History Brush, Eraser, or Dodge tools, then click the Set to enable airbrush capabilities button on the options bar.

USE THE MAGIC WAND
TOOL TO SELECT OBJECTS

What You'll Do

In this lesson, you'll open a new image, use the Magic Wand tool to select an image in the new image, and move it to the Market Fresh image. You'll also readjust the Eyedropper tool sample size, reselect and move the image so you can compare the selection difference, then delete the incomplete layer and position the complete layer in the Market Fresh image.

Understanding the Magic Wand Tool

You can use the Magic Wand tool to select an object by selecting the color range of the object. The **Magic Wand tool** lets you choose pixels that are similar to the ones where you first click in an image. You can control how the Magic Wand tool behaves by specifying tolerance settings and whether or not you want to select only contiguous pixels on the options bar. The Magic Wand tool options bar is shown in Figure 22.

Learning About Tolerance

The tolerance setting determines the range of colors you can select with the Magic Wand tool. For example, if you select a low tolerance and then click an image of the sky, you will only select a narrow range of blue pixels and probably not the entire sky. However, if you set a higher tolerance, you can expand the range of blue pixels selected by the Magic Wand tool. Each time you click the Magic Wand tool, you can choose from one of four buttons on the options bar to select a new

area, add to the existing area (the effect is cumulative; the more you click, the more you add), subtract from the existing area, or intersect with the existing area.

> **QUICK**TIP
>
> You can also press and hold [Shift] and repeatedly click to add pixels to your selection, or press and hold [Alt] (Win) or [option] (Mac), then click to subtract pixels from your selection.

Using the Eyedropper Tool and the Magic Wand Tool

The Contiguous and Tolerance settings are not the only determinants that establish the pixel area selected by the Magic Wand tool. The area that the Magic Wand tool selects also has an intrinsic relationship with the settings for the Eyedropper tool. The sample size, or number of pixels used by the Eyedropper tool to determine the color it picks up, affects the area selected by the Magic Wand tool. To understand this, you need to first examine the Eyedropper tool settings.

Enhancing Specific Selections

Understanding Sample Size

When the Eyedropper tool sample size is set to Point Sample, it picks up the one pixel where you click on the image. When the sample size is set to 3 by 3 Average, the Eyedropper tool picks up the color values of the nine pixels that surround the pixel where you click the image and averages them. The sample area increases exponentially to 25 pixels for the 5 by 5 Average setting. The sample size of the Eyedropper tool influences the area selected by the Magic Wand tool. Figure 23 shows how different Eyedropper tool sample sizes change the Magic Wand tool selections, even when you sample an image at the same coordinates and use the same tolerance setting. As you become familiar with the Magic Wand tool, it's a good idea to verify or change the Eyedropper tool sample size as needed, in addition to changing the tolerance setting.

FIGURE 22

Magic Wand tool options

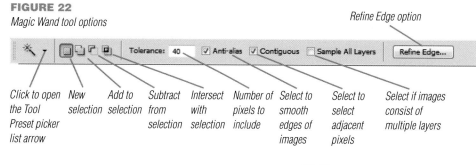

Refine Edge option

Click to open the Tool Preset picker list arrow · New selection · Add to selection · Subtract from selection · Intersect with selection · Number of pixels to include · Select to smooth edges of images · Select to select adjacent pixels · Select if images consist of multiple layers

FIGURE 23

Selection affected by Eyedropper tool sample size

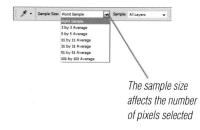

The sample size affects the number of pixels selected

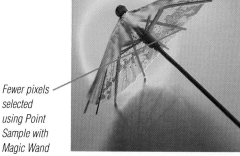

Fewer pixels selected using Point Sample with Magic Wand

Using the Refine Edge option

The Refine Edge button is on the options bar of a variety of tools, including the Magic Wand tool. It lets you improve the quality of a selection's edges and allows you to view the selection against different backgrounds, making editing easier. Once you've made a selection, click Refine Edge. Using the Refine Edge dialog box, you can make adjustments in the Radius (which determines the size of the region around the selection), Contrast (which sharpens selection edges), Smooth (which reduces irregular areas), Feather (which creates a soft-edged transition), and Contract/Expand (which shrinks or enlarges the selection).

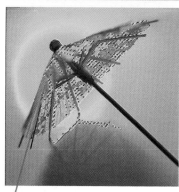

More pixels selected using 5 by 5 Average sample with Magic Wand

Select an object using the Magic Wand tool

1. Verify that the **Fruit and Vegetables layer** is the active layer.

2. Open PS 9-2.psd from the drive and folder where you store your Data Files, then save it as **Peppermint.psd**.

3. Drag the **Peppermint.psd window** to the right side of the workspace, and resize your windows so that they look similar to those shown in Figure 24.

4. Click the **Eyedropper tool** 🔍 on the Tools panel, then set the Sample Size to **5 by 5 Average** on the options bar.

5. Click the **Magic Wand tool** 🔍 on the Tools panel.

6. Type **50** in the Tolerance text box on the options bar, then press **[Enter]** (Win) or **[return]** (Mac).

7. Deselect the **Contiguous check box** (if it is selected).

> TIP If the Contiguous check box is selected, you'll select only the adjoining pixels that share the same color values.

8. In the Peppermint window, click the **bottom-left leaf** at approximately **20 X/175 Y** to select the peppermint plant, as shown in Figure 25.

9. Click the **Move tool** ▶⊕ on the Tools panel.

10. Position the **Move pointer** ▶⊕ over the **bottom-left leaf**, drag the **plant** in front of the lower orange quarter (and in front of the apples) in the Market Fresh image, then compare your image to Figure 26.

You opened a new file, set the Eyedropper tool sample size to a different selection setting, used the Magic Wand tool to select the Peppermint image you opened, then moved the selected image into the Market Fresh image.

FIGURE 24
New image opened and positioned

FIGURE 26
Selected object moved to current image

FIGURE 25
Selection indicated by marquee

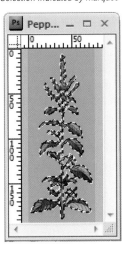

FIGURE 27
Comparison of selections

Selection made with 5 by 5 Average sample size captures more pixels

Selection made with Point Sample size captures fewer pixels

FIGURE 28
Selection positioned in image

1. Click **Window** on the Application bar, then click **Peppermint.psd**.

2. Click **Select** on the Application bar, then click **Deselect**.

3. Repeat Steps 4 through 10 in the previous steps, but this time, set the sample size for the Eyedropper tool to **Point Sample** in Step 4 and drag the plant above the green apple in Step 10.

4. Verify that the **Show Transform Controls check box** is selected on the options bar, then compare the two plants in the Market Fresh image, as shown in Figure 27.

   TIP You can see the difference in the plants more easily if you hide and then display the Apples layer. Your results may vary from the sample.

5. Delete **Layer 2** on the Layers panel.

6. Verify that the **Move tool** is selected and **Layer 1** (with the Peppermint plant) is active, click the **top of the peppermint plant** with the **Move pointer** ▶⊹, then drag it so it is centered behind the far left tomato at approximately **70 X/200 Y**.

7. Hide the rulers, deselect the **Show Transform Controls check box,** save your work, then compare your image to Figure 28.

You changed the Eyedropper tool sample size to its smallest setting, reselected the plant, moved it to the Market Fresh image, deleted one new layer, then repositioned the peppermint plant image.

LEARN HOW TO
CREATE SNAPSHOTS

What You'll Do

 In this lesson, you'll create a snapshot on the History panel, edit an image, then use the snapshot to view the image as it existed prior to making changes.

Understanding Snapshots

As mentioned earlier in this chapter, it is a good work habit to make a copy of an original layer to help you avoid losing any of the original image information. Creating a snapshot is like creating that new copy. The History panel can only record a maximum of 20 tasks, or states, that you perform. When the History panel reaches its limit, it starts deleting the oldest states to make room for new states. You can create a **snapshot**, a temporary copy of your image that contains the history states made to that point. It's a good idea to take a snapshot of the History panel image before you begin an editing session and after you've made crucial changes because you can use snapshots to revert to or review your image from an earlier stage of development. You can create multiple snapshots in an image, and you can switch between snapshots as necessary.

Creating a Snapshot

To create a snapshot, you can click the Create new snapshot button on the History panel, or click the History panel list arrow and then click New Snapshot, as shown in Figure 29. Each new snapshot is numbered consecutively; snapshots appear in order at the top of the History panel. If you create a snapshot by clicking the New Snapshot command, you can name the snapshot in the Name text box in the New Snapshot dialog box. Otherwise, you can rename an existing snapshot in the same way that you rename a layer on the Layers panel: double-click the snapshot, then edit the name once the existing name is highlighted. You can create a snapshot based on the entire image, merged layers, or just the current layer. A snapshot of the entire image includes all layers in the current image. A snapshot of merged layers combines all the layers in the current image on a single layer, and a snapshot of the current layer includes only the layer active at the time you took the snapshot. Figure 30 shows the New Snapshot dialog box.

Changing Snapshot Options

By default, Photoshop automatically creates a snapshot of an image when you open it.

To change the default snapshot option, click the History panel list arrow, click History Options, then select one of the check boxes shown in Figure 31. You can open files faster by deselecting the Automatically Create First Snapshot check box.

QUICKTIP

Photoshop does not save snapshots when you close a file.

FIGURE 29

Snapshot commands on the History panel

Default snapshot created when file is opened

New snapshot

Create new snapshot button

Opens the New Snapshot dialog box

Changes default snapshot options

FIGURE 30

New Snapshot dialog box

Selects which layers to include in the snapshot

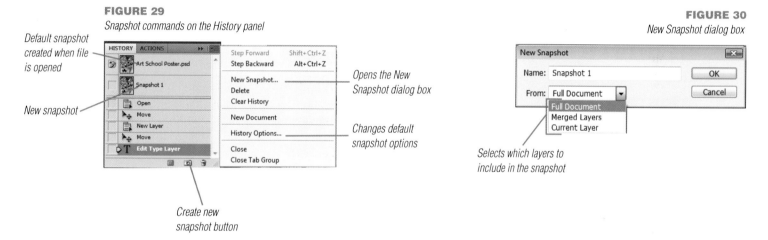

FIGURE 31

History Options dialog box

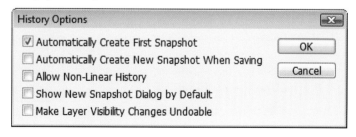

Lesson 6   Learn How to Create Snapshots

Create a snapshot

1. Deselect any selections in Peppermint.psd.

2. Click the **Invert button** 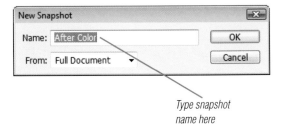 on the Adjustments panel, then compare your screen to Figure 32.

3. Change the workspace to **History and Layers**.

4. Click the **History panel list arrow**, then click **New Snapshot**.

5. Type **After Color** in the Name text box, as shown in Figure 33.

6. Click **OK**.

   The newly named snapshot appears on the History panel beneath the snapshot Photoshop created when you opened the image.

You deselected the selection in the Peppermint image, inverted the color in the image, then created and named a new snapshot.

FIGURE 32
Inverted image

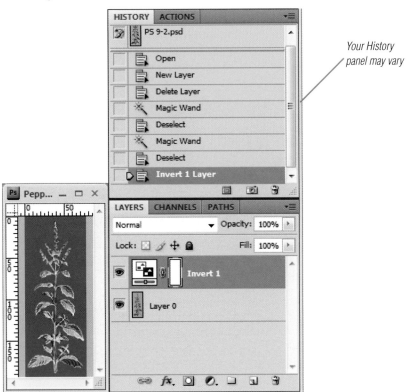

Your History panel may vary

FIGURE 33
New Snapshot dialog box

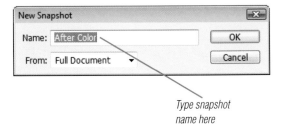

Type snapshot name here

FIGURE 34
Original snapshot view

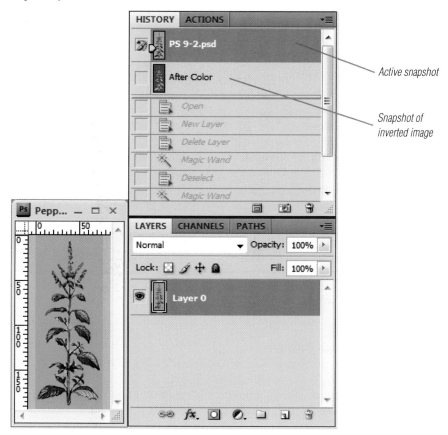

Active snapshot

Snapshot of inverted image

Use a snapshot

1. Scroll up (if necessary), click the **PS 9-2.psd snapshot** on the History panel, then compare your image to Figure 34.

   The image returns to its original color.

2. Click the **After Color snapshot** on the History panel.

3. Reset the panels to the **Essentials** workspace.

4. Close Peppermint.psd, save any changes.

You used the snapshot to view the image as it was before you made changes.

CREATE MULTIPLE-IMAGE LAYOUTS

What You'll Do

In this lesson, you'll create a picture package of the current image and then create a folder containing a contact sheet of images.

Understanding a Picture Package

With all the choices available for creating different variations of your images, you might get the idea that keeping track of all these choices is time-consuming or difficult. Not so; to facilitate the task, Adobe Bridge lets you generate multiple-image layouts. **Multiple-image layouts** are useful when you need to gather one or more Photoshop images in a variety of sizes for a variety of uses. For example, if you create an advertisement, you might want to have multiple image layouts for printing in different publications. Can you imagine what would be involved to create this type of arrangement of images manually? For each duplicate image, you'd have to create a layer, resize it, then position it correctly on the page. A lot of work! You can generate a single layout, also known as a **picture package**, which contains multiple images in a single file, as shown in Figure 35. The picture package option lets you choose from eight possible predesigned layouts of the same image, plus a custom layout, and then arranges them in a single printable image.

Creating a Web Gallery

You can display your image files on a website by creating a Web Photo Gallery. A Web Photo Gallery contains a thumbnail index page of all files you choose. To create a Web Photo Gallery, open Bridge, click the Output tab in the Application bar and the Web Gallery button in the Output panel. Click the Folders tab and the location of the files you want to include, then click Refresh Preview in the Output panel to see the gallery display in Bridge, or click the Preview in Browser to see the images in your browser.

Assembling a Contact Sheet

Previewing and cataloging several related images could be a time-consuming and difficult chore, but Bridge makes it easy.

It allows you to assemble a maximum of 30 thumbnail images in a specific folder, called a **contact sheet**, as shown in Figure 36. If the folder used to compile the contact sheet contains more than 30 files, Bridge automatically creates new sheets so that all the images appear.

FIGURE 35
Sample picture package

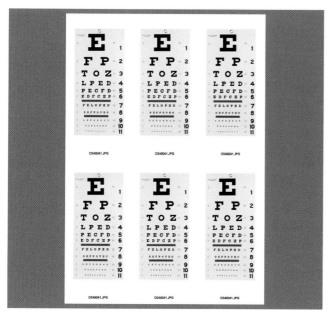

FIGURE 36
Sample contact sheet

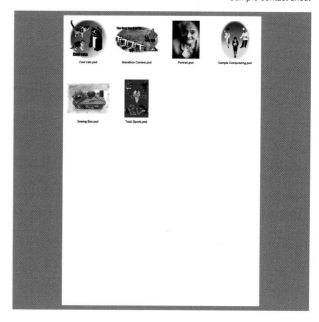

Create a Multi-image layout

1. Click the **Launch Bridge button** ▸Br on the Application bar.

2. Click the **Folders tab** FOLDERS if necessary.

3. Click the Folder where you store your Data Files, use the Content tab slider to locate the Market Fresh file, then click **Market Fresh.psd**.

4. Click **Output** at the top of the Bridge window, click the **PDF button** in the Output panel (if necessary), then click the **Repeat One Photo per Page check box** in the Layout section, and compare your settings to those shown in Figure 37, then click the **Refresh Preview** button.

5. Scroll down to the **Watermark section** of the Output panel, click the **View PDF After Save checkbox**, then click **Save**.

6. Save the multi-image layout in the location where you store your Chapter 9 Data Files, as **Picture Package.pdf**, then close the file.

You opened Adobe Bridge to create a multi-image layout, selected a layout for a picture package, then created and saved a layout using the Market Fresh image.

FIGURE 37
Multi-image settings in Adobe Bridge

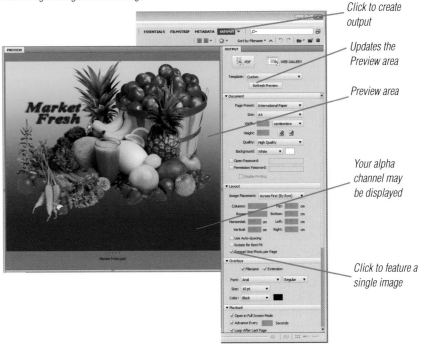

Click to create output

Updates the Preview area

Preview area

Your alpha channel may be displayed

Click to feature a single image

FIGURE 38
Layout section of the Output panel

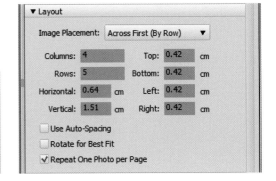

Customizing a Layout

With so many layout options available, you might think it would be impossible to customize any further. Well, you'd be wrong. Using the Layout section of the Output panel, shown in Figure 38, you can change the number of columns and rows, the amount of space in the margins, and rotate the page for the best fit.

FIGURE 39
Contact Sheet settings

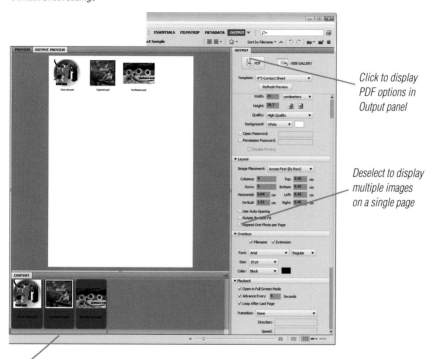

Click to display
PDF options in
Output panel

Deselect to display
multiple images
on a single page

Selected images in
Content panel: your
images will differ

Create a contact sheet

1. Create a folder on your computer that contains copies of at least three Photoshop images you have created, then name the folder **Contact Sample**.

2. Click the **Folders tab** in Adobe Bridge, click the **Contact Sample folder**, then click the **PDF button** in the Output panel.

3. Select the files in the Contact Sample folder in the Content tab (use [Shift] to select multiple files), and use the settings in the Output panel shown in Figure 39, then click **Refresh Preview**.

   Photoshop opens the files and places them in a new file to which you can assign a meaningful name.

4. Scroll down to the Watermark section of the Output panel, click **Save**, type the name **ContactSheet-001.pdf**, click **Save**, then close the file and exit Bridge and Photoshop.

You created a folder and placed images in it, and then used Adobe Bridge to select files from which you created a contact sheet of the images.

Automating Photoshop

Photoshop offers several automation options. You can also use the Automate command (on the File menu) to create batches, crop and straighten crooked images, change color modes conditionally, fit an image to a specified size (without distorting the image), and merge multiple images to create panoramas. You may notice that there is some duplication between Photoshop and Bridge. For example, you can use the Photomerge command in Bridge by clicking the Tools menu, pointing to Photoshop, then clicking Photomerge.

Power User Shortcuts

to do this:	use this method:
Clone Stamp tool	or **S**
Create a snapshot	
Duplicate selection and move 1 pixel: Left Right Up Down	Press and hold [Ctrl][Alt] (Win) or ⌘ [option] (Mac), then press ← → ↑ ↓
Move selection 10 pixels: Left Right Up Down	Press and hold [Shift] (Win) or ⌘ [shift] (Mac), then press ← → ↑ ↓

to do this:	use this method:
Eraser tools	E
Magic Wand tool	or **W**
Move selection 1 pixel: Left Right Up Down	 ← → ↑ ↓

Key: Blue bold letters are shortcuts for selecting tools on the Tools panel.

Enhancing Specific Selections

Create an alpha channel.

1. Open PS 9-3.psd from the drive and folder where you store your Data Files, then save it as **Tools**.
2. Make sure the rulers appear in pixels, then enlarge the image to 200%.
3. Display the Channels panel.
4. Select the Rectangular Marquee tool, then change the Feather to **25** on the options bar.
5. Create a selection from 70 X/50 Y to 400 X/270 Y (use the guides as a reference).
6. Save the selection, using your choice of name, on the Channels panel, then display the Alpha 1 channel.
7. Deselect the selection.
8. Open the Channel Options dialog box, select a blue color swatch of your choice at 50% Opacity, then close the Select channel color dialog box and the Channel Options dialog box.
9. Hide the Alpha 1 channel.
10. Save your work.

Isolate an object.

1. Display the Layers panel.
2. Duplicate the Tools layer, then name it **Red Tape**.
3. Use the Elliptical Marquee tool to surround the outer edge of the roll of red tape.
4. Select the inverse of the selection, then delete the selection.
5. Use the Elliptical Marquee tool to select the interior (hole) of the roll of red tape.
6. Delete the selection, then deselect the selection.
7. Save your work.

Erase areas in an image to enhance appearance.

1. Hide the Red Tape layer.
2. Make the Tools layer active.
3. Enlarge your view of the red tape.
4. Using the Background Eraser tool, erase the roll of red tape.
5. Make the Red Tape layer active.
6. Adjust the Color Balance settings on the Red Tape layer to +75, −57, and −10, so that the adjustment affects only the Red Tape layer. (*Hint*: Click the Color Balance button on the Adjustments panel.)
7. Save your work.

Use the Clone Stamp tool to make repairs.

1. Make the Tools layer active.
2. Select the Clone Stamp tool on the Tools panel.
3. Use the Hard Round 5 pixels brush tip. (*Hint*: Use the Brush Preset picker.)
4. Sample the area at 345 X/50 Y by pressing [Alt] (Win) or [option] (Mac) and clicking over the wire cutters.
5. Click the red dot (at approximately 310 X/85 Y) to remove this imperfection.
6. Save your work.

Use the Magic Wand tool to select objects.

1. Open PS 9-4.psd, then save it as **Wrench**.
2. Select the Magic Wand tool, deselect the Contiguous check box (if it is selected), then set the Tolerance to 0.
3. Click the wrench image anywhere on the white background.
4. Select the inverse of the selection.
5. Move the selection to the Tools image.
6. Move the top of the handle of the wrench to approximately 270 X/150 Y.
7. Deselect the selection, then close Wrench.psd.

Learn how to create snapshots.

1. Use the History panel list arrow to create a new snapshot.
2. Name the snapshot **New**.
3. Save your work, zoom out to 100% magnification, hide the rulers, then compare your image to Figure 40.

Create multiple-image layouts.

1. Use Bridge to create a 3 column, 4 row sheet containing the Tools image.
2. Save the file as **Picture Package-Tools** and close it.
3. Create a folder called Contact Sample 2 with image files to use for a 4 column, 4 row contact sheet.
4. Save this file as ContactSheet-002, then close it.
5. Close Bridge.

FIGURE 40
Completed Skills Review

Science Discovery, a traveling educational show for children, is planning a piece on earth science. For the first segment, the puppets will teach about different shapes, starting with spheres. You're going to design the spot graphic that will link users to the Science Discovery web page.

1. Obtain the following images for the graphic: a background that contains one or more round objects, at least two images that contain spheres whose content you can select, and any other images as desired. You'll use two of the sphere images for a clipping group.

2. Create a new Photoshop image, then save it as **Spheroid**.

3. Apply a color or style to the Background layer, or use any of the techniques you learned in this chapter to select and drag the image that will be the background to the Spheroid image, then apply at least one style to it. (*Hint*: An Adjustment layer is applied to the grapes.)

4. Use any of the techniques you learned in this chapter to select and drag the image that will be the base of the clipping group to the Spheroid image above the Background layer, and modify it as desired. (*Hint*: The tennis ball in the sample is the base image and has been duplicated.)

5. Use any of the techniques you learned in this chapter to select and drag an image that will be the target of a clipping mask to the Spheroid image, and modify it as necessary. (*Hint*: The golf balls in the sample are the target image.)

6. Create a clipping mask using the two images, then modify the result as desired. (*Hint*: The tennis ball has been copied to another layer, which was adjusted to a lower opacity setting and moved above the clipping mask to create the illusion that the golf balls are inside it.)

7. Create an alpha channel and ensure that it is visible in the image. (*Hint*: The tennis ball has a selected area alpha channel applied to it.)

8. Create type layers as desired, and apply at least one style or filter to at least one of the type layers. (*Hint*: The Nature's perfect snack type has a Dissolve blending mode, and the Drop Shadow and Gradient Overlay styles applied to it.)

9. Drag or copy any remaining images to the Spheroid image, transform them or apply at least one style or filter to them, then close the image files.

10. Save your work, then compare your image to the sample in Figure 41.

FIGURE 41
Completed Project Builder 1

Enhancing Specific Selections

Several resort hotels want to accommodate the unique vacation needs of their younger guests. They're going to give each child under 12 a bag of equipment, books, games, and other items that match their interests. Your job is to design the cover of the information booklet that will be included in the package.

1. Obtain images for the cover that are centered on a beach vacation theme. Include images whose content you can select or extract, and any other images as desired. You can use scanned images or images that are available on your computer, or you can connect to the Internet and download images. You'll need a background image and at least one layer to serve as the focal point.

2. Create a new Photoshop image, then save it as **Perfect Oasis**.

3. Apply a color or style to the Background layer, or use any of the techniques you learned in this chapter to select and drag the image that will be the background to the Perfect Oasis image.

4. Use any of the techniques you learned in this chapter to select and drag the image that will be the focal point of the Perfect Oasis image. (*Hint*: In the sample shown, the image of the boy and girl has a layer mask applied to it, and has been copied to another layer that has an elliptical marquee

with Drop Shadow and Bevel and Emboss styles applied to it.)

5. Open the surrounding image files, then use any of the techniques you learned in this chapter to select and drag the images to the Perfect Oasis image.

6. Add layer masks, transform, or apply filters or styles to the images as desired. (*Hint*: In the sample, the image of the boy and girl has been enhanced and has a layer mask; the surf also has been enhanced.)

7. Create type layers as desired and apply filters or styles to at least one of them. (*Hint*: The Could be right in your own backyard type has Drop Shadow, Bevel and Emboss, and Gradient Overlay styles applied to it.)

8. Create a layer set called **Title**, add a color to the layer set, and then add the type layers to it.

9. Save your work, close the image files, then compare your image to the sample in Figure 42.

FIGURE 42
Completed Project Builder 2

You're the senior graphics engineer at a 3D software simulation company and have just hired a few new graphic designers. Some of the work at your company involves reverse engineering, a process that your new artists will need to understand and capture visually. To better orient them to the practice, you've asked them to deconstruct a Photoshop image on the web, and then reinterpret the image using the techniques they identified. Before you assemble the staff, you want to walk through the process yourself.

1. Connect to the Internet, and use your browser to find information containing digital artwork that contains images and type that appears to have styles or filters applied. (Make a record of the site you found so you can use it for future reference, if necessary.)
2. Create a new Photoshop image and save it as **My Vision**.
3. Create a type layer named **Techniques**, then on the layer, type the skills and features that you believe were used to create the appearance of each letter and its background image. In addition to addressing the specifics for each letter, be sure to include the following general analyses:
    - Identify the light source for the image, and how light is handled for each letter and its background.
    - Discuss the relationship between the styles applied to the type and the styles or filters applied to the background image.
    - Evaluate any seemingly conflicting or unidentifiable techniques.
4. Complete your analyses and print the image.
5. Hide the Techniques layer, then obtain images to use for your own interpretation of the digital artwork. You can use scanned images or images that are available on your computer, or download images from the Internet.

6. Place the images in your image, create type layers for the letters, and then apply the techniques you identified. Compare your image to the sample shown in Figure 43.
7. Create a snapshot, then update the Techniques layer as necessary, print the image so that the Techniques layer prints clearly, then compare your before and after analyses. (*Hint*: Hide distracting layers if necessary.)
8. Hide the Techniques layer, make the other layers active, then save your work.

FIGURE 43
Design Project Website

After years of lackluster advertising campaigns, you've decided to combine the talent of local photographers and your Photoshop skills to create new artwork for a local beach. You know that this is a grand public relations opportunity not to be missed. You decide to design a poster and a companion bumper sticker that highlights the beach. You can use any appropriate images of your choice in the design.

1. Obtain images for the poster and bumper sticker. Include those whose content you can select or extract, and any other images as desired. You can use scanned images, or images that are available on your computer, or connect to the Internet and download images. You'll need a background image that might or might not include the animal, at least one small image (such as a snack, toy, or flower) to accompany the animal, and as many other images as desired.

2. Create a new Photoshop image and save it as **Beach Poster**.

3. Drag or copy the background to the Beach Poster image above the Background layer, then delete the Background layer, if necessary.

4. Select the animal in its image file, then copy the image to a new layer in the Beach Poster file. (*Hint*: The horses were selected using the Quick Selection tool.)

5. Duplicate the animal layer if desired, and apply filters or styles to it. (*Hint*: The horses

were selected, then copied.)

6. Create type layers for the bumper sticker as desired, include something unique about the species you selected, and apply at least one style or filter to them. (*Hint*: The background of the bumper sticker was created with the Rectangle tool and has Drop Shadow and Stroke effects applied to it, the heart was created with the Custom Shape tool, and the cut corners were created with the Eraser tool.)

7. Drag or copy the small image, transform it as needed, and then apply at least one style or filter to it. (*Hint*: The type has been scaled, rotated, and background erased.)

8. Drag or copy other images as desired, then apply filters or styles to them.

9. Be prepared to discuss the effects you can generate when you select an image, copy it, and apply different opacity settings, filters, or styles to each copy.

10. Save your work, then compare your image to the sample in Figure 44.

FIGURE 44
Completed Portfolio Project

Enhancing Specific Selections

1. Correct and adjust color

2. Enhance colors by altering saturation

3. Modify color channels using levels

4. Create color samplers with the Info panel

Enhancing Color

Photoshop places several color-enhancing tools at your disposal. By changing tonal values, these tools make it possible to change the mood or "personality" of a color. **Tonal values**, also called **color levels**, are the numeric values of an individual color and are crucial if you ever need to duplicate a color. For example, when you select a specific shade in a paint store that requires custom mixing, a recipe that contains the tonal values is used to create the color.

Using Tools to Adjust Colors

You can use color adjustment tools to make an image that is flat or dull appear to come to life. You can mute distracting colors to call attention to a central image. You can choose from several adjustment tools to achieve the same results, so the method you use depends on which one you *prefer*, not on which one is *better*.

Reproducing Colors

Accurate color reproduction is an important reason to learn about color measurement and modification. Because colors vary from monitor to monitor, and can be altered during the output process, you can specify exactly how you want them to look. Professional printers know how to take your Photoshop settings and adapt them to get the colors that match your specifications. Color levels, depicted in a **histogram** (a graph that represents the frequency distribution—for example, the number of times a particular pixel color occurs), can be modified by making adjustments in the input and output levels. When working with color levels, moving the input sliders toward the center of the histogram increases the tonal range, resulting in increased contrast in the image. Moving the output sliders toward the center decreases the tonal range, resulting in decreased contrast.

QUICKTIP

You can make color adjustments directly on a layer, or by using an adjustment layer. Directly applying a color adjustment affects only the layer to which it is applied. Applying a color adjustment using an adjustment layer affects all visible layers beneath it.

Tools You'll Use

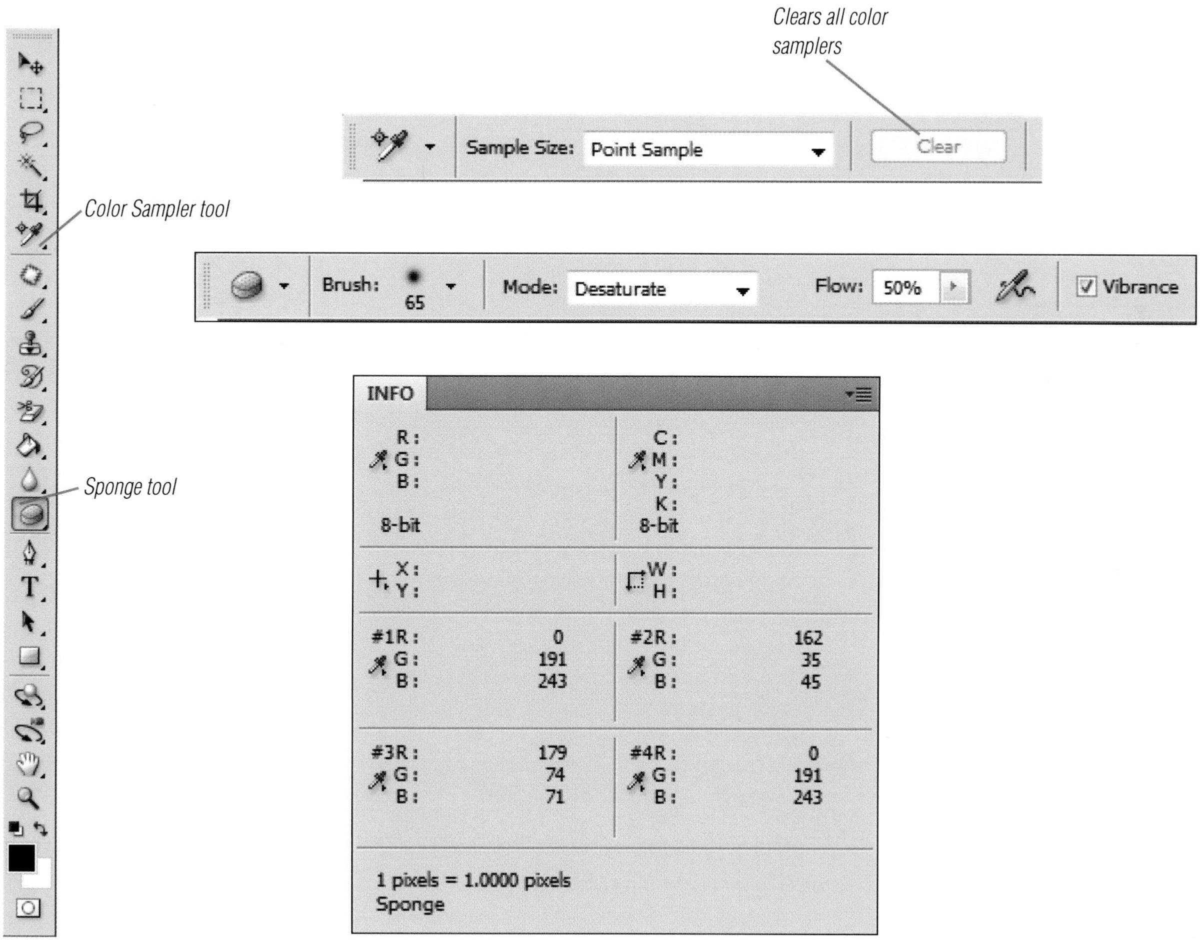

Clears all color
samplers

Sample Size: Point Sample ▾   Clear

Color Sampler tool

Brush: 65 ▾   Mode: Desaturate ▾   Flow: 50% ▸   ☑ Vibrance

Sponge tool

INFO	
R:	C:
G:	M:
B:	Y:
	K:
8-bit	8-bit

X:	W:
Y:	H:

#1R:	0	#2R:	162
G:	191	G:	35
B:	243	B:	45

#3R:	179	#4R:	0
G:	74	G:	191
B:	71	B:	243

1 pixels = 1.0000 pixels
Sponge

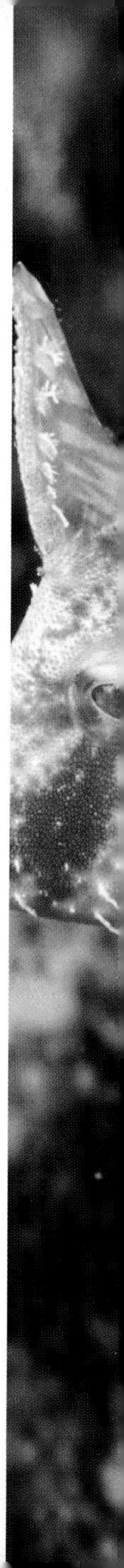

CORRECT AND
ADJUST COLOR

What You'll Do

 In this lesson, you'll modify settings for color balance and curves to make dull colors look more vivid.

Making Color Corrections

Learning to recognize which colors need correction is one of the hardest skills to develop. Adjusting colors can be very difficult because, while there is a science to color correction, you must also consider the aesthetics of your image. Beauty is in the eye of the beholder, and you must choose how you want your work to look and feel. Add to this the problem of reconciling hardware differences, where *my* red may look very different from *your* red, and you can see how color management can become a can of worms. A **color management system** reconciles the differences between different devices.

> **QUICK**TIP
>
> Most color corrections can be made by clicking the appropriate button on the Adjustments panel, or by using a dialog box that is opened by clicking the Image menu on the Application bar, then clicking Adjustments.

Using a Color Management System

Photoshop has a way to deal with hardware discrepancies: the device profile. A **profile** (also called an ICC profile) can be created for specific devices and embedded in an image, and is used to define how colors are interpreted by a specific device. ICC stands for International Color Consortium. You can create a profile by clicking Edit on the Application bar, then clicking Color Settings. Use the list arrows in the Working Spaces section. An image's working space tells the color management system how RGB or CMYK values are interpreted. You don't have to use profiles, but you can assign a specific profile by selecting the ICC Profile check box (Win) or the Embed Color Profile check box (Mac) in the Save As dialog box. Doing so embeds the profile in the working space of an image. Assigning an ICC profile is different from converting to an ICC profile. Converting occurs during output preparation, when you can select color management options in the Adobe PDF Options dialog box.

Balancing Colors

You can **balance colors** by adding and subtracting tonal values from those already existing in a layer. You do this to correct oversaturated or undersaturated color and to remove color casts from an image. The Color Balance dialog box or Adjustments panel contains three sliders: one for Cyan-Red, one for Magenta-Green and one for Yellow-Blue. You can adjust colors by dragging each of these sliders or by typing in values in the Color Levels text boxes. You

FIGURE 1
Variations dialog box

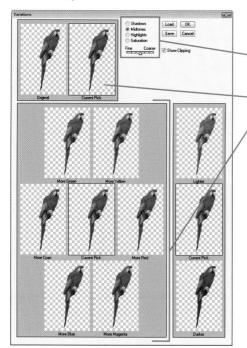

Additional adjustment options

Current selection

Color variations

can also use the Color Balance dialog box to adjust the color balance of shadows or highlights by clicking the Shadows or Highlights option buttons.

QUICKTIP

Color cast is a situation in which one color dominates an image to an unrealistic or undesirable degree, such as the yellowing of a photograph.

Modifying Curves

Using the Curves Adjustments panel or dialog box, you can alter the output tonal value of any pixel input. Instead of just being able to make adjustments using three variables

(highlights, shadows, and midtones), you can change as many as 16 points along the 0–255 scale in the Curves dialog box. The horizontal axis in the Curves dialog box represents the original intensity values of the pixels (the Input levels), and the vertical axis represents the modified color values (the Output levels). The default curve appears as a diagonal line that shares the same input and output values. Each point on the line represents each pixel. You add curves to the line to adjust the tonal values.

Analyzing Colors

When you look at an image, ask yourself, "What's wrong with this picture?" Does the image need more blue than yellow? Preserve your work by creating an adjustment layer, then try adjusting the color sliders, and see how the image changes. Then try modifying the curves. Much of the color correction process involves experimentation—with you, the artist, learning and applying the subtleties of shading and contrast.

Using Variations to adjust color

You can make color adjustments by viewing thumbnails of color variations on your current image. You can see a variety of thumbnails that show you some specific results of color correction. Start by clicking the layer you want to adjust. Click Image on the Application bar, point to Adjustments, then click Variations. The Variations dialog box, as shown in Figure 1, will open, showing your current layer with its settings, and thumbnails of the same layer with lighter, darker, or more of the individual colors from the Color Balance dialog box. This tool lets you see what a layer would look like if it had more of a particular color, *without* making any modifications to the actual image. You can use the Variations dialog box as a tool to help you develop your color correction skills.

Modify color balance settings

1. Start Photoshop, open PS 10-1.psd from the drive and folder where you store your Data Files, update the text layers (if necessary), then save the file as **Scarlet Macaws**.

2. Click the **Default Foreground and Background Colors button** on the Tools panel (if necessary).

3. Display the **Color and Tone** workspace.

   TIP   Some workspaces, such as Color and Tone, have the option of displaying additional information. You can display this additional information by clicking the list arrow in the top panel, then clicking Expanded View. Use the display that best meets your needs.

4. Click the **Large Macaw layer** on the Layers panel.

5. Click the **Color Balance button** on the Adjustments panel.

6. Drag the **sliders** so that the Midtones settings in the Color Levels text boxes are **60** for Cyan/Red, **–40** for Magenta/Green, and **–50** for Yellow/Blue, verify that the Preserve Luminosity check box is selected, then click the **Return to adjustment list button**.

7. Compare your image to Figure 2.

You modified the color balance settings by using the sliders. As you drag the sliders, you can see changes in the image on the active layer.

FIGURE 2
Color balanced layer

Intensified reds, magentas, and yellows

Using the Auto Adjustments commands

You can make color adjustments by clicking Image on the Application bar and using one of the Auto Adjustments commands. You can use three Auto Adjustments commands (Auto Tone, Auto Contrast, and Auto Color) to make color adjustments automatically without any additional input. The Auto Tone command adjusts the intensity levels of shadows and highlights by identifying the lightest and darkest pixel in each color channel and then redistributing the pixel's values across that range. You can use the Auto Contrast command to make simple adjustments to the contrast and mixture of colors in an RGB image; it works by analyzing the distribution of colors in the composite image, not in the individual color channels. The Auto Color command adjusts the contrast and color mixtures using the image itself to make the adjustment, resulting in neutralized midtones.

FIGURE 3
Curves graph in Adjustments panel

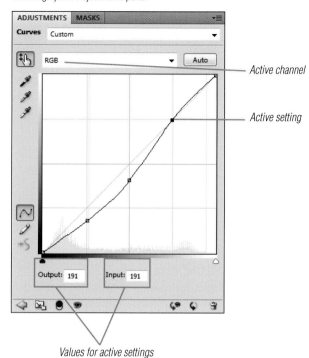

Active channel

Active setting

Output: 191   Input: 191

Values for active settings

FIGURE 4

Image with modified curves

Modify curves

1. Click the **Large Macaw layer**, then click the **Curves button** on the Adjustments panel.

2. Click the **center of the graph** at the point on the line where the input and output values both equal **128**.

   TIP   When you position the pointer over the Curves graph, input and output values display beneath the graph.

3. Drag the point down so that the input value equals **128** and the output value equals **104**.

   TIP   This is not an exact science. Don't worry if you can't get the input and output values to be exactly as stated in the steps.

   Did you notice that the image's colors change as you drag the line? If you use the Curves dialog box, you can see the changes if the preview check box is checked.

4. Click the **point where the curve intersects the right vertical gridline** (input value equals approximately **191**, and output value equals approximately **178**).

   TIP   The point that you click in the Curves dialog box is called the **active setting**.

5. Drag the **active setting** up as needed until the input and output values both equal **191**, as shown in Figure 3.

   TIP   After you select the active setting, you can also change its location by changing the values in the Input and Output boxes.

6. Click the **Return to adjustment list button** .

7. Save your work, then compare your screen to Figure 4.

You modified curves settings by using Curves on the Adjustments panel.

Using the Color Settings dialog box

You can use the Color Settings dialog box to save common color management controls, such as working spaces, color management policies, conversion options, and advanced controls. You might want to create a custom color setting, for example, to match a specific proofing setup used by a commercial printer. To open the Color Settings dialog box, click Edit on the Application bar, then click Color Settings. In most cases, it's best to use preset color settings that have been tested by Adobe Systems unless you are knowledgeable about color management. If you do make changes, you can save them as a preset using the Color Settings dialog box.

ENHANCE COLORS BY
ALTERING SATURATION

What You'll Do

In this lesson, you'll modify the appearance of an image by altering color saturation.

Understanding Saturation

Saturation is the purity of a particular color. A higher saturation level indicates a color that is more intense. To understand saturation, imagine that you are trying to lighten a can of blue paint. For example, if you add some gray paint, you decrease the purity and the intensity of the original color or desaturate it. Photoshop provides two methods of modifying color saturation: the Hue/Saturation dialog box and the Sponge tool.

Using the Sponge Tool

The Sponge tool is located on the Tools panel, and is used to increase or decrease the color saturation of a specific area within a layer. Settings for the Sponge tool are located on the options bar and include settings for the brush size, whether you want the sponge to saturate or desaturate, and how quickly you want the color to flow into or from the Sponge tool.

Using the Hue/Saturation Dialog Box

Hue is the amount of color that is reflected from or transmitted through an object. Hue is assigned a measurement (between 0 and 360 degrees) that is taken from a standard color wheel. In conversation, hue is the name of the color, such as red, blue, or gold and described in terms of its tints or shades, such as yellow-green or blue-green. Adjusting hue and saturation is similar to making modifications to color balance. You can make these adjustments by using the Hue, Saturation, and Lightness sliders, which are located in the Hue/Saturation dialog box. When modifying saturation levels using the Hue/Saturation dialog box, you have the option of adjusting the entire color range, or preset color ranges. The available preset color ranges are shown in Figure 5. To choose any one of these color ranges, click the Edit list arrow in the Hue/Saturation setting on the Adjustments panel *before* modifying any of the sliders.

Using Saturation to Convert a Color Layer to Grayscale

Have you ever wondered how an image could contain both a color and a grayscale object, as shown in Figure 6? You can easily create this effect using the Hue/Saturation setting on the Adjustments

panel. This image was created by clicking the layer containing the ice chest, clicking the Hue/Saturation button on the Adjustments panel, then changing the Saturation setting to –100.

FIGURE 5

Preset color ranges in the Hue/Saturation setting on the Adjustments panel

Select colors to be changed

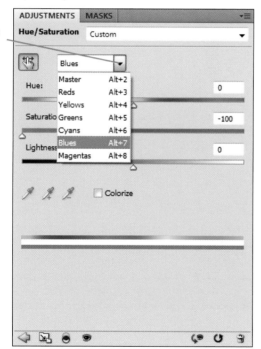

FIGURE 6

Grayscale layer

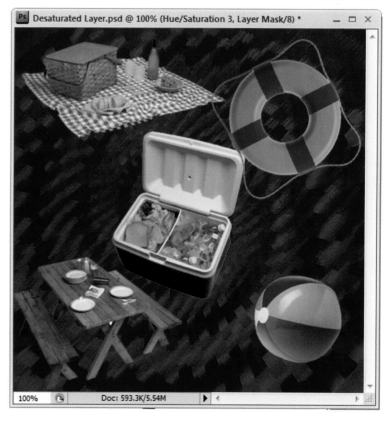

Saturate a color range

1. Click the **Small Macaw 1 layer** on the Layers panel to make it active, then make the layer visible.

2. Click the **Indicates layer visibility button** 👁 on the Large Macaw layer to hide it.

3. Click the **Hue/Saturation button** 🔲 on the Adjustments panel.

   TIP   When making color adjustments, you can use the preset buttons on the Adjustments panel, or use the Adjustments command on the Image menu.

4. Click the **Edit list arrow**, then click **Blues**.

5. Drag the **Saturation slider** to **+40**.

6. Click the **Edit list arrow**, then click **Yellows**.

7. Drag the **Saturation slider** to **+30**.

   The image's blues and yellows are intensified.

8. Click the **Return to adjustment list button** 🔽, then compare your image to Figure 7.

You changed the saturation of two preset color ranges. As you altered the saturation, the richness of the colors became more defined.

Getting more color data using HDR images

High Dynamic Range images, which use 32 bits per channel, allow real-world levels of illumination to be represented. The level of detail afforded by using 32 bits per channel means that imagery is more realistic and better able to simulate light conditions and a wider range of color values. You can create an HDR image using multiple photographs, each captured at a different exposure. In Photoshop, you can create HDR images from multiple photographs by clicking File on the Application bar, pointing to Automate, then clicking Merge To HDR command.

FIGURE 7
Modified blues and yellows

Scarlet Macaws.psd @ 100% (Hue/Saturation 1, Layer Mask/8)

Saturated yellow

Saturated blue

100%   Doc: 703.1K/2.98M

FIGURE 8
Reds saturated with the Sponge tool

Saturated red areas

Scarlet Macaws.psd @ 100% (Small Macaw 1, RGB/8#)

Scarlet Macaws

100%   Doc: 703.1K/2.98M

1. Click the **Small Macaw 1 layer** to make it active.

2. Click the **Sponge tool** on the Tools panel.

   TIP The Sponge tool is grouped with the Dodge tool and the Burn tool on the Tools panel.

3. Click the **Click to open the Brush Preset picker list arrow**, then double-click the **Hard Round 13 pixels brush tip**.

4. Click the **Mode list arrow** on the options bar, click **Saturate**, then set the Flow to **100%**.

5. Click and drag the pointer over the **red areas** (head, body, and tail feathers) of the parrot.

   The red color in the saturated area is brighter.

6. Save your work, then compare your screen to Figure 8.

You used the Sponge tool to saturate specific areas in an image. The Sponge tool lets you saturate spot areas rather than an entire color on a layer.

Correcting faulty exposures

The Exposure adjustment feature lets you correct for under- or over-exposure in images. By making adjustments to the black points (which can result in an image being too dark) or the white points (which can result in an image appearing too light), you can make corrections that will make an image's exposure settings just right. You can make exposure adjustments by clicking Image on the Application bar, pointing to Adjustments, then clicking Exposure, or by clicking the Exposure button on the Adjustments panel.

MODIFY COLOR CHANNELS
USING LEVELS

What You'll Do

In this lesson, you'll use levels to make color adjustments.

Making Color and Tonal Adjustments

You can make color adjustments using the Levels button on the Adjustments panel or the Levels dialog box (which can be opened by clicking Image on the Application bar, pointing to Adjustments, then clicking Levels). This feature lets you make modifications across a tonal range, using the composite color channel or individual channels. The Levels setting takes the form of a histogram and displays light and dark color values on a linear scale. The plotted data indicates the total number of pixels for a given tonal value.

There is no "ideal" histogram shape. The image's character and tone determine the shape of the histogram. Some images will be lighter and their histogram will be bunched on the right; some will be darker and their histogram will be bunched on the left. When working with the Levels setting, three triangular sliders appear beneath the histogram representing shadows, midtones, and highlights. Three text boxes appear for input levels (one box each for the input shadows, midtones, and highlights). Two text boxes appear for output levels (one for output shadows and one for highlights).

Correcting Shadows and Highlights

You can modify the settings for shadows and highlights independently. By moving the output shadows slider to the right, you can decrease contrast and *lighten* the image on an individual layer. You can decrease contrast and *darken* an image by moving the output highlights slider to the left in the Levels setting.

Adjusting Colors

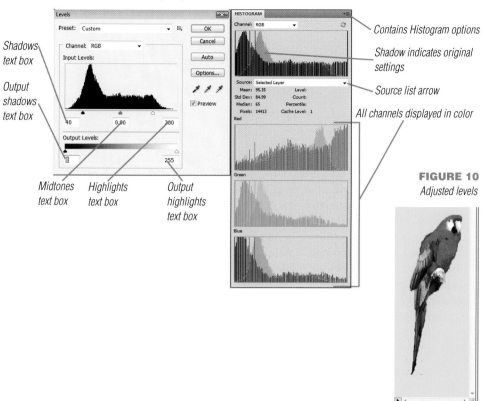

FIGURE 9
Levels dialog box and Histogram panel

Shadows text box

Output shadows text box

Contains Histogram options

Shadow indicates original settings

Source list arrow

All channels displayed in color

Midtones text box

Highlights text box

Output highlights text box

FIGURE 10
Adjusted levels

Understanding the Histogram panel

Using the Histogram panel, you can watch as you adjust color settings such as levels, curves, color balance, and hue/saturation. When the Histogram panel opens, you'll see the compact view: a single chart containing a composite channel for the image. You can view all the channels in color using the menu options on the list arrow on the panel. As you make color adjustments, the Histogram panel is updated. In addition to the modifications, the original settings are displayed as a light-colored shadow. This makes it easy to see how the settings have changed.

Adjust color using the Levels setting

1. Click the **Small Macaw 2 layer** on the Layers panel to make it active, then make the layer visible.

2. Click the **Indicates layer visibility button** on the Small Macaw 1 layer to hide it.

3. Drag the **Histogram panel tab** [HISTOGRAM] out of the dock (to the left of its current location).

4. Click the **Histogram panel list arrow**, then click **Expanded View** (if it is not already expanded).

5. Click the **Histogram panel list arrow**, then click **All Channels View**.

6. Click the **Histogram panel list arrow**, verify that the **Show Statistics** and **Show Channels in Color commands** contain check marks, then click RGB in the Channels list arrow (if necessary).

7. Click the **Small Macaw 2 layer**, click the **Source list arrow** on the Histogram panel, then click **Selected Layer**.

8. Click **Image** on the Application bar, point to **Adjustments**, then click **Levels** to open the Levels dialog box. Type **40** in the Shadows text box, press **[Tab]**, type **.90** in the Midtones text box, press **[Tab]**, then type **200** in the Highlights text box. See Figure 9.

9. Click **OK**, reset the **Color and Tone** workspace, then compare your work to Figure 10.

10. Save your work.

You modified levels for shadows, midtones, and highlights. You were also able to see how these changes were visible on the Histogram panel.

CREATE COLOR SAMPLERS
WITH THE INFO PANEL

What You'll Do

In this lesson, you'll take multiple color samples and use the Info panel to store color information.

Sampling Colors

In the past, you've used the Eyedropper pointer to take a sample of an existing color. By taking the sample, you were able to use the color as a background or a font color. This method is easy and quick, but it limited you to one color sample at a time. Photoshop has an additional feature, the **Color Sampler tool**, that makes it possible to sample—and store—up to four distinct color samplers.

> QUICKTIP
>
> The color samplers are saved with the image in which they are created.

Using Color Samplers

You can apply each of the four color samplers to an image or use the samplers to make color adjustments. Each time you click the Color Sampler tool, a color reading is taken and the number 1, 2, 3, or 4 appears on the image, depending on how many samplers you have already taken. See Figure 11. A color sampler includes all visible layers and is dynamic. This means that if you hide a layer from which a sampler was taken, the next visible layer will contain a sampler that has the same coordinates of the hidden layer, but the sampler will have the color reading of the visible layer.

Using the Info Panel

The Info panel is grouped with the Actions and Histogram panels in the Color and Tone workspace. The top-left quadrant displays actual color values for the current color mode. For example, if the current mode is RGB, then RGB values are displayed. The Info panel also displays CMYK values, X and Y coordinates of the current pointer location, and the width and height of a selection (if applicable), as shown in Figure 12. When a color sampler is created, the Info panel expands to show the color measurement information from that sample. Figure 13 shows an Info panel containing four color samplers. After you have established your color samplers but no longer want them to be displayed, click the Info panel list arrow, then deselect Color Samplers. You can display hidden color samplers by clicking the Info panel list arrow, then clicking Color Samplers.

Manipulating Color Samplers

Color samplers, like most Photoshop features, are designed to accommodate change. Each color sampler can be moved by dragging the sampler icon to a new location. After the sampler is moved to its new location, its color value information is updated on the Info panel. You can individually delete any of the samplers by selecting the Color Sampler tool, holding

[Alt] (Win) or [option] (Mac), then clicking the sampler you want to delete. You can also delete all the samplers by clicking the Clear button on the options bar.

QUICKTIP

Each time a color sampler is deleted, the remaining samplers are automatically renumbered. If you have defined four samplers and you want to add another sampler, you need to first clear an existing sampler.

FIGURE 11
Color samplers

Color samplers

FIGURE 12
Information displayed in the Info panel

Actual (RGB) color values

Pointer coordinates

User-chosen (CMYK) color values

Width and height of a selected area

HISTOGRAM	INFO	ACTIONS		
R:	146	C:	27%	
G:	21	M:	100%	
B:	30	Y:	98%	
		K:	27%	
8-bit		8-bit		
X:	280	W:	27	
Y:	97	H:	25	

FIGURE 13
Info panel with color samplers

HISTOGRAM	INFO	ACTIONS		
R:	0	C:	67%	
G:	191	M:	2%	
B:	243	Y:	0%	
		K:	0%	
8-bit		8-bit		
X:	121	W:		
Y:	220	H:		
#1R:	0	#2R:	162	
G:	191	G:	35	
B:	243	B:	45	
#3R:	179	#4R:	0	
G:	74	G:	191	
B:	71	B:	243	

Color samplers

Create color samplers

1. Click the **Indicates layer visibility button** for the Large Macaw and Small Macaw 1 layers on the Layers panel, so that all layers in the image are visible.

2. Display the rulers in pixels (if they are not already displayed).

3. Click the **Info panel tab** INFO to display the Info panel (if it is not displayed).

4. Click the **Color Sampler tool** on the Tools panel.

   TIP The Color Sampler tool is grouped with the Eyedropper tool, the Ruler tool, the Note tool, and the Count tool on the Tools panel.

5. Using Figure 14 as a guide, click the image in four locations.

6. Click the **Info panel list arrow**, then click **Color Samplers** to hide the color samplers.

7. Click the **Info panel list arrow**, then click **Color Samplers** to display the color samplers.

8. Hide the rulers.

You sampled specific areas in the image, stored that color data on the Info panel, then hid and revealed the color samplers.

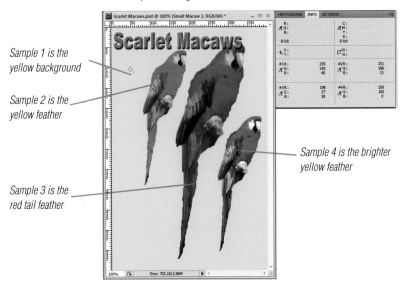

FIGURE 14
Color samplers in image

Sample 1 is the yellow background

Sample 2 is the yellow feather

Sample 4 is the brighter yellow feather

Sample 3 is the red tail feather

Creating a spot color channel

Printing a Photoshop image can be a costly process, especially if a spot color is used. A **spot color** is one that can't easily be re-created by a printer, such as a specific color used in a client's logo. By creating a spot color channel, you can make it easier for your printer to create the ink for a difficult color, assure yourself of accurate color reproduction, and save yourself high printing costs. If you use this feature, you won't have to provide your printer with substitution colors: the spot color contains all of the necessary information. You can create a spot color channel by displaying the Channels panel, clicking the Channels panel list arrow, then clicking New Spot Channel. Create a meaningful name for the new spot channel, click the Color box, click the Color Libraries button in the Select spot color dialog box, click the Book list arrow located at the top of the Color Libraries dialog box, click a color-matching system, then click a color from the list. You can also create a custom color by clicking the Picker button in the Custom Libraries dialog box. If you have created a color sampler, you can use this information to create the custom color for the spot color channel. Click OK to close the Color Libraries dialog box, then click OK to close the New Spot Channel dialog box.

FIGURE 15
Unsharp Mask dialog box

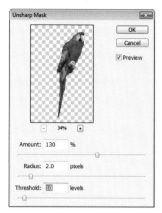

FIGURE 16
Lighting Effects dialog box

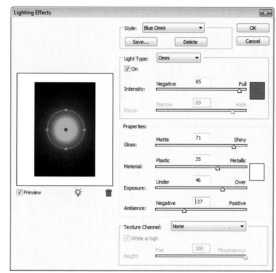

FIGURE 17
Lighting effect applied

Unsharp Mask changes the appearance of the Large Parrot layer

Your background colors may vary

Lighting effect changes the appearance of the Backdrop layer

Apply a color sampler and filter and add a lighting effect

1. Make the **Large Macaw layer** active.

2. Click **Filter** on the Application bar, point to **Sharpen**, then click **Unsharp Mask**.

   You are now ready to put the finishing touches on your color-corrected image.

3. Adjust your settings in the Unsharp Mask dialog box as necessary so they match those shown in Figure 15, then click **OK**.

   These settings emphasize the edges and create the illusion of a sharper image.

4. Make the **Backdrop layer** active.

5. Click **Filter** on the Application bar, point to **Render**, then click **Lighting Effects**.

6. Adjust your settings in the Lighting Effects dialog box so they match those shown in Figure 16, then click **OK**.

7. Double-click the **Scarlet Macaws layer thumbnail**, then click **Set the text color box** on the options bar.

8. Type the R, G, and B values in sample 3 on the Info panel in the R, G, and B text boxes in the Select text color dialog box, click **OK**, then click the **Commit any current edits button** ✔ on the options bar.

9. Save your work, hide the color samplers, then compare your screen to Figure 17.

10. Close the Scarlet Macaws image, then exit Photoshop.

You added the Unsharp Mask and Lighting Effects filters to make the objects stand out more dramatically against the background. You also changed the type color using the values from a sampled color.

Power User Shortcuts

to do this:	use this method:
Adjust color with thumbnails	Window ➤ Adjustments panel ➤ Variations
Adjust saturation	▦ on Adjustments panel
Balance colors	⚖ on Adjustments panel
Choose color range	Click Edit list arrow in Hue/Saturation dialog box, click color range
Convert color layer to grayscale	▦ or ▰ on Adjustments panel
Create color sampler	Click ✎, click image using ✐
Create spot color channel	Click CHANNELS, click ▾≣, New Spot Channel
Delete color sampler	Click ✎, press [Alt] (Win) or option (Mac), click sampler using ✄

to do this:	use this method:
Modify curves	▨ on Adjustments panel
Modify levels	▥ on Adjustments panel
Move color sampler	Press [Ctrl] (Win) or ⌘ (Mac), then click sampler with ▸
Open Histogram panel	HISTOGRAM
Open Info panel	INFO
Saturate with Sponge tool	◯ or O
Show/Hide color samplers	Click INFO, click ▾≣ ➤ Color Samplers

Key: Menu items are indicated by ➤ between the menu name and its command. Blue bold letters are shortcuts for selecting tools on the Tools panel.

Correct and adjust color.

1. Start Photoshop.
2. Open PS 10-2.psd from the drive and folder where your Data Files are stored, then save it as **Big Bird**.
3. Make the Bird layer active (if it is not already active), then display the Color and Tone workspace.
4. Display the Color Balance adjustment settings.
5. Change the Magenta-Green setting to +62, then return to the adjustment list.
6. Display the Curves adjustment settings.
7. Click the point where the Input and Output both equal 64.
8. Drag the curve up so that the Output equals 128 while the Input remains at 64, then return to the adjustment list.
9. Save your work.

Enhance colors by altering saturation.

1. Display the Hue/Saturation settings.
2. Edit the Greens color range.
3. Change the Hue to –70 and the Saturation to –15, then return to the adjustment list.
4. Use the Sponge tool to further saturate the green, light blue, and dark blue areas of the bird.
5. Save your work.

Modify color channels using levels.

1. Display the Levels adjustment settings.
2. Modify the Blue channel Input Levels to 95, 1.60, 185.
3. Modify the Red channel Output Levels to 0, 2, 200.
4. Return to the adjustment list and save your work.

FIGURE 18
Completed Skills Review

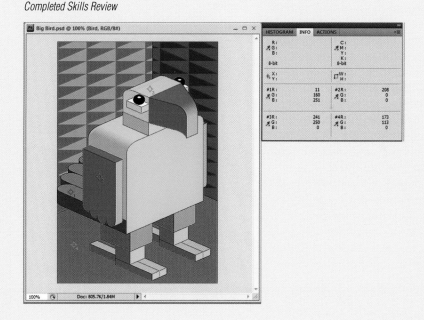

Create color samplers with the Info panel.

1. Click the Color Sampler tool.
2. Display the Info panel.
3. Create samplers for the following areas: the light blue feathers, the red wing, the yellow head, and the tan floor.
4. Compare your image to the sample shown in Figure 18.
5. Hide the color samplers.
6. Save your work.

The Artworks Gallery has commissioned you to create a promotional poster for an upcoming art show called Moods and Metaphors, which will be held during September of this year. The only guidance they have provided is that they want a piece that looks moody and evocative. You have already created a basic design, and you want to use color adjustments to heighten the mood.

1. Open PS 10-3.psd, then save it as **Gallery Poster**.
2. Make the Backdrop layer active (if necessary).
3. Display the Curves settings and adjust your settings so they match those shown in Figure 19.
4. Make the Shadow Man layer active.
5. Display the Hue/Saturation settings and change the Saturation setting to +60.
6. Create two color samplers: one using the color of the man's tie, and the other using the yellow under the spotlight.
7. Create two type layers: one for the date and location of the art show and one for expressive language that encourages people to come to the show, then position them appropriately in the image. Use either of the colors in the samplers for the font colors. For example, you can enter the color sampler RGB values in the Color Picker dialog box to create that color. (*Hint*: You can use any font and font size you want. The font used in the sample is Bernhard MT Condensed; the font size

is 85 pt for the Hurry . . . Don't miss it! layer and 36 pt for the Date and location layer.)
8. Hide the samplers.
9. Apply the following colors to the layer thumbnails: Hurry . . . Don't miss it! = Red, Date and location = Green. (*Hint*: Make these modifications using the Layer Properties command.)
10. Apply any styles to the type you feel are appropriate. (*Hint*: The Bevel and Emboss style is applied to the Hurry . . . Don't miss it!

type layer in the sample. The Outer Glow and the Inner Glow styles are applied to the Date and location layer in the sample.)
11. Apply any lighting effect you feel adds to the theme of the show. (*Hint*: The Flood Light style and Spotlight light type are applied to the Backdrop layer in the sample.)
12. Save your work, then compare your image to the sample in Figure 20.

FIGURE 19
Curves adjustment panel

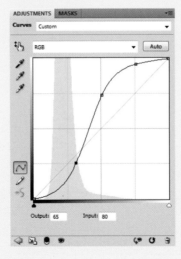

FIGURE 20
Completed Project Builder 1

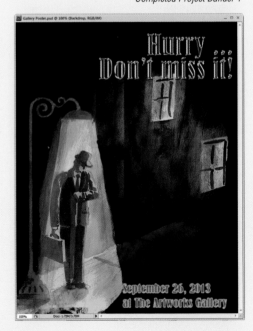

A new, unnamed e-commerce company has hired you to create an advertisement for their upcoming debut. While they are leaving the design to you, the only type they want in the imagery is "Find your inner self." They want this ad to be a teaser; more descriptive type will be added in the future. This is a cutting-edge company, and they want something really striking.

1. Open PS 10-4.psd, then save it as **Heads Up**.
2. Make the Backdrop layer active if it is not already active.
3. Use the Levels settings to modify the Input Levels of the RGB color settings. (*Hint*: The settings used in the sample are 82, 1.46, 200.)
4. Make the Head layer active.
5. Use the Hue/Saturation settings to modify the Head layer. (*Hint*: The settings used in the sample are Hue = –25, Saturation = +30, Lightness = –5.)
6. Create a color sampler for the color of the head, then hide the sampler.
7. Create a type layer for the image, then position it appropriately. (*Hint*: You can use any font, font size, and color you want. The font used in the sample is a blue OCRA Extended; the font size is 72 pt.)

8. Apply the color Yellow to the type layer thumbnail.
9. Apply any styles to the type you feel are appropriate. (*Hint*: The Drop Shadow and Bevel and Emboss styles are applied to the type layer in the sample.)

FIGURE 21
Sample Project Builder 2

10. Apply any filter you feel adds to the image. (*Hint*: The Lens Flare filter is applied to the Head layer in the sample.)
11. Save your work, then compare your image to the sample in Figure 21.

A friend of yours is a textile artist; she creates artwork that is turned into materials for clothing, curtains, and bedding. She has turned to you because of your Photoshop expertise and wants your advice on how she can jazz up her current project. You love the design, but think the colors need correction so they'll look more dynamic. Before you proceed, you decide to explore the Internet to find information on how Photoshop color correction techniques can be used to create an effective design.

1. Connect to the Internet, and use your browser to find information about adjusting colors in Photoshop. (Make a record of the site you found so you can use it for future reference, if necessary.)

2. Read about color correction and take notes on any information that will help you incorporate new ideas into the image.

3. Open PS 10-5.psd, then save the file as **Puzzle Pieces**.

4. Use the skills you have learned to correct or adjust one or more of the colors in this image.

5. Create two color samplers from colors used in the image.

6. Apply any filter you feel enhances the image. (*Hint*: The Smudge Stick filter is applied to the Yellow Pieces layer in the sample. The Texture Craquelure filter is applied to the Blue Pieces layer.)

7. Save your work, then compare your image to the sample in Figure 22.

FIGURE 22
Sample Design Project

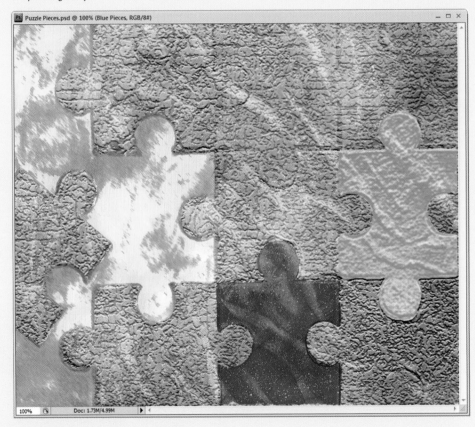

Each year, your company, OnTarget, has an art contest, and the winning entry is used as the cover of the Annual Report. OnTarget encourages employees to enter the contest. You decide to use your Photoshop skills to craft a winning entry. The OnTarget logo will be added once a winner of the contest has been selected.

1. Create an image with the dimensions 500 × 650 pixels.
2. Locate several pieces of artwork to use in the design. These can be located on your computer, from scanned images, or on the Internet. Remember that the images can show anything, but you want to show the flexibility of Photoshop and the range of your skills.
3. Save this file as **Annual Report Cover**.
4. Use any skills you have learned to correct or adjust the colors in this image.
5. Create a color sampler for at least two colors in the image, then hide the samplers.

6. Create one or two type layers for the name of the image (OnTarget Annual Report), then position the layer(s) appropriately in the image. Use your choice of font colors. (*Hint*: You can use any font and font size you want. The font used in the sample is Tempus Sans ITC; the font size is 110 pt in the title and 48 pt in the subtitle.)

FIGURE 23
Sample Portfolio Project

7. Add any necessary effects to the type layer(s).
8. If necessary, apply any filters you feel add to the image.
9. If desired, apply sampled colors within the image.
10. Save the image, then compare your image to the sample in Figure 23.

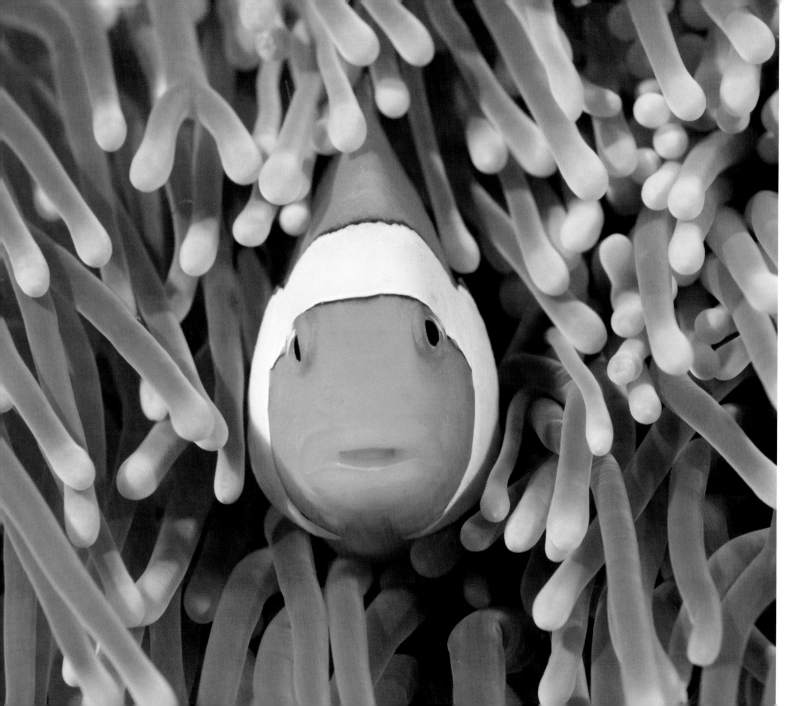

chapter

11

USING CLIPPING MASKS,
PATHS, & SHAPES

1. Use a clipping group as a mask

2. Use pen tools to create and modify a path

3. Work with shapes

4. Convert paths and selections

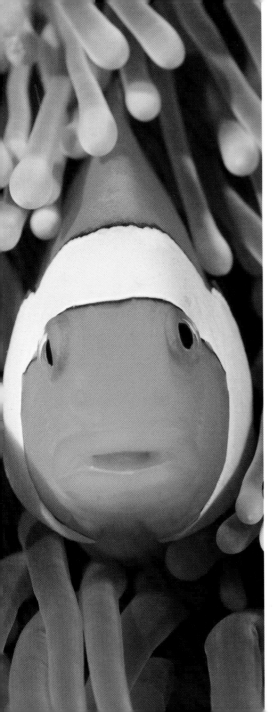

Working with Shapes

Photoshop provides several tools that help add stylistic elements, such as shapes, to your work. You can add either a shape or a rasterized shape to an image. A **shape** is simply a vector object that keeps its crisp appearance when it is resized, edited, moved, reshaped, or copied. A **rasterized shape** is converted into a bitmapped object that cannot be moved or copied; the advantage is that it can occupy a small file size, if compressed. The disadvantage is that a bitmapped object is resolution dependent. You can add either kind of shape as a predesigned shape, such as an ellipse, circle, or rectangle, or you can create a unique shape using a pen tool.

Defining Clipping Masks and Paths

A **clipping mask** (also called a **clipping group**) creates an effect in which the bottommost layer acts as a mask for all other layers in the group. You can use a **path** to turn an area defined within an object into a separate individual object—like an individual layer. A **path** is defined as one or more straight or curved line segments connected by **anchor points**, small squares similar to fastening points. Paths can be either open or closed. An **open path**, such as a line, has two distinct **endpoints**, anchor points at each end of the open path. A **closed path**, such as a circle, is one continuous path without endpoints. A **path component** consists of one or more anchor points joined by line segments. You can use another type of path called a **clipping path**, to extract a Photoshop object from within a layer, place it in another program (such as QuarkXPress or Adobe Illustrator), and retain its transparent background.

> QUICKTIP
>
> A shape and path are basically the same: the shape tools allow you to use an existing path instead of having to create one by hand. A path has a hard edge and is vector-based.

Creating Paths

Using a path, you can manipulate images on a layer. Each path is stored on the **Paths panel**. You can create a path using the Pen tool or the Freeform Pen tool. Each **pen tool** lets you draw a path by placing anchor points along the edge of another image, or wherever you need them, to draw a specific shape. As you place anchor points, line segments automatically fall between them. The **Freeform Pen tool** acts just like a traditional pen or pencil. Just draw with it, and it automatically places *both* the anchor points and line segments wherever necessary to achieve the shape you want. With these tools, you can create freeform shapes or use existing edges within an image by tracing on top of it. After you create a path, you can use the **Path Selection tool** to select the entire path, or the **Direct Selection tool** to select and manipulate individual anchor points and segments to reshape the path. Unlike selections, multiple paths can be saved using the Paths panel. When first created, a path is called a **work path**. The work path is temporary, but becomes a permanent part of your image when you name it. Paths, like layers, can be named, viewed, deleted, and duplicated.

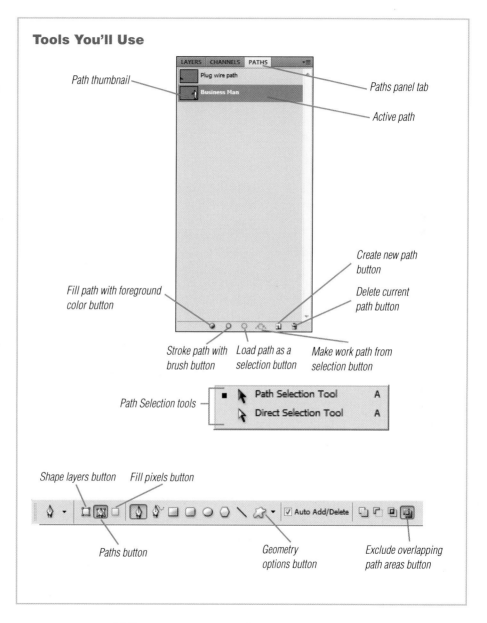

Tools You'll Use

Path thumbnail

Paths panel tab

Active path

Create new path button

Delete current path button

Fill path with foreground color button

Stroke path with brush button

Load path as a selection button

Make work path from selection button

Path Selection tools

Path Selection Tool — A
Direct Selection Tool — A

Shape layers button

Fill pixels button

Auto Add/Delete

Paths button

Geometry options button

Exclude overlapping path areas button

USE A CLIPPING
GROUP AS A MASK

What You'll Do

In this lesson, you'll rasterize a type layer, then use a clipping group as a mask for imagery already in an image. You'll also use the Transform command to alter an object's appearance.

Understanding the Clipping Mask Effect

If you want to display type in one layer using an interesting image or pattern in another layer as the fill for the type, then look no further. You can create this effect using a clipping mask (also called a clipping group). With a clipping group, you can isolate an area and make images outside the area transparent. This works very well with type, and can be used with a variety of images. Figure 1 shows an example of this effect in which type acts as a mask for imagery. In this effect, the (rasterized type) layer becomes a mask for the imagery. The image of the roses is *masked* by the text. For this effect to work, the layer that is being masked (the imagery, in this case) *must* be positioned above the mask layer (in this case, the type layer) on the Layers panel.

FIGURE 1
Sample clipping group effect

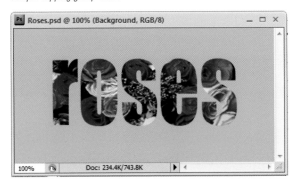

Rasterizing Text and Shape Layers

To use type or a shape in a clipping mask, the type or shape layer must first be rasterized, or changed from vector graphics into a normal object layer. Rasterizing changes the vector graphic into a bitmapped object, one that is made up of a fixed number of colored pixels. **Vector graphics** are made up of lines and curves defined by mathematical objects called vectors. The advantage to using vector graphics for shapes is that they can be resized and moved without losing image quality.

QUICKTIP

Bitmapped images contain a fixed number of pixels; as a consequence, they can appear jagged and lose detail when resized.

Using Transform Commands

Before you create a clipping mask, you might want to use one of the transform commands on the Edit menu to reshape layer contents so the shapes conform to the imagery that will be displayed. The transform commands are described in Table 1. Samples of the transform commands are shown in Figure 2. When a transform command is selected, a **bounding box** is displayed around the object. The bounding box contains **handles** that you can drag to modify the selection. A **reference point** is located in the center of the bounding box. This is the point around which the transform command takes place.

QUICKTIP

You can change the location of the reference point by dragging the point to a new location within the bounding box.

TABLE 1: Transform Commands

command	use
Scale	Changes the image size. Press [Shift] while dragging to scale proportionally. Press [Alt] (Win) or [option] (Mac) to scale from the reference point.
Rotate	Allows rotation of an image 360º. Press [Shift] to rotate in increments of 15º.
Skew	Stretches an image horizontally or vertically, but cannot exceed the image boundary.
Distort	Stretches an image horizontally or vertically, and can exceed the image boundary.
Perspective	Changes opposite sides of an image equally, and can be used to make an oval appear circular, or change a rectangle into a trapezoid.
Rotate 180º	Rotates image 180º clockwise.
Rotate 90º CW	Rotates image 90º clockwise.
Rotate 90º CCW	Rotates image 90º counterclockwise.
Flip Horizontal	Produces a mirror image along the vertical axis.
Flip Vertical	Produces a mirror image along the horizontal axis.

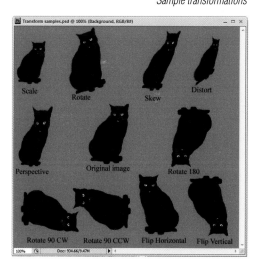

FIGURE 2
Sample transformations

Transform a type layer for use in a clipping mask

1. Open PS 11-1.psd from the drive and folder where you store your Data Files, update the text layers, then save the file as **Stamps**.

   The STAMPS type layer is active.

2. Click **Layer** on the Application bar, point to **Rasterize**, then click **Type**.

   The STAMPS layer is no longer a type layer, as shown in Figure 3.

3. Click the **Move tool** ⊹ on the Tools panel (if necessary).

4. Click **Edit** on the Application bar, point to **Transform**, then click **Skew**.

5. Type **-15** in the Set horizontal skew text box on the options bar, as shown in Figure 4, so the type is slanted.

   TIP You can also drag the handles surrounding the object until the skew effect looks just right.

6. Click the **Commit transform (Return) button** ✔ on the options bar.

7. Turn off the guides if they are displayed, and then compare your image to Figure 5.

   TIP There are two methods you can use to turn off the display of guides: you can hide them (using the Show command on the View menu) or clear them (using the Clear command on the View menu). Hiding the guides means you can display them at a later date, while clearing them means they will no longer exist in your document. Unless you know that you'll never need the guides again, it's a good idea to hide them.

You rasterized the existing type layer, then altered its shape using the Skew command and the Set horizontal skew by entering the value in the text box on the options bar. This transformation slanted the image.

FIGURE 3
Rasterized layer

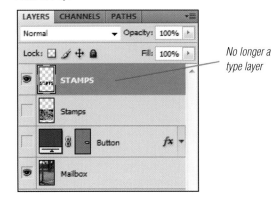

No longer a type layer

FIGURE 4
Skew options bar

Set horizontal skew text box

FIGURE 5
Skewed layer

FIGURE 6

Preparing to create the clipping group

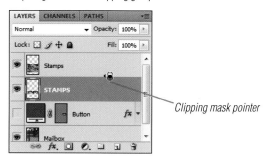

Clipping mask pointer

FIGURE 8

Layers and History panels

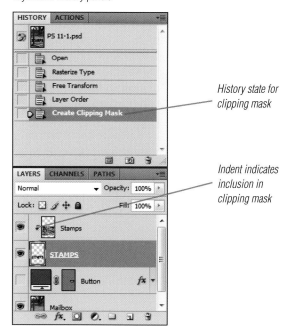

History state for clipping mask

Indent indicates inclusion in clipping mask

FIGURE 7

Effect of clipping mask

Stamps background visible through text

1. Drag the **STAMPS layer** beneath the Stamps layer.

   TIP Having multiple layers with the same or similar names is not a problem for Photoshop. To help out, try varying layer names or using upper and lowercase letters.

2. Click the **Indicates layer visibility button** on the Stamps layer on the Layers panel.

   The Stamps layer will serve as the fill for the clipping mask.

   TIP It's a good idea to first position the layer that will act as a mask *above* the layer containing the pattern so that you can adjust its size and shape. After the size and shape are the way you want them, reposition the mask layer *beneath* the pattern layer.

3. Use the workspace switcher to display the **History and Layers** workspace (created in Chapter 1).

4. Point to the **horizontal line** between the STAMPS and Stamps layers, press and hold **[Alt]** (Win) or **[option]** (Mac), then click, as shown in Figure 6.

5. Release **[Alt]** (Win) or **[option]** (Mac).

   The clipping mask is created. The stamps background becomes visible through the text.

6. Save your work, then compare your image to Figure 7 and the Layers panel to Figure 8.

7. Restore the **Essentials** workspace.

You created a clipping mask using the STAMPS and Stamps layers. This effect lets you use the imagery in one layer as the fill for an object in another layer.

Lesson 1   Use a Clipping Group as a Mask

USE PEN TOOLS TO CREATE
AND MODIFY A PATH

What You'll Do

In this lesson, you'll create and name a path, expand the path to give it a wider, more curved appearance, then fill it with the foreground color.

Using Pen and Shape Tools

You have seen how you can use a clipping mask to create a mask effect. You can also create a path to serve as a mask by using any of the shape tools—the Pen tool, the Freeform Pen tool, or the Magnetic Pen tool. You can modify a path using any of the following Pen and Path Selection tools: the Add Anchor Point tool, Delete Anchor Point tool, Convert Point tool, Direct Selection tool, and the Path Selection tool. Table 2 describes some of these tools and their functions. When you select a pen tool, you can choose to create a shape layer or a path by choosing the appropriate option on the options bar.

Creating a Path

Unlike temporary selections, paths you create are saved with the image they were created in and stored on the Paths panel. Although you can't print paths unless they are filled or stroked, you can always display a path and make modifications to it. You can create a path based on an existing object, or you can create your own shape

with a pen tool. To create a closed path, you must position the pointer on top of the first anchor point. A small circle appears next to the pointer, indicating that the path will be closed when the pointer is clicked. Figure 9 shows an image of a young woman and the Paths panel containing four paths. The active path (Starfish 1) displays the starfish in the lower-right corner. Like the Layers panel, each path thumbnail displays a representation of its path. You can click a thumbnail on the Paths panel to see a specific path. The way that you create a path depends on the tool you choose to work with. The Pen tool requires that you click using the pointer each time you want to add a smooth (curved) or corner anchor point, whereas the Freeform Pen tool only requires you to click once to begin creating the path, and places the anchor points for you as you drag the pointer.

Modifying a Path

After you establish a path, you can modify it and convert it into a selection. For example, you can add more curves to an existing

Using Clipping Masks, Paths, & Shapes

path, widen it, or fill a path with the foreground color. Before you can modify an unselected path, you must select it with the Direct Selection tool. When you do so, you can manipulate its individual anchor points without affecting the entire path. Moving an anchor point automatically forces the two line segments on either side of the anchor point to shrink or grow, depending on which direction you move the anchor point. You can also click individual line segments and move them to new locations. If you are working with a curved path, you can shorten or elongate the direction handles associated with each smooth point to adjust the amount of curve or length of the corresponding line segment.

Other methods for modifying a path include adding anchor points, deleting anchor points, and converting corner anchor points into smooth anchor points, or vice versa. Adding anchor points splits an existing line segment into two, giving you more sides to your object. Deleting an anchor point does the reverse. Deleting anchor points is helpful when you have a bumpy path that is the result of too many anchors. Converting corner points into smooth points can give your drawing a softer appearance; converting smooth points into corner points can give your drawing a sharper appearance.

QUICKTIP
Each time you click and drag using the Add Anchor pointer, you are adding smooth anchor points. You use two direction handles attached to each anchor point to control the length, shape, and slope of the curved segment.

QUICKTIP
You can press [Alt] (Win) or [option] (Mac) while you click a path thumbnail to view the path and select it at the same time.

FIGURE 9
Multiple paths for the same image

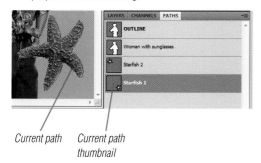

Current path   Current path
thumbnail

TABLE 2: Pen Tools

tool	button	use
Pen tool		Creates curved or straight line segments, connected by anchor points.
Freeform Pen tool		Creates unique shapes by placing anchor points at each change of direction.
Magnetic Pen tool	☑ Magnetic	Selecting the Magnetic check box on the options bar lets the Freeform Pen tool find an object's edge.
Add Anchor Point tool		Adds an anchor point to an existing path or shape.
Delete Anchor Point tool		Removes an anchor point from an existing path or shape.
Convert Point tool		Converts a smooth point to a corner point and a corner point to a smooth point.

Create a path

1. Click the **Indicates layer visibility button** 👁 on the STAMPS layer on the Layers panel so that it is no longer visible.

2. Click the **Mailbox layer** on the Layers panel.

   Hiding layers makes it easier to work on a specific area of the image.

3. Click the **Freeform Pen tool** ✒ on the Tools panel.

4. Click the **Paths button** 🔲 on the options bar (if it is not already selected).

5. Click the **Geometry options list arrow** on the options bar, then adjust the settings so that your entire options bar matches Figure 10.

6. Use the **Freeform Pen tool pointer** ✒ to trace *the vertical and horizontal posts* that hold the mailbox.

7. Click when you reach the starting point and the small 'O' appears in the pointer.

8. Click the **Paths panel tab** PATHS.

9. Double-click the **Work Path layer** on the Paths panel.

10. Type **Post path** in the Name text box.

11. Click **OK**, then compare your path and Paths panel to Figure 11.

You created a path using the Freeform Pen tool, then named the path in the Paths panel.

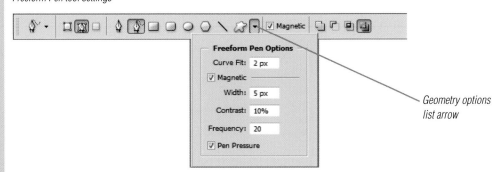

FIGURE 10
Freeform Pen tool settings

Geometry options list arrow

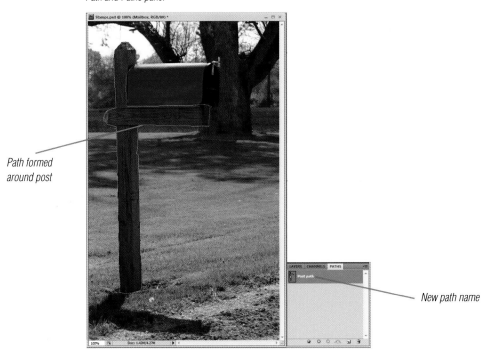

FIGURE 11
Path and Paths panel

Path formed around post

New path name

FIGURE 12
Points added to path

FIGURE 13
Fill Path dialog box

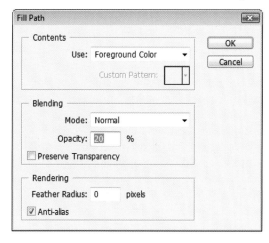

FIGURE 14
Modified path

Modify a path

1. Zoom into the mailbox so the zoom factor is **200%**, then click the **Add Anchor Point tool** ◊⁺ on the Tools panel.

2. Click a **point near the curve at the top of the mailbox**, then drag a **handle** so the curve conforms to the left side of the mailbox, using Figure 12 as a guide.

   As you drag the new anchor points, direction handles appear, indicating that you have added smooth points instead of corner points. You can drag any of these points so they conform to the shape you want for the path.

3. Zoom out to the 100% magnification, then click the **Eyedropper tool** ✐ on the Tools panel.

4. Click the **mailbox** to sample its color.

5. Click the **Paths list arrow** ▾≣ on the Paths panel, click **Fill Path**, modify the settings in the Fill Path dialog box using Figure 13 as a guide, then click **OK**.

   TIP   The Mailbox layer on the Layers panel must be selected or the Fill Path option on the Paths panel will not be available.

6. Deselect the path by clicking a blank area of the Paths panel.

7. Save your work, then compare your image to Figure 14.

You modified an existing path, then filled it with a color from a color existing in the image.

WORK WITH SHAPES

What You'll Do

In this lesson, you'll create two shapes, then modify and add a style to a shape layer.

Using Shape Tools

You might find that the imagery you are working with is not enough, and you need to create your own shapes. There are six shape tools on the Tools panel for creating shapes. A shape can occupy its own layer, called a **shape layer**. When you select a shape or pen tool, three buttons appear on the options bar to let you specify whether you want your shape to be on a new or existing shape layer, be a new work path, or be rasterized and filled with a color. Shapes and paths contain **vector data**, meaning that they will not lose their crisp appearance if resized or reshaped. You can create a rasterized shape using the Fill pixels button, but you cannot resize or reshape the rasterized shape.

Creating Rasterized Shapes

You cannot create a rasterized shape on a vector-based layer, such as a type or shape layer. So, to create a rasterized shape, you must first select or create a non-vector-based layer, select the shape you desire, then click the Fill pixels button on the options bar. You can change the blending mode to alter how the shape affects existing pixels in the image. You can change the opacity setting to make the shape more transparent or opaque. You can use the anti-aliasing option to blend the pixels on the shape's edge with the surrounding pixels. If you want to make changes to the content of a shape's blending mode, opacity, and anti-aliasing, you must make these changes *before* creating the rasterized shape; since the rasterization process converts the detail of the shape to an object layer. After you rasterize the shape, you can make changes to blending mode and opacity to the *layer* containing the shape.

Creating Shapes

A path and a shape are essentially the same, in that you edit them using the same tools. For example, you can modify a path and a shape using the Direct Selection tool. When selected, the anchor points are white or hollow, and can then be moved to alter the appearance of the shape or path. When you click a shape or

Using Clipping Masks, Paths, & Shapes

path with the Path Selection tool, the anchor points become solid. In this case, the entire path is selected, and the individual components cannot be moved: the path or shape is moved as a single unit. A shape can be created on its own layer and can be filled with a color. Multiple shapes can also be added to a single layer, and you can specify how overlapping shapes interact.

(Painting tools are used when individual pixels are edited, such as by changing a pixel's color on a rasterized shape.)

Embellishing Shapes

You can apply other features such as the Drop Shadow and the Bevel and Emboss style, or filters, to shapes. Figure 15 shows the Layers panel of an image containing two layer shapes. The top layer (in Yellow) has the Bevel and Emboss style applied to it.

QUICKTIP

When you first create a shape, it is automatically filled with the current foreground color.

FIGURE 15
Shape layers on Layers panel

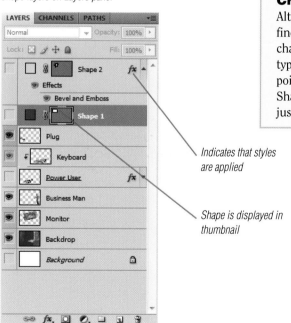

Indicates that styles are applied

Shape is displayed in thumbnail

Creating custom shapes

Although Photoshop comes with many interesting custom shapes, you still may not find the one you're looking for. If that's the case, consider creating your own using characters found within any symbol fonts installed on your computer. First create a type layer using the symbol of your choosing, then click Layer on the Application bar, point to Type, and click the Convert to Shape command. Use the Define Custom Shape command on the Edit menu to create your own custom shape. The shape you just created now appears at the bottom of the panel containing custom shapes.

Create a shape

1. Click the **Rectangle tool**  on the Tools panel.

2. Click the **Shape layers button** on the options bar.

3. Make sure the Style picker list arrow displays the Default Style (None) Style: □.

4. Display the rulers in pixels and display the guides.

5. Verify that the **Mailbox layer** is active.

6. Drag the **Marquee pointer** + from approximately **0 X/510 Y** to **555 X/685 Y** using the guides to draw the rectangle. Compare your Paths panel to Figure 16.

7. Compare your image to Figure 17.

   The shape is added to the image, and the Rectangle tool is still active.

You created a new shape layer, using the Rectangle tool. The new shape was created on its own layer.

FIGURE 16
Path created by shape

FIGURE 17
Shape in image

New shape

Export a path into another program

As a designer, you might find yourself working with other programs, such as Adobe Illustrator, or QuarkXPress. Many of the techniques you have learned, such as working with paths, can be used in all these programs. For example, you can create a path in Photoshop, then export it to another program. Before you can export a path, it must be created and named. To export the path, click File on the Application bar, point to Export, then click Paths to Illustrator (Win) or Write to Illustrator (Mac). The Paths list arrow (Win) or Write list arrow (Mac) in the Export Paths dialog box lets you determine which paths are exported. You can export all paths or one specific path. After you choose the path(s) that you want to export, choose a name and location for the path, then click Save.

FIGURE 18

Additional shape in image

FIGURE 19

Styles added to custom shape

New shape

*Custom shape with Drop Shadow
and Bevel and Emboss styles*

FIGURE 20

Style added to shape

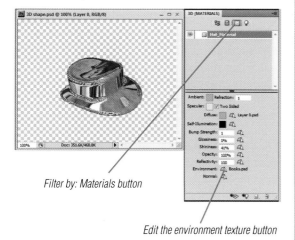

Filter by: Materials button

Edit the environment texture button

Creating realistic 3D shapes

Using the Advanced 3D workspace and your knowledge of shapes, you can create and rotate realistic 3D shapes that show naturalistic reflection. To do this, create an RGB file, then fill the layer with any pattern. Display the Advanced 3D workspace, click the 3D menu on the Application bar, point to New Shape from Layer, then click one of the shapes listed, such as the Hat. The image in the layer (the fill pattern) is wrapped around the 3D shape. Click the 3D Rotate tool in the Tools panel, position the pointer over the shape, then drag the shape to reposition it. Take note of the lifelike shadows and highlights as you reposition the shape. Using the 3D panel, you can treat the contents of a graphics file as a texture and wrap it around a shape, as shown in Figure 20. To do this, click the Filter By: Materials button in the 3D panel, click the Edit the environment texture button, then click Load Texture. Click a file, then click Open. The original layer will automatically be converted into a Smart Object. (You may see a warning box if your video card does not meet the requirements necessary for 3D rendering.)

Create and modify a custom shape

1. Click the **Layers panel tab** LAYERS , then select and make the **Button layer** visible.

2. Click the **Custom Shape tool button** on the options bar.

3. Click the **Click to open Custom Shape picker list arrow** → ˙ , then double-click **Envelope 2** (the first shape from the right in the second row).

4. Drag the **Marquee pointer** + over the flat surface of the button from approximately **390 X/470 Y** to **510 X/505 Y**.

5. Display the **Swatches panel**, click **white swatch** on the Swatches panel, then click **OK** to close the Pick a solid color dialog box. Compare your image to Figure 18.

6. Verify that the **Shape 2 mask thumbnail** on the Layers panel is selected.

7. Click the **Add a layer style button** *fx.* on the Layers panel.

8. Click the **Drop Shadow**, click **Bevel and Emboss**, then click **OK** to accept the current settings.

9. Save your work, turn off the guides and rulers, then compare your image to Figure 19.

You created an additional shape layer, changed the color of the shape, then applied a style to the shape.

CONVERT PATHS AND SELECTIONS

What You'll Do

In this lesson, you'll convert a selection into a path, then apply a stroke to the path.

Converting a Selection into a Path

You can convert a selection into a path so that you can take advantage of clipping paths and other path features, using a button on the Paths panel. First, create your selection using any technique you prefer, such as the Magic Wand tool, lasso tools, or marquee tools. After the marquee surrounds the selection, press and hold

Customizing print options

Because a monitor is an RGB device and a printer uses the CMYK model to print colors even a well-calibrated monitor will never match the colors of your printer. Therefore, professional printers use standardized color systems such as Pantone or Toyo.

In the course of working with an image, you may need to print a hard copy. In order to get the output you want, you can set options in the Page Setup dialog box. To open this dialog box, click File on the Application bar, then click Page Setup. The relationship of the length to the width of the printed page is called **orientation**. A printed page with the dimensions 8½" W × 11" L is called **portrait orientation**. A printed page with dimensions 11" W × 8 ½" L is called **landscape orientation**.

For additional printing options, click File on the Application bar, click Print, then in the Print dialog box click the Output from the list arrow at the top of the dialog box (that has Color Management as the default selection). Here you can gain increased control over the way your image prints. For example, pages printed for commercial uses might often need to be trimmed after they are printed. The trim guidelines are called **crop marks**. These marks can be printed at the corners, center of each edge, or both. You can select the Corner Crop Marks check box and/or Center Crop Marks check box to print these marks on your image.

[Alt] (Win) or [option] (Mac), then click the Make work path from selection button on the Paths panel, as shown in Figure 21.

Converting a Path into a Selection

You also can convert a path into a selection. You can do this by selecting a path on the Paths panel, then clicking the Load path as a selection button on the Paths panel.

Choosing the Right Method

Are you totally confused about which method to use to make selections? You might have felt equally at sea after learning about all your paint tool choices. Well, as with painting, you need to experiment to find the method that works best for you. As you gain experience with Photoshop techniques, your comfort level—and personal confidence—will grow, and you'll learn which methods are *right for you*.

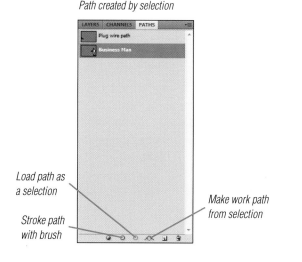

Load path as
a selection

Stroke path
with brush

Make work path
from selection

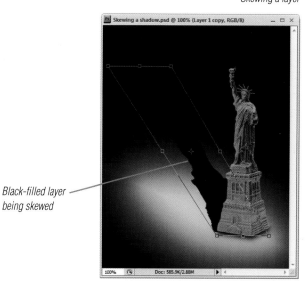

Black-filled layer
being skewed

Using the Transform command to create a shadow

You've already experienced using the Transform command to change the existing shape of an object or type. You can also use this command to simulate a shadow. To do so, you simply duplicate a layer, then fill the copy of the layer with black by changing the background color to black, then press [X] to swap foreground and background colors. Make the black copy the active layer, then use the Transform command to skew the object. Figure 22 shows an example of this technique.

Convert a selection into a path

1. Display the **STAMPS layer** and the **Stamps layer**.

2. Click the **STAMPS layer** on the Layers panel.

3. Click the **Magic Wand tool** ✺ on the Tools panel, and verify that the Contiguous checkbox is selected.

4. Click anywhere in the **burgundy color** behind the word STAMPS.

5. If necessary, click the **Add to selection button** 🔲 on the options bar, click the open area in the **A,** click the open area in the letter **P,** click **Select** on the Application bar, then click **Inverse.** Compare your image to Figure 23.

6. Click the **Paths panel tab** PATHS.

7. Press and hold **[Alt]** (Win) or **[option]** (Mac), click the **Make work path from selection button** ⌢ on the Paths panel, then release **[Alt]** (Win) or **[option]** (Mac).

   TIP Pressing [Alt] (Win) or [option] (Mac) causes the Make Work Path dialog box to open. You can use this to change the Tolerance setting. If you don't press and hold this key, the current tolerance setting is used.

8. Type **1.0** in the Tolerance text box, then click **OK**.

9. Double-click **Work Path** on the Paths panel.

10. Type **Stamps path** in the Name text box of the Save Path dialog box, then click **OK**. Compare your Paths panel to Figure 24.

You created a selection using the Magic Wand tool, then converted it into a path using the Make work path from selection button on the Paths panel.

FIGURE 23
Selection in image

Selected object

FIGURE 24
Selection converted into path

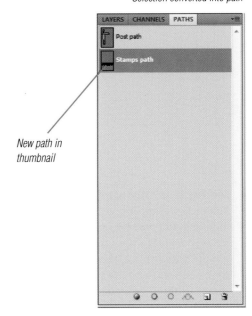

New path in thumbnail

FIGURE 25
Stroked path

New stroked path in thumbnail

FIGURE 26
Layers panel

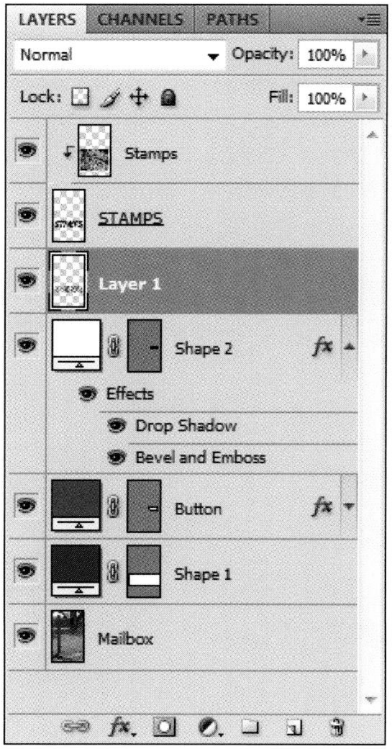

FIGURE 27
Completed image

Stroke a path

1. Click the **Eyedropper tool** on the Tools panel.

2. Click the **black swatch** on the Swatches panel.

3. Activate the **Shape 2 layer** on the Layers panel, then create a new layer above it.

4. Click the **Stamps path** on the Paths panel, then click **Brush tool** on the Tools panel, and select the **Hard Round 9 pixels brush size** with 100% opacity (if necessary).

   TIP You can select a path as a *selection* (rather than as a path) by holding [Ctrl] (Win) or ⌘ (Mac) while clicking the name of the path. When you do this, marching ants surround the path, which indicate that it's a *selection*.

5. Click the **Paths list arrow** on the Paths panel, click **Stroke Path**, click the **Tool list arrow** in the Stroke Path dialog box, click **Brush** (if necessary), then click **OK**.

6. Click anywhere on the **Paths panel** to deselect the path, then compare your panel to Figure 25.

7. Click the **Layers panel tab** LAYERS, then compare your Layers panel to Figure 26.

8. Save your work, then compare your image to Figure 27.

9. Close the file and exit Photoshop.

You stroked a path, using a color from the Swatches panel and a command from the Paths list arrow.

Power User Shortcuts

Key: Menu items are indicated by ➤ between the menu name and its command. Blue bold letters are shortcuts for selecting tools on the Tools panel.

to do this:	use this method:
Add an anchor point	[icon]
Change perspective	Edit ➤Transform ➤Perspective
Convert a selection into a path	[icon]
Convert a point	[icon]
Create a clipping group	Press and hold [Alt] (Win) or [option] (Mac), position pointer between layers, then click using [icon]
Create a custom shape	[icon] or [Shift] **U**
Create a line	[icon] or [Shift] **U**
Create a new shape layer	[icon]
Create a new work path	[icon]
Create a polygon	[icon] or [Shift] **U**
Create a rectangle	[icon] or [Shift] **U**
Create a rounded rectangle	[icon] or [Shift] **U**
Create an ellipse	[icon] or [Shift] **U**
Delete an anchor point	[icon]

to do this:	use this method:
Deselect a path	Click an empty space on Paths panel
Distort a selection	Edit ➤ Transform ➤Distort
Draw freeform shapes	[icon] or [Shift] **P**
Draw paths	[icon] or [Shift] **P**
Draw along the object's edge	Click the Magnetic check box
Export a path	File ➤ Export ➤ Paths to Illustrator
Fill a layer with background color	[Ctrl][Shift][Backspace] (Win) or [shift][$\mathcal{H}$][delete] (Mac)
Flip a selection	Edit ➤ Transform ➤ Flip Horizontal or Flip Vertical
Load path as a selection	[icon]
Repeat last transform command	Edit ➤ Transform ➤ Again or [Shift][Ctrl][T] (Win) or [shift][$\mathcal{H}$][T] (Mac)
Rotate a selection	Edit ➤Transform ➤ Rotate
Scale a selection	Edit ➤ Transform ➤ Scale
Skew a selection	Edit ➤ Transform ➤ Skew
Stroke a path	[icon]

Use a clipping group as a mask.

1. Open PS 11-2.psd from the drive and folder where you store your Data Files, then save it as **Mathematics**. (Substitute a font available on your computer for the Mathematics type layer, if necessary. The font used in the sample is a 72 pt Arial.)
2. Rasterize the Mathematics type layer, then click the Move tool on the Tools panel.
3. Transform the rasterized type layer by distorting it, using Figure 28 as a guide.
4. Drag the Mathematics layer beneath the Symbols layer on the Layers panel.
5. Create a clipping group with the Mathematics and Symbols layers.
6. Apply the Bevel and Emboss style (using the existing settings) to the Mathematics layer.
7. Save your work.

Use pen tools to create and modify a path.

1. Make the Man layer active.
2. Click the Freeform Pen tool on the Tools panel.
3. Click the Paths button and verify that the Magnetic check box is selected.
4. Open the Paths panel.
5. Trace the figure, *not the shadow*.
6. Change the name of the Work Path to **Figure path**.
7. Use the Eyedropper tool on the Tools panel to sample Pure Yellow Green using the Swatches panel.
8. Fill the path with the Foreground Color using 100% opacity.

9. Deselect the Figure path on the Paths panel.
10. Save your work.

Work with shapes.

1. Activate the Layers panel, then make the Megaphone layer active.
2. Use the Eyedropper tool to sample the RGB Red swatch on the Swatches panel.
3. Click the Custom Shape tool on the Tools panel.
4. Click the Shape layers button on the options bar.
5. Open the Custom Shape picker on the options bar, then select the Scissors 2 custom shape.
6. Create the shape from 200 X/50 Y to 330 X/220 Y.
7. Apply a Bevel and Emboss style (using the existing settings) to the Shape 1 layer.
8. Save your work.

Convert paths and selections.

1. Make the Megaphone layer active.
2. Hide the Backdrop, Mathematics, and Shape 1 layers.
3. Use the Magnetic Lasso tool to select the megaphone. (*Hint*: Try using a 0-pixel Feather, a 5-pixel Width, and 10% Edge Contrast.)

4. Display the Paths panel, then make a path from the selection.
5. Change the name of the Work Path to **Megaphone path**.
6. Use the Eyedropper tool to sample the Dark Violet Magenta swatch on the Swatches panel, then fill the megaphone path with this color.
7. Deselect the path, display the Layers panel, then show all layers.
8. Clear the guides, hide the rulers, then adjust the contrast of the Symbols layer to +42.
9. Apply a Radial Blur filter, using the Spin method with Good quality and the Amount = 10, to the Backdrop layer.
10. Apply a 100% Spherize filter (Distort Filter) to the Backdrop layer.
11. Save your work, then compare your image to Figure 28.

FIGURE 28
Completed Skills Review

A cable manufacturer wants to improve its lackluster image—especially after a scandal that occurred earlier in the year. The company has hired you to create a dynamic image of one of its bestselling products, which they plan to use in an image advertising campaign. You have been provided with a picture of the product, and your job is to create a more exciting image suitable for print ads.

1. Open PS 11-3.psd, then save it as **Power Plug**.
2. Duplicate the Power Plug layer.
3. Add a type layer (using any font available on your computer) that says Power Plug. (In the sample, a 146.82 pt Cooper font is used.)
4. Rasterize the type layer.
5. Transform the rasterized type layer, using a method of your choosing.
6. Apply any layer styles. (In the sample, a contoured Bevel and Emboss style and Drop Shadow is applied.)
7. Move the rasterized layer below the Power Plug copy layer, then create a clipping mask.
8. Adjust the Saturation of the Power Plug copy layer to +90.

9. Create an adjustment layer that changes the Yellow/Blue Color Balance of the Power Plug copy layer to +65.
10. Create an adjustment layer that changes the Color Balance of the (original) Power Plug layer so that the text is more visible. (In the sample, the color levels of the midtones are −80, +80, −80.)
11. Modify the Opacity of the Power Plug layer to 85%.
12. Save your work, then compare your image to the sample in Figure 29.

FIGURE 29
Sample Project Builder 1

Using Clipping Masks, Paths, & Shapes

The National Initiative to Promote Reading has asked you to come up with a preliminary design for their upcoming season. They have provided you with an initial image you can use, as well as the promise of a fat paycheck if you can finish the project within the day. You can use any additional imagery to complete this task.

1. Open PS 11-4.psd, then save it as **Booklovers**.
2. Locate at least one piece of appropriate artwork—either on your computer, in a royalty-free collection, or from scanned images—that you can use in this image.
3. Use any appropriate methods to select imagery from the artwork.
4. After the selections have been made, copy them into Booklovers.
5. Transform any imagery (if necessary).
6. Use your skills to create at least two paths in the image.
7. Add any special effects to a layer, such as a style or a vignette.
8. Add descriptive type to the image, using the font and wording of your choice. (In the sample, an 80 pt Onyx font is used.) You can rasterize the type and create a mask (if necessary).
9. Make any color adjustments, or add filters, (if necessary).
10. Save your work, then compare your image to the sample in Figure 30.

FIGURE 30

Sample Project Builder 2

Using Clipping Masks, Paths, & Shapes

You can pick up some great design tips and tricks from the Internet. Because you are relatively new to using Photoshop shapes, you decide to see what information you can find about shapes on the Web. Your goal is not only to increase your knowledge of shapes and paths, but to create attractive artwork.

1. Connect to the Internet and use your browser to find information about using paths and shapes in Photoshop. (Make a record of the site you found so you can use it for future reference, if necessary.)

2. Create a new Photoshop image, using the dimensions of your choice, then save it as **Shape Experimentation**.

3. Use paths and shapes to create an attractive image.

4. Create an attractive background, using any of your Photoshop skills.

5. Create at least two paths, using any shapes you want.

6. Add any special effects to the paths.

7. Make any color adjustments, or add filters, (if necessary).

8. If you want, add a type layer, using any fonts available on your computer. (In the sample, an Caslon Pro font of varying size is used.)

9. Save your work, then compare your image to the sample in Figure 31.

FIGURE 31
Sample Design Project

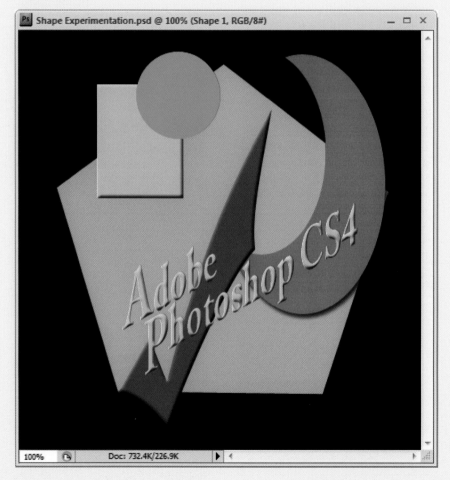

A Photoshop design contest, sponsored by a high-powered advertising agency, has you motivated. You have decided to submit the winning entry. Your entry must be completely original, and can use any imagery available to you.

1. Start Photoshop and create an image with any dimensions you want.
2. Save this file as **Contest Winner**.
3. Locate several pieces of artwork—either on your computer, in a royalty-free collection, or from scanned images. Although the images can show anything, remember that you want to show positive imagery so that the judges will select it.
4. Select imagery from the artwork and move it into Contest Winner.
5. Use your knowledge of shapes and paths to create interesting effects.
6. Add text to the image, and use any transform commands to enhance the text.
7. Add any filter effects if you decide they will make your image more dramatic. (In the sample, the Spatter filter was applied to the Computer layer.)
8. Make any color adjustments (if necessary).
9. Add type in any font available on your computer. (A 60 pt Britannic Bold font is shown in the sample. The following styles have been applied: Drop Shadow and Bevel and Emboss.)

10. Save your work, then compare your image to the sample in Figure 32.

FIGURE 32
Sample Portfolio Project

12

TRANSFORMING
TYPE

1. Modify type using a bounding box

2. Create warped type with a unique shape

3. Screen back type with imagery

4. Create a faded type effect

Working with Type

Type is usually not the primary focus of a Photoshop image, but it can be an important element when conveying a message. You have already learned how to create type and to embellish it using styles, such as the Drop Shadow and the Bevel and Emboss styles, and filters, such as the Twirl and Wind filters. You can further enhance type using techniques such as transforming or warping.

Transforming and Warping Type

When you want to modify text in an image, you can simply select the type layer, select the Horizontal Type tool, then make changes using the options bar. You can also modify type by dragging the handles on the type's bounding box. A **bounding box** (or transform controls box) is a rectangle that surrounds type and contains handles that are used to change the dimensions. Many of the Photoshop features that can be used to modify images can also be used to modify type layers. For example, type can be modified using all the transform commands on the Edit menu except Perspective and Distort. For more stylized type, you can use the Create warped text button to create exciting shapes by changing the dimensions. **Warping** makes it possible to distort type so that it conforms to a shape. Some of the distortions available through the warp feature are Arc, Arch, Bulge, Flag, Fish, and Twist. You do not need to rasterize type to use the warp text feature, so you can edit the type as necessary after you have warped it.

QUICKTIP

If you want to use the Perspective or Distort commands, or you want to apply a filter to type or create a clipping mask, you must first rasterize the type.

Using Type to Create Special Effects

In addition to adding styles to type, you can also create effects with your type and the imagery within your image. One popular effect is **fading type**, where the type appears to originate in darkness and then gradually gets brighter, or vice versa. You can use the Gradient tool to fade type. The **screening back** effect displays imagery through the layer that contains type. One way to create the screened back effect is to convert a type layer into a shape layer, add a mask, and then adjust the levels of the shape layer. As with graphic objects, adding special effects to type changes the mood, style, and message of the content. You'll probably want to experiment with all your choices to strike just the right note for a particular project.

Tools You'll Use

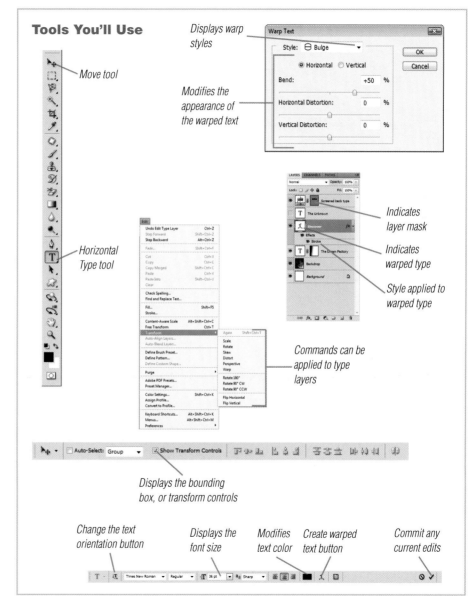

Displays warp styles

Modifies the appearance of the warped text

Move tool

Horizontal Type tool

Indicates layer mask

Indicates warped type

Style applied to warped type

Commands can be applied to type layers

Displays the bounding box, or transform controls

Change the text orientation button

Displays the font size

Modifies text color

Create warped text button

Commit any current edits

12-3

MODIFY TYPE USING
A BOUNDING BOX

What You'll Do

In this lesson, you'll change the dimensions of type using a bounding box.

Selecting the Bounding Box

A bounding box, such as the one shown in Figure 1, is a tool you can use to control the size and proportions of existing type. You can display the bounding box by clicking the Move tool on the Tools panel, then selecting the Show Transform Controls check box on the options bar. After the transform controls (also known as the bounding box) feature is turned on, it will appear around type whenever a type layer is selected. As soon as you

click a handle on the bounding box, the dotted lines of the box become solid, as shown in Figure 2. At the center of the bounding box (by default) is the **reference point**, the location from which distortions and transformations are measured.

FIGURE 1
Bounding box around type

Handle

Bounding box

Reference point

FIGURE 2
Resizing the bounding box

Preparing to resize the bounding box

Outline becomes solid when clicked

Changing the Bounding Box

When the bounding box around type is selected, the options bar displays additional tools for transforming type. Table 1 describes the bounding box options in detail. You can change the size of the bounding box by placing the pointer over a handle. When you do this, the pointer changes to reflect the direction in which you can pull the box. When you resize a bounding box, the type within it reflows to conform to its new shape. As you can see from the table, some of these tools are buttons and some are text boxes.

QUICKTIP
You can use the text boxes on the Transform Controls option bar to make entries or to visually inspect the results of your changes.

TABLE 1: Transform Control Tools

tool	button	use
Reference point location button		The black dot determines the location of the reference point. Change the reference point by clicking any white dot on the button.
Set horizontal position of reference point text box	X: 249.1 px	Allows you to reassign the horizontal location of the reference point.
Use relative positioning for reference point button	△	Determines the point you want used as a reference.
Set vertical position of reference point text box	Y: 194.8 px	Allows you to reassign the vertical location of the reference point.
Set horizontal scale text box	W: 80%	Determines the percentage of left-to-right scaling.
Maintain aspect ratio button		Keeps the current proportions of the contents within the bounding box.
Set vertical scale text box	H: 156.3%	Determines the percentage of top-to-bottom scaling.
Set rotation text box	△ 0.0 °	Determines the angle the bounding box will be rotated.
Set horizontal skew text box	H: 0.0 °	Determines the angle of horizontal distortion.
Set vertical skew text box	V: 0.0 °	Determines the angle of vertical distortion.
Switch between free transform and warp modes button		Toggles between manual entry of scaling and warp styles.
Cancel transform (Esc) button	⊘	Returns to the image without carrying out transformations.
Commit transform (Return) button	✓	Returns to the image after carrying out transformations.

Display a bounding box

1. Open **PS 12-1.psd** from the drive and folder where you store your Data Files, update the text layers as needed, then save the file as **Happy Hound**.

   TIP The fonts in this file are various point sizes of Times New Roman and Arial. Please substitute another font if these are not available on your computer.

2. Display the rulers in pixels and display the **Typography workspace**.

3. Click the **Happy Hound layer** on the Layers panel.

4. Click the **Move tool** ⊹ on the Tools panel (if it is not already selected).

5. Click the **Show Transform Controls check box** on the options bar. Compare your image to Figure 3.

   Transform control handles surround the bounding box. When you place the pointer on or near a handle, you can transform the shape of a bounding box. Table 2 describes the pointers you can use to transform a bounding box.

You displayed the bounding box of a text selection to make it easier to adjust the size and shape of the layer contents. Resizing a bounding box is the easiest way to change the appearance of an object or type layer.

FIGURE 3
Displayed bounding box

Selected check box indicates that bounding box is displayed

Move tool selected

Bounding box surrounds active type layer

TABLE 2: Transform Pointers

pointer	use to
↗	Resize bounding box; drag upper-right and lower-left handles.
↖	Resize bounding box; drag upper-left and lower-right handles.
↔	Resize bounding box; drag middle-left and middle-right handles.
↕	Resize bounding box; drag upper-center and lower-center handles.
↵	Rotate bounding box; appears below the lower-right handle.
↳	Rotate bounding box; appears below the lower-left handle.
↰	Rotate bounding box; appears above the upper-right handle.
↱	Rotate bounding box; appears above the upper-left handle.
↻	Rotate bounding box; appears to the left of the middle-left handle.
↘	Rotate bounding box; appears below the lower-center handle.
▷	Skew type. Press and hold [Ctrl] (Win) or ⌘ (Mac) while dragging a handle.

FIGURE 4
Modified bounding box

Enlarged type and
bounding box

FIGURE 5
Bounding box before modification

Bounding box (and
text it contains takes
up less room)

FIGURE 6
Transform settings

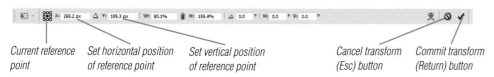

Current reference
point

Set horizontal position
of reference point

Set vertical position
of reference point

Cancel transform
(Esc) button

Commit transform
(Return) button

Modify type using a bounding box

1. Drag the **top-center handle** ↕ with the Resizing pointer until you see that the Set vertical position of reference point text box (Y:) displays approximately **195 px**. Compare your bounding box to Figure 4.

   > TIP When you begin dragging the resizing handles, the option bar changes to display the bounding box transform tools. You can also type values in these text boxes.

2. Drag the **right-center handle** ↔ until the Set horizontal scale text box (W:) displays approximately **80%**.

3. Compare your bounding box to Figure 5 and your options bar to Figure 6. Your settings might differ.

   > TIP You can use the Transform commands (Rotate, Scale, Skew, Distort, Perspective, and Warp) with any of the resizing pointers to distort a bounding box using an angle other than 90°.

4. Click the **Commit transform (Return) button** ✔ on the options bar.

5. Save your work.

Using the bounding box, you modified the type by scaling disproportionately.

DESIGNTIP **Thinking out side the (bounding) box**

You're probably used to thinking in terms of font size: 10pt, 12pt, etc. Once you understand how to resize type using the bounding box, you'll realize that the rigid font size you apply from a list arrow is just a starting point. You really can have *any size* font you want!

CREATE WARPED TYPE
WITH A UNIQUE SHAPE

What You'll Do

In this lesson, you'll warp text, then enhance the text with color and a layer style.

Warping Type

Have you ever wondered how designers create those ultra-cool wavy lines of text? They're probably using the Create warped text feature, which gives you unlimited freedom to create unique text shapes. You can distort a type layer beyond the limits of stretching a bounding box by using the Create warped text feature. You can choose from 15 warped text styles. These styles are shown in Figure 7. You can warp type horizontally or vertically.

FIGURE 7
Warp text styles

Default setting —— None

☐ Arc
☐ Arc Lower
☐ Arc Upper

☒ Arch
☐ Bulge
☐ Shell Lower
☐ Shell Upper

☒ Flag
☒ Wave
☐ Fish
☐ Rise

☒ Fisheye
☐ Inflate
☒ Squeeze
☒ Twist

Adding Panache to Warped Text

After you select a warp text style, you can further modify the type using the Bend, Horizontal Distortion, and Vertical Distortion sliders in the Warp Text dialog box. These settings and what they do are described in Table 3. A sample of warped text is shown in Figure 8. You adjust the warped style by using the sliders shown in Figure 9.

QUICKTIP

You cannot use the Distort and Perspective transform commands on non-rasterized type; however, you can achieve similar results by warping type.

Combining Your Skills

By this time, you've learned that many Photoshop features can be applied to more than one type of Photoshop object. The same is true for warped text. For example, after you warp text, you can apply a style to it, such as the Bevel and Emboss style, or a filter. You can also use the Stroke style to really make the text pop.

FIGURE 8
Sample of warped type

Bounding box surrounds warped type

FIGURE 9
Warp Text dialog box

Current style

Selects a new style

Options are displayed when style other than 'None' is selected

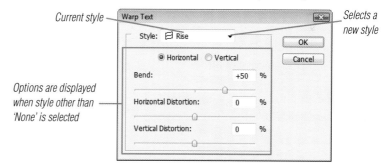

TABLE 3: Warped Type Settings

setting	use
Horizontal	Determines the left-to-right direction of the warp style.
Vertical	Determines the top-to-bottom direction of the warp style.
Bend	Determines which side of the type will be affected.
Horizontal Distortion	Determines if the left or right side of the type will be warped.
Vertical Distortion	Determines if the top or bottom of the type will be warped.

Create warped text

1. Click the **Gourmet Bones Edition layer** on the Layers panel.

2. Zoom into the image until the magnification factor is **100%**.

3. Double-click the **Gourmet Bones Edition layer thumbnail** T on the Layers panel.

4. Click the **Set the font size list arrow** on the options bar, then click **12 pt**.

5. Click the **Create warped text button** 飞 on the options bar.

6. Click the **Style list arrow** in the Warp Text dialog box, then click **Arc Upper**.

7. Verify that the **Horizontal option button** is selected.

8. Change the settings for the **Bend**, **Horizontal Distortion**, and **Vertical Distortion text boxes** so that they match those shown in Figure 10.

9. Click **OK** to close the Warp Text dialog box, commit any current edits, then compare your type to Figure 11.

10. Use the **Move tool** ⊕ on the Tools panel to drag or nudge the type so it is centered over the logo of the bones as shown in Figure 12.

> TIP You can also use the (keyboard) arrow keys to nudge objects when the Move tool is active.

You transformed existing type into a unique shape using the Create warped text button. This feature lets you make type a much more dynamic element in your designs.

FIGURE 10
Warp Text dialog box

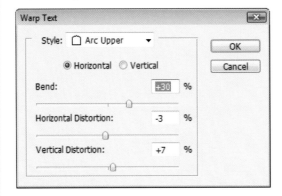

FIGURE 11
Warped type

FIGURE 12
Moved type

Selected warped type

FIGURE 13
Sampled area

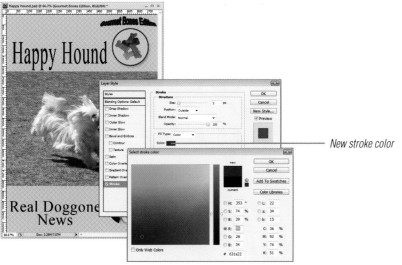

New stroke color

FIGURE 15
Layers panel

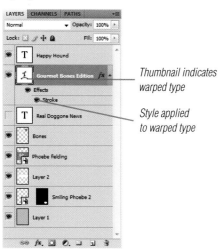

Thumbnail indicates
warped type

Style applied
to warped type

FIGURE 14
New color applied to warped type

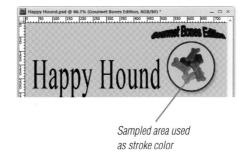

Sampled area used
as stroke color

1. Zoom out until the magnification level is at **66.7%**.

2. Click the **Add a layer style button** 𝑓𝑥. on the Layers panel, then move the Layer Style dialog box so the warped type is visible (if necessary).

3. Click **Stroke**.

4. Click the **Set color of stroke button** in the Layer Style dialog box.

5. Verify that the **Only Web Colors check box** is not selected, then click the image anywhere on the **maroon bone** (at approximately **650 X/130 Y**), as shown in Figure 13.

6. Click **OK** to close the Select stroke color dialog box.

7. In the Layer Style dialog box, make sure the Size is set to **3 px** and the Position is set to **Outside**, click **OK**, then turn off the bounding box display (if necessary).

8. Save your work, then compare your image to Figure 14 and the Layers panel to Figure 15.

You added a Stroke style to the warped text and changed the color of the stroke using a color already present in the image.

Lesson 2   Create Warped Type with a Unique Shape

LESSON 3

SCREEN BACK TYPE
WITH IMAGERY

What You'll Do

In this lesson, you'll convert type to a shape layer using the Convert to Shape command, then adjust the levels to create a screened back effect.

Screening Type

Using many of the techniques you already know, you can create the illusion that type appears to fade into the imagery below it. This is known as **screening back** or **screening** type. You can create a screened back effect in many ways. One method is to adjust the opacity of a type layer until you can see imagery behind it. Another method is to convert a type layer into a shape layer, which adds a vector mask, then adjust the levels of the shape layer until you achieve the look you desire. A **vector mask** makes a shape's edges appear neat and defined on a layer. As part of this screening back process, the type assumes the shape of its mask. Figure 16 shows a sample of screened back type. Notice that the layer imagery beneath the type layer is visible.

FIGURE 16
Screened back type

Image visible beneath screened back text

Screened back text

Creating the Screened Back Effect

Before converting a type layer, it's a good idea to duplicate the layer. That way, if you are not satisfied with the results, you can easily start from scratch with the original type layer. After the duplicate layer is created, you can convert it into a shape layer, using the Layer menu. After the layer is converted, make sure the original layer is hidden. Using the Levels setting in the Adjustments panel, you can increase or decrease the midtones and shadows levels, as shown in Figure 17, to create different effects in the screened back type.

Adding Finishing Touches

Adding effects to a layer can give your screened back type a more textured or three-dimensional look. For example, you can add the Bevel and Emboss style to a screened back shape layer, as shown in Figure 18. Here, the Bevel and Emboss style serves to accentuate the type. You can also add filter effects such as noise or lighting to make the text look more dramatic.

FIGURE 17
Levels setting in Adjustments panel

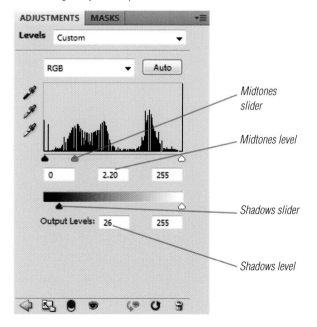

FIGURE 18
Screened back type with Bevel and Emboss style

Convert a type layer to a shape layer

1. Click the **Real Doggone News layer** on the Layers panel.

2. Click the **Layers panel list arrow** ▼≣.

3. Click **Duplicate Layer**.

   TIP When duplicating a layer, you have the option of keeping the duplicate in the current image, placing it in another image that is currently open, or in a new image, by clicking the Document list arrow in the Duplicate Layer dialog box, then clicking another filename or New.

4. Type **Screened back type** in the As text box, then click **OK**.

5. Click the **Indicates layer visibility button** 👁 on the Real Doggone News layer on the Layers panel, then compare your Layers panel to Figure 19.

6. Use the workspace switcher to display the **History and Layers workspace** (created in Chapter 1).

7. Click **Layer** on the Application bar, point to **Type**, then click **Convert to Shape**, as shown in Figure 20.

   The type layer is converted to a shape layer. Figure 21 shows the Layers panel (with the converted type layer state and vector mask thumbnail) and the History panel (with the Convert to Shape state).

In preparation for screening back type, you created a duplicate layer, then hid the original from view. You then converted the duplicate layer into a shape layer.

FIGURE 19
Duplicate layer

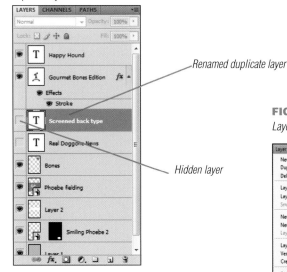

Renamed duplicate layer

Hidden layer

FIGURE 20
Layer menu

Converts a type layer to a shape layer

FIGURE 21
History and Layers panel

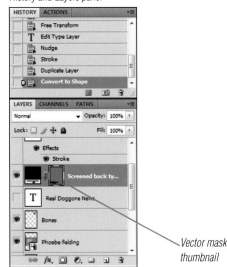

Vector mask thumbnail

FIGURE 22
Levels setting in Adjustments panel

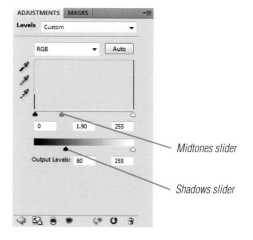

Midtones slider

Shadows slider

Adjust layer content

1. Click the **Levels button** 📈 on the Adjustments panel, then click the **This adjustment affects all the layers below (click to clip to layer) button** 🌑 .

2. Drag the **Input Levels midtones slider** to the left, until the middle Input Levels text box reads approximately **1.90**.

   The content of the layer is now less transparent.

3. Drag the **Output Levels shadows slider** to the right until the left Output Levels text box reads **80** as shown in Figure 22.

   The content of the layer now looks lighter.

4. Click the **Return to adjustment list button** 🔙 on the Adjustments panel.

5. Click **Layer 1** on the Layers panel.

6. Save your work, then compare your image to Figure 23.

7. Display the **Essentials workspace**.

You modified the midtones and shadows levels on the shape layer to make the text less transparent. You adjusted the Output Levels shadows slider to make the pixels that make up the text appear brighter.

FIGURE 23
Screened back type

Screened back layer

CREATE A FADED
TYPE EFFECT

What You'll Do

In this lesson, you'll use the Gradient tool to make text appear faded in one area and brighter in another. You'll also apply a lighting filter.

Creating a Fade Effect

In addition to being able to change the font, size, color, and shape of your text, you might want to create the illusion that type is fading away in order to add an element of mystery to your masterpiece. You can create this effect using a type layer, a layer mask, and the Gradient tool. You can apply this effect to part of a type layer, if you want the text to look as if it's fading in or out, or to the entire layer.

QUICKTIP

Type does not have to be rasterized to create the fade effect.

Creating semitransparent type

You can use blending options to create what appears to be semitransparent type. To do this, create a type layer and apply any layer styles you want. The Satin style, for example, can be used to darken the type, and the Pattern Overlay style can be used to create a patterned effect. In the Layer Style dialog box, drag the Set opacity of effect slider to the left and watch the preview until you get the amount of transparency you like. Any background images behind the type will appear as the fill of the type.

Adding Styles to Type

You may have noticed the rather colorful Styles panel included in the Typography workspace as well as the Essentials, Painting, and Web workspaces, although its location varies. You can apply these (preset) styles to any layer, much as you can use the (adjustable) layer styles button on the Layers panel.

FIGURE 24

White chrome type effect

Using the Gradient Tool

Before you can apply the fade effect, you need to create a layer mask for the type layer. You create the layer mask by clicking the Add layer mask button on the Layers panel. Then, you click the Gradient tool on the Tools panel. You can experiment with different types of gradient styles, but to create simple fading type, make sure

Linear Gradient is selected on the options bar, click the Click to open Gradient picker list arrow, then click the Black, White button on the Gradient panel.

Creating white chrome type

By now, you've come to realize that not only can you create cool type by warping and fading it, you can also apply other techniques to create a variety of unique effects. For instance, you can give type the illusion of white chrome, and even add color to the chrome effect. To create this effect, start with black type in a large point size. Add a drop shadow, switch the foreground color to white, then fill the type with the new foreground color by pressing [Alt][Backspace] (Win) or [option][delete] (Mac). Add an Inner Shadow style, then the Satin style (with a low Distance setting). See the top of Figure 24. To add color to the effect (at the bottom of Figure 24), modify the Hue/Saturation setting and the Curves setting.

Create a fade effect

1. Click the **Phoebe fielding layer** on the Layers panel.

2. Click the **Horizontal Type tool** T. on the Tools panel, click above the **dog's tail** at approximately **100 X/360 Y**, set the font to **Arial** or **Arial Black**, the font size to **48 pt**, the alignment to **Left align text**, then type **Times** as shown in Figure 25.

3. Click the **Commit any current edits button** ✓ on the options bar.

4. Click the **Add layer mask button** 🔘 on the Layers panel.

5. Click the **Gradient tool** 🔲 on the Tools panel.

   TIP The Gradient tool might be hidden under the Paint Bucket tool on the Tools panel.

6. Click the **Linear Gradient style** 🔲 on the options bar (if necessary).

7. Click the **Click to open Gradient picker list arrow** on the options bar.

8. Double-click the **Black, White style** (top row, third from left), then adjust the settings on your options bar to match Figure 26.

9. Verify that the **layer mask** is selected, press and hold **[Shift]**, drag the **Gradient pointer** ✛ from the bottom of the Times text letter 'm' halfway up in the letter 'm', then release **[Shift]**. Compare your text to Figure 27.

10. Save your work.

You added a layer mask and a gradient to create a faded type effect.

FIGURE 25
New type in image

New type layer

FIGURE 26
Options for the Gradient tool

Black, White gradient   Linear Gradient   Reverse check box reverses the direction of the fade

FIGURE 27
Faded text in image

Bottom half of type is faded

FIGURE 28
Styles panel

FIGURE 29
Lighting effect

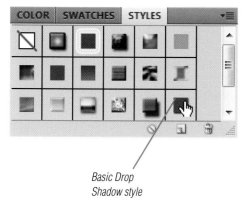

Basic Drop
Shadow style

Apply a style to type

1. Click the **Happy Hound layer** on the Layers panel.
2. Click the **Basic Drop Shadow box** in the Styles panel, as shown in Figure 28.

You applied a preset style to type using the Styles panel.

Add a lighting effect

1. Click the **Smiling Phoebe 2 layer** on the Layers panel.

    Make sure the layer thumbnail is selected, not the mask thumbnail.

2. Click **Filter** on the Application bar, point to **Render**, then click **Lighting Effects**.
3. Make sure that the **Default style** and **Omni Light type** are selected, and that the light source is directly above the dog's left ear (in the black area), then click **OK**.
4. Hide the rulers, save your work, then compare your image to Figure 29.
5. Close the image, then exit Photoshop.

You added a lighting filter to give the image a more polished appearance.

Warping objects

You can warp any rasterized object by clicking Edit on the Application bar, pointing to Transform, then clicking Warp. When you do this, a grid displays around the object. Clicking and dragging any of the points on the grid allows you to transform the shape of the object. Once you have selected this command, the options bar displays the Warp list arrow. You can use a custom shape, in which you drag the handles that surround the object, or you can select a shape from the list to use to warp the object.

Lesson 4   Create a Faded Type Effect

Power User Shortcuts

to do this:	use this method:
Adjust color levels	⏸ on Adjustments panel
Change warp type color	Double-click 工 , click ▮
Commit a transformation	✔
Convert type to a shape	Layer ≻ Type ≻ Convert to Shape
Create faded type	▣ , ▣ , ▣ , click to open Gradient picker list, then drag pointer over type
Create warped type	Double-click T , click 工
Display a bounding box	▸⊕ or V, select ☐ Show Transform Controls

to do this:	use this method:
Scale a bounding box	Press [Shift] while dragging handle, click ✔
Screen back type	Duplicate layer, hide original layer, convert type to shape, then adjust Levels
Select Gradient tool	▣ or [Shift] G
Skew a bounding box	Press [Ctrl] (Win) or ⌘ (Mac) while dragging handle, ✔
Stroke a type layer	fx. , Stroke, Set color of stroke button
Turn off bounding box display	▸⊕ or V, deselect ☑ Show Transform Controls

Key: Menu items are indicated by ≻ between the menu name and its command. Blue bold letters are shortcuts for selecting tools on the Tools panel.

Modify type using a bounding box.

1. Open PS 12-2.psd, update the text layers (if necessary), then save it as **Charge Card**.
2. Substitute a font available on your computer (if necessary). (*Hint*: The fonts used in the sample are a 36 pt and 48 pt Courier New.)
3. Display the rulers in pixels and make sure the guides are showing.
4. Select the Move tool (if it is not already selected), and make sure that the Show Transform Controls check box is selected.
5. Make the Ace Shopper layer active, drag the bounding box to the left so that the left edge of the A is just to the left of the guide at 155 X, then drag the top-middle handle of the bounding box to 290 Y.
6. Use the Transform command on the Edit menu to skew the text by dragging the upper-right handle of the bounding box to 420 X.
7. Commit the transformations, then save your work.

Create warped type with a unique shape.

1. Double-click the layer thumbnail on the Photoshop type layer on the Layers panel.
2. Change the font size to 72 pt.
3. Commit the transformation, then drag the type's bounding box so that the bottom-left corner is at 135 X/150 Y. (*Hint*: this may take more than one step to complete.)
4. Open the Warp Text dialog box.
5. Change the Warp Text style to Arch.

6. Click the Horizontal option button (if it is not already selected).
7. Change the Bend setting to +42, the Horizontal Distortion setting to +42, and the Vertical Distortion setting to 0, then close the Warp Text dialog box.
8. Move the type so that the bottom-right corner of the bounding box is at 545 X/150 Y.
9. Change the type color using the Swatches panel (Dark Violet Magenta).
10. Apply the default Drop Shadow and Bevel and Emboss styles to the Photoshop type layer, then save your work.

Screen back type with imagery.

1. Make the CHARGE layer active.
2. Increase the font size to 80 pt.
3. Move the CHARGE layer so the bottom-left corner is at 90 X/275 Y.
4. Duplicate this layer, calling the new layer **Screened back type**.
5. Hide the CHARGE layer.

FIGURE 30
Completed Skills Review

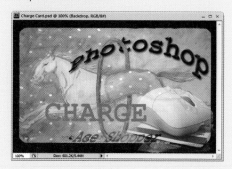

6. Convert the Screened back type layer to a shape layer.
7. Add a (clipped) Levels Adjustment layer that modifies the Midtones Input level to 0.45 and the Output levels shadow slider to 136, then close the Adjustment layer.
8. Make the Backdrop layer active, then use the Sponge tool to saturate the part of the image that is behind the text CHARGE.
9. Save your work.

Create a faded type effect.

1. Make the Ace Shopper layer active, then add a mask to this layer.
2. Select the Gradient tool, set the opacity to 70%, select the Linear Gradient style, then select Black, White on the Gradient picker.
3. Drag a straight line the length of the text, starting at approximately 155 X/315 Y and ending at the right edge of the image.
4. Clear the guides, then hide the rulers.
5. Add the Add Noise filter with a 50% Uniform Distribution to the Background layer.
6. Save your work, then compare your image to Figure 30.

You have been asked to create cover art for a new pop-psychology book entitled *Dueling Personalities: Outer Struggles*. The author has created some initial artwork that she wants on the cover. You can use any of your Photoshop skills to enhance this image, but you particularly want to transform the type to convey the mood and theme of the book.

1. Open PS 12-3.psd, then save it as **Dueling Personalities**.

2. Create two type layers: **Dueling Personalities** and **Outer Struggles**. (*Hint*: You can use any font available on your computer. In the sample, a 72 pt and 60 pt Trebuchet MS font is shown.)

3. Position the type layers appropriately.

4. Make sure the Show Transform Controls check box is selected.

5. Warp the Dueling Personalities type, using the Rise style and the settings of your choice in the Warp Text dialog box.

6. Use the bounding box to enlarge the warped text.

7. Duplicate the Outer Struggles type layer, choosing a suitable name for the duplicate layer.

8. Convert the copied layer to a shape, then change the levels using the settings of your choice. (In the sample, the Midtones input level is 2.26, and the Output shadows level is 20.)

9. Hide the original type layer.

10. Add a new type layer using the text and font of your choice in an appropriate location on the image.

11. Use the bounding box to scale the type layer to a smaller size.

12. Create a mask on this new layer.

13. Use the Gradient tool and the new type layer to create a fade effect.

FIGURE 31

Sample Project Builder 1

14. Change any font colors, and add any enhancing effects to the type layers.

15. Add any filter effects or color adjustments that you determine are necessary to complete the image. (In the sample, the Brightness is adjusted to −15, and the Contrast is adjusted to +15 using an Adjustment Layer.)

16. Save your work, then compare your image to the sample in Figure 31.

You work for Creativity, a graphic design firm that works almost exclusively with the high-tech business sector. As the newest member of the creative team, you have been assigned the design of the cover for the upcoming Annual Report. You have seen the Annual Reports for previous years, and they always feature dramatic, exciting designs. You have already started on the initial design, but need to complete the project.

1. Open PS 12-4.psd, then save it as **Creativity**.
2. Create a new layer containing just the dice. (*Hint*: You can duplicate the Backdrop layer, then use any of your Photoshop skills to isolate the dice in their own layer. Possible alternatives include creating a mask or erasing pixels.)
3. Modify the Backdrop layer so that only the pattern is displayed.
4. Create type layers for text appropriate for an annual report. (*Hint*: You can use any font available on your computer. In the sample, a Georgia font is shown.)
5. Position the type layers appropriately.
6. Warp at least one of the type layers, using the style and settings of your choice. (*Hint*: In the sample, the Bulge style was used.)
7. Enlarge or skew at least one type layer.
8. Create a screened back effect using one of the type layers and the settings of your choice. (In the sample, the Midtones input level is 2.26, and the Output shadows level is 20.)
9. Create a fade effect using one of the type layers.
10. Change any font colors (if necessary), then add any enhancing effects to the type layers.
11. Add any filter effects or color adjustments (using the existing and newly created and modified layers) that you determine are necessary. In the sample, the Brightness is adjusted to +25, and the Contrast is adjusted to +10. The area underneath the dice in the Backdrop layer was saturated using the Sponge tool, and the default Lighting Effects filter was applied to the Backdrop layer.
12. Save your work, then compare your image to the sample in Figure 32.

FIGURE 32
Sample Project Builder 2

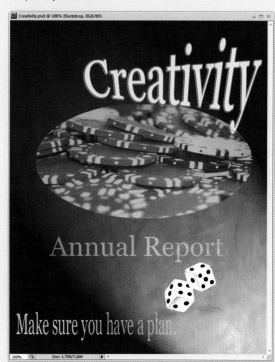

You have been asked to design an advertisement for your favorite television station. Before you begin, you decide to see what information you can find about type enhancements on the Internet. You intend to use the information you find to improve your skills and create a dramatic image. Be prepared to discuss the design elements used in this project. (*Hint*: If you don't have a favorite television station, invent call letters that you can use in this exercise.)

1. Connect to the Internet and use your browser to find information about transforming type in Photoshop. (Make a record of the site you found so you can use it for future reference, if necessary.)
2. Create a new Photoshop image, using the dimensions of your choice, then save it as **Television Station Ad**.
3. Create a type layer, using any color for the layer, any font available on your computer, and any text you want. (In the sample, an Onyx font is used.)
4. Create a warped type effect, using any style and settings of your choice. (In the sample, the Arc style is used.)
5. Create an attractive background, using any of your Photoshop skills or any imagery available to you. You can use scanned or digital camera images, purchased imagery,

or any images available on your computer.
6. Create any necessary additional type layers.
7. Resize any fonts, if necessary, using the bounding box.
8. Add any special effects to the type layers.

FIGURE 33

Sample Design Project

9. If necessary, make color adjustments or add filters.
10. Save your work, then compare your image to the sample in Figure 33.

You are a member of a fan club devoted to your favorite musical group. The fan club is holding a contest to choose a cover design for the band's new CD. You decide to put your expert Photoshop skills to work on this project. After the design is complete, take time to consider what you did, why you did it, and how your efforts contributed to the overall design of the image.

1. Create a Photoshop image using the dimensions of your choice, then save it as **CD Cover Artwork**.
2. Locate several pieces of artwork—either on your computer, in a royalty-free collection, or from scanned images. Although the images can show anything, you want to show positive imagery in keeping with the band's message.
3. Select imagery from the artwork and move it into CD Cover Artwork.
4. Create a warped type effect using any style and settings of your choice. (In the sample, the Viner Hand ITC font is used.)
5. Create any necessary additional type layers.
6. Resize any fonts, if necessary, using the bounding box.
7. Add any special effects to the type layers.
8. If necessary, make color adjustments or add filters.
9. Use at least one of the transformation skills you learned in this chapter to enhance the text.
10. Add any filter effects, if you decide they will make your image more dramatic. (In the sample, the Wind filter is applied to a layer.)
11. Make any color adjustments you feel would improve the look of the image.
12. Save your work, then compare your image to the sample in Figure 34.

FIGURE 34
Sample Portfolio Project

Transforming Type

13

LIQUIFYING
AN IMAGE

1. Use the Liquify tools to distort an image

2. Learn how to freeze and thaw areas

3. Use the mesh feature as you distort an image

Distorting Images

If you want to have some fun with an image, try your hand at the Liquify feature. Like the Smudge tool and the distort filters, you can use it to distort an image. But unlike those tools, the Liquify feature gives you much more control over the finished product. This feature contains ten distinct tools that you can use to create distortion effects.

Using the Liquify Feature

The Liquify feature lets you make an image look as if parts of it have melted. You can apply the eight Liquify distortions with a brush, and like other brush-based Photoshop tools, you can modify both the brush size and pressure to give you just the effect you want. You can use the two non-distortion Liquify tools to freeze and thaw areas within the image. Freezing protects an area from editing and possible editing errors, whereas thawing a frozen area allows it to be edited. With these two tools, you can protect specific areas from Liquify distortions, and can determine with great accuracy which areas are affected.

Using Common Sense

Because the effects of the Liquify feature are so dramatic, you should take the proper precautions to preserve your original work. You can work on a copy of the original image, or create duplicate layers to ensure that you can always get back to your starting point.

Tools You'll Use

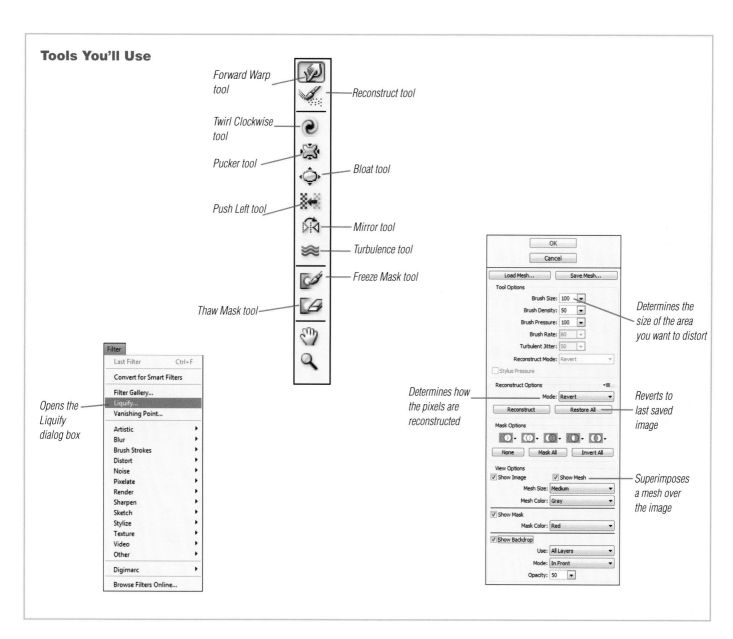

Forward Warp tool

Reconstruct tool

Twirl Clockwise tool

Pucker tool

Bloat tool

Push Left tool

Mirror tool

Turbulence tool

Freeze Mask tool

Thaw Mask tool

Filter

Last Filter	Ctrl+F
Convert for Smart Filters	
Filter Gallery...	
Liquify...	
Vanishing Point...	
Artistic	▶
Blur	▶
Brush Strokes	▶
Distort	▶
Noise	▶
Pixelate	▶
Render	▶
Sharpen	▶
Sketch	▶
Stylize	▶
Texture	▶
Video	▶
Other	▶
Digimarc	▶
Browse Filters Online...	

Opens the Liquify dialog box

Determines the size of the area you want to distort

Determines how the pixels are reconstructed

Reverts to last saved image

Superimposes a mesh over the image

USE THE LIQUIFY TOOLS
TO DISTORT AN IMAGE

What You'll Do

In this lesson, you'll use the Forward Warp tool in the Liquify dialog box to create distortions.

Using the Liquify Dialog Box

With the **Liquify feature**, you can apply distortions to any rasterized layer. When you use the Liquify command, the contents of the active layer appear in a large preview window in the Liquify dialog box. The distortion tools—used to apply the Liquify effects—are displayed on the left side of the dialog box; the tool settings are displayed on the right side. Unlike other tools that you use in the image window, you can only access the Liquify tools from the Liquify dialog box. (The Liquify feature is similar to the Vanishing Point feature in this respect.) In this dialog box, you can create eight different types of distortions.

QUICKTIP

As you apply distortions, the effects are immediately visible in the preview window of the Liquify dialog box.

Exploring the Possibilities

Compare Figures 1 (the original image) and 2 (the distorted image). As you can see from the altered image, you can use this feature to make drastic changes in an image. The following Liquify tools were used for the distorted image:

- The Twirl Clockwise tool was used repeatedly on the top book.
- The Pucker tool was used on the third book eight times. (The Pucker tool pulls the pixels toward the center of the brush tip.)
- The Bloat tool was used repeatedly on the second book. (The Bloat tool pushes pixels away from the center of the brush tip, which can create a more subtle effect.)

You can use distortions to create wild effects or to make subtle mood changes within an image. You can also use the Liquify tools to endow a person with instant weight gain—or weight loss!

Going Wild with Distortions

Of course, you can create wild, crazy distortions using the Liquify feature, and it is a lot of fun. As you can see from Figure 2, you can create some rather bizarre effects using these tools, but you can also use the distortion tools very conservatively to just correct a flaw or tweak an image.

FIGURE 1
Undistorted image in Liquify dialog box

Twirl Clockwise tool
Pucker tool
Bloat tool

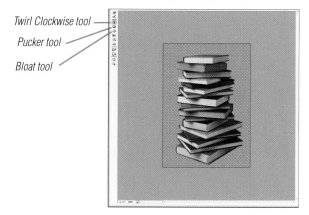

FIGURE 2
Distortion samples

Effect of the Twirl Clockwise tool

Effect of the Pucker tool

Effect of Bloat tool

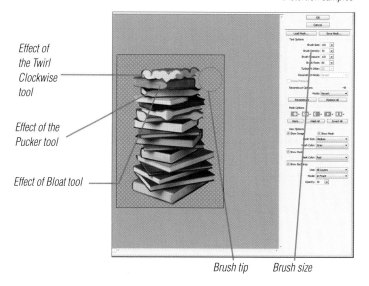

Brush tip   Brush size

Open the Liquify dialog box and modify the brush size

1. Open PS 13-1.psd from the drive and folder where you store your Data Files, then save the file as **Las Vegas**.

2. Click **Filter** on the Application bar, then click **Liquify**.

3. Click the **Zoom tool** 🔍 in the Liquify dialog box, then click the center of the image.

4. Make sure the following check boxes are *not* selected: **Show Mesh**, **Show Mask**, and **Show Backdrop**.

5. Click the **Forward Warp tool** 🖐 in the Liquify dialog box.

   The Liquify tools are described in Table 1.

6. Double-click the **Brush Size text box**, type **125**, then press **[Enter]** (Win) or **[return]** (Mac).

   TIP You can adjust the brush size by typing a value between 1 and 600 in the text box, pressing [[] to decrease by 2 or []] to increase by 2, or by clicking the Brush Size list arrow, then dragging the slider to a new value.

7. Adjust your settings in the Liquify dialog box so that they match those shown in Figure 3.

   TIP The Stylus Pressure check box option will appear dimmed if you do not have a graphics tablet attached to your computer.

You opened the Liquify dialog box, then chose the Forward Warp tool and a brush size.

FIGURE 3
Choosing a brush size

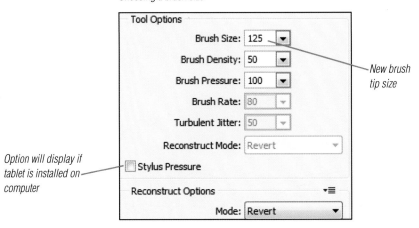

Option will display if tablet is installed on computer

New brush tip size

TABLE 1: Liquify Tools

tool	button	use
Forward Warp tool	🖐	Pushes pixels forward during dragging.
Reconstruct tool	🖌	Unpaints recently distorted pixels completely or partially.
Twirl Clockwise tool	⊙	Rotates pixels clockwise during dragging. (Hold [Alt] to twirl counter-clockwise.)
Pucker tool	⊠	Moves pixels toward the center of the active brush tip.
Bloat tool	◇	Moves pixels away from the center of the active brush tip.
Push Left tool	⁞⁞⁞	Moves pixels perpendicular to the brush stroke.
Mirror tool	⋈	Copies pixels to the brush area.
Turbulence tool	≋	Randomly scrambles pixels.
Freeze Mask tool	✎	Protects an area from distortion.
Thaw Mask tool	✎	Makes a frozen area available for distortions.

FIGURE 4
Positioned pointer

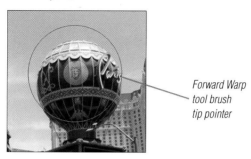

Forward Warp
tool brush
tip pointer

FIGURE 5
Enlarged globe

Enlarged globe is
distorted

FIGURE 6
Effect of Forward Warp tool

Your results will be different

Use the Forward Warp tool

1. Position the **Forward Warp tool pointer** ⊕ over the gold circle in the Paris balloon, as shown in Figure 4.

   TIP   Your results may vary slightly from those shown in the figures in this book.

2. Drag the **gold circle** up so it stretches the top of the globe, as shown in Figure 5.

   TIP   You can return an image to its previous appearance by clicking Restore All in the Reconstruction Options section of the Liquify dialog box. The Reconstruct button undoes each action of the brush, much like the Undo command or History panel.

3. Use the **Forward Warp tool pointer** ⊕ in different locations of the **gold circle** to create an enlarged balloon effect.

4. Click **OK** to close the Liquify dialog box.

5. Save your work, then compare your image to Figure 6.

You used the Forward Warp tool to distort the pixels of the balloon in an image. By dragging, you pushed the pixels forward, giving the balloon a larger, distorted appearance.

LEARN HOW TO FREEZE
AND THAW AREAS

What You'll Do

In this lesson, you'll freeze an area of an image, make distortions, then thaw the areas so that they can be edited.

Controlling Distortion Areas

Like storing food in the freezer to protect it from spoiling, you can **freeze** areas within an image so that the Liquify tools leave them unaffected. Using the Liquify dialog box, you can protect areas within an image, then **thaw** them—or return them to a state that can be edited—and make necessary distortions. You control which areas are distorted by using the Freeze Mask and Thaw Mask tools in the Liquify dialog box.

Freezing Image Areas

You can selectively freeze areas by painting them with a pointer. The View Options section in the Liquify dialog box lets you display frozen areas in the preview window. By default, frozen areas are painted in red, but you can change this color to make it more visible. For example, Figure 7 shows an image that has not yet been distorted. If you froze areas of this image using the default red color, they would not be visible because of the colors in this image.

QUICKTIP

To isolate the exact areas you want to freeze, try painting a larger area, then using the Thaw Mask tool to eliminate unwanted frozen areas.

Reconstructing Distortions

No matter how careful you are, you will most likely either create a distortion you don't like, or need to do some sort of damage control. Unlike typical Photoshop states, individual distortions you make using the Liquify feature do not appear on the History panel, and therefore cannot be undone. You can, however, use the History panel to delete the effects of an entire **Liquify session**. When you delete a Liquify state from the History panel, your image is restored to its original condition. In order to correct or delete the effects of a liquify tool during a Liquify session you need to use a reconstruction method. However, how distortions are reconstructed is determined by the mode used. If you want to reconstruct, you can do so by using one of five different reconstruction modes in the Liquify dialog box. Each mode affects the way pixels are

Liquifying an Image

reconstructed, relative to frozen areas in the image. This allows you to redo the changes in new and innovative ways.

Undergoing Reconstruction

Figure 8 shows several reconstructed areas as well as a frozen area painted in blue.

Using the Reconstruct tool and the Stiff mode, the tail feathers of the chicken were restored to their original condition. The Rigid mode was used on the feet, and the beak was reconstructed using the Loose mode. You can use several methods to reconstruct an image:

- Click Restore All in the Liquify dialog box.
- Choose the Revert mode, then click Reconstruct in the Liquify dialog box.

- Click the Reconstruct tool, choose the Revert mode, then drag the brush over distorted areas in the Liquify dialog box.
- Click the Cancel button in the Liquify dialog box.
- Make distortions in the Liquify dialog box, then drag the Liquify state to the Delete current state button on the History panel.

FIGURE 7
Original image

FIGURE 8
Frozen areas and distortions in preview window

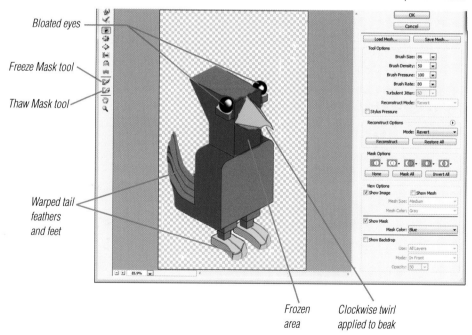

Bloated eyes

Freeze Mask tool

Thaw Mask tool

Warped tail feathers and feet

Frozen area

Clockwise twirl applied to beak

Freeze areas in an image

1. Click **Filter** on the Application bar, then click **Liquify**.

2. Use the **Zoom tool** 🔍 in the Liquify dialog box to magnify the image.

   TIP   Use the Zoom tool in the Liquify dialog box as needed to increase the size of objects you're working on. Use the Hand tool to reposition objects for better visibility.

3. Click the **Freeze Mask tool** in the Liquify dialog box.

4. Double-click the **Brush Size text box**, type **20**, then press **[Enter]** (Win) or **[return]** (Mac).

5. Click the **Show Mask check box**, click the **Mask Color list arrow**, then click **Red** (if it is not already selected). Compare your Liquify dialog box settings to Figure 9 and make any necessary adjustments.

6. Drag the **Freeze pointer** ⊕ around the perimeter of the top of the Eiffel Tower, using Figure 10 as a guide. (Don't worry if your results differ.)

   Table 2 describes the reconstruction modes available in the Liquify dialog box.

You modified Liquify settings, then froze an area within the image by using the Freeze Mask tool. Freezing the areas protects them from any Liquify effects you apply going forward.

FIGURE 9
Liquify settings

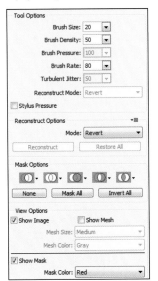

FIGURE 10
Frozen area

Red area is frozen

TABLE 2: Reconstruction Modes

mode	use
Revert	Changes areas back to their appearance before the dialog box was opened.
Rigid	Maintains right angles in the pixel grid during reconstruction.
Stiff	Provides continuity between frozen and unfrozen areas during reconstruction.
Smooth	Smoothes continuous distortions over frozen areas during reconstruction.
Loose	Smoothes continuous distortions similar to the Smooth mode but provides greater continuity between distortions in frozen and unfrozen areas.

FIGURE 11
Distortions in image

*Distortion
applied to spire*

*Mail truck is
reduced*

FIGURE 12
Distortions applied

FIGURE 13
History panel

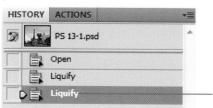

*State indicates most
recent distortions*

Distort unprotected areas of an image

1. Click the **Pucker tool** in the Liquify dialog box.

2. Change the brush size to **100**.

3. Position the center of the **Pucker pointer** ⊕ over the **US Postal truck**, then press and hold the mouse button until the truck is noticeably smaller.

4. Click the **Bloat tool** in the Liquify dialog box.

5. Center the **Bloat pointer** ⊕ over the center of the **top of the Eiffel Tower**, then press and hold the mouse button until the tip increases in size and fills the frozen area.

6. Compare your image to Figure 11.

7. Click **None** in the Mask Options section to remove the mask.

8. Click **OK**, then display the **History and Layers workspace**.

   The distortions are applied to the image.

9. Save your work, compare your image to Figure 12 and the History panel to Figure 13.

10. Display the **Essentials workspace**.

After distorting two areas, you removed the frozen mask and displayed two different workspaces.

USE THE MESH FEATURE AS
YOU DISTORT AN IMAGE

What You'll Do

In this lesson, you'll use the mesh feature to assist you when making distortions.

Using the Mesh Feature

The **mesh** is a series of horizontal and vertical gridlines superimposed on the preview window. You can easily see the effects of your distortions while working in an image by turning on the mesh. Although this feature is not necessary to create distortions, it can be helpful for seeing how much distortion you have added. The mesh can be controlled using the View Options section in the Liquify dialog box, shown in Figure 14. A magnified and distorted image, with the default medium-size, blue mesh displayed, is shown in Figure 15.

> QUICKTIP
>
> Distortions on the gridlines look similar to isobars on a thermal map or elevations on a topographic map.

Changing the Mesh Display

You can modify the appearance of the mesh so that it is displayed in another color or contains larger or smaller gridlines. You may want to use large gridlines if your changes are so dramatic that the use of smaller gridlines would be distracting. As shown in Figure 16, you can use the large gridlines to see where the distortions occur. If the mesh color and the colors in the image are similar, you may want to change the mesh color. For example, a yellow mesh displayed on an image with a yellow background would be invisible. A red mesh against a white background, as shown in Figure 16, is more noticeable.

Visualizing the Distortions

When the mesh feature is on and clearly visible, take a look at the gridlines as you make your distortions. Note where the gridlines have been adjusted and if symmetrical objects have equally symmetrical distortions. For example, distortions of a rectangular skyscraper can be controlled so that they are equivalent on all visible sides. If symmetry is what you want, the mesh feature gives you one method of checking your results.

Getting a Better View of Distortions

The active layer is always shown in the Liquify dialog box, but you might find it helpful to distort imagery with its companion layers visible. You can do this in two ways. One way is by selecting the Show Backdrop check box in the Liquify dialog box, and selecting which layer (or all layers) you want to be visible with the selected layer. You can then adjust the opacity of the backdrop layer(s) to make the layer(s) more visible. This technique distorts only the layer selected on the Layers panel. The other way is by merging visible layers: Click the highest layer on the Layers panel, click the Layers panel list arrow, then click Merge Visible. When you open the merged layers in the Liquify dialog box, all the imagery will be visible and can be altered by distortions. One way of ensuring that you can get back to your original layers—in case things don't turn out quite as you planned—is by making copies of the layers you want to combine before you merge the layers.

QUICKTIP

You can always turn off the mesh feature if it is distracting.

FIGURE 14
Mesh display options

Select to display mesh
Changes mesh size
Changes mesh color

FIGURE 15
Distorted image with default size and blue mesh

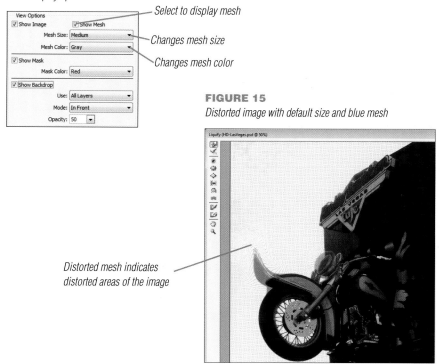

Distorted mesh indicates distorted areas of the image

FIGURE 16
Distorted image with large red mesh

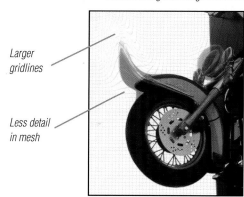

Larger gridlines

Less detail in mesh

Turn on the mesh

1. Click **Filter** on the Application bar, then click **Liquify**.

2. Use the **Zoom tool** 🔍 in the Liquify dialog box to magnify the image.

3. Click the **Bloat tool** ◈ in the Liquify dialog box, then verify that the brush size is **100**.

4. Select the **Show Mesh check box**.

5. Click the **Mesh Color list arrow**, then click **Red**.

6. Verify that the **Mesh Size** is set to **Medium** and the **Show Backdrop check box** is selected Compare your image and settings to Figure 17, then make any adjustments necessary so that your settings match those shown in the figure.

You turned on the mesh and changed the mesh color and verified the setting of the mesh size.

FIGURE 17
Medium red mesh over an image

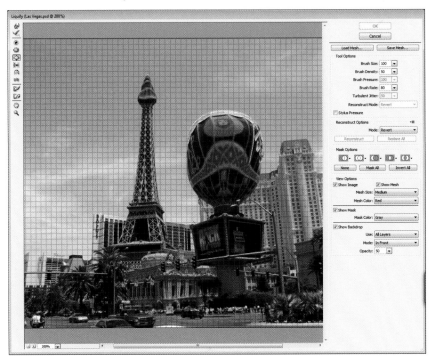

FIGURE 18
Warped Eiffel Tower and marquee

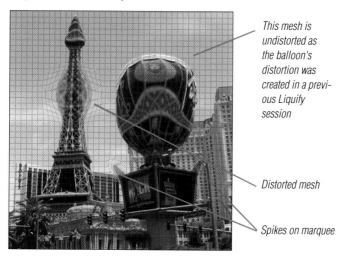

This mesh is undistorted as the balloon's distortion was created in a previous Liquify session

Distorted mesh

Spikes on marquee

FIGURE 19
Distortions applied to image

Distort an image with the mesh feature activated

1. Position the **Bloat pointer** ⊕ over the middle of the center of the Eiffel Tower, press and hold the mouse button until you see the mesh being distorted, then release the mouse button.

2. Click the **Forward Warp tool** 🖌 in the Liquify dialog box, then change the brush size to **25**.

3. Click the **Mesh Size list arrow**, then click **Large**.

   The gridlines appear larger.

4. Drag the **Forward Warp pointer** ⊕ in the top edge of the **Paris marquee** (the two framed screens beneath the Paris balloon) so that it forms spikes using medium horizontal strokes, as shown in Figure 18.

5. Click the **Show Mesh check box** to turn off the mesh.

6. Click **OK**.

7. Save your work, then compare your image to Figure 19.

8. Close the image, then exit Photoshop.

You added new distortions to the image and modified the mesh size. After viewing the distortions with the larger mesh, you turned off the mesh and viewed the image.

Power User Shortcuts

to do this:	use this method:
Bloat an area	Filter ➤ Liquify, ⬦ or B
Change freeze color	Filter ➤ Liquify, Mask Color list arrow
Change mesh color	Filter ➤ Liquify, select Show Mesh check box, click the Mesh Color list arrow
Change mesh size	Filter ➤ Liquify, select Show Mesh check box, click the Mesh Size list arrow
Change brush size	Filter ➤ Liquify, [100 ▸] or [[] or []]
Freeze pixels	Filter ➤ Liquify, ✐ or F
Open Liquify dialog box	Filter ➤ Liquify or [Shift][Ctrl][X] (Win) or ⌘ [shift][X] (Mac)
Pucker an area	Filter ➤ Liquify, ⬛ or S
Reconstruct pixels in an area	Filter ➤ Liquify, ✎ or R

to do this:	use this method:
Reflect pixels in an area	Filter ➤ Liquify, ⬛ or M
Return image to prewarp state	Click Restore All in Liquify dialog box, click Cancel in Liquify dialog box, or drag state to 🗑 on the History panel
Shift pixels in an area	Filter ➤ Liquify, ⬛ or O
Thaw frozen pixels	Filter ➤ Liquify, ⬛ or D
Turn mesh on/off	Filter ➤ Liquify, select Show Mesh check box
Turn Backdrop on/off	Filter ➤ Liquify, select Show Backdrop check box
Twirl an area clockwise	Filter ➤ Liquify, ● or C
Warp an area	Filter ➤ Liquify, ⬛ or W

Key: Menu items are indicated by ➤ between the menu name and its command. Blue bold letters are shortcuts for selecting tools in the dialog box.

Use the Liquify tools to distort an image.

1. Open PS 13-2.psd, then save it as **Blurred Vision**.
2. Open the Liquify dialog box.
3. Change the Brush Size to 65.
4. Select the Twirl Clockwise tool.
5. Twirl the F in Line 2.
6. Twirl the P in Line 2.
7. Close the Liquify dialog box, then save your work.

Learn how to freeze and thaw areas.

1. Open the Liquify dialog box.
2. Turn on the Show Mask feature, then change the Mask Color to Green.
3. Use the Freeze Mask tool to freeze the O in the middle of Line 3.
4. Select the Bloat tool.
5. Bloat each remaining letter in Line 3.

6. Use the Thaw Mask tool to thaw the frozen areas.
7. Click OK, then save your work.

Use the mesh feature as you distort an image.

1. Open the Liquify dialog box.
2. Turn on the Show Mesh feature.
3. Change the Mesh Color to Blue.
4. Change the Mesh Size to Large.
5. Select the Pucker tool, then change the Brush Size to 135.
6. Pucker the E on Line 1 and the number 7.
7. Use the Bloat tool and a 150 Brush Size to distort the green bar (between lines 6 and 7) and the red bar (between lines 8 and 9). Then distort the letter P in line 4.
8. Close the Liquify dialog box, save your work, then compare your image to Figure 20.

FIGURE 20
Completed Skills Review

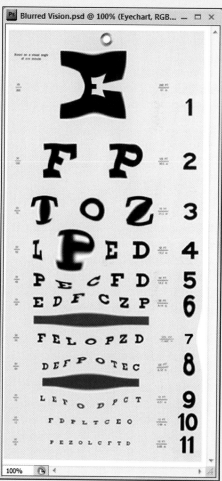

Your lifelong dream to open a restaurant is about to come true. In fact, even though you haven't found a location, you've already chosen a name: the Shooting Star Restaurant. Fortunately, you can use your Photoshop skills to save some money by designing your own promotional advertisements. You've created the initial background art, but need to complete the image.

1. Open PS 13-3.psd, then save it as **Shooting Star**.
2. Activate the Shooting Star layer, then open the Liquify dialog box.
3. Display the mesh in a size and color you think are appropriate.
4. Change the freeze mask color to Red (if necessary).
5. Use the brush size of your choice to freeze the face in the lower-left corner.
6. Use the Twirl Clockwise tool and a Brush Size of 25 to distort the bright shooting star.
7. Use the Bloat tool with a Brush Size of 250 to distort the shooting star.
8. Turn off the mesh, then click OK to close the Liquify dialog box.
9. Add a type layer that says **Shooting Star Restaurant**. (*Hint*: You can use any color and any font available on your computer. In the sample, a Poor Richard font is shown.)
10. Use the bounding box to change the size of the text.
11. Warp the type layer using the style and the settings of your choice. (*Hint*: Do not rasterize the type layer.)
12. Apply the type effects of your choice to the text.
13. Make any color adjustments you feel are necessary. (*Hint*: In the sample, the Levels were adjusted so that the input midtones are .69.)
14. Add any filter effects that you determine are necessary to enhance the image. (In the sample, the Lens Flare filter was set at 105mm Prime at 90% Brightness and positioned over the shooting star.)
15. Save your work, then compare your image to the sample in Figure 21.

FIGURE 21
Sample Project Builder 1

Your friend is a film photographer and doesn't understand the power of Photoshop and digital photography. His birthday is coming soon, and you think it is a great opportunity to show him how useful Photoshop can be and to have a little fun with him. One of the things you like best about your friend is his great sense of humor. You decide to use the Liquify tools to distort a photo of him so it looks like a caricature.

1. Open PS 13-4.psd, then save it as **Buddy Boy**.
2. Locate at least one piece of appropriate artwork—either a scanned image of a friend, an image on your computer, or an image from a royalty-free collection—that you can use in this file.
3. Use any appropriate methods to select imagery from the artwork.
4. After the selections have been made, copy each selection into Buddy Boy.
5. Transform any imagery, if necessary.
6. Change the colors of the gradient fill in the Backdrop layer to suit the colors in your friend's image.
7. Open the Liquify dialog box.
8. Display any size mesh in any color you find helpful.
9. Change the freeze mask color to a color you find helpful.
10. Use the brush size of your choice to freeze an area within the image. (*Hint*: In the example,

the face was protected while the hair was enlarged and brushed back.)
11. Use any distortion tool in any brush size of your choice to distort an area near the frozen area.
12. Thaw the frozen areas.
13. Use any additional distortion techniques to modify the image and distort the physical characteristics, as a caricaturist would do.

FIGURE 22
Sample Project Builder 2

14. Turn off the mesh, then click OK to close the Liquify dialog box.
15. Add a type layer with a clever title for your friend. You can position it in any location you choose.
16. Save your work, then compare your image to the sample in Figure 22.

Liquifying an Image

You really love the Photoshop Liquify feature and want to see other samples of how this tool can be used. You decide to look on the Internet, find a sample, then cast a critical eye on the results.

1. Connect to the Internet and use your browser to find information about the Liquify feature in Photoshop. (Make a record of the site you found so you can use it for future reference, if necessary.) You might find an image similar to a liquified image such as the sample shown in Figure 23.
2. Ask yourself the following questions about a specific image to which the Liquify feature has been applied.
   - Do you like this image? If so, why?
   - Does the distortion prevent you from determining what the image is?
   - In your opinion, does the distortion make the image more or less effective?
   - How was the distortion created?
   - After seeing this sample, what is your opinion as to the overall effectiveness of the Liquify feature? How can it best be used?
3. Be prepared to discuss your answers to these questions either in writing, in a group discussion, or in a presentation format.

FIGURE 23
Sample Design Project

You have been asked to give a presentation to a group of students who are interested in taking computer design classes. The presentation should include general topics, such as layers, type, and making selections, and can also include more exotic features, such as Liquify. Make it clear that the Liquify feature can be used on people, objects, or abstract images. Create an image that you can use in your presentation.

1. Create a new Photoshop image with any dimensions.
2. Save the file as **Photoshop Presentation**.
3. Locate several pieces of artwork—either on your computer, in a royalty-free collection, or from scanned images. Remember that the images can show anything, but you want to demonstrate the flexibility of Photoshop and the range of your skills.
4. Select imagery from the artwork and move it into Photoshop Presentation.
5. Open the Liquify dialog box.
6. Display any size mesh in any color you find helpful.
7. Use the Freeze Mask tool and the brush size of your choice to isolate areas that you don't want to distort.

8. Use any distortion tool in any brush size of your choice to distort an area in the image.
9. Thaw the frozen areas.
10. Use any additional distortion techniques to modify the image.
11. Turn off the mesh, then click OK to close the Liquify dialog box.
12. Use any transformation skills to enhance the image.
13. Add any filter effects, if you decide they will make your image more dramatic. (In the sample, the Fresco filter was applied to the Abstract layer.)

14. Make any necessary color adjustments.
15. Add at least one type layer in any font available on your computer. (A Constantia font is shown in the sample.)
16. Use your knowledge of special effects and the bounding box to enhance the type layer. (The following effects have been applied: Flag-style warped text, Drop Shadow style, Stroke style, and Bevel and Emboss style.)
17. Save your work, then compare your image to the sample in Figure 24.

FIGURE 24
Sample Portfolio Project

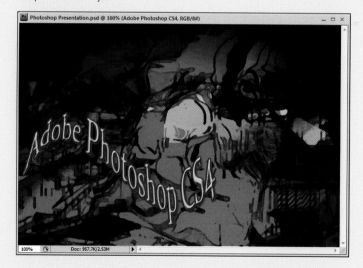

chapter 14

PERFORMING IMAGE
SURGERY

1. Delete unnecessary imagery

2. Correct colors in an image

3. Tweak an image

Understanding the Realities

By now you've realized that working with Photoshop is not always about creating cool effects and exciting images. Sometimes, your main task is problem-solving.

For example, you don't always have access to perfect images. If you did, you wouldn't need the arsenal of tools that Photoshop provides. Often, we find ourselves with images that need some "help." Perhaps the colors in an image are washed out, or maybe the image would be perfect except for one element that you don't want or need.

Assessing the Situation

In some situations, there may be many obvious ways to achieve the look you want in an image. A smart Photoshop user knows what tools are available, evaluates an image to see what is needed, then decides which methods are best to fix the problem areas in the image.

Applying Knowledge and Making Decisions

People who can apply their Photoshop knowledge effectively are in demand in today's job market. The ability to assess which tools are needed in the first place is as much a part of Photoshop expertise as knowing how to use the tools. You can approach the same design problem in many ways; your job is to determine which approach to take in order to make an image look right. And it is up to you to determine what "right" is. By the time your image is finished, you may feel as if it has undergone major surgery.

QUICKTIP

Image surgery often goes unappreciated. You may spend a lot of time cleaning up edges and eliminating "dirt" and "smudges"—defects that often are noticeable in an image only when they've been neglected!

Tools You'll Use

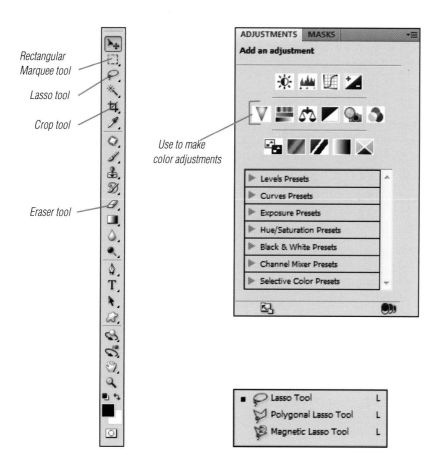

Rectangular
Marquee tool

Lasso tool

Crop tool

Use to make
color adjustments

Eraser tool

	Lasso Tool	L
	Polygonal Lasso Tool	L
	Magnetic Lasso Tool	L

DELETE UNNECESSARY IMAGERY

What You'll Do

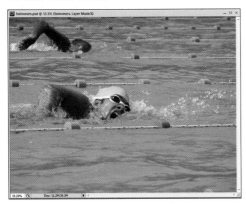

In this lesson, you'll use your skills and a variety of tools to conceal unwanted imagery. You'll also add a new layer from a selection and add a layer mask.

Evaluating the Possibilities

Now that you have some experience creating and editing images, your assessment abilities have probably sharpened. You are more accustomed to deciding what imagery is useful for a particular project. You may also find that you've begun looking at images in terms of their potential usefulness for other projects. You might, for example, see a great element in one image and think, "That object has a crisp edge. I could isolate it using the Magnetic Lasso tool and use it for this other project."

QUICKTIP

Don't be surprised when a simple touch-up job that you thought would take a few minutes actually takes hours. Sometimes a seemingly simple effect is the one that requires the most work.

Performing Surgery

Removing unwanted imagery can be time-consuming and frustrating, but it can also be extremely gratifying (after you're finished). It's detailed, demanding, and sometimes complicated work. For example, Figures 1 and 2 show the same image *before* and *after* it underwent the following alterations:

- The .tif file was saved as a Photoshop .psd file.
- Selection tools were used to create separate layers for the background, the backdrop, and the candles.
- The candles layer was duplicated, as insurance—just in case it became necessary to start over. See the Layers panel in Figure 3.
- The backdrop color was changed from black to pure blue violet.
- The candles on the left and right sides were eliminated by using eraser tools.
- Extraneous "dirt" and "smudges" were eliminated by using eraser tools.
- Contrast was added to the candles by using an adjustment layer.
- The Liquify feature was used to extend the individual flames and to smooth out the candle holder at the bottom of the image.
- The Noise filter was applied to the Backdrop layer, to give it more texture and dimension.

Understanding the Alternatives

Could these effects be achieved using other methods? Of course. For example, the bottom of the image was modified using the Forward Warp tool in the Liquify dialog box, but a similar effect could have been created using a painting tool such as the Smudge tool. The effect of the Noise filter could also have been created using the Grain filter. How many different ways can you think of to get the imagery from Figure 1 into the separate layers shown in Figure 2? It's possible that you can create these effects in many ways. For example, you might want to use the Magnetic Lasso tool to select areas with clearly defined edges, then zoom in and use the Eraser tool to clean up dirt and smudges. Or you just may decide to keep it simple and use the Rectangular Marquee tool to copy and paste pixels from one area to another.

Preparing for Surgery

Even if you think you've got it all figured out, sometimes things do not go the way you planned. Doesn't it make sense to take the time to prepare for a worst-case scenario when using Photoshop? Of course. You can easily protect yourself against losing hours of work by building in some safety nets as you work. For example, you can duplicate your original image (or images) just in case things go awry. By creating a copy, you'll never have to complain that your original work was ruined. You can also save interim copies of your image at strategic stages of your work. Above all, make sure you plan your steps. To do this, perform a few trial runs on a practice image before starting on the *real* project. Until you get comfortable reading the states on the History panel, write down what steps you took and what settings you used. Careful planning will pay off.

FIGURE 1
Original TIFF file

FIGURE 2
Modified image

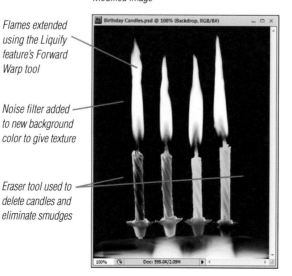

Flames extended using the Liquify feature's Forward Warp tool

Noise filter added to new background color to give texture

Eraser tool used to delete candles and eliminate smudges

FIGURE 3
Layers panel of modified image

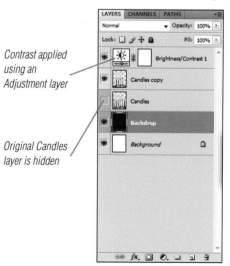

Contrast applied using an Adjustment layer

Original Candles layer is hidden

Lesson 1   Delete Unnecessary Imagery

Prepare the image for surgery

1. Open PS 14-1.jpg from the drive and folder where you store your Data Files.

2. Use the **Format list arrow** in the Save As dialog box to change the file from a JPG to the **Photoshop (*.PSD, *.PDD)** format, then save the file as **Swimmers.psd**.

3. Change the workspace to **History and Layers** (created in Chapter 1).

4. Click **Layer** on the Application bar, point to **New**, then click **Layer From Background**.

5. Type **Swimmers** in the Name text box.

6. Click the **Color list arrow** in the New Layer dialog box, click **Green**, then click **OK**.

7. Drag the **Swimmers layer** on the Layers panel to the **Create a new layer button** 🔲 .

   A copy of the Swimmers layer (named Swimmers copy) is created. Compare your image and History and Layers panels to Figure 4.

8. Click the **Swimmers layer** on the Layers panel.

9. Click the **Indicates layer visibility button** 👁 on the Swimmers copy layer.

   Table 1 reviews some of the many possible selection methods you can use to remove unwanted imagery.

You saved a .jpg file in the Photoshop PSD format, converted a Background layer into an image layer, then made a copy of the image layer.

FIGURE 4
Duplicated layer

New file format

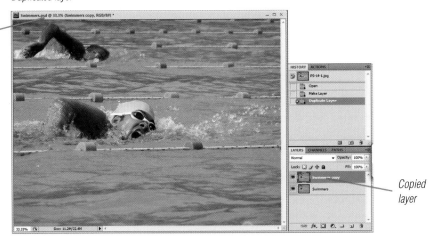

Copied layer

TABLE 1: Image Removal Methods

tool	name	method
🖌	Magnetic Lasso tool	Trace an object along its edge, then click Edit ➤ Clear.
✳	Magic Wand tool	Select by color, then click Edit ➤ Clear.
🖌	Clone Stamp tool	Press and hold [Alt] (Win) or [option] (Mac), click sample area, release [Alt] (Win) or [option] (Mac), then click areas you want to remove.
⬚	Rectangular Marquee tool	Select area, select Move tool, press and hold [Alt] (Win) or [option] (Mac), drag selection to new location.
◯	Elliptical Marquee tool	Select area, select Move tool, press and hold [Alt] (Win) or [option] (Mac), drag selection to new location.
▱	Eraser tool	Drag over pixels to be removed.
◈	Patch tool	Select source/destination, then drag to destination/source.

FIGURE 5
Selection in image

Imagery surrounded
by marquee

FIGURE 6
Cleared selection

Area with
deleted pixels

Lesson 1   Delete Unnecessary Imagery

Select imagery with the Rectangular Marquee tool

1. Verify that the rulers are displayed in pixels, then click the **Zoom tool** 🔍 on the Application bar.

   TIP   Make sure the Resize Windows To Fit check box on the options bar is selected.

2. Click the **lowest-left piece of yellow rope** until the zoom level is 50%.

3. Click the **Rectangular Marquee tool** ⬚ on the Tools panel, then change the Feather setting to **0 px**, if necessary.

4. Drag the **Rectangular Marquee pointer** ╋ around the rectangular section of yellow rope to the left of the orange buoy (from approximately **220 X/1070 Y** to **540 X/1100 Y**).

   Compare your selection to Figure 5.

5. Click **Edit** on the Application bar, then click **Clear**.

   TIP   You can also use the Eraser tool to delete the rope hidden by the water, although it would be difficult to erase all the nooks and crannies. You can also choose to cover these pixels rather then remove them.

6. Click **Select** on the Application bar, then click **Deselect**.

   Compare your image to Figure 6.

   TIP   You can also cut a selection by clicking Edit on the Application bar, then clicking Cut, which allows you to paste the selection elsewhere by clicking Edit on the Application bar, then clicking Paste.

You used the Zoom tool to get a closer look at an image, then used the Rectangular Marquee tool to eliminate unwanted imagery.

Duplicate imagery

1. Verify that the **Rectangular Marquee tool** is selected.

2. Select a rectangular area of rope that is clearly visible above the water from approximately **1000 X/1050 Y** to **1350 X/1100 Y**. Compare your selection to Figure 7.

3. Press and hold **[Ctrl][Alt]** (Win) or ⌘ **[option]** (Mac), drag the selection to the area displaying the deleted pixels, then release **[Ctrl][Alt]** (Win) or ⌘ **[option]** (Mac).

   The selection is duplicated over the deleted pixels.

   TIP Pressing and holding [Ctrl] [Alt] (Win) or ⌘ [option] (Mac) lets you temporarily convert the current tool to the Move tool.

4. Click **Select** on the Application bar, then click **Deselect**.

5. Use any Photoshop tools, such as the Clone Stamp tool, to fill in any missing areas until you are satisfied with the results.

   Compare your screen to Figure 8.

   TIP You can use pixels from anywhere in the image.

6. Display the **Essentials workspace**.

You selected areas within the image and then duplicated them to cover deleted imagery and make the image look more natural.

FIGURE 7
Selected area

FIGURE 8
Image with duplicated pixels

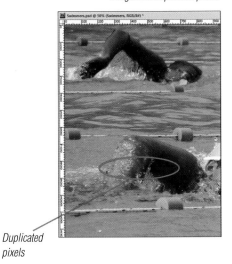

Duplicated pixels

DESIGNTIP Fooling the eye

You can fool the eye when you replace pixels in an image. Even if the replacement pixels are not completely accurate, the eye can be tricked into thinking that the image looks reasonable. For example, you can duplicate ground and sky pixels, and most viewers will accept them as looking "right." However, the reverse is not necessarily true. If you remove something from an image but leave some pixels behind, viewers are likely to think that something is wrong. For example, if you erase the figure of a woman from an image, but you neglect to eliminate all the pixels for the woman's hair, the reader's eye would probably recognize the incongruity. Remnants of dangling hair would almost certainly bring into question the accuracy of the image.

FIGURE 9
Image with new layer and mask

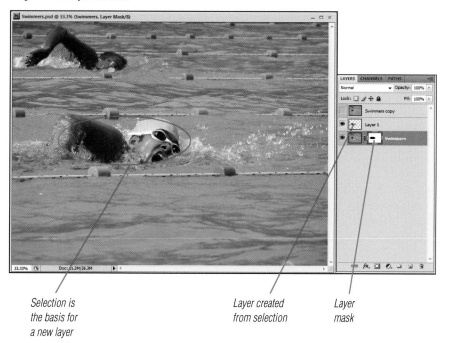

Selection is
the basis for
a new layer

Layer created
from selection

Layer
mask

Correcting color

You can make color corrections on a layer in a number of ways. One option is to make your corrections directly on the original layer. Another option is to make a copy of the original layer *before* making the corrections on the layer. You can also make your corrections using adjustment layers, and then merge the layers down when you are satisfied with the results. You can add an adjustment layer to the current layer by clicking Layer on the Application bar, pointing to New Adjustment Layer, then clicking the type of adjustment you want to make, or by clicking a preset button on the Adjustments panel.

Create a layer from a selection

1. Click the **Elliptical Marquee tool** ◯ on the Tools panel, then verify that the Feather setting is set to **0 px**.

2. Drag the **Marquee pointer** ✛ around the swimmer with the yellow cap from approximately **200 X/660 Y** to **1300 X/1070 Y**.

3. Click **Layer** on the Application bar, point to **New**, then click **Layer via Copy**.

   A new layer containing the selection is created and is the active layer.

4. Click the **Swimmers layer** on the Layers panel.

5. Drag the **Marquee pointer** ✛ around the swimmer with the yellow cap but slightly smaller than the oval used in Step 2 from approximately **250 X/670 Y** to **1260 X/1050 Y**.

6. Click **Layer** on the Application bar, point to **Layer Mask**, then click **Hide Selection**.

   A layer mask is placed over the selection on the Swimmers layer. The mask will be used to conceal pixels while highlighting the image of the swimmer.

7. Hide the rulers.

8. Click the **Zoom tool** 🔍 on the Application bar.

9. Press and hold **[Alt]** (Win) or **[option]** (Mac), click the image until the zoom level is **33.3%**, then release **[Alt]** (Win) or **[option]** (Mac).

10. Save your work, then compare your image to Figure 9.

You created a new layer from a selection, then created a layer mask from a selection.

CORRECT COLORS IN
AN IMAGE

What You'll Do

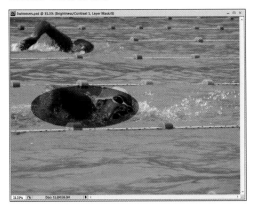

In this lesson, you'll make color adjustments to a specific layer.

Revitalizing an Image

You may find that you are working with an image that looks fine except that it seems washed out or just leaves you in the doldrums. You may be able to spice up such an image by adjusting the color settings. By modifying the color balance, for example, you can increase the red tones while decreasing the green and blue tones to make the image look more realistic and dramatic. After you select the layer that you want to adjust, you can make color-correcting adjustments by displaying the Adjustments panel, then clicking the type of color adjustment you want to make.

Making Color Adjustments

So, the image you're working with seems to need *something*, but you're not quite sure what. Until you become comfortable making color corrections, do everything in your power to provide yourself with a safety net. Create duplicate layers and use adjustment layers instead of making corrections directly on the original layer. Before you begin, take a long look at the image and ask yourself, "What's lacking?" Is the problem composition, or is it truly a color problem? Do the colors appear washed out rather than vibrant and true to life? Is the color deficiency really a problem, or does the image's appearance support what you're trying to accomplish?

Assessing the Mood

Color can be a big factor in establishing mood in an image. For example, if you are trying to create a sad mood, increasing the blue and green tones may be more effective than modifying specific imagery. If you decide that your image does need color correction, start slowly. Try balancing the color and see if that gives you the effect you want. Keep experimenting with the various color correction options until you find the method that works for you.

FIGURE 10
Hue/Saturation Adjustments panel

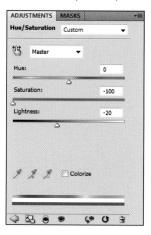

FIGURE 11
Brightness/Contrast Adjustments panel

FIGURE 12
Color corrected image

Adjusted pixels
created from
selection

FIGURE 13
Layers panel

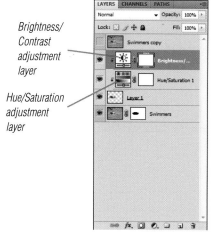

Brightness/
Contrast
adjustment
layer

Hue/Saturation
adjustment
layer

1. Click **Layer 1** on the Layers panel.

2. Click the **Hue/Saturation button** on the Adjustments panel.

3. Click the **This adjustment affects all layers below (click to clip to layer) button** on the Adjustments panel.

4. Change the settings in the Hue/Saturation dialog box so that they match those shown in Figure 10, then click the **Return to adjustment list button** on the Adjustments panel.

5. Click the **Brightness/Contrast button** on the Adjustments panel.

6. Click on the Adjustments panel.

7. Change the settings so that they match those shown in Figure 11, then click on the Adjustments panel.

8. Save your work, then compare your image to Figure 12 and your Layers panel to Figure 13.

You adjusted the hue/saturation and brightness/contrast in the layer created from a selection, making the image of the swimmer's face stand out. You made color adjustments using adjustment layers, which you grouped with Layer 1.

Lesson 2   Correct Colors in an Image

TWEAK AN IMAGE

What You'll Do

In this lesson, you'll crop out unnecessary imagery. You'll also add a layer style to enhance the image, and draw attention away from the background.

Evaluating What's Next

Every image has its own unique problems, and you'll probably run into a few final challenges when coordinating an image to work with other elements in a final publication or finished product. The last step in preparing an image for production is to decide what final fixes are necessary so that it serves its intended purpose.

Cropping an Image

Sometimes an image contains more content than is necessary. In the image of the swimmers, there's too much water. Of course, *you* have to determine the central focus of the image and what it is you want the reader to see. Is the subject of the image the water, or the swimmers? If your image suffers from too much of the wrong imagery, you can help your reader by getting rid of the unnecessary and possibly distracting imagery. This type of deletion not only removes imagery, but changes the size and shape of the image. You can make this type of change using the Crop tool on the Tools panel. When you make a selection within an image, you can use cropped area settings (the Shield check box and the Opacity list arrow) on the options bar to see how the image will appear after it has been cropped.

Adding Layer Styles

Image layers can also benefit from the same layer styles that can be applied to type layers, such as a Drop Shadow.

FIGURE 14
Cropped area in image

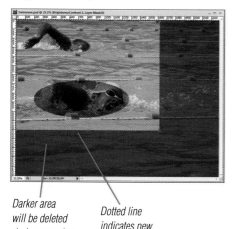

Darker area
will be deleted
during cropping

Dotted line
indicates new
boundaries

FIGURE 15
Completed image

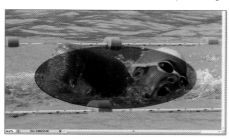

FIGURE 16
Layers panel for completed image

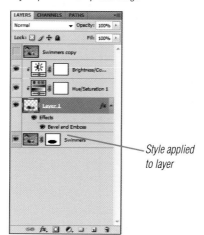

Style applied
to layer

Crop the image

1. Display the rulers in pixels.
2. Click the **Crop tool** ⌗, on the Tools panel.
3. Drag the **Crop pointer** ⌗ in a rectangular area surrounding the two swimmers from approximately **0 X/0 Y** to **1620 X/1200 Y**.

   The area that will be cropped from the image appears darker, as shown in Figure 14.
4. Click the **Commit current crop operation button** ✔ on the options bar.

   The cropped imagery is discarded.
5. Hide the rulers, then resize the image so it fits your screen.
6. Click **Layer 1** on the Layers panel.
7. Click the **Add a layer style button** *fx*, on the Layers panel.
8. Click **Bevel and Emboss**, accept the existing settings, then click **OK**.
9. Save your work, then compare your image to Figure 15 and your Layers panel to Figure 16.
10. Close the image file and exit Photoshop.

You cropped the image, then applied the Bevel and Emboss style to the layer created from a selection.

Rotate and pan-and-zoom a canvas

Perhaps you need to rotate an image from its current axis in order to paint or draw on it. If this is the case, you can click the Rotate View tool on the Application bar, then drag any corner of the image. The Rotate View tool allows you to rotate a canvas *non-destructively*: it does not transform the image. As you drag, a compass displays in the center of the image which indicates how much rotation you have added to the original image. (The amount of rotation is also shown in the Rotation Angle text box in the options bar.) If you are using Photoshop Extended, you can use the *pan and zoom feature*. If you have a graphics card and your computer has OpenGL enabled (in Preferences), you can zoom in and out by holding the Zoom tool (rather than just clicking) without loss of resolution. You can pan by holding the [spacebar] while pressing the Zoom tool.

Power User Shortcuts

to do this:	use this method:
Add layer style	*fx.*, click style(s)
Clear selection	[Delete] (Win) or [delete] (Mac)
Clone an area	🖃. or [Shift] S, press and hold [Alt] (Win) or option (Mac), click sample area, release [Alt] (Win) or option (Mac), then click areas you want cloned
Create an adjustment layer	Layer ➢ New Adjustment Layer ➢ type of adjustment
Create layer from selection	[Ctrl][J] (Win) or ⌘[J] (Mac)
Crop an image	🔲.
Cut selection	Edit ➢ Cut or [Ctrl][X] (Win) or ⌘[X] (Mac)
Deselect selection	Select ➢ Deselect or [Ctrl][D] (Win) or ⌘[D] (Mac)

to do this:	use this method:
Duplicate a layer	Drag layer to 🔲
Duplicate a selection and move it to a new location	🔲. or ◯ or [Shift] M, create selection, press and hold [Ctrl][Alt] (Win) or ⌘ option (Mac), then drag selection to new location
Erase pixels	🖊. or [Shift] E, drag pointer over pixels to be removed
Magnify an area	🔍 or Z, then click image
Paste selection	Edit ➢ Paste or [Ctrl][V] (Win) or ⌘[V] (Mac)
Select a complex object	📓 or [Shift] L
Select and delete by color	✎ or W, then click Edit ➢ Clear

Key: Menu items are indicated by ➢ between the menu name and its command. Blue bold letters are shortcuts for selecting tools on the Tools panel.

Delete unnecessary imagery.

1. Open PS 14-2.psd from the drive and folder where you store your Data Files, then save it as **Paradise Lost**.
2. Zoom in on the metronome.
3. Use the tool of your choice to select as much of the metronome as possible *without* selecting the toy boat or telephone. (*Hint*: You can use the Add to selection button on the options bar, or you can make multiple selections.)
4. Clear the metronome selection from the image.
5. Deselect the selection.
6. Use the Eraser tool and any size brush tip to get rid of any remaining metronome pixels.
7. Create a selection around the telephone and its cord using the tool of your choice. (*Hint*: You can use multiple selections to select this object.)
8. Clear the selection. (*Hint*: You will repair the defects created by this step later.)
9. Deselect the selection.
10. Use the Eraser tool and any size brush tip to get rid of any remaining telephone pixels.
11. Sample the red color of the toy boat image near the damaged area on the shell of the boat.
12. Use the Brush tool and any size brush tip to repair the damaged toy boat (where the telephone was removed).
13. Zoom out to the original magnification.
14. Save your work.

Correct colors in an image.

1. Make the Whistle layer active and visible.
2. Create a Color Balance adjustment layer that is clipped to the Whistle layer.
3. Correct the Cyan/Red level to +73, and the Magenta/Green level to –57.
4. Create a Brightness/Contrast adjustment layer that is clipped to the previous layer.
5. Change the Brightness slider to –10 and the Contrast slider to +15.
6. Use the bounding box feature to rotate the whistle, then nudge the object up using the sample in Figure 17 as a guide.
7. Make the Toy Boat layer active.
8. Create a Hue/Saturation adjustment layer that is clipped to the Toy Boat layer.
9. Change the Hue slider to +45 and the Saturation slider to +60.
10. Save your work.

Tweak an image.

1. Hide the Background layer.
2. Make the Push Pins layer active.
3. Use the tool of your choice, such as the Clone Stamp tool or the Magnetic Lasso tool and the Patch tool, to remove the two shadows above and below of the body of the whistle using Figure 17 as a guide. (*Hint*: You can magnify the area, if necessary.)

4. Apply the Ocean Ripple (Distort) filter using the following settings: Ripple Size = 3, Ripple Magnitude = 6.
5. Display the Background layer.
6. Change the opacity of the Push Pins layer to 60%.
7. Apply the Drop Shadow style to the Toy Boat layer using the default settings.
8. Make the Push Pins layer active.
9. Use the Horizontal Type tool to create a red type layer in the upper-right corner of the image that says Paradise Lost. (In the sample, a Matura MT Script Capitals font is used.)
10. Add the following styles to the type: Drop Shadow, Stroke, and Bevel and Emboss.
11. Save your work, then compare your image to the sample in Figure 17.

FIGURE 17
Completed Skills Review project

An exclusive women's clothing shop, First Class Woman, has hired you to revamp its image by creating the first in a series of advertisements. First Class Woman has been known for some time as a stuffy clothing store that sells pricey designer originals to the over-60 set. The time has come to expand its customer base to include women between the ages of 30 and 60. Their advertising agency recommended you, having seen samples of your work. They want you to inject some humor into your creation. They have provided you with some whimsical images they want to see in the ad.

1. Open PS 14-3.psd, then save it as **First Class Woman**.
2. Separate each of the items in the Glasses, Necklace, Bags layer into their own layers. (*Hint*: You can use the selection method(s) of your choice.)
3. Rename the layers using appropriate names.
4. Apply colors to each renamed thumbnail on the Layers panel.
5. Rearrange the objects as you see fit.
6. Turn on the Show Transform Controls feature. Use a bounding box to resize the glasses, bags, or neckace, if you choose.
7. Make the Fan layer active and visible, then transform the size of the fan so it is smaller. (*Hint*: Click Edit on the Application bar, point to Transform, then use the Scale command.)

8. Make a duplicate of the Glasses layer, accepting the default name.
9. Hide the original Glasses layer.
10. Use the Liquify feature on the duplicate Glasses layer using your choice of effects.
11. Add at least one adjustment layer, as you feel necessary. (*Hint*: In the sample, the Brightness was adjusted to –8, and the Contrast was adjusted to +35 in the Bags layer. In the Necklace layer, the following color balance adjustments were made: Cyan/Red level to +53, the Magenta/Green level to –65, and the Yellow/Blue level to –49. In the Roses layer, the Brightness was adjusted to –55, and the Contrast to –1.)

12. Add a type layer that says **First Class Woman**. (*Hint*: You can use any color and any font available on your computer. In the sample, a 48 pt Snap ITC font is shown.)
13. Warp the type layer using the style and the settings of your choice.
14. Apply the styles of your choice to the text.
15. Adjust the opacity of the Roses layer using any setting you feel is appropriate.
16. Add any filter effects you want. (In the sample, the Smudge Stick filter is applied to the Roses layer, and the Lens Flare filter is applied to the Glasses copy layer.)
17. Save your work, then compare your image to the sample in Figure 18.

FIGURE 18
Sample Project Builder 1

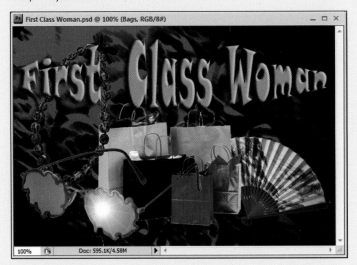

Your local chamber of commerce has asked you to volunteer your services and design a new advertisement for the upcoming membership drive. The theme of this year's membership drive is "The Keys to the City." They have supplied you with an initial image, but the rest is up to you.

1. Open PS 14-4.psd, then save it as **Membership Drive**.
2. Convert the Background layer into an image layer.
3. Rename the layer using any name you want, then apply a color to the thumbnail.
4. Create a new layer, then convert it into a Background layer.
5. Locate at least one piece of appropriate artwork—either a scanned image, an image on your computer, one from a digital camera, or an image from a royalty-free collection—that you can use in this image.
6. Use any appropriate methods to select imagery from the artwork.
7. After the selections have been made, copy them into Membership Drive.
8. Transform any imagery you feel will improve the finished product.
9. Use any method to eliminate some of the keys in the image. (In the sample, the third key from the bottom is eliminated.)
10. Add a type layer using the text and style of your choice to create a catch phrase for the ad. (*Hint*: You can use any color and any font available on your computer. In the sample, a Perpetua font in various sizes is shown.)
11. Add another type layer that contains the chamber of commerce name. (*Hint*: You can use the name of the town in which you live.)
12. Add additional type layers, if desired.
13. Add an adjustment layer to at least one of the layers.
14. Modify the layer containing the keys using any method(s) you want. (In the sample, the Opacity is lowered to 86%, and the Tiles filter is applied.)
15. Save your work, then compare your image to the sample in Figure 19.

FIGURE 19
Sample Project Builder 2

You have seen how you can use Photoshop to take ordinary photographs and manipulate them into exciting artistic creations. You can use the web to find imagery created by many new and exciting artists who specialize in photo manipulation. To broaden your understanding of Photoshop, you decide to closely examine an artistic work, then *deconstruct it* to speculate as to how it was accomplished.

1. Connect to the Internet and use your browser to find digital artwork. (Make a record of the site you found so you can use it for future reference, if necessary.)
2. Click the links for the images until you find one that strikes you as interesting. A sample image is shown in Figure 20.
3. Examine the image, then ask yourself the following questions:
   - What images would you need to create this montage? In what format would you need them (electronic file, hard-copy image, or photograph)?
   - What techniques would you use to create this effect?
   - Do you like this image? If so, why?

4. Be prepared to discuss your answers to these questions, either in writing, in a group discussion, or in a presentation format.

FIGURE 20
Sample Design Project

5. Using your favorite word processor, create a document called **Digital Art Analysis** that records your observations.

Morguefile: (c) 2006 anairam_zeravla. http://www.morguefile.com/archive/?display=134637

You are about to graduate from The Art League, a local, independently-owned institution that trains artists in the use of all art media. Because of your talent, you have been asked to create next year's poster for the school.

1. Develop a design concept for the poster.
2. Create a new Photoshop image with your choice of dimensions.
3. Save this file as **Art School Poster**.
4. Locate several pieces of artwork—either on your hard disk, in a royalty-free collection, from a digital camera, or from scanned images. The images can show anything that is art-related and can be part of other images.
5. Create a layer for each image, then name each layer and apply a color to each layer thumbnail.
6. Transform any imagery you feel will enhance the design.

7. Add a type layer using a style and color of your choosing that contains a phrase you like. (*Hint*: You can use any font available on your computer. A Papyrus font in various sizes is used in the sample.)

8. Add an adjustment layer to at least one of the layers.
9. Add any filter effects, if you decide they will make your image more dramatic.
10. Save your work, then compare your image to the sample in Figure 21.

FIGURE 21
Sample Portfolio Project

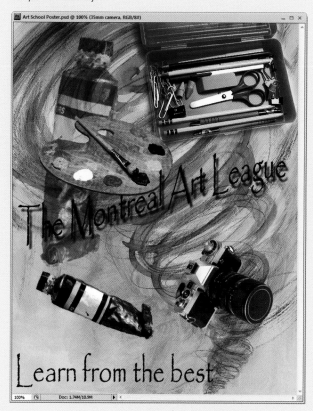

chapter

15

ANNOTATING AND AUTOMATING AN IMAGE

1. Add annotations to an image

2. Create an action

3. Modify an action

4. Use a default action and create a droplet

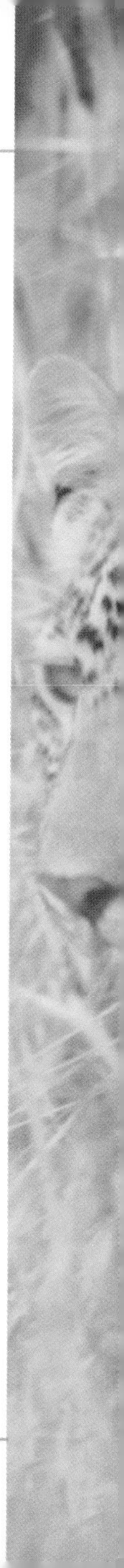

15 ANNOTATING AND
AUTOMATING AN IMAGE

Creating Notes

Have you ever wished you could paste a sticky note on an image, to jot down an idea or include a message to someone who will be reviewing the design? Well, in Photoshop you can, using notes.

Communicating Directly to Your Audience

By creating written **notes**, you can communicate directly to anyone viewing your image. You can place written comments—electronic sticky notes—right in the file. Once a note is in place, anyone opening your image in Photoshop can double-click the note icon and read your comments.

Using Automation

Have you ever performed a repetitive task in Photoshop? Suppose you create an image with several type layers containing different fonts, and then you decide that each of those type layers should use the same font family. To make this change, you would have to perform the following steps on each type layer:

- Select the layer.
- Double-click the layer thumbnail.
- Click the Set the font family list arrow.
- Click the font you want.
- Click the Commit any current edits button.

Wouldn't it be nice if there were a way to speed up commonly performed tasks like this one? That's where automation, courtesy of the Actions feature, comes in. Using this feature you can record these five steps as one action. Then, rather than having to repeat each of the steps, you just play the action.

QUICKTIP

Many programs have a feature that records and then can play back repetitive tasks. Other programs call this feature a macro, script, or behavior.

Tools You'll Use

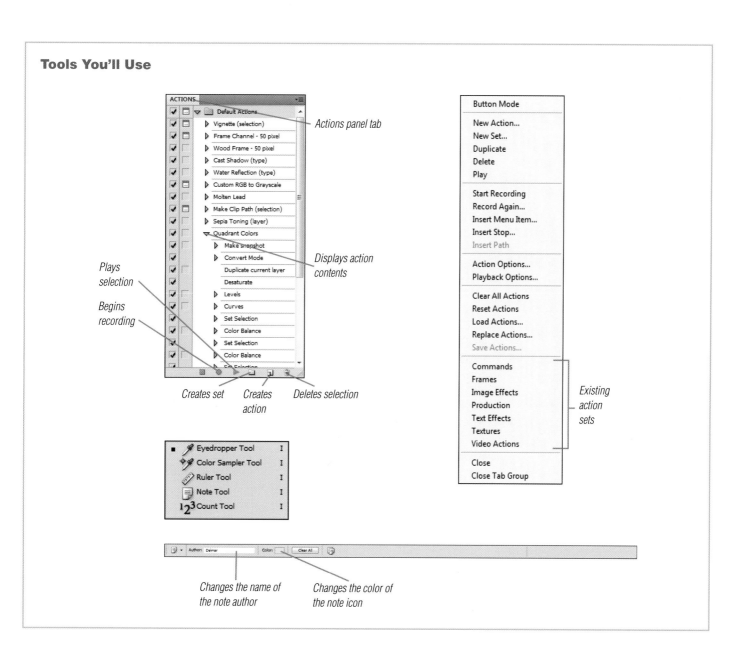

Actions panel tab

Plays selection

Begins recording

Creates set   Creates action   Deletes selection

Displays action contents

Button Mode

New Action...
New Set...
Duplicate
Delete
Play

Start Recording
Record Again...
Insert Menu Item...
Insert Stop...
Insert Path

Action Options...
Playback Options...

Clear All Actions
Reset Actions
Load Actions...
Replace Actions...
Save Actions...

Commands
Frames
Image Effects
Production
Text Effects
Textures
Video Actions

Existing action sets

Close
Close Tab Group

Eyedropper Tool   I
Color Sampler Tool   I
Ruler Tool   I
Note Tool   I
Count Tool   I

Changes the name of the note author

Changes the color of the note icon

ADD ANNOTATIONS TO
AN IMAGE

What You'll Do

In this lesson, you'll create a note.

Creating an Annotation

Annotations are similar to the yellow sticky notes you might attach to a printout. You can create a annotation by clicking the Note tool on the Tools panel (in the Eyedropper group), clicking in the image where you want the note to appear, then typing the contents. Each note within a file has an icon that appears on the image in the work area, as shown in Figure 1, while the contents of the note displays in the Notes panel.

Reading Notes

To open a closed note, double-click the note icon. You can also right-click (Win) or [control]-click (Mac) the note icon, then click Open Note, as shown in Figure 1. You can move the note within the image by dragging the note's icon.

QUICKTIP

You can differentiate between active and inactive notes by the appearance of the note icons. The icon for an inactive note has a solid color, while the icon for an active note displays a pencil.

Using the Notes Panel

The contents of a note displays in the Notes panel, which can be opened by double-clicking a note icon, clicking the Show or hide the notes panel button on the Note tool options bar, or clicking Notes on the Window menu. Scroll bars display in the Notes panel if the contents exceed the window display, although you can resize the Notes panel by dragging any of the edges (Win) or the bottom edge (Mac) to the desired dimension. The status bar (at the bottom of the Notes panel) contains left and right arrows that let you navigate all the notes within an image, a counter to tell you which note is currently active, and a trash can that lets you delete the active note.

QUICKTIP

You can delete a selected note by clicking the Delete note button in the Notes panel, pressing [Delete], or by right-clicking the note (Win) or [control]-clicking the note (Mac), then clicking Delete Note.

Personalizing a Note

By default, the note icon is a pale yellow color. You can change this color by clicking the Note color box on the options bar. When the Select note color dialog box opens, you can use any method to change the color, such as sampling an area within an existing image. You can also change the author of the note by selecting the contents in the Name of author for notes text box, typing the information you want, then pressing [Enter] (Win) or [return] (Mac).

The font size of the note can be changed using the Type section of the Preferences command in the Edit menu (Win) or Photoshop menu (Mac).

FIGURE 1
Open note in an image

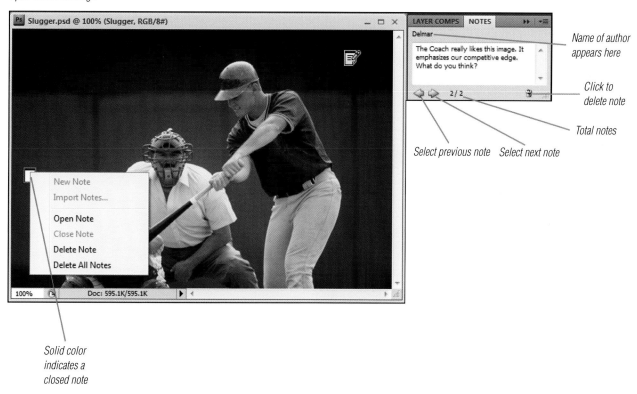

Name of author appears here

Click to delete note

Total notes

Select previous note   Select next note

Solid color indicates a closed note

Create a note

1. Open PS 15-1.psd from the drive and folder where you store your Data Files, update the text layers (if necessary), save the file as **Hawaiian Vacation**, then turn off any displayed guides (if necessary).

2. Click the **Note tool** ![note icon] on the Tools panel.

3. If your name does not appear in the Name of author for notes text box on the options bar, select the contents of the text box, type **Your Name**, then press **[Enter]** (Win) or **[return]** (Mac).

4. Click the **Swatches panel tab** SWATCHES , click the **Note color box** ☐ on the options bar, then click **RGB Cyan** (the fourth swatch from the left in the first row) on the Swatches panel.

5. Click **OK**. Compare your options bar to Figure 2. The Note color box is cyan.

6. Display the rulers in pixels, then click in the water above the far left button at approximately **30 X/220 Y**.

7. Type the text shown in Figure 3.

8. Click the **Show or hide the notes panel button** ![icon] in the Note tool options bar, then compare your image to Figure 4.

You used the Note tool to create a note within an image. You specified an author for the note, and you changed the color of the note icon using the Swatches panel. Notes are a great way to transmit information about an image.

FIGURE 2
Options for the Note tool

Your name will
be different

Click to display the
Notes panel

FIGURE 3
Note annotation in image

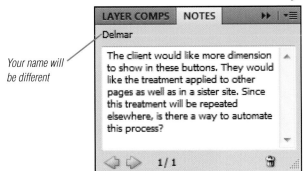

Your name will
be different

FIGURE 4
Note icon

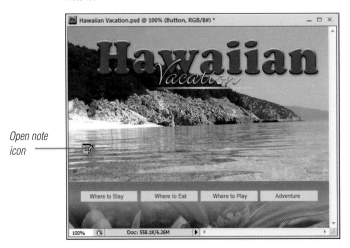

Open note
icon

FIGURE 5
Notes panel contents

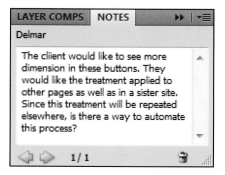

FIGURE 6
Note icon in image

Modify a note annotation

1. Click the **Show or hide the notes panel button** in the Note tool options bar.

2. Click to the **left of 'more'** in the first line of the note, type **to see**, select **to show (and its trailing space)**, then press **[Delete]**.

    Compare your note to Figure 5.

3. Click the image in the **shaded mountain** to the right of the island (beneath the 'n').

4. Type **The client may want to find another image for the next advertising cycle**.

5. Click the **Select previous note button**.

    The first note displays in the Notes panel.

6. Click the **Select next note button** in the Notes panel.

7. Click the **Delete note button** in the Notes panel, then click **Yes** to delete the note.

    One note remains in the image.

8. Save your work, then compare your image to Figure 6.

You modified an existing note, added a new note, viewed each of the notes using buttons in the Notes panel, then deleted the second note.

CREATE AN ACTION

What You'll Do

In this lesson, you'll create an action that applies a style to a layer by creating a snapshot that is used to restore your file to its original condition, then you'll record steps using the Actions panel.

Simplifying Common Tasks

Suppose you are responsible for maintaining the ad slicks for all your company's products (and there are a lot of them). What would you do if the company decided to change their image designs so that each existing product advertisement is shown with Drop Shadow and Inner Shadow styles? (Resigning your position is *not* an option.) Instead, you can create an action to speed up this monumental task.

Understanding Actions

Most tasks that you perform using a button or menu command can be recorded as an action. Each action can contain one or more steps and can also contain a **stop**, which lets you complete a command that can't be recorded (for example, the use of a painting tool). Actions can be stored in sets, which are saved as .atn files and are typically named by the category of actions they contain. For example, you can create multiple type-related actions, then store them in a set named Type Actions. You access actions from the Actions panel,

which is normally grouped with the History panel. You can view actions in List Mode or in Button Mode on the Actions panel. The **List Mode**, the default, makes it possible to view the details within each action. The **Button Mode** displays each action without details.

QUICKTIP

The act of creating an action is not recorded on the History panel; however, the steps you record to define a new action are recorded on the History panel.

Knowing Your Options

You use commonly recognizable media player buttons to operate an action. These buttons are located at the bottom of the Actions panel and let you play, record and stop, as well as move forward and backward in an action.

QUICKTIP

The Actions panel displays in the Automation workspace.

Annotating and Automating an Image

Recording an Action

When recording is active, the red Recording button on the Actions panel appears. The action set also opens as soon as you begin recording to show all the individual actions in the set.

QUICKTIP

To test your actions, first you can create a snapshot of your image. Then you work on an action, make any changes, or record new steps. Use the snapshot to restore the image to its original state. After the image is restored, you can play the action to verify that the steps work.

Playing Back Actions

You can modify how actions are played back using the Playback Options dialog box, as shown in Figure 7. The playback options are described in Table 1. You can open the Playback Options dialog box by clicking the Actions panel list arrow, then clicking Playback Options. The Accelerated, Step by Step, and Pause For options control the speed at which the steps are performed.

QUICKTIP

An action creates internal automation, while **a script** (or scripting) creates external automation from an outside source. JavaScript, for example, lets you write Photoshop scripts that run on Windows or Mac OS.

FIGURE 7
Playback Options dialog box

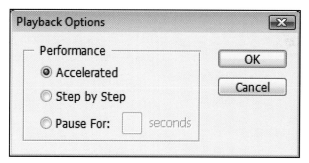

TABLE 1: Action Playback Options

option	description
Accelerated	Plays all steps within an action, then makes all changes.
Step by Step	Completes each step in an action and redraws the image before advancing to the next step.
Pause For	Lets you specify the number of seconds that should occur between steps in an action.

Create an action

1. Display the **Automation** workspace.
2. Click **Window** on the Application bar, click **History** to display the History panel, then click the **Create new snapshot button** 📷 .
3. Drag the **History panel tab** `HISTORY` out of the Actions panel group so it appears separately to the left of the Actions panel.

   TIP By default, the History panel window is small. Enlarge it by dragging the bottom edge.

4. Verify that the **triangle** to the left of the Default Actions set on the Actions panel is facing to the right and that the set is closed. Compare your panel to Figure 8.

   TIP You can toggle the button mode on and off by clicking the list arrow on the Actions panel, then clicking Button Mode.

   You can click the triangle next to a *set* to show or hide the actions in it. You can also click the triangle next to an *action* to show or hide the steps in it.

   TIP When you create an action in the Default Actions set, or in any set, the action is available in all your Photoshop images.

5. Click the **Create new action button** 🔲 on the Actions panel. The New Action dialog box opens.
6. Type **Button Drop Shadow** in the Name text box.
7. Click the **Color list arrow**, click **Violet**, then compare your dialog box to Figure 9.
8. Click **Record**. Did you notice that the red Recording button is displayed on the Actions panel and all default actions opened? See Figure 10.

You created a snapshot to make it possible to easily test the new action. You used the Create new action button on the Actions panel to create an action called Button Drop Shadow.

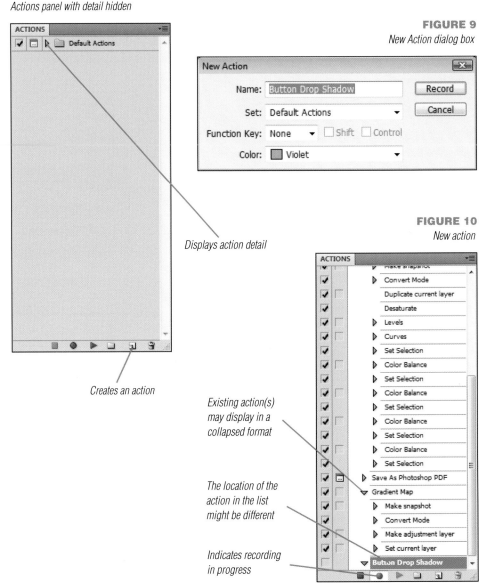

FIGURE 8
Actions panel with detail hidden

FIGURE 9
New Action dialog box

Displays action detail

Creates an action

FIGURE 10
New action

Existing action(s) may display in a collapsed format

The location of the action in the list might be different

Indicates recording in progress

Annotating and Automating an Image

FIGURE 11

Layer Style dialog box

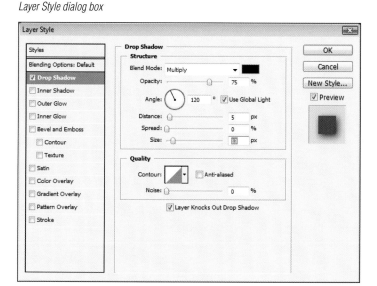

FIGURE 12

Selected action

FIGURE 13

Modified image

— Drop shadow
behind buttons

Record an action

1. Click the **Button layer** on the Layers panel (if it is not already selected).

2. Click the **Add a layer style button** *fx.* on the Layers panel, click **Drop Shadow**, then change your Layer Style dialog box settings so they match those shown in Figure 11.

3. Click **OK**.

4. Click the **Stop playing/recording button** on the Actions panel.

5. Click the **Button Drop Shadow action** on the Actions panel. See Figure 12.

6. Scroll to the top of the History panel (if necessary), then click **Snapshot 1**.

   The Button layer returns to its original appearance.

7. With the **Button Drop Shadow action** still selected, click the **Play selection button** on the Actions panel.

8. Save your work, then compare your screen to Figure 13.

You recorded steps for the Button Drop Shadow action. After the recording was complete, you used a snapshot to restore the image to its original state, \then you played the action to test it. Testing is an important step in creating an action.

MODIFY AN ACTION

What You'll Do

In this lesson, you'll modify the recently created action by adding new steps to it.

Getting It Right

Few of us get everything right the first time we try to do something. After you create an action, you might think of other steps that you want to include, such as changing the order of some or all of the steps, or altering an option. The beauty of Photoshop actions is that you can make modifications and additions to them with little effort.

Revising an Action

You can modify an existing action by clicking the step that is just above where you want the new step(s) to appear. Click the Begin recording button on the Actions panel, record your steps (just as you did when you initially created the action), then click the Stop playing/recording button when you're finished. The new steps are inserted after the selected step.

QUICKTIP

Because users may not know how to resume playback after encountering a stop, it's a good idea to include a helpful tip that tells them to click the Play selection button after encountering the stop.

Changing the Actions Panel View

In addition to dragging the borders to change the shape of the Actions panel, you can also change the way the steps are displayed. By default, actions are displayed in a list; the steps appear as a list below each action included in them. Figure 14 shows the actions in the Default Actions set in a list in which all the detail is accessible but hidden. (Remember that you can display the detail for each action by clicking the triangle next to the action, to expand it.)

Working in Button Mode

In Button Mode, each action is displayed as a button—without the additional detail found in the list format. Each button is displayed in the color selected when the action was created and the Play button is not displayed. In Button Mode, all you need to do to play an action is to click the button. Figure 15 shows the same actions in Button Mode. You can toggle between these two modes by clicking the Actions panel list arrow, then clicking Button Mode, as shown in Figure 16.

Annotating and Automating an Image

FIGURE 14

Actions displayed in a list

FIGURE 15

Actions displayed in Button Mode

FIGURE 16

Actions panel menu

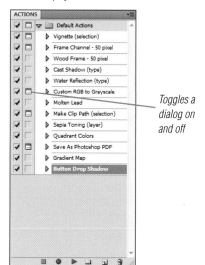

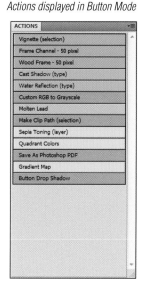

Toggles a dialog on and off

Switches between list and button modes

Understanding a stop

In addition to containing any Photoshop task, an action can include a stop, which is a command that interrupts playback to allow you to perform other operations—particularly those that cannot be recorded in an action, or those that might change each time you play the action. You insert a stop by clicking the step *just above* where you want the pause to take place. Click the Actions panel list arrow, then click Insert Stop. The Record Stop dialog box opens, allowing you to enter a text message that appears when the action is stopped, as shown in Figure 17. You select the Allow Continue check box to include a Continue button in the message that appears when the action is stopped. You can resume the action by clicking this button. An action that contains a dialog box—such as an action that contains a stop—displays a toggle dialog on/off icon to the left of the action name on the Actions panel. This icon indicates a **modal control**, which means that dialog boxes are *used* in the action, but are not displayed. When the action is resumed, the tasks begin where they were interrupted. You can resume the action by clicking the Play selection button on the Actions panel.

FIGURE 17

Record Stop dialog box

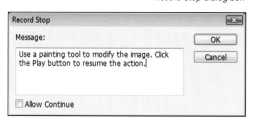

Add steps to an action

1. Verify that the **Button layer** is active on the Layers panel.

2. Click the **Set Layer Styles of current layer step** (the first step) in the Button Drop Shadow action on the Actions panel.

3. Click the **Begin recording button**  on the Actions panel.

4. Click **Image** on the Application bar, point to **Adjustments**, then click **Brightness/Contrast**. Change the settings in your dialog box to match the settings in Figure 18.

5. Click **OK**.

6. Click the **Stop playing/recording button** on the Actions panel. Compare your Actions panel to Figure 19.

   The Button Drop Shadow action has a new step added to it.

7. Click **Snapshot 1** on the History panel.

8. Click the **Button Drop Shadow action** on the Actions panel, then click the **Play selection button** on the Actions panel. Compare your screen to Figure 20.

You added a new step (which modified the brightness/contrast) to the Button Drop Shadow action. You then tested the modified action by using a snapshot and playing the action.

FIGURE 18
Brightness/Contrast dialog box

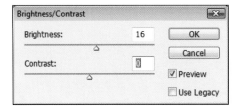

FIGURE 19
New steps added to the Button Drop Shadow action

FIGURE 20
Result of modified action

Annotating and Automating an Image

FIGURE 21
Modified image

Automating with data sets

You can use the Photoshop Variables feature to combine text and images into a graphic template. Imagine a Photoshop image that contains placeholders for the name of a car, it's make and model, price, and an image of the car. Use as many layers as you like to put all the graphic elements needed to finish the completed files, such as .jpgs for each car, in a single folder, click Image on the Application bar, point to Variables, then click Define. Use the Variables dialog box to assign variables for text and graphic layers, and use a text editor to create a document containing variables separated by commas. To create the data sets, click Image on the Application bar, point to Variables, point to Data Sets, then click Import. You can export the data sets as individual files by clicking File on the Application bar, pointing to Export, then clicking Data Sets as Files. Once you've made any changes to the individual files, you can use the Image Processor in Bridge to create flattened copies.

1. Click the **Brightness/Contrast step** on the Actions panel (the second step in the Button Drop Shadow action).

2. Click the **Begin recording button** ● on the Actions panel.

3. Click the **Add a layer style button** *fx.* on the Layers panel.

4. Click **Bevel and Emboss**, then click **OK** to accept the existing settings.

5. Click the **Stop playing/recording button** ▪ on the Actions panel.

   The new step is added to the existing action. Table 2 describes other ways to modify actions.

6. Click **Snapshot 1** on the History panel.

7. Click the **Button Drop Shadow action** on the Actions panel, then click the **Play selection button** ▶ on the Actions panel.

8. Save your work, then compare your image to Figure 21.

You added the Bevel and Emboss style to an action, then you tested the action.

TABLE 2: Methods for Modifying an Action

modification type	method
Rearrange steps	Move an existing step by dragging the step to a new location in the action.
Add new commands	Click the step above or below where you want the new step to appear, then click ▶.
Rerecord existing commands	Click the step you want to recreate, click ▾☰, then click Record Again.
Duplicate existing commands	Click the step you want to duplicate, click ▾☰, then click Duplicate.
Delete actions	Click the action you want to delete, then click 🗑.
Delete a step in an action	Click the step you want to delete, then click 🗑.
Change options in an action	Click the step that has options you want to change, click ▾☰, then click Action Options or Playback Options.

USE A DEFAULT ACTION
AND CREATE A DROPLET

What You'll Do

In this lesson, you'll use actions from other sets and create a droplet.

Taking Advantage of Actions

Photoshop actions can really help your session by automating tedious tasks. You can add a default action to any action you've created. A **default action** is an action that is prerecorded and tested, and comes with Photoshop. You can incorporate some of these nifty actions that come with Photoshop into those you create.

Identifying Default Actions

The default actions that come with Photoshop are Vignette, Frame Channel, Wood Frame, Cast Shadow, Water Reflection, Custom RGB to Grayscale, Molten Lead, Make Clip Path (selection), Sepia Toning (layer), Quadrant Colors, Save As Photoshop PDF, and Gradient Map. In addition, there are seven action sets that come with Photoshop: Commands, Frames, Image Effects, Production, Text Effects, Textures, and Video Actions. You can load any of these action sets by clicking the Actions panel list arrow, then clicking the name of the set you want to load.

Using Default Actions

You can incorporate any of the default actions that come with Photoshop—or those you get from other sources—into a new action by playing the action in the process of recording a new one. Each time an existing action is played, a new snapshot is created on the History panel, so don't be surprised when you see additional snapshots that you never created. To incorporate an existing action into a new action, first select the step that is *above* where you want the new action to occur. Begin recording your action, then scroll through the Actions panel and play the action you want to include. When the action has completed all steps, you can continue recording other steps or click the Stop playing/recording button if you are done. That's it: all of the steps in the default action will be performed when you play your new action.

Loading Sets

In addition to the Default Actions, the seven additional sets of actions are listed at the bottom of the Actions panel menu.

If you store actions from other sources on your computer you can load those actions by clicking the Actions panel list arrow, clicking Load Actions, then choosing the action you want from the Load dialog box. The default sets that come with Photoshop are stored in the Actions folder that is in the Presets folder of the Adobe Photoshop CS4 folder.

QUICKTIP

If you want to save actions to distribute to others, you must first put them in a set. You create a set by clicking the Create new set button on the Actions panel (just like creating a Layer set). Place the action or actions in a set, select the set, click the Actions panel list arrow, then click Save Actions.

Understanding a Droplet

A **droplet** is a stand-alone action in the form of an icon. You can drag one or more closed Photoshop files onto a droplet icon to perform the action on the file or files. You can store droplets on the hard drive on your computer, place them on your desktop, or distribute them to others using other storage media. Figure 22 shows an example of a droplet on the desktop. Droplets let you further automate repetitive tasks.

Creating a Droplet

You create a droplet by using the Automate command on the File menu, an existing action, and the Create Droplet dialog box. In the Create Droplet dialog box, you use the Set list arrow to choose the set that

contains the action you want to use to create the droplet, then use the Action list arrow to choose the action. Finally, you can choose the location on your computer where you'll store the droplet.

QUICKTIP

When placed on the desktop, a droplet has a unique down-arrow icon filled with the Photoshop logo. The droplet name appears below the icon.

FIGURE 22
A droplet on the desktop

Photoshop droplet

Icons on your desktop will be different

Automating using batches

There may be times when you might need to perform the same action on multiple files. Rather than dragging each image onto a droplet, one at a time, you can combine all of the images into a batch. A **batch** is a group of images designated to have the same action performed on them simultaneously. You can create a batch using all of the files in one specific folder or using all of the Photoshop images that are currently open. When you have opened or organized the files you want to include in a batch, click File on the Application bar, point to Automate, then click Batch. The Batch dialog box opens, offering you options similar to those used for creating droplets. You can also use Adobe Bridge as a source of creating batches by clicking Tools on the Adobe Bridge menu bar, pointing to Photoshop, then clicking Batch.

Include a default action within an action

1. Verify that the **Set Layer Styles of current layer step** at the bottom of the Actions panel is active (the last step in the Button Drop Shadow action).

   > TIP If your Actions panel becomes too messy, you can clear it by clicking the Actions panel list arrow, then clicking Clear All Actions. To restore the Default Actions set, click the Actions panel list arrow, then click Reset Actions.

2. Verify that the **Button layer** is active in the Layers panel.

3. Click the **Begin recording button** ⏺ on the Actions panel.

4. Scroll to the top of the Actions panel, then click the **Cast Shadow (type) action**, as shown in Figure 23.

You prepared to insert the Cast Shadow default action into the Button Drop Shadow action. If this action had been applied to a type layer, the type would have been rasterized before the effect could be applied.

FIGURE 23

Action to be added to the Button Drop Shadow action

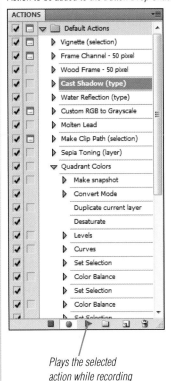

Plays the selected
action while recording

FIGURE 24

Example of a website that offers Photoshop Actions

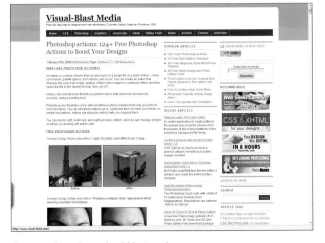

Courtesy of http://www.visual-blast.com/

FIGURE 25

*Cast Shadow action in the Button Drop
Shadow action*

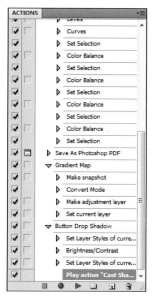

FIGURE 26

Modified Layers panel

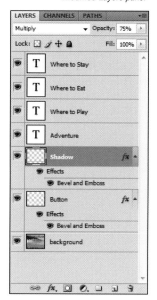

Play an existing action in a new action

1. Click the **Play selection button** ▶ on the Actions panel.

2. Click the **Stop playing/recording button** ■ on the Actions panel. A new layer is created in the Layers panel. Compare your Actions panel to Figure 25.

3. Click **Snapshot 1** on the History panel.

   TIP Some default actions create a snapshot as their initial step. For this reason, you might see multiple snapshots on the History panel.

4. Click the **Button Drop Shadow action** on the Actions panel.

5. Click the **Play selection button** ▶ on the Actions panel.

6. Save your work, then compare your Layers panel to Figure 26.

   The Cast Shadow action added a reflection beneath the buttons.

You included the Cast Shadow action in the Button Drop Shadow action. You used the snapshot to revert to the image's original appearance and replayed the action, which modified the image.

Understanding scripts and actions

Like an action, a script is a series of commands that manipulates objects in Photoshop and the other programs of the Creative Suite. While individual actions are tremendous time-savers, you can use Photoshop Scripts to save even more time performing repetitive tasks. A script has the following advantages over an action in that it can:

- contain conditional logic, giving it the ability to make decisions based on content.
- perform actions that involve multiple applications, such as those programs found in the Creative Suite.
- open, save, and rename files.
- be copied from one computer to another. An action would have to be recreated or turned into a droplet.
- use variable file paths to locate and open a file.

You can manage scripts within Photoshop using the Script Events Manager, which is accessed by clicking File on the Application bar, pointing to Scripts, then clicking Script Events Manager.

Create a droplet

1. Click **File** on the Application bar, point to **Automate**, then click **Create Droplet**.

2. Click **Choose** in the Create Droplet dialog box.

   The Save dialog box opens.

3. Type **Button Drop Shadow-Cast Shadow** in the File name text box (Win) or Save As text box (Mac) in the Save dialog box.

4. Click the **Save in list arrow** (Win) or **Places panel** (Mac), then click **Desktop**, as shown in Figure 27.

   > TIP You can create a droplet and save it anywhere on your computer by clicking the Save in list arrow (Win) or Places panel (Mac), and clicking the location where you want to store the file.

5. Click **Save**.

6. Click the **Action list arrow** in the Create Droplet dialog box, then click **Button Drop Shadow** (if it is not already selected). Compare your dialog box settings to Figure 28.

7. Click **OK**.

You created a droplet using the Button Drop Shadow action and saved it to the desktop for easy access.

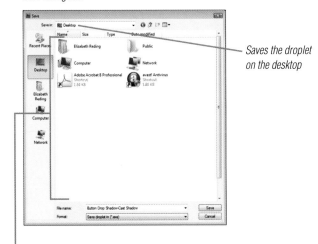

FIGURE 27
Save dialog box

Saves the droplet on the desktop

Your list will be different

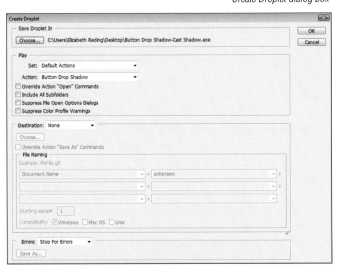

FIGURE 28
Create Droplet dialog box

Annotating and Automating an Image

FIGURE 29
Droplet on desktop

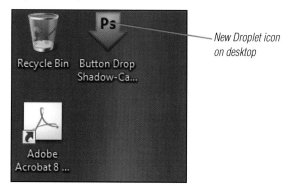

New Droplet icon
on desktop

FIGURE 30
Image updated by droplet

Run a droplet

1. Minimize all open windows so the desktop is visible, then compare your desktop to Figure 29.

2. Maximize the Photoshop window.

3. Click **Snapshot 1** on the History panel.

4. Save your work, close the Hawaiian Vacation image, then minimize Photoshop (Win) or Hide Photoshop (Mac).

    TIP   When Photoshop is *not* running, activating a droplet automatically launches the program.

5. Locate the closed Hawaiian Vacation image on your computer, using the file management program of your choice, then adjust the windows so you can see the Hawaiian Vacation file and the droplet icon on the desktop.

6. Drag the **Hawaiian Vacation file** onto the droplet icon on the desktop.

    The Photoshop window is restored, the Hawaiian Vacation image opens, and the action is replayed.

    TIP   Sometimes a file automatically closes after a droplet has been applied. To see the applied droplet, you must reopen the file.

7. Display the **Essentials workspace**, save your work, then compare your screen to Figure 30.

8. Close the file and exit Photoshop, then drag the **droplet** to the location where you store your Data Files.

You returned the image to its original appearance by using Snapshot 1 on the History panel, and closed the file. Then you tested the droplet by dragging the Hawaiian Vacation file onto the droplet.

Power User Shortcuts

to do this:	use this method:
Apply droplet	Drag closed Photoshop file onto droplet
Change author display	📄 or [Shift] I, then type name in Name of author for notes text box
Change Note icon color	📄 or [Shift] I, click Note color color box, choose color, then click OK
Close an open note	Click 📄
Collapse action detail	▼
Create a batch	File ➤ Automate ➤ Batch
Create a droplet	File ➤ Automate ➤ Create Droplet
Create a note	📄 or [Shift] I, then click where you want the note to appear
Create a snapshot	📷 on the History panel
Create an action	⬛ on the Actions panel, select options, then click ●
Delete a note	Select note, press [Delete] (Win), or click 🗑

to do this:	use this method:
Expand action detail	▷
Open a closed note	Double-click note icon
Play an action	▶
Record an action	● , then perform tasks
Record an action from another set	● , click existing action in another set, click ▶, then click ⬛
Return Actions panel to original size and location	Workspace Switcher➤ Automation
Revert image to original appearance using a snapshot	HISTORY , click snapshot
Stop recording	⬛
Toggle Actions panel between List and Button Modes	▼≣, then click Button Mode
Select next note	▷
Select previous note	◁

Key: Menu items are indicated by ➤ between the menu name and its command. Blue bold letters are shortcuts for selecting tools on the Tools panel.

Add annotations to an image.

1. Open PS 15-2.psd from the drive and folder where you store your Data Files, then save it as **Team Players**.
2. Select the Note tool.
3. Enter your name as the Author of the note (if necessary).
4. Change the Note color to Pure Magenta (the second box from the right in the fifth row of the Swatches panel).
5. Display the rulers (if necessary).
6. Click the image at 30 X/650 Y, then type the following: **This will make a great motivational poster for our department**.
7. Close the note.
8. Hide the rulers, then save your work.

Create an action.

1. Make the A Source of Strength and Stability layer active (if it is not already active).
2. Display the Automation workspace and the History panel, and create a new snapshot using the History panel, then display the Actions panel.
3. Collapse the Default Actions set (if necessary).
4. Create a new action using the Actions panel.
5. Name the new action **Motivation**, and apply the color Yellow to it.
6. Record the action using the following steps:
   a. Make the Team Players layer active.
   b. Change the font in this layer to an 85 pt Impact (or another font available on your computer).
   c. Stop recording.

7. Click Snapshot 1 on the History panel to restore the original appearance of the image.
8. Replay the Motivation action.
9. Save your work.

Modify an action.

1. Select Set current text layer of the Motivation action at the bottom of the Actions panel.
2. Begin recording the following steps:
   a. Make the A Source of Strength and Stability layer active.
   b. Change the font in this layer to a 36 pt Impact (or another font available on your computer).
   c. Make the Team Players layer active.
   d. Add the default Bevel and Emboss style with Contour to the layer.
   e. Stop recording.
3. Click Snapshot 1 on the History panel to restore the original appearance of the image.
4. Replay the Motivation action.
5. Save your work.

Use a default action and create a droplet.

1. Make the A Source of Strength and Stability layer active.
2. Select the Set Layer Styles of current layer step (the last step in the Motivation action).
3. Begin recording the following steps:
   a. Make the Team Players layer active.
   b. Play the Water Reflection (type) action in Default Actions. (Substitute another action if this one is not available.)
   c. Stop recording.

4. Click Snapshot 1 on the History panel to restore the original appearance of the image.
5. Replay the Motivation action.
6. Restore Snapshot 1, then save your changes.
7. Create a droplet on the desktop called **Motivation** using the Motivation action, save your work, then exit Photoshop.
8. Drag the Team Players file onto the Motivation droplet. See Figure 31.
9. Drag the droplet to the location where you store your Data Files.

FIGURE 31
Completed Skills Review project

As the newest member of the Game Corporation design team, you have noticed that some of your fellow designers perform many repetitive tasks and could really benefit from using actions. One of these repetitive tasks is taking a single-layer image, creating a layer from the Background layer, creating a new layer, then turning the new layer into the Background layer. This way, they can preserve the Background layer while modifying the image that was on the existing Background layer. You want to make their lives easier, so you decide to create an action that completes this task. To circulate the action among your co-workers, you decide to create a droplet for this action that you can e-mail or post to the network. (*Hint:* There are a variety of steps in a varied sequence you can take to create this action.)

1. Open PS 15-3.psd, then save it as **New Layers**.
2. Create a snapshot of the current image using the default name.
3. Hide any displayed action details (if necessary).
4. Write down the steps you will need to perform to create this action. (You can use a word processor or a sheet of paper, or you can use the Notes panel in Photoshop.)
5. Create a new action in the Default Actions set called **New Layers**.

6. Apply the Orange color to the action.
7. Record the necessary steps to complete the action.
8. Use the snapshot to return the image to its original condition.
9. Play the action to verify that it works as you expected.
10. If the action does not perform as expected, make any necessary modifications to it.

FIGURE 32
Sample Project Builder 1

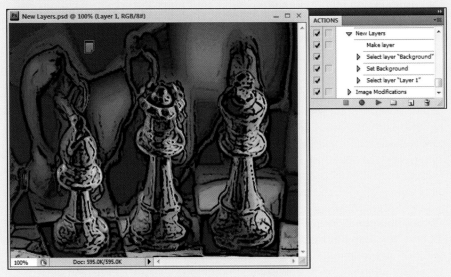

11. Save your work, then compare your screen, Layers panel, and Actions panel to the sample in Figure 32.
12. Create a droplet for the action named **New Layers**, then save it in the drive and folder where you store your Data Files.

An anniversary is coming up for some friends of your family. You and your twin have decided to collaborate on a gift, even though you live at opposite sides of the country. You each have a great photo of the couple that you'd like to modify in the same way, using Photoshop. Because your twin has a slow Internet connection, you decide to create a droplet (which is significantly smaller in size than a completed Photoshop image), then e-mail the droplet so that your twin can apply it to the photo. The droplet can be used to apply your proposed modifications to the picture.

1. Open PS 15-4.psd, then save it as **Anniversary Gift**.
2. Create a snapshot of the current image using the default name.
3. After examining the image, decide what changes you want to make. Write down the steps you will need to perform to create this action, including any stops. (*Hint*: You can use any of your Photoshop skills and any Photoshop features. It is recommended that you create a layer from the Background layer, then create a new layer to be used as the Background layer. Include any necessary color corrections in adjustment layers.)
4. Create a new action in the Default Actions set called **Image Modifications**.
5. Apply the red color to the action (for the Button Mode).

6. Record the steps you wrote down. (*Hint*: In the sample, a 48 pt Trebuchet MS font is used. You do not have to include a type layer, but if you do, use any font available on your computer.)
7. Use the snapshot to return the image to its original condition.
8. Play the action to verify that it works as you expected.

FIGURE 33
Sample Project Builder 2

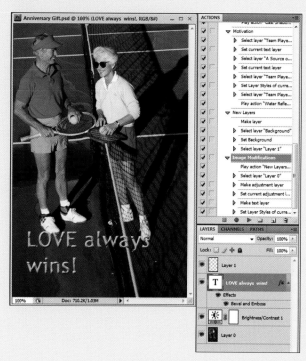

9. If the action does not perform as expected, make any necessary corrections to it.
10. Save your work, then compare your image, Layers panel, and Actions panel to the sample in Figure 33.
11. Create a droplet for the new action called **Gift Image**, and save it to the drive and folder where you store your Data Files.

Annotating and Automating an Image

The Internet is a great resource for actions and droplets. You can find many actions that incorporate sophisticated design concepts. Some websites let you download actions for free, while others might charge a subscription fee. As you perfect your skills using actions, you decide to scour the web and see what cool actions you can find.

1. Connect to the Internet and use your browser to find Photoshop actions. (Make a record of the site you found so you can use it for future reference, if necessary.)
2. Download an action that you want to try.
3. Create a new Photoshop image called **Action Sample** using any dimensions.
4. Supply any imagery and/or type layers by using any electronic images you can acquire through Internet purchase, from your hard disk, or by using a scanner. Use any fonts available on your computer.
5. Duplicate the image and type layers to preserve your original image.
6. Create a note anywhere on the image, indicating the source of the action (include the URL).
7. Create a snapshot of the image.
8. Load and play the action in the image. If necessary, click Continue or OK to accept any messages or settings in dialog boxes that open.
9. Create a droplet called **Play Downloaded Action**.
10. Save your work to the drive and folder where you store your Data Files, then compare your
11. screen (and the partial view of the downloaded action) to the sample in Figure 34.
12. Review the design features used in your downloaded action.

FIGURE 34
Sample Design Project

Creating an interesting design can be a challenge. As a motivational exercise, the head of your department has asked you to create an image to inspire a positive working environment using Photoshop actions, along with your raw creativity and imagination. You can choose any topic for the artwork, work with any existing or scanned imagery, and use any new or existing actions. As you determine what actions to create, think about why a series of tasks is worthy of an action. How will automating a task benefit you, your co-workers, and your organization? Think efficiency; think quality.

1. Create a new Photoshop image with any dimensions.
2. Save this file as **Game Plan**.
3. Locate artwork—either on your computer, in a royalty-free collection, or from scanned images.
4. Sketch a rough draft of your layout.
5. Add any necessary type layers using any fonts available on your computer. (*Hint*: In the sample, a Comic Sans MS font is used.)
6. Create a note that lists the actions you used. (*Hint*: You can use actions created in this chapter, or you can create one or more new actions, if necessary.)

7. Write down the steps that were used in any new actions. Review the following questions: Why did you create the actions that you did? What factors determined that a task should be converted into an action?

8. Be prepared to prove that the actions work correctly.
9. Save your work, then compare your image, Layers panel, and Actions panel to the sample in Figure 35.

FIGURE 35
Sample Portfolio Project

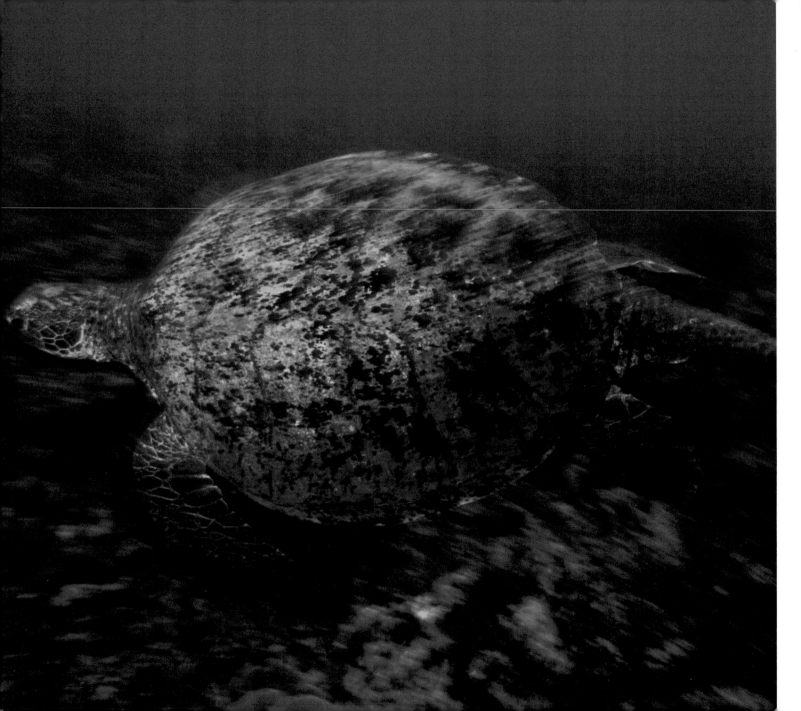

chapter

16

CREATING IMAGES FOR
THE WEB

1. Learn about web features

2. Optimize images for web use

3. Create a button for a web page

4. Create slices in an image

5. Create and play basic animation

6. Add tweening and frame delay

7. Modify video in Photoshop

8. Use Camera Raw features

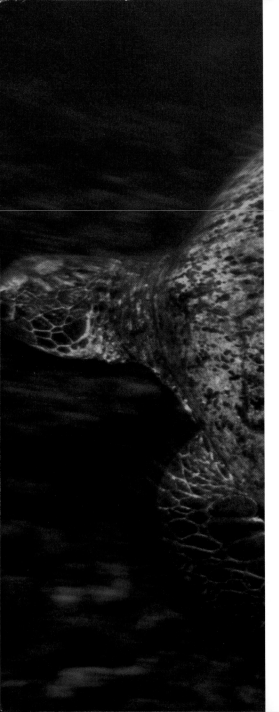

16 CREATING IMAGES FOR
THE WEB

Using Photoshop for the Web

In addition to creating exciting images that can be professionally printed, you can use the tools in Photoshop to create images for use on the web. Once you have a Photoshop image, you can use additional web-specific tools and features to add the dimension and functionality required by today's web audience.

Understanding Web Graphics

Images and graphics can be tailored specifically for the web by creating buttons and other features unique to web pages. Using Photoshop, you can combine impressive graphics with interactive functionality to create an outstanding website.

> **QUICK**TIP
>
> Photoshop provides the capabilities for dividing one image into smaller, more manageable parts, and for creating more efficient web-ready files.

Extending Skills to Video

Photoshop Extended and QuickTime can be used to play and modify video. Almost any Photoshop skill you can apply to images can be applied to video clips.

Fine-Tuning Images with Camera Raw

Images that you take with your own digital camera can be tweaked using Adobe Bridge and the Camera Raw dialog box. You can use the Camera Raw dialog box to adjust images in RAW format (as well as those in JPG and TIFF formats) while preserving all the original image data.

Tools You'll Use

Slice tool

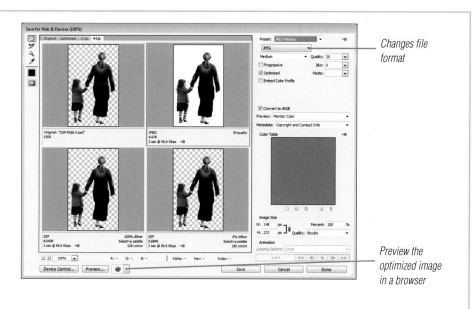

Changes file format

Preview the optimized image in a browser

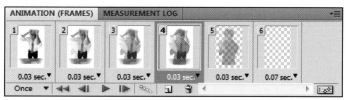

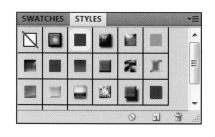

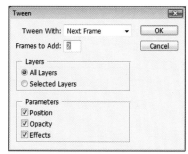

LEARN ABOUT
WEB FEATURES

What You'll Do

In this lesson, you'll open and rename a file in Photoshop, create slices and then turn off the display of the slices.

Using Photoshop to Create Web Documents

Using Photoshop to create web documents is similar to creating any other image, except that there are new features that you will use. These new features include **slices** (subsections of an image to which you can assign additional functionality) and the Animation panel. The Animation panel does exactly what it's name suggests: it is used to apply movement to layers in an image.

QUICKTIP

Photoshop contains a web-specific workspace (called Web) that contains panels you're likely to use when creating documents for the web.

Previewing Files for the Web

You can add many sophisticated web effects to the files you create in Photoshop, such as slices and animation, as shown in Figure 1. To insert and view them in a web page, you need to follow the procedures dictated by your HTML editor. HTML (Hypertext Markup Language) is the language used for creating web pages. You can preview most web effects directly in Photoshop. You can preview your files in your browser by clicking the Preview the optimized image in a browser button in the Save For Web & Devices dialog box.

QUICKTIP

Because monitor quality, operating systems, and browsers will vary from user to user, you should preview your images on as many different systems as possible before you finalize an image for the web.

Creating Navigational and Interactive Functionality

You can divide an image you create for a website into many smaller sections, or slices. You use a **slice** to assign special features, such as links and animation, to specific areas within an image. **Links** allow you to direct the reader to sites specifically related to a particular topic. An image sequence, or **animation**, simulates an object moving on a web page. You can create an animation by making slight changes to several images, and then adjusting the timing between their appearances. When you convert an image to HTML, slices become cells in an HTML table, and animations become files in object folders.

QUICKTIP

If the Animation panel is not visible, you can display it by clicking Window on the Application bar, then by clicking Animation.

FIGURE 1
Image with web features

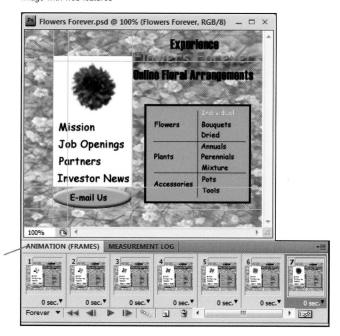

Creates the appearance of animation

View Slices

1. Start Photoshop, open PS 16-1.psd from the drive and folder where you store your Data Files, then save it as **Europa Market**.

   | TIP   Update the text layers if you see a message box stating that some text layers need to be updated before they can be used for vector-based output.

2. Click the **Default Foreground and Background Colors button** on the Tools panel.

3. Verify that the rulers display in pixels.

4. Click the **Slice tool** on the Tools panel.

   | TIP   The Slice tool is grouped with the Crop tool and the Slice Select tool.

5. Display the **Web** workspace.

6. Use the **Zoom tool** on the Application bar to change the magnification level to 200% (selecting the Resize Windows to Fit check box, if necessary).

7. Click **Window** on the Application bar, then click **Animation**.

   The Animation panel and the slices in the Europa Market image are visible. Compare your screen to Figure 2.

You opened an image in Photoshop, then displayed the document slices and the Animation panel.

FIGURE 2
Image with slices and Animation panel

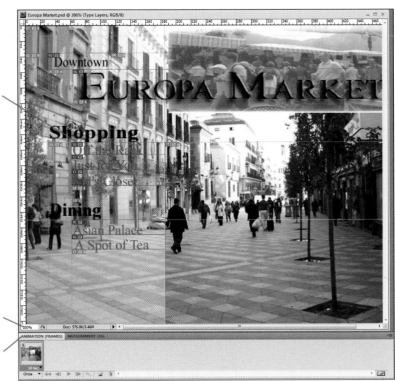

Individual slice

Magnification level

Animation panel

Creating Images for the Web

FIGURE 3
Slices turned off

Your magnification level may differ

1. Click **View** on the Application bar, point to **Show** then deselect **Slices**.

2. Click the **Fit Screen button** [Fit Screen] on the options bar.

   The size of the document may change (depending on the size of your monitor and your resolution setting) after clicking the Fit Screen button. This button is just one more tool you can use to create your ideal work environment.

3. Verify that the guides are displayed, then compare your image to Figure 3.

You adjusted your view of the image, turned off the display of the Slices, then verified that the guides are displayed.

OPTIMIZE IMAGES
FOR WEB USE

What You'll Do

In this lesson, you'll optimize an image for the web in Photoshop. Then you'll modify the optimized image and add it to an existing file.

Understanding Optimization

You can create an awesome image in Photoshop and merge and flatten layers conscientiously, but still end up with a file so large that no one will wait for it to download from the web. An **optimized** file is as beautiful as a non-optimized file; it's just a fraction of its original size.

Optimizing a File

When you optimize a file, you save it in a format that balances the need for detail and accurate color against file size. Photoshop allows you to compare an image in the following common web formats:

- JPEG (Joint Photographic Experts Group)
- GIF (Graphics Interchange Format)
- PNG (Portable Network Graphics)
- WBMP (a Bitmap format used for mobile devices, such as cell phones)

In Photoshop, the Save For Web & Devices dialog box has four view tabs: Original, Optimized, 2-Up, and 4-Up. See Figure 4. The Original view displays the graphic without any optimization. The Optimized, 2-Up, and 4-Up views display the image in its original format, as well as other file formats. You can change the file format being displayed by selecting one of the windows in the dialog box, then clicking the Optimized file format list arrow.

Exporting an image

You can export an image with transparency in Photoshop by saving your file in either a PNG or GIF format, then converting the image's background layer to an image layer. Select any elements in the layer you want as transparent, delete them from the layer, then save your changes.

You can also use the Photoshop Save As command on the File menu to quickly save a file in a different graphics format by using Photoshop's default settings. Using the Save As command, however, will *not* preserve web features such as slices, links, or animations.

Understanding Compression

GIF, JPEG, and PNG compression create compressed files without losing substantial components. Figuring out when to use which format can be challenging. Often, the decision may rest on whether color or image detail is most important. JPEG files are compressed by discarding image pixels; GIF and PNG files are compressed by limiting colors. GIF is an 8-bit format (the maximum number of colors a GIF file can contain is 256) that supports one transparent color; JPEG does not support transparent color. Having a transparent color is useful if you want to create a fade-out or superimposed effect. Because the JPEG format discards, or *loses*, data when it compresses a file, it is known as **lossy**. GIF and PNG formats are **lossless**—they compress solid color areas but maintain detail.

Hand tool

Slice Select tool

Zoom tool

Eyedropper tool

Eyedropper Color

Toggle Slices Visibility tool

Original image format and size

FIGURE 4
Optimizing files in Photoshop

Optimized file format list arrow

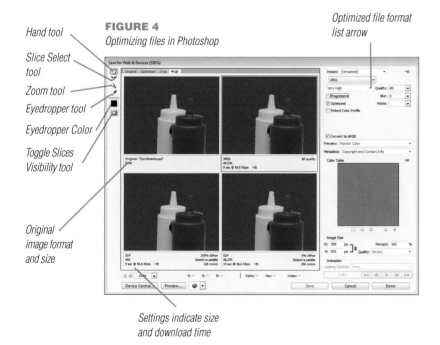

Settings indicate size and download time

FIGURE 5
Comparing file formats

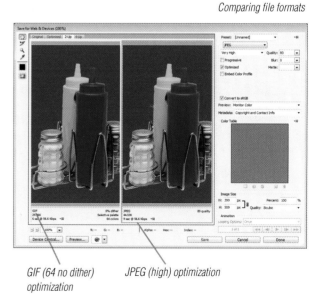

GIF (64 no dither) optimization

JPEG (high) optimization

Comparing Image Types

Figure 5 compares optimization of a photograph with a solid color background optimized in both GIF and JPEG formats. If you look closely, you'll see that the GIF colors look streaky and appear to be broken-up, while the JPEG colors appear crisp and seamless. Table 1 lists optimization format considerations. Because you cannot assume that other users will have access to the latest software and hardware, it's a good idea to compare files saved under different formats and optimization settings, and preview them in different browsers and on different computers. Yes, this can be time-consuming, but you'll end up with images that look great in all web browsers.

FIGURE 6
Adobe Device Central CS4

TABLE 1: Optimization Format Considerations

format	file format	use with
JPEG (very common)	All 24-bit (works best with 16 M colors)	Photographs, solid colors, soft edges
GIF (very common)	8-bit (256 colors)	Detailed drawings, sharp edges (logos, vector graphics), animation
PNG (less common)	24-bit (16 M colors)	Detailed drawings, logos, bitmap graphics
WBMP (less common)	1-bit (2 colors)	Cell phones and other mobile devices

Using Adobe Device Central CS4

Adobe Device Central CS4 is designed to give more flexibility to those professionals who create content for mobile phones and other consumer electronic devices. You can use the window shown in Figure 6 to obtain detailed specifications needed to design content for consumer electronic devices you may not have at your fingertips. You can then use the Emulator tab to preview your content on those same devices. This feature lets you increase your range of consumer electronic devices and can be updated to keep pace with new products, as well as manufacturer updates and improvements to existing products.

FIGURE 7
Save For Web & Devices dialog box

Outline surrounds selected format

List arrow changes format

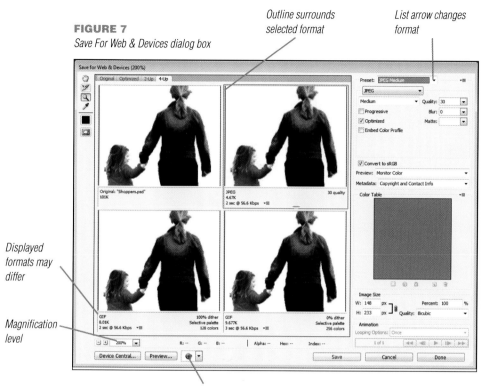

Displayed formats may differ

Magnification level

Preview in the optimized image in a browser button

1. Open PS 16-2.psd from the drive and folder where you store your Data Files, then save it as **Shoppers** in the folder where you store your Data Files.

2. Click **File** on the Application bar, then click **Save for Web & Devices**.

3. Click the **4-Up tab**.

4. Click the **Zoom tool** 🔍 on the left side of the Save For Web & Devices dialog box.

   TIP You can use the Hand tool to reposition the image.

5. Click the **top-right image** until all four images are enlarged to **200%**.

   TIP The zoom level is displayed in the lower-left corner of the Save For Web & Devices dialog box. You can also click the Zoom Level list arrow and select a magnification.

6. Click the **Preset list arrow**, click **JPEG Medium**, then compare your dialog box to Figure 7.

   The Save button saves a file in the selected format, the Cancel button resets the settings and closes the dialog box, and the Done button remembers the current settings and closes the dialog box.

   TIP To complete optimization of the file, you can click the desired format in the dialog box, click Save, enter a new name (if necessary) in the Save Optimized As dialog box, then click Save.

You opened a file, then used the Save for Web & Devices command on the File menu to open the Save For Web & Devices dialog box. You observed the differences between possible formats.

Using Transparency and Matte options

When using the Save for Web & Devices command, you can determine how the Transparency and Matte options are optimized within an image. Using both of these tools in a variety of combinations, you can blend fully or partially transparent pixels with a color from the Color Picker or Matte menu.

Complete image optimization

1. Click the **Preset list arrow**, then click **GIF 128 Dithered**. Compare your image to Figure 8.

   TIP The Preset list arrow contains 12 predesigned settings, while the Optimized file format list arrow lets you create your own unique settings with any options you choose.

2. Click **Save**.

3. Navigate to the folder where you store your Data Files, verify that **Shoppers** is in the File name text box (Win) or the Save As text box (Mac), then click **Save**.

   TIP Click OK if a warning box displays.

   The optimized file is similar in color quality, but approximately one-tenth the size of the original file (118 KB vs. 11.3 KB).

   TIP The optimized file is saved in the designated file format and folder. If your optimized file had spaces in its name, you would notice that the spaces in the optimized file name were replaced with hyphens.

4. Close the Shoppers.psd file without saving any changes.

You optimized a file, and then saved the optimized file. When you optimize a file, a copy of the file is saved, and no changes are made to the original.

FIGURE 8
Image optimized

Outline surrounds selected format

Click to select a predesigned format

List arrow changes format

File size

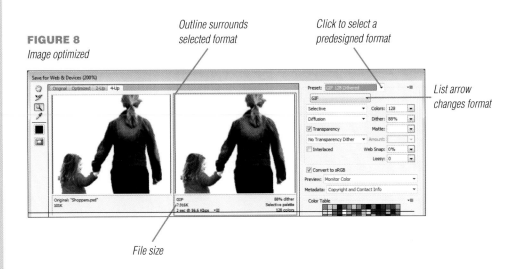

Using High Dynamic Range (HDR) images

HDR images are used in motion pictures, special effects, 3D work, and high-end photography. An HDR image is one that stores pixel values that span the whole tonal range. HDR images store linear values, meaning that the value of each pixel is proportional to the amount of light measured by the camera. Each HDR image stores 32-bits per color channel, and is coded using floating point numbers. In Photoshop, an HDR image is converted to an 8-bit/channel or 16-bit/channel image mode. You can use the HDR Conversion dialog box to adjust the brightness and contrast using one of the following methods: Exposure and Gamma, Highlight Compression, Equalize Histogram, or Local Adaptation.

FIGURE 9

Optimized file moved to image

GIF image
in document

1. Verify that the Europa Market.psd is active, then select the **Shoppers layer**.

2. Open Shoppers.gif.

3. Click **Select** on the Application bar, click **Color Range**, then verify that the **Image option button** is selected and that the Fuzziness text box is set to **0**.

4. Click the **white background** of the image in the Color Range dialog box, select the **Invert check box**, then click **OK**.

5. Click the **Move tool** on the Tools panel, verify that the **Show Transform Controls check box** is *not* selected, then use the **Move pointer** to drag the selection to the Europa Market image.

6. Drag the **Shoppers** so the top of the woman's head is below the "R" in Market, and below the guideline at 150Y.

7. Defringe the contents of Layer 2 using a setting of 2 pixels.

8. Click the **Layers panel list arrow**, then click **Layer Properties**.

9. Type **2 Shoppers** in the Name text box, then click **OK**.

10. Close the Shoppers.gif file, save your work, then compare your screen to Figure 9.

You opened an optimized file, selected the file and dragged it into the Europa Market image, defringed the image, then renamed the layer. The optimized file will be easier for a viewer to load in any browser.

CREATE A BUTTON FOR
A WEB PAGE

What You'll Do

In this lesson, you'll create and name a layer, then create a button to use in a web page. You'll add type to the button, apply a style, and then link the type and button layers so they can be used as a single object in a web page.

Learning About Buttons

A **button** is a graphical interface element that helps visitors navigate through and interact with a website with ease. Photoshop provides several ways for you to create buttons. You can create your own shape, apply a preformatted button style, or import a button you've already created. You can also assign a variety of actions to a button so that the button completes the required task when clicked or moused-over by someone viewing the site in a browser.

Creating a Button

You can create a button by drawing a shape with a shape tool, such as a rectangle, on a layer. After you create the shape, you can stylize it by applying a color or style, and then add text that will explain what will happen when it's clicked.

Saving a file for the web

Before you can use Photoshop files on the web, you must first convert them to the HTML format. Photoshop uses default settings when you save optimized images for the web. You can specify the output settings for HTML format, your HTML editor, and the way image files, background files, and slices are named and saved. To change the output settings in Photoshop, click the Preset list arrow in the Save For Web & Devices dialog box, select a file and compression type, then click the file format and compression quality list arrows to 'dial-in' the exact settings you want. To change a file to the HTML format, open the file in the Save for Web & Devices dialog box, click the Save as type list arrow, click one of the HTML options, then click Save.

Applying a Button Style

You can choose from the many pre-designed Photoshop button styles on the Styles panel, or you can create your own.

To apply a style to a button, you must first select a style, then create a button shape. Before creating the button, draw a shape for the button (using the Rectangle tool, for example) double-click one of the button styles on the Styles panel, which appear as thumbnails, or click a style name from the Set style for new layer list arrow on the options bar. Figure 10 shows the button styles on the Styles panel. You can also modify a button with a style already applied to it by first selecting the button and then choosing a new style from the Styles panel.

FIGURE 10
Button styles

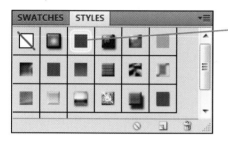

Style thumbnail

Changing a web image using Variables

When designing a web page, you may want to experiment with a variety of text samples (such as text on a button) or with different imagery for different occasions. You can do this in Photoshop using Variables. This feature lets you define many data sets, each containing different text or pixel information. You can then insert each data set and easily make changes to your web page. You define data sets by clicking Image on the Application bar, pointing to Variables, then clicking Define. Each data set is defined for a specific layer, which is selected from the Layer list arrow in the Variables dialog box. You can also view existing data sets for the active file by clicking Next in the Variables dialog box. Once the data sets are defined, you can quickly switch between them by clicking Image on the Application bar, then clicking Apply Data Set. This dialog box lets you apply a specific data set by clicking its name.

Create a button

1. Click the **Zoom tool** 🔍 on the Application bar.

2. Click the **Fit Screen button** [Fit Screen] on the options bar.

3. Verify that the **2 Shoppers layer** on the Layers panel is selected.

4. Click the **Create a new layer button** ◰ on the Layers panel.

   A new layer, Layer 2, appears above the 2 Shoppers layer, and beneath the Type Layers set.

5. Double-click the name **Layer 2** on the Layers panel, type **QuickGift Button**, then press **[Enter]** (Win) or **[return]** (Mac).

6. Click the **Rounded Rectangle tool** ▭ on the Tools panel.

7. If necessary, click the **Shape layers button** ▢ on the options bar.

   TIP The Rounded Rectangle tool is grouped with the Rectangle tool.

8. Click the **Click to open Style picker list arrow** on the options bar, click the **list arrow**, click **Buttons**, then click **Append**.

9. Using the guides as a reference to create a shape beneath the word A in A Spot of Tea, drag the **Marquee pointer** ╋ from approximately **60 X/320 Y** to **185 X/350 Y**.

10. Click the **Click to open Style picker button**, scroll to the bottom of the list, then click **Star Glow**, as shown in Figure 11.

    You created the shape that will be used for a button.

You verified settings, created a new layer, selected the Rounded Rectangle tool, selected a button style on the options bar, and then created a button.

FIGURE 11
Button style list

List arrow displays style panel

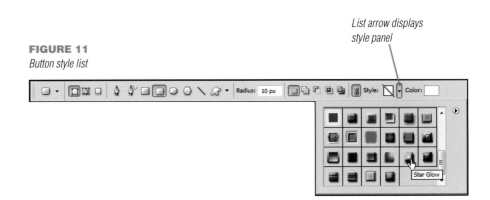

FIGURE 12
Button created in image

1. Click the **Horizontal Type tool** T. on the Tools panel.

2. Click the **button shape** at approximately **70 X/335 Y**.

3. Click the **Set the text color box** on the options bar, sample the red in the existing type, then click **OK**.

4. Click the **Set the font family list arrow** on the options bar, then click **Arial**.

5. Click the **Set the font size list arrow** on the options bar, then click **18 pt**.

6. Type **QuickGift**, then commit the current edits.

7. Right-click the **QuickGift layer**, then click **Convert to Smart Object**.

   The Smart Object and button shape layers are linked.

8. Click the **Move tool** on the Tools panel, then center the type on the button.

9. Save your work, then compare your work to Figure 12.

You added type to a button, and then converted the QuickGift type layer to a Smart Object.

CREATE SLICES IN
AN IMAGE

What You'll Do

In this lesson, you'll view the existing slices in the Europa Market image, create slices around the Shopping and Dining type, resize a slice, and assign a web address to the slice. You'll also create a new slice from the 2 Shoppers layer on the Layers panel.

Understanding Slices

You not only have the ability to work with images in layers, but you can also divide an image into unlimited smaller sections, or slices. Photoshop uses slices to determine the appearance of special effects in a web page. A **slice** is a rectangular section of an image that you can use to apply features, such as rollovers and links, and can be created automatically or by using any marquee tool or the Slice tool.

QUICKTIP
A slice is always rectangular, even if you create it using an elliptical marquee.

Using Slices

There are two kinds of slices: a **user-slice**, which you create, and an **auto-slice**, which is created in response to your user-slice. You can use the Slice tool to create a slice by dragging the pointer around an area. Every time you create a slice,

Photoshop automatically creates at least one auto-slice, which fills in the area around the newly created slice. Photoshop automatically numbers user- and auto-slices and updates the numbering according to the location of the new user-slice. User-slices have a solid line border, auto-slices have a dotted line border, and any selected slices have a yellow border. A selected user-slice contains a bounding box and sizing handles. You can resize a slice by dragging a handle to a new location, just as you would resize any object.

Learning About Slice Components

By default, a slice consists of the following components:

- A colored line that helps you identify the slice type
- An overlay that dims the appearance of the unselected slices
- A number that helps you identify each individual slice
- A symbol that helps you determine the type of slice

Adjusting Slice Attributes

You can adjust slice attributes by clicking Guides, Grid & Slices under the Preferences command. Figure 13 shows slice preferences. You can choose how to display slice lines and line color.

FIGURE 13
Preferences dialog box

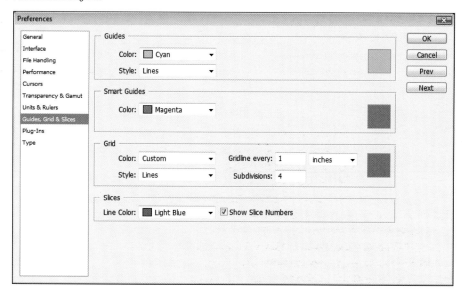

Slice numbering changes as you add or delete slices. Each user-slice contains a symbol indicating if it is an image slice or a layer-based slice, if the slice is linked, or if it includes a rollover effect. See Table 2 for a description of the symbols used to identify user-slices.

QUICKTIP

It doesn't matter which layer, if any, is active when you create slices using the Slice tool or any of the marquee tools.

Using a Layer-Based Slice

In addition to drawing a slice using the Slice tool, you can use the New Layer-Based Slice command on the Layer menu to create a slice from a layer on the Layers panel. This is an easy way of creating a slice *without* having to draw an outline.

Creating a Layer-Based Slice

Creating a layer-based slice automatically surrounds the image on the layer with a slice, which can be useful if you want to

create a slice quickly or if you want a large slice. Photoshop updates the slice whenever you modify the layer or its content. For example, the slice automatically adjusts if you move its corresponding layer on the Layers panel, or you erase pixels on the layer. In Figure 14, the active slice is an Image slice.

QUICKTIP

To delete a layer-based slice, user-slice, or auto-slice, select the slice, then press [Delete] (Win) or [delete] (Mac).

TABLE 2: User-Slice Symbols

symbol	used to identify
⊠	Image slice
✦	Layer-based slice
⊠	No image slice

Using the Slice Options Dialog Box

The Slice Options dialog box is used to set options such as content type, name, and URL for a specific slice. You open this dialog box by double-clicking a slice with the Slice Select tool. You use the list arrows in the Slice Options dialog box to assign individual settings, features, and effects to the slices you've created in your image. For example,

you could set a slice to initiate an action, such as displaying the linked file in a new browser window, or displaying the linked file in the same frame using the Target field.

Assigning a Web Address to a Slice

You can assign a web page to a selected slice by typing its Uniform Resource Locater (URL) in the URL text box. The URL is the

web page's address that appears in the Address box in your browser. You can designate how that web page will be displayed in your browser by choosing one of the options on the Target list.

FIGURE 14
Sliced image

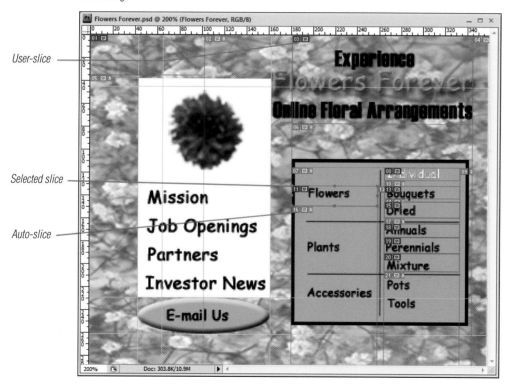

User-slice

Selected slice

Auto-slice

Create a slice using the Slice tool

1. Click the **Zoom tool** 🔍 on the Application bar.

2. Click the image of the **Shopping text** until the zoom percentage is **200%**.

3. Click the **Slice tool** ✄ on the Tools panel.

   The existing slices in the image are visible.

   > TIP You can also create a slice by creating a selection with any marquee tool, clicking Select on the Application bar, then clicking Create Slice from Selection.

4. Drag the **Slice pointer** ✄ around the **Shopping type** (from approximately **30 X/125 Y** to **185 X/150 Y**).

5. Drag the **Slice pointer** ✄ around the **Dining type** (from approximately **30 X/225 Y** to **120 X/250 Y**), fit the image to the screen, then compare your slices to Figure 15.

You viewed the existing slices in the Europa Market image and created two user-based slices, one for the Shopping text and one for the Dining text.

FIGURE 15
New slices added to image

Newly added slice

Selected slice

Slice numbering automatically changes with each modification (your numbers might be different)

FIGURE 16

New layer-based slice

Layer-based slice does not
display sizing handles

Create a layer-based slice

1. Click the **2 Shoppers** on the Layers panel.

2. Click **Layer** on the Application bar, click **New Layer-Based Slice**, then compare your screen to Figure 16.

   A new slice surrounds the 2 Shoppers layer object. Slice numbering automatically changes with each modification so your numbers might be different.

   TIP   You can also create a layer-based slice by right-clicking the layer, and then clicking New Layer-Based Slice.

You made the 2 Shoppers layer active on the Layers panel, then created a slice based on this layer.

Resize a slice

1. Click the **Slice Select tool**  on the Tools panel.

2. Click the **Dining slice**.

3. Drag the **right-middle sizing handle** ↔ to **185 X**, compare your slice to Figure 17, then release the mouse button.

   TIP   Because layer-based slices are fitted to pixels on the layer, they will not display sizing handles when selected.

You resized the Dining slice.

FIGURE 17
Resized slice

Drag handle to
new position

FIGURE 18

URL assigned to slice

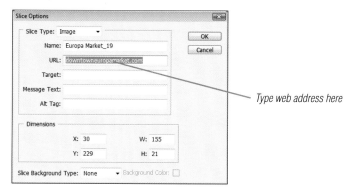

Type web address here

FIGURE 19

Slice with URL assigned

Assign a web address to a slice

1. Double-click the **Dining slice** with the **Slice Select tool** .

   The Slice Options dialog box opens when you double-click a slice with the Slice Select tool.

2. Type **downtowneuropamarket.com** in the URL text box, then compare your Slice Options dialog box to Figure 18.

   | TIP   Your slice numbers might vary.

3. Click **OK** to close the Slice Options dialog box.

4. Click an area outside of the slice to deselect the Dining slice, then compare your image to Figure 19.

   | TIP   To hide slices in your image, click View on the Application bar, point to Show, then click Slices.

5. Save your work, then close Europa Market.psd.

You assigned a web address to a slice using the Slice Options dialog box, then deselected the slice.

CREATE AND PLAY
BASIC ANIMATION

What You'll Do

 In this lesson, you'll create basic animation by creating animation frames. For each newly created frame, you'll modify layers by hiding and showing them, and changing their opacity. You'll also play and preview the animation, to test your work.

Understanding Animation

You can use nearly any type of graphics image to create interesting animation effects. You can move objects in your image or overlap them so that they blend into one another. Once you place the images that you want to animate in an image, you can determine when and how you want the animation to play.

Creating Animation on the Animation Panel

Remember that animation is nothing more than a series of still images displayed rapidly to give the illusion of motion. The Animation panel displays a thumbnail of the animation image in each frame. A **frame** is an individual image that is used in animation. When you create a frame on the Animation panel, you create a duplicate of the current frame, and can then modify it as desired. The layers that are visible on the Layers panel appear in the selected frame, and thus, in the animation. Here's all that's involved in creating a simple animation:

- Place images on layers in the image.
- Hide all but one layer.
- Duplicate the frame, turn off the displayed layer, then turn on the layer you want to see.

Animating Images

If you look at the Layers panel in Figure 20, you'll see that there are images on two layers. The Animation panel contains two frames: one for each of the layers. When frame 1 is selected, the man appears in the image; when frame 2 is selected, the woman appears. When the animation is played, the images of the man and woman alternate.

Moving and Deleting Frames

To move a frame to a different spot, click the frame on the Animation panel, and drag it to a new location. To select contiguous frames, press and hold [Shift], and then click the frames you want to include. To select noncontiguous frames, press and hold [Ctrl] (Win) or ⌘ (Mac), and then click the frames you want to include. You can delete a frame by clicking it on the Animation panel, then dragging it to the Deletes selected frames button on the Animation panel.

Looping the Animation

You can set the number of times the animation plays by clicking the Selects looping options list arrow on the Animation panel, then clicking Once, Forever, or Other. When you select Other, the Set Loop Count dialog box opens, where you can enter the loop number you want.

Previewing the Animation

When you're ready to preview an animation, you have a few choices:

- You can use the buttons on the bottom of the Animation panel. When you click the Plays/stops animation button, the animation plays.
- You can preview and test the animation in your browser by clicking the

Preview the optimized image in a browser button in the Save for Web & Devices dialog box.

QUICKTIP

You can change the size of the Animation panel thumbnails by clicking the panel list arrow, clicking Panel Options, clicking a thumbnail size, and then clicking OK. You can select a different-sized thumbnail for each panel.

FIGURE 20
Sample of basic animation

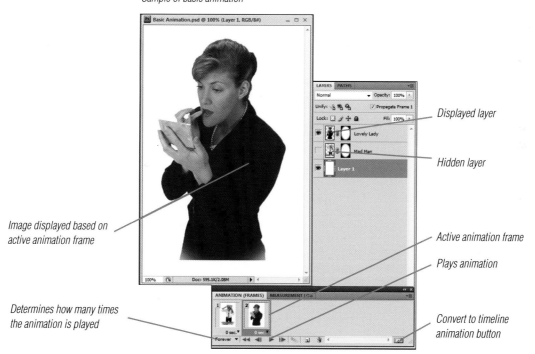

Displayed layer

Hidden layer

Image displayed based on active animation frame

Active animation frame

Plays animation

Determines how many times the animation is played

Convert to timeline animation button

Converting Animation Frames to a Timeline

By default, the Animation panel displays frames, but you can change the display so it shows a timeline. You can change the display by clicking the Convert to timeline animation button in the lower-right corner of the Animation (Frames) panel. (Change back to displaying frames by clicking the Convert to frame animation button when the timeline is displayed.) Figure 21 shows the Animation (Timeline) panel. As you drag the bars for each of the layers in the animation, the image updates to show the effect of your changes.

QUICKTIP

If the Animation panel displays the timeline, the Convert to frame animation button displays. The Convert to timeline animation button displays in the Animation (Frames) panel.

FIGURE 21
Animation (Timeline) panel

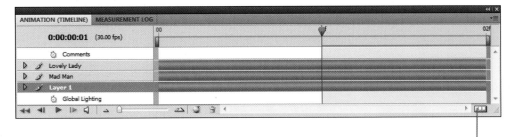

Convert to frame animation button

FIGURE 22
Zoomify Export dialog box

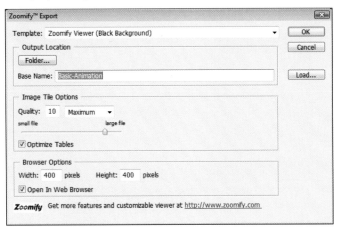

Exporting to Zoomify™
Using the Export to Zoomify feature, you can post your high-resolution images on the web so viewers can pan and zoom them in more detail. Using this feature, your image will download in the same time as an equivalent size JPEG file. Figure 22 shows the Zoomify Export dialog box which you can open by clicking File on the Application bar, point to Export, then click Zoomify.

FIGURE 23
Frames created on Animation panel

Indicates state has an animation

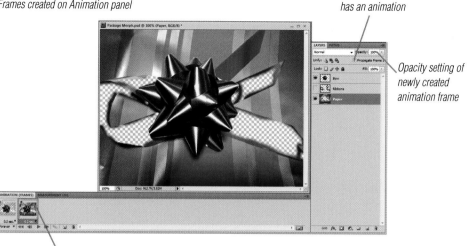

Opacity setting of newly created animation frame

New animation frame

FIGURE 24
Completed animation frames

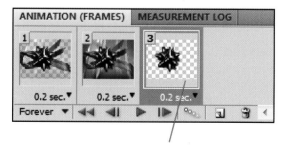

New animation frame

Create and duplicate animation frames

1. Open PS 16-3.psd from the drive and folder where you store your Data Files, then save it as **Package Morph**.

2. Click **Window** on the Application bar, then click **Animation** to open the Animation panel (if it is not already open) and display the rulers in pixels.

3. Adjust the opacity setting of the Paper layer to **50%** on the Layers panel.

4. Click the **Duplicates selected frames button** 🔲 on the Animation panel.

   A new Animation frame is created and is now the active frame.

5. Adjust the opacity setting of the Paper layer to **100%**, then compare your Animation panel to Figure 23.

6. Click the **Duplicates selected frames button** 🔲 on the Animation panel.

7. Click the **Indicates layer visibility button** 👁 on the Paper layer on the Layers panel.

8. Click the **Indicates layer visibility button** 👁 on the Ribbons layer on the Layers panel to hide this layer.

9. Click the **Bow layer** to make it active.

   The content from the Bow layer appears in frame 3 of the Animation panel. See Figure 24.

You created an animation frame, duplicated existing frames, and adjusted the opacity of the frames. Duplicating frames with different levels of opacity creates an animated effect when viewed in a browser.

Adjust animation frames

1. Set the opacity setting of the Bow layer to **50%**.

2. Click the **Duplicates selected frames button** on the Animation panel, then adjust the opacity setting of the Bow layer to **100%**.

3. Click the **Duplicates selected frames button** on the Animation panel. You have now created five frames.

4. Click the **Indicates layer visibility button** on the Bow layer to hide it.

5. Click the **Ribbons layer** on the Layers panel to make it active, then click the **Indicates layer visibility button** on the Layers panel for this layer.

6. Adjust the opacity setting to **50%**.

7. Click the **Duplicates selected frames button** on the Animation panel, then adjust the opacity setting of the Ribbons layer to **100%**. Compare your screen to Figure 25.

You adjusted the opacity of frames using the Layers panel. The adjustment of frame settings lets you simulate movement when the animation is played.

FIGURE 25
Completed animation frames

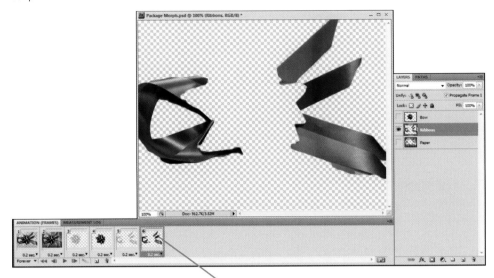

New animation frame

Using video layers in Photoshop Extended

If you have QuickTime 7.1 or higher installed on your computer, you can use Photoshop Extended to edit individual frames of video and image sequence files. You can also edit and paint on video, apply filters, masks, transformations, layer styles, and blending modes. When you open a video file in Photoshop Extended, the frames are contained within a video layer (indicated by a filmstrip icon in the Layers panel). You can create a video layer in an active document by displaying the Animation panel in Timeline mode, clicking Layer on the Application bar, pointing to Video Layers, then clicking New Video Layer from File.

FIGURE 26
Animation displayed in browser

Your browser may be different

Animation automatically begins when you open the image

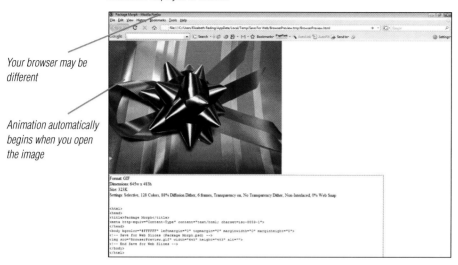

TABLE 3: Animation Tools

tool	tool name	description
▼	Selects looping options	Determines how many times the animation plays
◀◀	Selects first frame	Makes the first frame on the panel active
◀❙	Selects previous frame	Makes the previous frame on the panel active
▶	Plays animation	Plays the animation
■	Stops animation	Stops the animation
❙▶	Selects next frame	Makes the next frame to the right on the panel active
°°°°	Tweens animation frames	Creates frames in slight increments
▣	Duplicates selected frames	Creates a duplicate of selected frames
▦	Deletes selected frames	Disposes of selected frames

Play animation in the image and browser

1. Verify that **Forever** displays in the Selects looping options text box, click the **first frame** in the Animation panel, then click the **Plays/stops animation button** ▶ on the Animation panel.

   The Plays/stops animation button changes its appearance depending on the current state of the animation. See Table 3 for a description of the buttons on the Animation panel.

2. Click the **Plays/stops animation button** ■ on the Animation panel.

   The animation stops, displaying the currently active frame.

3. Save your work.

4. Click **File** on the Application bar, click **Save for Web & Devices**, then click the **Preview the optimized image in a browser button** 🔘 (at the bottom of the dialog box to the right of the Preview button) then compare your preview to Figure 26.

   TIP   The first time you use this feature you will have to add a browser.

5. Close your browser, then click **Cancel** in the Save for Web & Devices dialog box.

   TIP   The animation might play differently in your browser, which is why it is important to preview your files on as many different systems as possible.

You played the animation in your image, then viewed it in a browser.

ADD TWEENING AND
FRAME DELAY

What You'll Do

 In this lesson, you'll add tweening to animation and adjust the frame delay for a frame on the Animation panel.

Understanding Tweening

To create animation, you assemble a series of frames, then play them quickly to create the illusion of continuous motion. Each frame represents a major action point. Sometimes the variance between actions creates erratic or rough motion. To blend the motion *in between* the frames, you can tween your animation. **Tweening** adds frames that change the action in slight increments from one frame to the next. The origin of this term predates computer animation, when an artist known as an *inbetweener* hand-drew each frame that linked major action frames (at 24 frames per second!), and thus the term tweening was born.

Using Tweening on the Animation Panel

You can add tweening to a frame by clicking the Tweens animation frames button on the Animation panel, and then entering the number of in-between frames you want in the Tween dialog box. You can choose whether you want the tweening to affect all layers or just the selected layer, and if you want the image to change position or opacity. You can also specify the frame on which you want the tweening to start, and specify the number of frames to add in between the frames (you can add up to 100 frames in a single tween). Figure 27 shows a two-frame animation after four tween frames were added. The opacity of the man is 100% in the first frame and 0% in the last frame. Adding five tween frames causes the two images to blend into each other smoothly, or **morph** (metamorphose).

> QUICKTIP
> You can select contiguous frames and apply the same tweening settings to them simultaneously.

Understanding Frame Delays

When you create frames on the Animation panel, Photoshop automatically sets the **frame delay**, the length of time that each frame appears. You can set the delay time in whole or partial seconds by clicking the Selects frame delay time list arrow below each frame. You can set the frame delay you want for each frame, or you can select several frames and apply the same frame delay to them.

Setting Frame Delays

To change the delay for a single frame, click a frame, click the Selects frame delay time list arrow, then click a time. To change the delay for contiguous frames, press and hold [Shift], click the frames you want to include, and then click the Selects frame delay time list arrow on *any* of the selected frames. To change the delay for noncontiguous frames, press and hold [Ctrl] (Win) or ⌘ (Mac), click the frames you want to include, then click the Selects frame delay time list arrow on any of the selected frames.

FIGURE 27
Animation panel

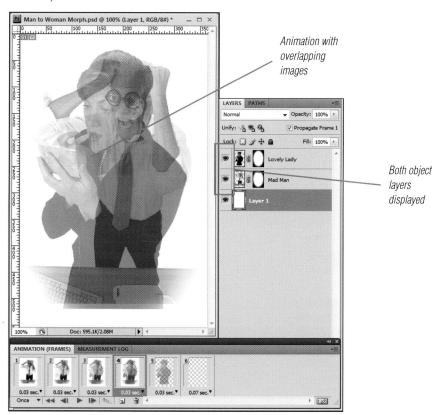

Animation with overlapping images

Both object layers displayed

Correcting pixel aspect ratio in video

This feature automatically corrects the ratio of pixels displayed for the monitor in use. Without this correction, pixels viewed in a 16:9 monitor (such as a widescreen TV) would look squashed in a 4:3 monitor (typical rectangular TV). Use the Pixel Aspect Ratio Correction command to turn off the scaling correction and view the image as it looks on a computer (square pixel) monitor. Photoshop automatically converts and scales the image to the pixel aspect ratio of the non-square pixel document. Images brought in from Adobe Illustrator will also be properly scaled. You can assign a pixel aspect ratio to a document by clicking View on the Application bar, pointing to Pixel Aspect Ratio, then selecting a pixel aspect ratio. When you have selected a pixel aspect ratio, the Pixel Aspect Ratio Correction option will be checked on the View menu.

Tween animation frames

1. Click **frame 3** on the Animation panel.

2. Click the **Tweens animation frames button** ⚬⚬⚬ on the Animation panel.

3. Adjust the settings in your Tween dialog box so that they match those shown in Figure 28.

4. Click **OK**.

   Two additional frames are added after frame 3.

5. Click the **Plays/stops animation button** ▷ on the Animation panel, then view the animation.

6. Click the **Plays/stops animation button** ■ on the Animation panel, then compare your panel to Figure 29, which now has eight frames.

You used the Tweens animation frames button on the Animation panel to insert two new frames, then played the animation to view the results. Did you notice that the overall effect is smoother and more fluid motion?

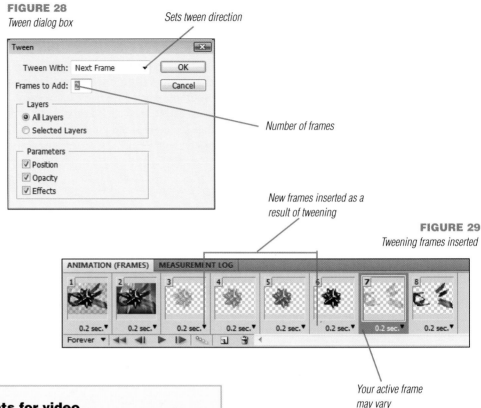

FIGURE 28
Tween dialog box

Sets tween direction

Number of frames

New frames inserted as a result of tweening

FIGURE 29
Tweening frames inserted

Your active frame may vary

Previewing Photoshop documents for video

When you're working on a Photoshop image that you plan to include in a digital video or video presentation, you can use the Video Preview plug-in (included with Photoshop) to see real-time results as you work. Because the images you create in Photoshop are made up of square pixels, and video editing programs usually convert these to non-square pixels for video encoding, distortion can result when you import an image into a video editing program. But with Video Preview, you can check for distortion and make changes before finalizing your image. When the Video Preview plug-in is installed, and your computer is connected to a video monitor via FireWire, you can access Video Preview by clicking File on the Application bar, pointing to Export, then clicking Video Preview. This command also lets you adjust the aspect ratio as necessary for different viewing systems, such as NTSC, PAL, or HDTV.

FIGURE 30
Frame delay menu

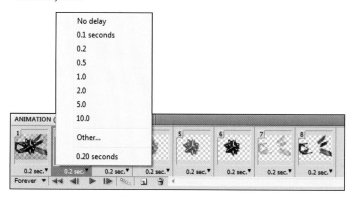

1. Click **frame 2** on the Animation panel.

2. Click the **Selects frame delay time list arrow** `0.2 sec.▼` at the bottom of the selected frame.

3. Compare your frame delay menu to Figure 30, then click **0.5**.

   The frame delay for frame 2 changes to 0.5.

4. Click the **Plays/stops animation button** ▶ on the Animation panel, then view the animation.

5. Click the **Plays/stops animation button** ■ on the Animation panel.

6. Open the **Save for Web & Devices dialog box**, then click the **Preview the optimized image in a browser button** 🌐 .

7. Close your browser.

8. Save your work, then compare your image and Animation panel to Figure 31.

9. Close the Animation panel, then close the image.

You fine-tuned your animation by changing the frame delay for frame 2, then previewed the animation in your browser. It's important to preview animations in multiple web browsers on as many computers and operating systems as you can manage, so that you can see your work as others will view it.

FIGURE 31
Frame delay in Animation panel

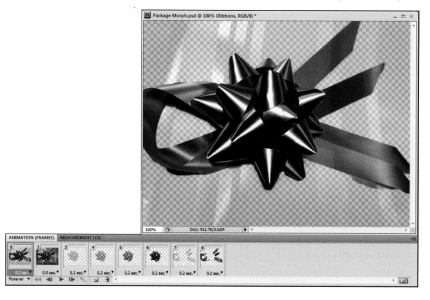

MODIFY VIDEO IN
PHOTOSHOP

What You'll Do

In this lesson, you'll open a video file and save it in a Photoshop format. You'll rotate the frame, apply several effects, and change the starting and ending points of the video sequence.

Playing Video

It might surprise you to know that you can play video using Photoshop Extended (with QuickTime 7.1 or higher installed), but then again, you might have guessed that it was possible after creating animation sequences using individual frames, since video is the natural next step after working with individual images.

> **QUICK**TIP
>
> You can create your own video sequences using most digital cameras. You may have to modify your camera settings or flip a switch on the camera body.

Working with Video

When you open a video file in Photoshop Extended, individual frames are contained in a video layer, and the layer appears in the Layers panel with a special filmstrip icon, shown in Figure 32. You can use your existing Photoshop skills (such as creating and editing adjustment layers, adjusting opacity, making selections, adding masks, painting, and cloning) on the video layer.

Table 4 lists the movie file extensions that can be opened in Photoshop Extended.

Frame Versus Timeline in the Animation Panel

Although the Animation panel has two modes (frame and timeline), you use the timeline mode when working with video. The timeline mode tools at the bottom of the Animation panel, shown in Figure 33, allow you to navigate the sequence. In addition to the tools in the Animation panel, you can use the spacebar to start and stop playing the animation. The Frame mode shows frame duration and layer animation properties; timeline mode shows frame duration and keyframed layer properties.

> **QUICK**TIP
>
> If you convert a video sequence from timeline to frame animation, you will be left with a single frame in the Animation panel.

Enhancing Video

Changes you can make to layers in a Photoshop image can also be applied to video layers. For example, you can apply adjustment layers to lighten or darken the overall look of a video sequence. Such enhancements can be used throughout a video sequence or can be controlled so that they only affect specific areas of the timeline. Figure 34 shows several adjustment layers, although only the Levels adjustment layer affects the entire sequence.

FIGURE 32
Filmstrip icon in Layers panel

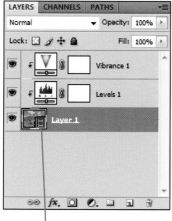

Filmstrip icon in thumbnail

FIGURE 33
Animation panel

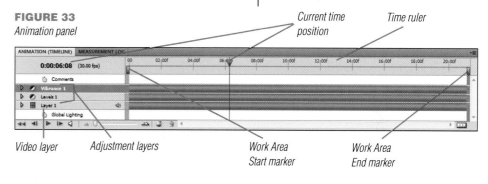

Current time position

Time ruler

Video layer   *Adjustment layers*   *Work Area Start marker*   *Work Area End marker*

Adjustment level affecting part of video sequence

FIGURE 34
Animation panel with adjustment layers

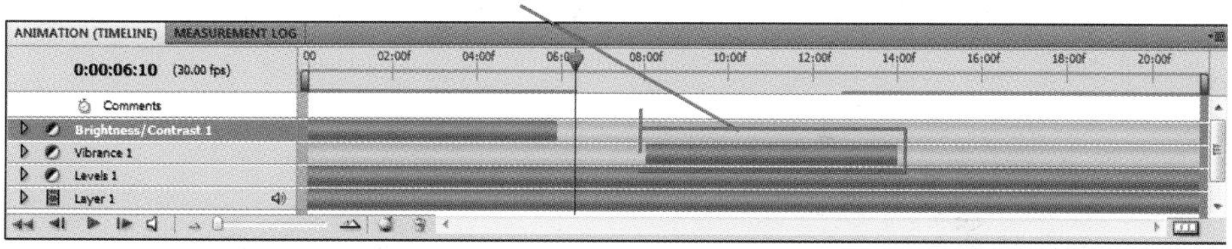

TABLE 4: Usable Movie File Types in Photoshop Extended

name	stands for	additional information
AVI	Audio Video Interleave	Developed by Microsoft
FLV	Flash video	Streaming video files
MOV	QuickTime format	Developed for Mac. Can be uploaded toYouTube without additional conversion
MPEG-1	Moving Pictures Expert Group	Used on the web for short video and animation files
MPEG-2 (with encoder)		Used for higher resolution video, digital television and DVDs
MPEG-4		Used for compression of AV data and CD distribution

Apply an adjustment layer

1. Open PS 16-4.avi from the drive and folder where you store your Data files, then save it as **Forum Shops Escalator.psd**.

   TIP When you save a video file in Photoshop, the file format is changed to .psd, which can be edited in many Adobe video programs.

2. Click **Image** on the Application bar, point to **Image Rotation**, click **90° CW**, then click **Convert** to transform the video layer into a Smart Object layer.

   The image is rotated, and the filmstrip icon on the thumbnail in the Layers panel is changed to a Smart Object. See Figure 35.

3. Switch to the **Essentials workspace**, display the Animations panel, then click the **Brightness/Contrast button** ☼ on the Adjustments panel.

4. Change the Brightness to **10** and the Contrast to **10**, then click the **Return to Adjustment list button** ◁ on the Adjustments panel.

5. Click the **Play button** ▷ on the Animation panel.

6. When you are finished watching the video, click the **Stop button** ▣ , then compare your work to Figure 36.

   TIP In addition to using the familiar DVD buttons in the Animation panel, you can also press the spacebar (on the keyboard) to start and stop video playback.

You saved a movie file in the Photoshop format, rotated the image, added an adjustment layer, then played the video.

FIGURE 35
Rotated image with Smart Object

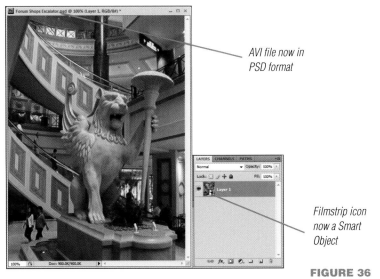

AVI file now in PSD format

Filmstrip icon now a Smart Object

FIGURE 36
Adjustment layer in video sequence

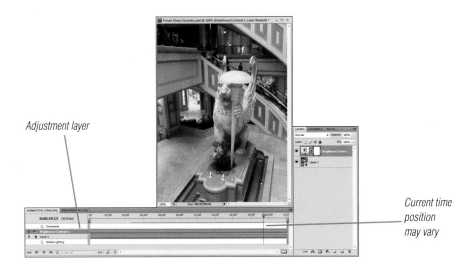

Adjustment layer

Current time position may vary

FIGURE 37

Modifying starting point of Adjustment layer

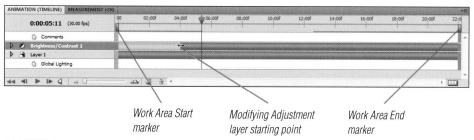

Work Area Start
marker

Modifying Adjustment
layer starting point

Work Area End
marker

FIGURE 38

Modified video settings

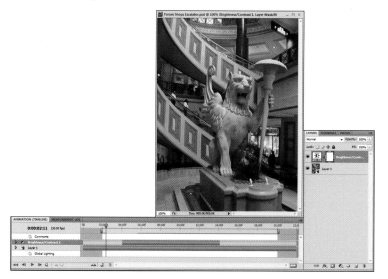

Modify video settings

1. Make Layer 1 the active layer.

2. Drag the **Starting point of the Brightness/Contrast 1 layer** to approximately **4:00f** on the time ruler, as shown in Figure 37.

3. Drag the **Ending point of the Brightness/Contrast layer** to approximately **14:00f** on the time ruler.

4. Drag the **Work Area Start marker** to approximately **2:00f** on the time ruler.

5. Drag the **Work Area End marker** to approximately **20:00f** on the time ruler.

6. Press the **spacebar** on the keyboard to play the video, then press the **spacebar** when you are finished watching.

7. Save your work, compare your Animation panel to Figure 38, then close the file.

You modified the starting and ending point of an Adjustment layer, changed the position of the work area markers on the time ruler, then played the video sequence.

Using Video Document Presets for video

When you open a new document in Photoshop, you're presented with a blizzard of choices, and these choices extend to video. You can see the Video presets that are available by clicking File on the Application bar, then clicking New. Click the Preset list arrow, then click Film & Video. Click the Size list arrow and you'll see all the size presets that are available.

USE CAMERA RAW FEATURES

What You'll Do

In this lesson, you'll learn how to use the Camera Raw dialog box to make adjustments to images in the Raw, TIFF, and JPEG formats.

Using Raw Data from Digital Cameras

When you consider all the elements you'll need to get your website up and running, you'll probably want to use your own camera as a source of imagery. If you're a digital camera photographer, or have access to digital photos, you'll appreciate the ability to use images in the 16-bit Camera Raw format because it contains so much controllable data. Sure, the files are twice the size, but the resolution contains 65,000 data points (versus the 256 data points in an 8-bit image). Once an image with raw data is opened, the Camera Raw interface appears. This interface contains magnification and color correction options.

FIGURE 39

Camera Raw dialog box

Camera description

Camera raw Image

Buttons cancel, save changes, or open Photoshop

The Camera RAW dialog box shown in Figure 39 contains three buttons in the lower-right corner: Open Image, Cancel, and Done, and one button in the lower-left corner: Save Image. The Open Image button applies changes and opens the image. The Save Image button converts and saves an image. The Done button applies the changes and closes the dialog box without opening the image. The Cancel button closes the dialog box without accepting any changes. In addition to files in the RAW format, JPEG and TIFF digital images can also be opened using the Camera Raw dialog box, enabling you to take advantage of the same powerful setting options. To do this, right-click the image in Adobe Bridge, then click Open in Camera Raw.

Don't be alarmed if you see a caution icon in the Camera Raw dialog box. This icon indicates that the preview image has been generated from a camera raw image.

Modifying Camera Raw Images

An image in the camera raw format can be opened using the File menu or Adobe Bridge, but the image initially opens in the Camera Raw dialog box rather than in the Photoshop window. This dialog box creates a sidecar XMP file that contains metadata and accompanies the camera raw file. An image that has been modified using the Camera Raw plug-in is accompanied by an icon in Bridge, as shown in Figure 40.

QUICKTIP

You can synchronize image settings from one to many images in Camera Raw by selecting an image (in Filmstrip View), clicking the Synchronize button at the top of the Filmstrip pane, then clicking the Synchronize button.

Using Camera Raw Settings and Preferences

The Camera Raw file format is similar to a digital negative. It contains all the information a camera has about a specific image. It is also similar to the TIFF format in that it does not discard any color information, yet it is smaller than an uncompressed TIFF. Camera Raw settings can be saved (up to 100 settings) and then applied to a specific camera or for specific lighting conditions. The Apply Camera Raw Settings menu allows you to save current settings and add them to the Settings menu, as well as modify settings for Exposure, Shadows, Brightness, Contrast, and Saturation.

QUICKTIP

You can use Adobe Bridge to copy and paste Camera Raw settings from one image to another. To do this, open Adobe Bridge, select a file, click Edit on the Application bar, point to Develop Settings, then click Copy Camera Raw Settings. Once this is complete, select one or more (other) Raw images in Bridge, click Edit on the Application bar, point to Develop Settings, then click Paste Camera Raw Settings.

FIGURE 40
Raw image in Adobe Bridge

Icon indicates
edits to raw file

DSCF1280.RAF

Using Camera Raw adjustment settings

Because the Camera Raw format for each digital camera is different, you can adjust the Camera Raw settings to recreate the colors in a photo more accurately. Using the Camera Calibration button located in the Image Adjustment tabs, you can select a profile: ACR 4.4 (the built-in camera profile for Photoshop CS4). Use the Hue and Saturation sliders to adjust the red, green, and blue in the image. Camera Raw adjustments made to the original image are always preserved, so you can adjust them repeatedly if necessary. The adjustment settings are stored within the Camera Raw database file or in a sidecar XMP file that accompanies the original Camera Raw image in a location of your choosing.

Understanding the Camera Raw Dialog Box

When you open multiple camera raw images, the Camera Raw dialog box displays a filmstrip, as shown in Figure 41. The left panel of the dialog box, which only appears when multiple images are open, displays camera raw, TIFF, or JPEG files opened in the Camera Raw dialog box. The center panel displays the view controls, the selected image, zoom levels, and navigation arrows. The right panel displays a histogram for the active image, the image adjustment tabs, and adjustment sliders.

QUICKTIP

Open multiple camera raw images by selecting image thumbnails in Adobe Bridge, pressing and holding [Shift] right-clicking, then clicking Open in Camera Raw.

FIGURE 41

Multiple open images in Camera Raw dialog box

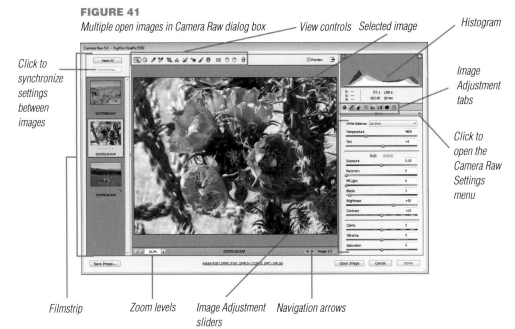

Click to synchronize settings between images

View controls   *Selected image*   *Histogram*

Image Adjustment tabs

Click to open the Camera Raw Settings menu

Filmstrip   *Zoom levels*   *Image Adjustment sliders*   *Navigation arrows*

Using the Digital Negative format (DNG)

Adobe DNG (Digital Negative format) is an archival format for camera raw files that contains the raw image data created within a digital camera, as well as the metadata that define what that data means. This format is designed to provide compatibility among the increasing number of Camera Raw file formats. The following Saving options are available:

- Compressed (lossless), which applies a lossless compression to the DNG file.
- Convert to Linear Image, which stores the image data in an interpolated format.
- Embed Original Raw File, which stores the entire original camera raw image data in the DNG file, and JPEG Preview, which specifies whether to embed a JPEG preview in the DNG file.

Export Camera Raw settings

The settings you created and stored in the Camera Raw database can be exported to a sidecar XMP file, embedded in a DNG file, or can be used to update JPEG previews embedded in DNG files. To export Camera Raw settings, open the files in the Camera Raw dialog box, switch to the Filmstrip view if necessary, then select the thumbnail(s) whose settings you want to export. Open the Camera Raw Settings menu in the Camera Raw dialog box, then click Export Settings to XMP. An XMP file will be created in the folder where the Raw image is located.

Modifying Images in the Camera Raw Dialog Box

You can make many image modifications right in the Camera Raw dialog box. Some of the tools should look familiar to you, as you've already seen or used them in Photoshop. Figure 42 identifies unfamiliar view control tools as well as the additional tools that are displayed when the Retouch tool is selected. Using the Retouch tool, you can heal or clone defective areas of an image *before* bringing it into Photoshop.

You can make changes to colors using tabs in the Image Adjustments area in the right panel. Adjustments you can make include the following:

- Basic: adjusts white balance, color saturation, and tonality.
- Tone Curve: fine-tunes tonality using a Parametric curve and a Point curve.
- HSL/Grayscale: fine-tunes colors using Hue, Saturation, and Luminance adjustments, as shown in Figure 43.
- Split Toning: lets you color monochrome images or create special effects with color images.

- Detail: Sharpens images or reduces noise.
- Lens Corrections: compensates for chromatic aberration and vignetting caused by a camera lens.
- Camera Calibration: corrects a color cast in shadows and adjusts non-neutral colors to compensate for the differences between camera behavior and the Camera Raw profile for your particular camera model.
- Presets: lets you save and apply sets of image adjustment settings.

FIGURE 42

Camera Raw view controls

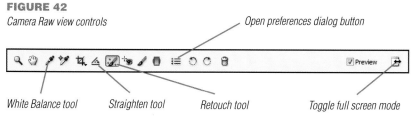

White Balance tool   Straighten tool   Retouch tool   Toggle full screen mode

Open preferences dialog button

FIGURE 43

HSL/Grayscale Adjustment tab

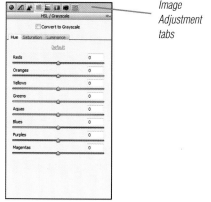

Image Adjustment tabs

FIGURE 44

Camera Raw Preferences dialog box

Changing Camera Raw Preferences

To change the preferences in the Camera Raw dialog box, click Edit in the Adobe Bridge Application bar, then click Camera Raw Preferences, or click the Open preferences dialog button in the view controls area of the Camera Raw dialog box. The Camera Raw Preferences dialog box lets you determine how image settings will be saved, and how default image settings are handled. See Figure 44.

Power User Shortcuts

to do this:	use this method:
Create a slice	✎ or [Shift][C]
Cycle shape tools	[Shift][U]
Deselect slices	[Ctrl][D] (Win) ⌘[D] (Mac)
Hide/show rulers	[Ctrl][R] (Win) ⌘[R] (Mac)
Preview in browser	🌐 or your browser button

to do this:	use this method:
Save for Web & Devices	[Ctrl][Shift][Alt][S] (Win) ⌘ [Shift] option [S] (Mac)
Select a slice	✎
Show Animation panel	[F11] (Win)
Start animation playback	▶
Stop animation playback	◼

Key: Menu items are indicated by ➤ between the menu name and its command. Blue bold letters are shortcuts for selecting tools on the Tools panel.

Creating Images for the Web

Learn about web features.

1. Start Photoshop, open PS 16-5.psd from the drive and folder where you store your Data Files, then save it as **Optimal Dolphin**.
2. Set the background and foreground colors to their default values.
3. Fit the image on the screen.

Optimize images for web use.

1. Open the Save For Web & Devices dialog box.
2. Display the 4-Up tab, then zoom in or out of the image (if necessary).
3. Verify the settings of the image to the right of the original image as GIF 64 Dithered.
4. Save the file as **Optimal-Dolphin-GIF.gif** to the drive and folder where you store your Data Files.
5. Open the Save for Web & Devices dialog box, click the first GIF image after the original image, change the settings to JPEG High, then compare your image to Figure 45.
6. Use the Save button to save the file as **Optimal-Dolphin-JPG.jpg**.
7. Close Optimal Dolphin *without* saving changes.

FIGURE 45
Completed Skills Review 1

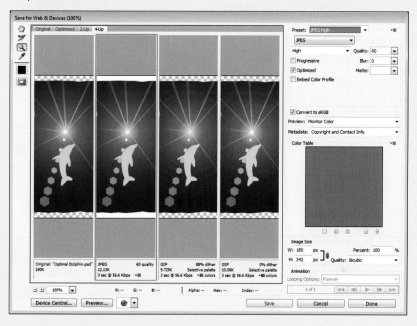

Create a button for a web page.

1. Open PS 16-6.psd, then save it as **Canine-Nation**.
2. If prompted, update the text layers.
3. Set the background and foreground colors to the default.
4. Fit the image on the screen, and display the rulers and slices (if necessary).
5. Select the Rounded Rectangle tool.
6. Activate the Board layer.
7. Select the Woodgrain style, then use the guides to help you draw a button from 15 X/340 Y to 135 X/390 Y.
8. Select the Type tool.
9. Click the image within the button type **Rescue** (use a White, Bold 18 pt Arial font), then center the text within the button.
10. Save your work.

Create slices in an image.

1. Draw a slice for the Train button from 15 X/150 Y to 135 X/200 Y.
2. Draw a slice for the Groom button from 15 X/210 Y to 135 X/260 Y.
3. Draw a slice for the Board button from 15 X/275 Y to 135 X/325 Y.
4. Draw a slice for the Rescue button from 15 X/340 Y to 135 X/390 Y.
5. Resize the Jack Russell slice (the image of the dog in the top-right portion of the image) so that the top is 90 Y and the bottom is 320 Y.
6. Type the following (fictitious) URL for the Jack Russell slice: **http://www.caninenation. com/breed/jackrussell_faq.html**.
7. Hide the slices and rulers.
8. Save your work, compare your image to Figure 46, then close Canine-Nation.

FIGURE 46
Completed Skills Review 2

Create and play basic animation.

1. Open PS 16-7.psd, then save it as **The Old Soft Shoe**.
2. Display the rulers (if necessary).
3. Display the Animation panel, duplicate frame 1, make the Cat Forward layer active, then drag the Cat Forward image to approximately 250 X.
4. Duplicate frame 2, then hide the Cat Forward layer and make the Cat Dancing layer visible.
5. Duplicate frame 3, then hide the Cat Dancing layer and make the Cat Forward layer visible.
6. Duplicate frame 4, hide the Cat Forward layer, make the Cat Dancing layer visible, then change the Opacity setting of the Cat Dancing layer to 0%.
7. Play the animation.
8. Save your work, then hide the rulers, if necessary.

Add tweening and frame delay.

1. Tween frame 2 using the previous frame and adding two frames.
2. Tween frame 5 using the previous frame and adding one frame.
3. Tween frame 6 using the previous frame and adding five frames.
4. Set the looping option to Forever, than play the animation.
5. Set the frame delay for frames 1, 4, 6, and 7 to 0.2 seconds.
6. Play the animation.
7. Preview the animation in your browser.
8. Save your work, then compare your image to Figure 47.

FIGURE 47
Completed Skills Review 3

Modify Video in Photoshop.

1. Open **PS 16-8.avi**, then save it as **Wind Trancer sculpture**.
2. Convert the video layer into a Smart Object.

3. Add a Color Balance adjustment layer using the following midtone settings:
   Cyan-Red: +41
   Magenta-Green: +37
   Yellow-Blue: +22

4. Clip the adjustment layer to the existing layer.
5. Add a Brightness/Contrast adjustment layer using a Brightness of −29 and a Contrast of +30.
6. Clip this adjustment layer to the existing layer, then compare your image to Figure 48.

FIGURE 48
Partially completed Skills Review 4

7. Change the starting point of the Color Balance 1 layer to approximately 9:00f.

8. Change the ending point of the Color Balance 1 layer to approximately 18:00f.

9. Change the starting point of the Brightness/Contrast 1 layer to approximately 3:00f.

10. Change the ending point of the Brightness/Contrast 1 layer to approximately 12:00f.

11. Play the video.

12. Decrease the work area by approximately one second at the beginning and ending of the video sequence.

13. Save your work, play the video, then compare your screen to Figure 49.

FIGURE 49
Completed Skills Review 4

A local long-distance runners group is sponsoring a cross-country run for charity. The event will offer short cross-country races for all ages and fitness levels. You've volunteered to use your skills to design an animation for their web page that encourages even the slowest runners to join in the fun.

1. Obtain the following images for the animation: one object that conveys the idea of movement and an obstacle it moves over, around, or toward. You can also obtain a background and any other images, as desired. You can draw your own images, use the images that are available on your computer, scan print media, create images using a digital camera, or connect to the Internet and download images.

2. Create a new Photoshop image and save it as **Xtream Charity**.

3. Apply a color or style to the Background layer. (*Hint*: The Background layer in the sample has a Pattern Overlay style applied to it.)

4. Add frames to the Animation panel. Make one a motion animation and the other a fade-out effect.

5. Tween each animation and add frame delays as necessary.

6. Preview the animation in your image and in your browser.

7. Save your work, then compare your screen to the sample shown in Figure 50.

FIGURE 50
Sample Project Builder

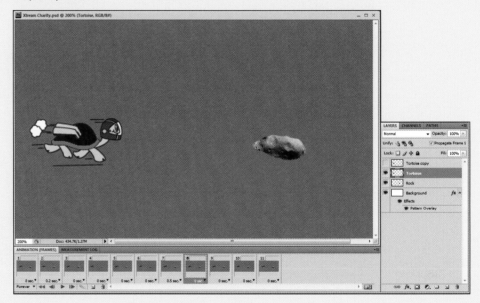

You've just been elected to the board of directors of a community access TV station. Each board member is expected to serve on at least one committee. You've chosen the Community Involvement Committee, and have been asked to design a snappy, numeric countdown animation that will introduce public service announcements.

1. Obtain images appropriate for a countdown. You can draw your own numbers, use the images that are available on your computer, scan print media, create images using a digital camera, or connect to the Internet and download images. You must include at least one other image, and can include any additional images, as desired.

2. Create a new Photoshop image, then save it as **Countdown**.

3. Apply a color or style to the Background layer, add images as desired, and apply effects to them. (*Hint*: The Background layer in the sample has a Pattern Overlay style applied to it.)

4. Create at least three type layers with numbers for a countdown, and apply styles or filters to them as desired. (*Hint*: Each number in the sample has a duplicate with different opacities.)

5. Create an animation that makes the numbers move across the image and fade into one another.

6. Duplicate the last number so that it changes appearance at least twice.

7. Tween each animation and add frame delays as necessary.

8. Preview the animation in your image and in your browser.

9. Save Countdown as **Countdown Browser**, then adjust tweening and frame delays so that it plays perfectly in your browser.

10. Save your work, then compare your screen to the sample shown in Figure 51.

FIGURE 51
Sample Project Builder 2

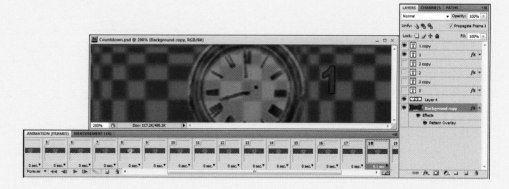

After your first experience with creating your own animation, you and your friends are hooked. You want to peruse the full range of animation on the web. You decide to study one aspect of web animation. Your first stop will be to check out the latest in animated banner ads.

1. Connect to the Internet and use your browser to find sites containing downloadable animation. (Make a record of the site you found so you can use it for future reference, if necessary.) A sample site is shown in Figure 52.

2. Create a new Photoshop image and save it as **Banners et al**.

3. Identify an animation that interests you by scrolling down the page or linking to one of the sites listed on the page.

4. Create a type layer named **Animation Techniques**, then type the animation techniques and Photoshop skills and features that you believe were used to create the appearance of the animation.

5. Be sure to add the following points to the Animation Techniques layer:
   - Identify how many different animations are active throughout the sequence and at any one time.
   - Identify instances of tweening and frame delay.
   - Give examples of techniques unknown to you.

6. When your analysis is complete, print the image.

7. Hide the Animation Techniques layer, then obtain images to use for your own interpretation of the animation. You can use the images that are available on your computer, scan print media, or download images from the Internet.

8. Place the images in your image, create type layers as needed, and then apply the animation techniques you identified.

9. Update the Animation Techniques layer as necessary, print the image so that the Animation Techniques layer prints clearly, then compare your before and after analyses. (*Hint*: Hide distracting layers.)

10. Hide the Animation Techniques layer, make the other layers active, then save your work.

FIGURE 52
Sample Design Project

Courtesy of Jupiterimages Corporation - http://www.animationfactory.com/en/

You and your team handle new product presentations for Never Too Late (NTL), an online message service that sends daily reminders to clients. NTL is teaming with an automated home electronics company to offer a new home-based service. They're going to provide an automatic wake-up call that turns on a client's computer, plays a wake-up message until the client responds, and then lists the day's important activities. You want to demonstrate a prototype that shows off the product at your next staff meeting. This prototype will transform a black-and-white line drawing into a color image as part of the wake-up call feature. You'll add appropriate sounds later.

1. Obtain images for the wake-up call. One image should be a black-and-white image that you can easily transform to color. You can draw your own images, use the images that are available on your computer, scan print media, create images using a digital camera, or connect to the Internet and download images.
2. Create a new Photoshop image, then save it as **Wake Up**.
3. Apply a color or style to the Background layer, add other images as desired, and apply effects to them. (*Hint*: The sample has three color layers that alternate as the background, two of which have gradients applied to them.)
4. Place the images in the file. (*Hint*: The black-and-white line art is a cartoon line drawing that was filled in to colorize it. You can color a similar image by choosing background colors on the Tools panel, selecting the Eraser tool, and then clicking the Lock transparent pixels button on the Layers panel.)
5. Create at least one type layer as desired and at least one other image or background.

6. Create an animation for the state you created.
7. Tween each animation, and add frame delays as necessary.
8. Preview the animation in your image and in your browser.
9. Save your work, then compare your screen to the sample shown in Figure 53.

FIGURE 53
Sample Portfolio Project

PORTFOLIO PROJECTS
AND EFFECTS

1. Create a pencil sketch from a photo

2. Create a montage effect with blocks

3. Simulate a slide mount

4. Create a reflection effect

5. Fake a motion blur

6. Improve a photo

7. Animate warped type

8. Fix photographic defects

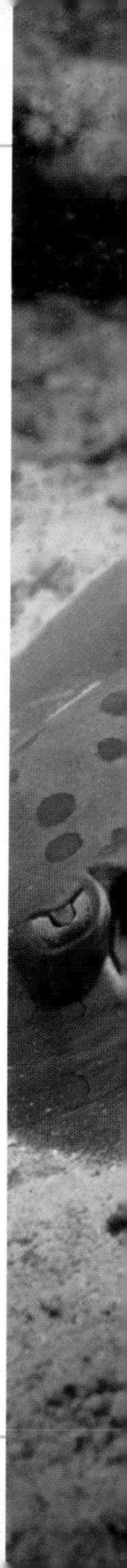

PORTFOLIO PROJECTS
AND EFFECTS

Introduction

Now that you've got all kinds of Photoshop skills under your belt, you're ready to discover real-world opportunities to use these skills and have some fun, too. This appendix presents seven projects that you can complete at your own pace using your own design choices. Rather than guiding you through each step, these projects suggest strategies and methods for achieving the finished product. As you complete these projects, you'll build on the knowledge you already have, and even learn a few new Photoshop tricks along the way.

Getting the Most from the Projects

Of the seven projects in this appendix, three are effects—smaller, mini-projects that you can use within other images. For example, the reflected object effect shown in Figure 1 could stand on its own or be used as a component in a larger image. The pulsing type and motion blur projects seen in Figures 2 and 3 could each easily be used in a web page. (You'll create

each of these effects later in this appendix.) Any of the techniques shown in this appendix could be increased or reduced. How much a technique is used depends entirely on what sort of effect you're going for and the results you see.

FIGURE 1
Sample 1

Using Multiple Skills

Like most real-life projects, the image in Figure 2 makes use of many different Photoshop skills. Look at the figure, then see how many tasks from the following list you can identify:

- Warped type
- Composite images
- Button images with type
- Type resized using its bounding box

Viewing Animation

It would be great to be able to see an animation on a static page, wouldn't it? Well, short of that, the effect shown in Figure 3 is achieved by turning on all the layers in the image so you can see approximately what the animation will look like when viewed in a browser.

FIGURE 2
Sample 2

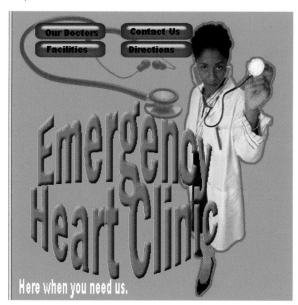

FIGURE 3
Sample 3

CREATE A PENCIL SKETCH
FROM A PHOTO

Skills You'll Use

In this lesson, you'll do the following:

- Save a digital image as a Photoshop file.
- Change the color mode.
- Duplicate and invert a layer.
- Change the blending mode.
- Apply a filter.
- Use the History Brush to restore color.

Creating a Unique Look

How about this? Take an ordinary photo, and give it a look that's not realistic at all. You can do this by duplicating a layer here and there, changing the color mode, applying a filter, and then selectively restoring color. How much you restore is entirely up to you!

> **QUICK**TIP
>
> As you work through each exercise, carefully examine the History panel of the completed project. It may help you understand the steps that were taken to achieve the final product.

Preparing for Magic

Figure 4 contains an ordinary portrait photo, but watch what happens. First, you turn this color image to grayscale mode (discarding the color information), then duplicate the existing background layer. Next, you invert the duplicate layer. This process (which you achieve by clicking Image on the Application bar, pointing to Adjustments, then clicking Invert) flips

the colors or tones of the active layer, so whatever is dark becomes light. Change the Blending Mode to Color Dodge. Don't panic: it looks like your image has disappeared, doesn't it? But apply a Gaussian Blur and a pencil-like sketch will be visible. Pretty cool, huh?

Using the History Brush Tool

You might be satisfied with the image the way it is, but wait—there's more! To add a little more pizzazz, you can selectively reapply some color. First, flatten the image, then change the mode back to RGB color. Now we're going to see some magic! Select the History Brush tool from the toolbox and selectively paint areas in the image. In Figure 5, for example, the face and hair are painted, but you could paint any areas you want.

> **QUICK**TIP
>
> The History Brush tool is a source of earlier pixel data, but can only be used within a single image.

FIGURE 4
Project 1 – Beginning

FIGURE 5
Project 1 – Completed

FIGURE 6
Project 1 – Portfolio Sample

Project 1   Create a Pencil Sketch from a Photo

Create a pencil sketch effect

1. Open PS APP-1.jpg from the drive and folder where you store your Data Files, then save it as **Colorized Pencil Sketch.psd**.

2. Use the following suggestions to guide you through completing the project:

   - Change the image mode to Grayscale.

   - Duplicate the background layer, then rename the duplicate.

   - Invert the new layer (click Image on the Application bar, point to Adjustments, then click Invert or click the Invert button on the Adjustments panel), then use the Layer Style dialog box to change the blending mode to Color Dodge.

   - Add a Gaussian Blur filter. (A setting of 4 pixels is used in the sample.)

   - Flatten the image, then change the mode to RGB Color.

   - Create a new layer, then set the blending mode to Multiply.

   - Use the History Brush to paint the woman's face, hair, and neck. (*Hint*: The image will look almost blank up to this point.)

3. Save your work, then compare your image to Figure 5.

   Figure 6 shows how this image might be used in a marketing piece to promote a product. In this example, type was added to promote the name of a photography studio.

You saved a digital image as a Photoshop file, changed the image mode, applied a filter, flattened the image, then used the History Brush to selectively restore color to the image.

CREATE A MONTAGE
EFFECT WITH BLOCKS

Skills You'll Use

In this lesson, you'll do the following:
- Save a digital image as a Photoshop file.
- Add a background layer.
- Resize imagery.
- Create layers from selections.
- Add layer styles.

Keeping It Simple

Sometimes all it takes to make an image stand out is a simple technique executed with artistic flair. Take, for example, the image shown in Figure 7. This is a nice photograph as is, but with a little Photoshop sleight-of-hand, you can really make it pop.

> **QUICK**TIP
>
> Most Photoshop tasks are easy to accomplish but may take longer than you think.

Getting Boxy

The boxy effect you see in Figure 8 is not difficult to create. Once you've added a background layer and resized the initial image (in this case, the quaint shop),

the real fun begins. Make the layer containing the actual image active, then randomly pick a spot and draw a rectangle with the Rectangular Marquee tool. Create a layer from the selection using the Layer via Copy command, then add a drop shadow to the layer. Then, to add to the effect, move the layer (the one you created from the selection) so it's slightly offset from the original. Repeat this process in different parts of the image until you're satisfied with the results. As you can see from the completed image, this effect was repeated eight times (resulting in eight new layers). Now, that wasn't hard, was it?

> **QUICK**TIP
>
> You could automate this process by creating an action for these repetitive steps.

FIGURE 7
Project 2 – Beginning

FIGURE 8
Project 2 – Completed

FIGURE 9
Project 2 – Portfolio Sample

Project 2   Create a Montage Effect with Blocks

Create a block montage effect

1. Open PS APP-2.jpg from the drive and folder where you store your Data Files, then save it as **Shopping.psd**.

2. Use the following suggestions to guide you through completing the project:

   ■ Create a new background layer using the color of your choice. (A medium brown is shown in the sample.)

   ■ Resize the original layer so it appears to be framed by the background layer.

   ■ Make a rectangular selection, create a layer from the selection, add a drop shadow or outer glow effect, then move the layer.

   ■ Repeat the process of creating a drop-shadowed or outer glowed, offset layer from a selection until you've achieved the look you want.

   TIP   You can easily copy formatting from one layer to another by selecting the layer containing the formatting you want to duplicate, press and hold [Alt] while dragging the formatting effect(s) to the layer where you want to apply the formatting.

3. Save your work, then compare your image to Figure 8.

   Figure 9 shows how this image could be used in a promotional poster.

You saved a digital image as a Photoshop file, added a new background layer, resized an object, created layers from selections, then added layer styles.

SIMULATE
A SLIDE MOUNT

Skills You'll Use

In this lesson, you'll do the following:
- Use a digital image in a Photoshop file.
- Draw a shape.
- Delete a selection.
- Add a drop shadow.
- Add type.
- Merge layers.
- Resize and skew or rotate a shape.

Creating an Illusion

You've probably seen photos that look like slides in a magazine or an ad somewhere, and asked "How'd they do that?" The illusion is actually very easy to create, using a few simple Photoshop tricks. Just draw a shape, add some text, and pop in an image.

Simulating a Slide

To create the effect of a slide, you create a new layer, change the foreground color to gray, then draw a rounded rectangle shape. (You don't want to draw a shape layer or a path, you want to fill pixels.) Draw a horizontal marquee within the rounded rectangle (this is where the slide image would appear), rasterize the shape, then delete the selection to 'punch a hole' in the slide. Add a drop shadow to the object, and your slide is finished. You can add text to the slide to make it look more realistic. When your slide looks just right, merge all the appropriate layers into a single slide layer.

> **QUICK**TIP
> You'll probably want to duplicate your blank slide so it'll be easier to use over and over. No point in reinventing the wheel!

Adding the Image to the Slide

The individual photos in Figure 10 will work fine for the individual slide images. Make sure you've got enough slide blanks, then select each photo and drag it into the slide image. Each photo will have to be resized to fit the hole in each slide, and you may want to skew the slides to make them look scattered, rather than perfectly aligned. This gives the slides a more realistic look.

FIGURE 10
Project 3 – Beginning

FIGURE 11
Project 3 – Completed

FIGURE 12
Project 3 – Portfolio Sample

Project 3   Simulate a Slide Mount

1. Open PS APP-3.jpg and PS APP-4.jpg from the drive and folder where you store your Data Files.

2. Open a new Photoshop image with the dimensions 450 X 225 pixels, then save it as **Slide Mount.psd**.

3. Use the following suggestions to guide you through completing the project:

   ■ Create a rounded-rectangular shape in a shade of gray.

   ■ Knock out a rectangle in the middle of the shape.

   ■ Add a drop shadow to the shape.

   ■ Add text to the image, then merge the layers so the slide is a single layer.

   ■ Copy the slide layer (you may want to make multiple copies, depending on your overall design goal).

   ■ Insert an image in the rectangular knock-out.

   ■ Rotate or skew the slide (if that is the look you want to achieve).

4. Save your work, then compare your image to Figure 11.

   TIP   The image on the right was converted into a Smart Object, then enhanced with the Sharpen filter.

   Figure 12 shows an example of how the slides could be used in a corporate advertisement.

You created a new Photoshop image, opened two digital image files to use in the new image, created a shape that looks like a slide, knocked out a rectangle in the slide, added type to the shape, inserted an image in the shape, and rotated or skewed it to make it look more realistic. You repeated this process for all the images you wanted to present as "slides."

CREATE A
REFLECTION EFFECT

Skills You'll Use

In this lesson, you'll do the following:

- Save a Photoshop image using a new name.
- Duplicate a layer.
- Flip and reposition an image.
- Apply a blur filter and a distort filter.
- Apply a mask and gradient.
- Adjust midtones.

Understanding Illusion

So much of what we do in Photoshop involves creating an illusion. As you saw in the previous project, you can create an image that looks like a photographic slide by using what you know about how real slides look to trick the eye. In this project, you trick the eye again—by making an object look as if it were reflected in rippling water. The beauty of Photoshop layers is that you can easily duplicate objects, then manipulate the images within selected layers. Once a layer is duplicated, it can be flipped, and then 'doctored' to display the ephemeral qualities that it might have by being reflected in a pool of water. Figure 13 shows objects against a background, and Figure 14 shows those same objects after a reflection effect was created.

QUICKTIP

Use your observations about real objects to create effective illusions. An object reflected in water would look blurrier than the original, maybe with some ripples, and the reflection would fade as it got farther from the original.

Creating a Reflection

You can begin creating the reflection effect by duplicating the Tools layer. Flip the duplicate vertically, and then drag it beneath the original. (The duplicate will serve as the reflected object.) Since a reflected object should not be a mirror-image, apply a Motion Blur filter, then apply a Ripple filter to give it that 'watery' look.

Applying a Fade

To give the reflection a faded look, apply a mask, then apply a gradient to the mask. You can give depth to the surface on which the object sits, by creating a marquee on the background layer, then adjusting the midtones in the Levels dialog box. *Voila!*

FIGURE 13
Project 4 – Beginning

Create a reflection effect

1. Open PS APP-5.psd from the drive and folder where you store your Data Files, then save it as **Reflected Object Effect.psd**.

2. Use the following suggestions to guide you through completing the project:

   - Duplicate the Tools layer.
   - Flip the image vertically on the duplicate layer.
   - Reposition the duplicate layer so it appears to be *beneath* the original layer.
   - Apply a Motion Blur filter to the duplicate layer.
   - Apply a Ripple filter to the duplicate layer.
   - Add a rectangular layer mask to the duplicate layer, then draw a linear gradient from the top of the reflection to the bottom of the image.
   - Select the Rectangular Marquee tool, then set the feather setting to 5 px.
   - With the Background layer active, draw a marquee around the bottom half of the image.
   - Open the Levels dialog box, then modify the midtones (the center slider) setting to darken the selection. (In the sample, the midtones are adjusted to .70.)

3. Save your work, then compare your image to Figure 14.

You saved a Photoshop file using a new name, duplicated and flipped an image, applied two filters, created a layer mask, then added a gradient and modified the midtones in the Levels dialog box.

FIGURE 14
Project 4 – Completed

FAKE A MOTION BLUR

Skills You'll Use

In this lesson, you'll do the following:
- Save a Photoshop image using a new name.
- Rasterize a type layer.
- Create multiple type layers by duplicating and editing a single layer.
- Apply a motion blur filter.
- Make frames from each layer.
- Add movement and time delays to an animation sequence.

Deciding What's Possible

Using a little imagination, you can create interesting animations for your website. You've seen words fly in from the side in what looks like a blur, right? This type of moving text is often used to call attention to a special event or important information, because it's more likely to catch a viewer's eye than static type. You can create this effect, often called a motion blur, using a few simple tools in Photoshop.

Dividing and Conquering

You start with a simple line of type, as shown in Figure 15, which you can rasterize and duplicate. Then you apply the motion blur filter to the duplicate layer. This is the layer that's going to simulate the movement. The next step is to separate each blurred word onto its own layer. (If your sanity is important to you, you'll probably want to do some layer renaming.) With the duplicate layer active, draw a marquee around a single word, then click Layer on the Application bar, point to New, then click Layer via Cut. (This step puts the selected object on its own layer.) Repeat this process until you have separated all the words—blurred and clear—as you want them. Moving the blurred words slightly left or right will make your animation more convincing.

QUICKTIP

The Layer via Cut command is similar to the Layer via Copy command, except that the source layer is modified.

Animating the Layers

Now the animation fun begins. Make frames from layers and reorder the layers (if necessary), then turn on and off layers for each frame depending on the effect you want. Move any layers that will add to the effect of movement, add time delays, then play the animation.

FIGURE 15
Project 5 – Beginning

FIGURE 16
Project 5 – Completed

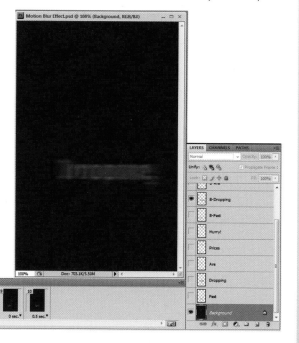

Fake a motion blur

1. Open PS APP-6.psd from the drive and folder where you store your Data Files, then save it as **Motion Blur Effect.psd**.

2. Use the following suggestions to guide you through completing the project:

   ▪ Rasterize the type layer.

   ▪ Duplicate the type layer.

   ▪ Add a motion blur filter to the duplicate layer. (In the sample, a setting of 50 pixels and a 0° angle is used.)

   ▪ Separate each blurred word from the duplicate layer.

   ▪ Separate each clear word from the original layer.

   ▪ Open the Animation panel, if it is not already displayed.

   ▪ Make frames from the layers.

   ▪ Turn on and off layers for each frame as necessary. Position the type so that the blurred type appears first, then the sharp type appears in a slightly different location, creating the illusion of movement.

   ▪ Add time delays.

   ▪ Play the animation in Photoshop and in a browser.

3. Save your work, then compare your image to Figure 16.

You saved a Photoshop file using a new name, rasterized and duplicated a type layer, added a motion blur filter, then separated each word onto its own layer. Using the Animation panel, you made frames from the layers, turned the layers on and off, added time delays, then played the animation.

IMPROVE A PHOTO

Skills You'll Use

In this lesson, you'll do the following:
- Save a digital image as a Photoshop file.
- Paint areas to make them brighter.
- Use Liquify to move pixels.

Dieting with Photoshop

This is better than cosmetic surgery—much faster and certainly much cheaper! Suppose you have a photo, like the one in Figure 17. Handsome guy, right? But he could stand some improvement. His teeth look a little dingy, and let's face it, there's a little too much to love here. But you can fix that!

Improving on Reality

You can whiten dingy teeth by simply painting them white, right? Sure, but that's not always the most effective technique—in fact, this can make someone look ridiculous. Impossibly white teeth can look unrealistic. A better approach is either to sample a brighter area of the existing teeth, or to find a brighter off-white that looks believable.

QUICKTIP

Remember that real-life objects are rarely made up of solid colors. That means that no one's teeth are completely one color. Look closely, and you'll see greens and blues in your teeth. This means that when coloring objects in Photoshop, you may need to mix colors rather than using only one shade.

Pushing Pixels

When you look at Figure 18, you can see what a difference these changes can make. Using the Liquify feature, pixels were pushed to slim the waist and neck areas. A mask was placed over the man's beard so it wouldn't get distorted when the neck pixels were moved.

QUICKTIP

To move pixels with greater control, use the Push Left tool in the Liquify feature.

FIGURE 17
Project 6 – Beginning

FIGURE 19
Project 6 – Portfolio Sample

FIGURE 18
Project 6 – Completed

Teeth whitened

Neck thinner

Waist thinner

Improve a photo

1. Open PS APP-7.jpg from the drive and folder where you store your Data Files, then save it as **Improved Image.psd**.

2. Use the following suggestions to guide you through completing the project:

   - Duplicate the original image, so that you can work on each area in a different layer.

   - Zoom into the teeth, select a small brush size, then paint the teeth.

   - Choose a lighter off-white, then paint the teeth. (In the sample, the foreground color was changed to R=234, G=231, B=216.)

   - Use the Liquify feature to reduce the waist and neck areas.

   - Add any necessary adjustment layers for color correction.

   TIP   The image was converted into a Smart Object, then enhanced with the Sharpen More filter.

3. Save your work, then compare your image to Figure 18.

   Figure 19 shows an example of how this improved photo could be used in an advertisement.

You saved a digital image as a Photoshop file, brightened teeth by painting them, and used the Liquify feature to make the image more flattering.

ANIMATE WARPED TYPE

Skills You'll Use

In this lesson, you'll do the following:

- Warp a type layer.
- Modify the warped type layer.
- Add frames to animation.
- Set time delays to animation.

Text with a Pulse

One of the simplest animations you can create with type is a pulsing effect. Similar to creating a motion blur with type, this effect can be used to call attention to information in a web page, but instead of text appearing to fly in from off-screen, it can seem to pulse or vibrate on its own.

Warping Type

To create this effect, you simply warp multiple frames of identical text in different ways. Start by warping a type layer. Modify the warp settings so each frame is different. Add and tween frames until you have a sufficient number to simulate movement. Add some time delays and you're ready to play the animation.

FIGURE 20

Project 7 – Completed

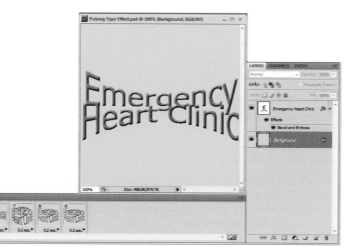

1. Open PS APP-8.psd from the drive and folder where you store your Data Files, then save it as **Pulsing Type Effect.psd**.

2. Use the following suggestions to guide you through completing the project:

   ■ Apply a warp to the type layer.

   ■ Open the Animation panel (if it is not already displayed), then create an additional frame.

   ■ Modify the warp for the new frame.

   ■ Tween the two frames.

   ■ Create additional frames as necessary, modifying the warp in each. In the sample, a Bulge style warp is used with different bend settings for each frame.

   ■ Add tweening and frame delays to smooth the animation effect.

   ■ Play the animation in a browser.

3. Save your work, then compare your image to Figure 20.

You saved a Photoshop file with a different name, then warped a type layer. Using the Animation panel, you added frames, modified the warp settings in each frame, tweened frames, added time delays, then played the animation.

FIX PHOTOGRAPHIC
DEFECTS

Skills You'll Use

In this lesson, you'll do the following:

- Duplicate an image.
- Clean dirt with the Spot Healing Brush tool.
- Eliminate the red eye effect.
- Brighten teeth.
- Add a vignette effect.
- Add a new layer.

Not-So-Perfect Pictures

Our new digital cameras will do almost everything for us, but they won't clean a dirty face, and they may not automatically get rid of red eye.

Isolating Defects

Figuring out problem areas in a photograph can be a challenge. If you're lucky, however, it can be easy. A dirty face, stained outfit, or misplaced blob is easily identified, but composition errors can be harder to spot.

> **QUICK**TIP
>
> It's easy to become fixated on every word and every pixel in your image. It is possible that no one else will notice something you consider a major problem. Learn to let go!

Defining Problems

Part of the problem in identifying problems in images is that we form irrational attachments to our artwork. An ugly sign in an otherwise beautiful image is not a reflection on you. And with Photoshop, you can improve on those defects. It's very difficult to look objectively at your work, but that skill is as essential as learning what Photoshop tool to use in a given situation.

FIGURE 21
Project 8 – Beginning

FIGURE 22
Project 8 – Completed

FIGURE 23
Project 8 – Portfolio Sample

Project 8   Fix Photographic Defects

Fix defects

1. Open PS APP-9.jpg from the drive and folder where you store your Data Files, then save it as **Happy Dog.psd**.

2. Use the following suggestions to guide you through completing the project:

   - Duplicate the original image so that you can work on each area in a different layer.

   - Zoom into the dog's face, then use the Spot Healing Brush tool (or Healing Brush tool) to clean the area around the mouth and under each eye.

   - Use the Red Eye tool to eliminate the red eye effect.

   - Use a light color to whiten the dog's teeth. (The 20% Gray swatch was used in the sample.)

   - Add a vignette effect. (The sample vignette has a 30 px feather.)

   - Add a layer that lies beneath the vignette. (The sample Layer 1 is filled with the swatch Pale Warm Brown.)

3. Save your work, then compare your image to Figure 22.

   Figure 23 shows an example of how this improved photo could be used for promotional purposes.

You saved a digital image as a Photoshop file, used the Spot Healing Brush tool to clean dirt, painted teeth to make them appear brighter, created a vignette effect, then added a layer filled with a complementary color.

ACE Certification Grid for Adobe Photoshop CS4

Topic Area	Objectives	Chapter(s)
1.0 General knowledge	1.1 Describe how to arrange panels and save workspaces. (Includes: arranging and docking panels, customizing menus and shortcuts, and saving workspaces.)	1 (p. 16-23)
	1.2 Describe how to use tabbed documents and the application frame. (Includes: window management (not panel/workspace management), includes screen modes, canvas rotation, n-up views.)	1 (p. 12, 20-23) 14 (p. 13)
	1.3 Describe options for changing the document view and zoom level. (Includes: GPU-assisted pan and zoom techniques.)	1 (p. 34-36) 14 (p. 13)
	1.4 Given a scenario, describe the best way to resize an image. (Includes: Canvas Size dialog box, Image Size dialog box, resampling options, Free Transform, Options bar, resolution concepts.)	1 (p. 23, 29) 12 (p. 4-7)
	1.5 Add metadata to an image in Adobe Photoshop.	1 (p. 9-10)
	1.6 Explain the advantages of and when you would use 32-bit, 16-bit, and 8-bit images.	16 (p. 10, 12, 40)
	1.7 Explain the advantages of different file format choices when saving a Photoshop document. (Includes: file formats, compression methods, color support.)	16 (p. 40-42)
2.0 Correcting, painting, and retouching	2.1 Explain how to correct tonal range and color in Photoshop by using the Adjust-ments panel. (Includes: setting black point and white point, using Curves/Levels, Hue/Saturation vs. Vibrance, Auto Color, new Curves interface, Selective Color, new color correction UI)	10 (p. 6-13)
	2.2 Given a painting tool, adjust options appropriately and paint on a layer. (Includes: Brush tool, Pencil tool, blending modes, Options bar.)	6 (p. 4-21)
	2.3 Create, edit, and save a custom brush.	6 (p. 10-13)
	2.4 Given a scenario, explain which retouching tool would be most effective. (Includes: Healing, Spot healing, Patch tools and options, Clone Source panel.)	6 (p. 4-21)
	2.5 Create and use gradients and patterns.	9 (p. 8-11)
	2.6 Explain how to use filters and the Filter Gallery.	8 (p. 12, 2-27)
3.0 Working with selections	3.1 Given a scenario, create a selection using the appropriate tool. (Includes: Quick Selection, Lasso tools, Magic Wand, Marquee tool, Color Range, luminosity shortcut.)	2 (p. 12-15) 3 (p. 4-19)
	3.2 Save and load selections.	3 (p. 9)
	3.3 Move and transform selections.	3 (p. 12-14)
	3.4 Modify and preview a selection using Refine Edge.	9 (p. 21)

Topic Area	Objectives	Chapter(s)
4.0 Creating and using layers	4.1 Create and arrange layers and layer groups.	1 (p. 24-27) 2 (p. 10, 16-19)
	4.2 Given a scenario, select, align, and distribute multiple layers in an image.	7 (p. 10-13)
	4.3 Explain the uses of layer comps, and compare to layer groups.	2 (p. 16-20)
	4.4 Given a scenario, explain the use of layer Blending Options.	7 (p. 14-17)
	4.5 Create and edit layer effects.	5 (p. 12-15, 24-27)
	4.6 Create and edit layer styles.	5 (p. 12-15 20-22)
	4.7 Explain how to convert an image to black and white with the most control.	4 (p. 22)
5.0 Working with masks and channels	5.1 Explain the uses of masks and channels.	7 (p. 6-20) 9 (p. 4-7)
	5.2 Given a scenario, use the Masks panel and painting tools to create and edit a layer mask.	7 (p. 4-9)
	5.3 Create, view, and edit channels.	9 (p. 4-7)
	5.4 Explain the difference between a layer mask and a vector mask.	7 (p. 4-12) 12 (p. 12)
	5.5 Explain why you would use a clipping mask.	7 (p. 26-29) 11 (p. 2-7)
	5.6 Convert to or from a selection, a channel, a layer mask, a vector mask, and a Quick Mask.	7 (p. 23, 28) 9 (p. 4) 11 (p. 8-9) 12 (p. 12-13)
6.0 Working with vector tools	6.1 Create shape layers and paths using the Pen and Shape tools.	11 (p. 8-19)
	6.2 Explain the advantages of using vector drawing tools versus pixel-based tools.	11 (p. 2-5, 12)
	6.3 Given a scenario, manage paths using the Paths panel.	11 (p. 8-11)
	6.4 Given a scenario, alter the properties of type.	12 (p. 4-19)

Topic Area	Objectives	Chapter(s)
7.0 Using Camera Raw and Bridge	7.1 Describe the advantages of using Adobe Camera Raw to process digital camera raw files.	16 (p. 40-42)
	7.2 Given a Camera Raw adjustment setting, explain the purpose of that setting.	16 (p. 40-42)
	7.3 Export files from Camera Raw.	16 (p. 42)
	7.4 Given a scenario, import files directly from a camera using Bridge. (Includes: Adobe Photo Downloader options.)	1 (p.13)
	7.5 Given a scenario, describe the best way to apply one image's adjustments to many others. (Includes: Synchronize in Camera Raw, or copy and paste settings in Bridge.)	16 (p. 41-42)
	7.6 Apply keywords and metadata to images by using Bridge. (Includes: Keywords panel, Metadata panel, and metadata templates.)	1 (p. 9-10)
	7.7 Given a scenario, find a specific group of files out of a large collection in Bridge.	1 (p. 9-10)
8.0 Automating tasks	8.1 Create and use actions.	15 (p. 8-19)
	8.2 Create and use a batch action.	15 (p. 16)
	8.3 List and describe the automation features in Photoshop.	1 (p. 15) 9 (p. 28-31)
	8.4 Given a scenario, describe the best way to process a large number of images through Photoshop.	9 (p. 31) 15 (p. 16)
	8.5 Describe the difference between actions and scripting.	15 (p. 19)
	8.6 Create variables.	16 (p. 15)
9.0 Working with filters	9.1 Describe the process and components of Photoshop color management. (Includes: profiles, working spaces, rendering intents, settings.)	4 (p. 7) 10 (p. 4, 7, 13)
	9.2 Configure the Color Settings dialog box.	10 (p. 7, 13)
	9.3 Given a scenario, describe the proper color conversion to apply. (Scenarios include: To CMYK for prepress, to a different color space for Web or video.)	10 (p. 4-7)
	9.4 Given a scenario about a color management problem, describe the proper action to take.	10 (p. 4-7)
	9.5 Discuss the relationship between color gamut and rendering intents.	4 (p. 7)
	9.6 Explain the purpose and use of the Proof Setup command.	1 (p. 35)

CERTIFICATION GRID

Topic Area	Objectives	Chapter(s)
10.0 Advanced knowledge	10.1 Given a scenario, create and edit a Smart Object. (Scenarios include: create from Camera Raw files, imported vector objects, and layers.)	7 (p. 19, 28) 11 (p. 15)
	10.2 Create and edit Smart Filters.	8 (p. 9, 12-13)
	10.3 Given a scenario, use Vanishing Point to edit in perspective.	8 (p. 28-31)
	10.4 Explain how to use features that handle images moving to and from video workflows. (Includes: Pixel aspect ratio, document presets, Video Preview.)	16 (p. 32-34, 39)
	10.5 Create, edit, and convert an HDR image.	10 (p. 10)
	10.6 Describe how to use Photomerge to create a panorama.	14 (p. 13)
11.0 Create output for print	11.1 Given a scenario, describe how to set up the Print dialog box.	1 (p. 32-37)
	11.2 Using the Print dialog, position an image at a given size and location on a sheet of paper.	1 (p. 35)
	11.3 Configure the Print dialog for color-managed output to a high-quality inkjet printer. (Includes: set the correct Color Management options, understand the relationship of Photoshop to the printer driver.)	1 (p. 9, 35)
	11.4 Given a scenario, prepare an image for use in a printed Adobe InDesign document. (Includes: flattened CMYK, layered RGB with layer comps, Photoshop PDF with vector layers.)	1 (p. 32-37) 2 (p. 17, 18, 21)
	11.5 Set up the Print dialog box to proof one device on another.	1 (p. 35)
12.0 Creating output for Web and mobile devices	12.1 Given a scenario, choose the appropriate Save for Web options for a Web graphic. (Includes: file format, transparency, and metadata inclusion.)	16 (p. 4-11, 41)
	12.2 Explain the options in the Save for Web and Devices dialog box.	16 (p. 8-13)
	12.3 Explain how to create an animated Web image.	16 (p. 26-35)
	12.4 Create and upload a complete Web gallery.	1 (p. 37)
	12.5 Explain how to create a sliced Web image.	16 (p. 18-25)
	12.6 Explain how to preview content for a device using Device Central.	16 (p. 10)

Data Files List

Chapter	Data File Supplied	Student Creates File	Used in
Chapter 1	PS 1-1.psd PS 1-2.tif		Lessons 2–8
		Review.psd	Skills Review
	PS 1-3.psd		Skills Review
	PS 1-4.psd		Project Builder 2
		Critique-1.psd Critique-2.psd	Design Project
Chapter 2	PS 2-1.psd PS 2-2.psd		Lessons 1–4
	PS 2-3.psd PS 2-4.psd		Skills Review
	PS 2-5.psd PS 2-6.psd		Project Builder 1
	PS 2-7.psd PS 2-8.psd		Project Builder 2
	PS 2-9.psd PS 2-10.psd		Design Project
	PS 2-11.psd		Portfolio Project
Chapter 3	PS 3-1.psd PS 3-2.psd PS 3-3.psd PS 3-4.psd PS 3-5.psd PS 3-6.psd		Lessons 1–4
	PS 3-7.psd PS 3-8.tif PS 3-9.tif PS 3-10.tif		Skills Review
	PS 3-11.psd		Project Builder 1
	PS 3-12.psd		Project Builder 2
		Sample Compositing.psd	Design Project
	PS 3-13.psd		Portfolio Project

Chapter	Data File Supplied	Student Creates File	Used in
Chapter 4	PS 4-1.psd		Lessons 1–4, 6-7
	PS 4-2.psd		Lessons 5–6
	PS 4-3.tif		Lesson 7
	PS 4-4.psd PS 4-5.psd PS 4-6.tif		Skills Review
	PS 4-7.psd		Project Builder 1
	PS 4-8.psd		Project Builder 2
	PS 4-9.psd		Design Project
	PS 4-10.psd		Portfolio Project
Chapter 5	PS 5-1.psd		Lessons 1–7
	PS 5-2.psd		Skills Review
	PS 5-3.psd		Project Builder 1
	PS 5-4.psd		Project Builder 2
	PS 5-5.psd		Design Project
		Community Promotion.psd	Portfolio Project
Chapter 6	PS 6-1.psd		Lessons 1–4
	PS 6-2.psd		Skills Review
	PS 6-3.psd		Project Builder 1
	PS 6-4.psd		Project Builder 2
		Art Course.doc	Design Project
		Dealership Ad.psd	Portfolio Project
Chapter 7	PS 7-1.psd		Lessons 1–6
	PS 7-2.psd		Skills Review
	PS 7-3.psd		Project Builder 1
		Cleanup.psd Cleanup copy.psd	Project Builder 2
		Currency.psd Currency copy.psd	Design Project
		Poetry Poster.psd	Portfolio Project

Chapter	Data File Supplied	Student Creates File	Used in
Chapter 8	PS 8-1.psd		Lessons 1–6
	PS 8-2.psd		Lesson 6
	PS 8-3.psd PS 8-4.psd		Skills Review
		Play.psd	Project Builder 1
		Jazz and Blues.psd	Project Builder 2
	PS 8-5.psd		Design Project
		Dance.psd	Portfolio Project
Chapter 9	PS 9-1.psd		Lessons 1–7
	PS 9-2.psd		Lessons 5–6
		Picture Package.pdf /Contact Sample ContactSheet-001.pdf	Lesson 7
	PS 9-3.psd PS 9-4.psd	Picture Package-Tools.pdf /Contact Sample 2 ContactSheet-002.pdf	Skills Review
		Spheroid.psd	Project Builder 1
		Perfect Oasis.psd	Project Builder 2
		My Vision.psd	Design Project
		Beach Poster.psd	Portfolio Project
Chapter 10	PS 10-1.psd		Lessons 1–4
	PS 10-2.psd		Skills Review
	PS 10-3.psd		Project Builder 1
	PS 10-4.psd		Project Builder 2
	PS 10-5.psd		Design Project
		Annual Report Cover.psd	Portfolio Project
Chapter 11	PS 11-1.psd		Lessons 1–4
	PS 11-2.psd		Skills Review
	PS 11-3.psd		Project Builder 1
	PS 11-4.psd		Project Builder 2
		Shape Experimentation.psd	Design Project
		Contest Winner.psd	Portfolio Project

Chapter	Data File Supplied	Student Creates File	Used in
Chapter 12	PS 12-1.psd		Lessons 1–4
	PS 12-2.psd		Skills Review
	PS 12-3.psd		Project Builder 1
	PS 12-4.psd		Project Builder 2
		Television Station Ad.psd	Design Project
		CD Cover Artwork.psd	Portfolio Project
Chapter 13	PS 13-1.psd		Lessons 1–3
	PS 13-2.psd		Skills Review
	PS 13-3.psd		Project Builder 1
	PS 13-4.psd		Project Builder 2
		Photoshop Presentation.psd	Portfolio Project
Chapter 14	PS 14-1.jpg		Lessons 1–3
	PS 14-2.psd		Skills Review
	PS 14-3.psd		Project Builder 1
	PS 14-4.psd		Project Builder 2
		Digital Art Analysis.doc	Design Project
		Art School Poster.psd	Portfolio Project
Chapter 15	PS 15-1.psd		Lessons 1–4
	PS 15-2.psd		Skills Review
	PS 15-3.psd		Project Builder 1
	PS 15-4.psd		Project Builder 2
		Action Sample.psd (downloaded action - varies) Play Downloaded Action.exe	Design Project
		Game Plan.psd	Portfolio Project

Chapter	Data File Supplied	Student Creates File	Used in
Chapter 16	PS 16-1.psd		Lessons 1–6
	PS 16-2.psd		Lesson 2
	PS 16-3.psd		Lesson 5
	PS 16-4.avi		Lesson 7
	PS 16-5.psd		Skills Review
	PS 16-6.psd		
	PS 16-7.psd		
	PS 16-8.avi		
		Xtream Charity.psd	Project Builder 1
		Countdown.psd	Project Builder 2
		Countdown Browser.psd	
		Banners et al.psd	Design Project
		Wake Up.psd	Portfolio Project
Appendix	PS APP-1.jpg		Project 1
	PS APP-2.jpg		Project 2
	PS APP-3.jpg		Project 3
	PS APP-4.jpg		
	PS APP-5.psd		Project 4
	PS APP-6.psd		Project 5
	PS APP-7.jpg		Project 6
	PS APP-8.psd		Project 7
	PS APP-9.jpg		Project 8

Action
A series of tasks that you record and save to play back later as a single command.

Active layer
The layer highlighted on the Layers panel. The active layer's name appears in parentheses in the image window title bar.

Active setting
In the Curves dialog box, the point that you click and drag to change the input and output values.

Additive colors
A color system in which, when the values of R, G, and B are 0, the result is black; when the values are all 255, the result is white.

Adjustment layer
An additional layer for which you can specify individual color adjustments. The adjustment layer allows you to temporarily alter a layer before making the adjustment permanent.

Adjustment panel
Visible panel that makes creation of adjustment layers easy.

Adobe Bridge
A stand-alone application that serves as the hub for the Adobe Create Suite. It can be used for file management tasks such as opening, viewing, sorting, and rating files.

Adobe Device Central
Gives flexibility to those who create content for mobile phones and other consumer electronic devices. The Emulator tab allows you to preview your content on a variety of devices.

Alpha channel
Specific color information added to a default channel. Also called a *spot channel*.

Altitude
A Bevel and Emboss setting that affects the amount of visible dimension.

Ambience property
Controls the balance between the light source and the overall light in an image.

Anchor points
Small square handles, similar to fastening points, that connect straight or curved line segments.

Angle
In the Layer Style dialog box, the setting that determines where a drop shadow falls relative to the text.

Animation
The illusion of motion, created by placing a series of images in the same location and adjusting the timing between their appearances.

Animation panel
Panel that is used to display and edit frames and video (in Timeline mode).

Annotation
A written note embedded in a Photoshop file.

Anti-aliasing
Partially fills in pixel edges, resulting in smooth-edge type. This feature lets your type maintain its crisp appearance and is especially useful for large type.

Application bar
The area containing the menu bar (containing Photoshop commands), additional buttons, and the title bar (displaying the program name).

Arrangement
How objects are positioned relative to one another.

Artistic filters
Used to replicate natural or traditional media effects.

Asymmetrical balance
When objects are placed unequally on either side of an imaginary vertical line in the center of the page.

Auto-slice
A slice created by Photoshop. An auto-slice has a dotted-line border.

Background color
Used to make gradient fills and to fill in areas of an image that have been erased. The default background color is white.

Background Eraser tool
Used to selectively remove pixels from an image, just as you would use a pencil

eraser to remove unwanted written marks. The erased areas become transparent.

Balance colors
Process of adding and subtracting colors from those already existing in a layer.

Base color
The original color of an image.

Base layer
The bottom layer in a clipping group, which serves as the group's mask.

Baseline
An invisible line on which type rests.

Baseline shift
The distance type appears from its original position.

Batch
A group of files designated to have the same action performed on them simultaneously.

Bitmap
A geometric arrangement of different color dots on a rectangular grid.

Bitmap mode
Uses black or white color values to represent image pixels; a good choice for images with subtle color gradations, such as photographs or painted images.

Bitmap type
Type that may develop jagged edges when enlarged.

Blend color
The color applied to the base color when a blending mode is applied to a layer.

Blend If color
Determines the color range for the pixels you want to blend.

Blending mode
Affects the layer's underlying pixels or base color. Used to darken or lighten colors, depending on the colors in use.

Blur filters
Used to soften a selection or image.

Bounding box
A rectangle with handles that appears around an object or type and can be used to change dimensions, also called a *transform controls box*.

Bridge
See Adobe Bridge.

Brightness
The measurement of relative lightness or darkness of a color (measured as a percentage from 0% [black] to 100% [white]).

Brush library
Contains a variety of brush tips that you can use, rename, delete, or customize.

Brush Strokes filters
Used to mimic fine arts effects such as a brush and ink stroke.

Button
A graphical interface that helps visitors navigate and interact with a website easily.

Button mode
Optional action display in which each action available in Photoshop is displayed as a button—without additional detail.

Camera Raw
Allows you to use digital data directly from a digital camera. The file extension that you see will vary with each digital camera manufacturer.

Channels
Used to store information about the color elements contained in each channel.

Channels panel
Lists all channel information. The top channel is a composite channel—a combination of all the default channels. You can hide channels in the same manner that you hide layers: click the Indicates layer visibility button.

Character panel
Helps you control type properties. The Toggle the Character and Paragraph panel button is located on the options bar when you select a Type tool.

Clipboard
Temporary storage area, provided by your operating system, for cut and copied data.

Clipping mask (Clipping group)
A group of two or more contiguous layers linked for the purposes of masking. Effect used to display the image or pattern from one layer into the shape of another layer.

Clipping path
Used when you need to extract a Photoshop object from within a layer, then place it in another program (such as QuarkXPress or Adobe Illustrator), while retaining its transparent background.

Closed path
One continuous path without endpoints, such as a circle.

CMYK image
An image using the CMYK color system, containing at least four channels (one each for cyan, magenta, yellow, and black).

Color cast
A situation in which one color dominates an image to an unrealistic or undesirable degree.

Color channel
An area where color information is stored. Every Photoshop image has at least one channel and can have a maximum of 24 color channels.

Color management system
Keeps colors looking consistent as they move between devices.

Color mode
Used to determine how to display and print an image. Each mode is based on established models used in color reproduction.

Color Picker
A feature that lets you choose a color from a color spectrum.

Color Range command
Used to select a particular color contained in an existing image.

Color Sampler tool
Feature that samples—and stores—up to four distinct color samplers. This feature is used when you want to save specific color settings for future use.

Color separation
Result of converting an RGB image into a CMYK image; the commercial printing process of separating colors for use with different inks.

Composite channel
The top channel on the Channels panel that is a combination of all the default channels.

Compositing
Combining images from sources such as other Photoshop images, royalty-free images, pictures taken from digital cameras, and scanned artwork.

ConnectNow
An Adobe tool that allows for online collaboration with others.

Contact sheet
Compilation of a maximum of 30 thumbnail images (per sheet) from a specific folder.

Contiguous
Items that are next to one another.

Crisp
Anti-aliasing setting that gives type more definition and makes it appear sharper.

Crop
To exclude part of an image. Cropping hides areas of an image without losing resolution quality.

Crop marks
Page notations that indicate where trimming will occur and can be printed at the corners, center of each edge, or both.

Darken Only option
Replaces light pixels with darker pixels.

Default action
An action that is prerecorded and tested, and comes with Photoshop.

Default channels
The color channels automatically contained in an image.

Defringe command
Replaces fringe pixels with the colors of other nearby pixels.

Deselect
A command that removes the marquee from an area so it is no longer selected.

Destructive editing
Changes to pixels that are irreversible and *cannot be undone* once the current Photoshop session has ended.

Diffuse filter
Used to make layer contents look less focused.

Digimarc filter

Embeds into an image a digital watermark that stores copyright information.

Digital camera

A camera that captures images on electronic media (rather than film). Its images are in a standard digital format and can be downloaded for computer use.

Digital image

A picture in electronic form. It may be referred to as a file, document, picture, or image.

Digital Negative Format

An archival format for camera raw files that contains the raw image data created within a digital camera as well as its defining metadata. Also called *Adobe DNG*.

Direct Selection tool

Used to select and manipulate individual anchor points and segments to reshape a path.

Distance

Determines how far a shadow falls from the text. This setting is used by the Drop Shadow and Bevel and Emboss styles.

Distort filters

Create three-dimensional or other reshaping effects. Some of the types of distortions you can produce include Glass, Pinch, Ripple, Shear, Spherize, Twirl, Wave, and ZigZag.

Dithering

Occurs when a web browser attempts to display colors that are not included in its native color palette.

Dock

A collection of panels or buttons surrounded by a dark gray bar. The arrows in the dock are used to maximize and minimize the panels.

Droplet

A stand-alone action in the form of an icon.

Drop Shadow

A style that adds what looks like a colored layer of identical text behind the selected type. The default shadow color is black.

Drop Zone

A blue outline area that indicates where a panel can be moved.

Endpoints

Anchor points at each end of an open path.

Eraser tool

Has the opposite function of a brush in that it eliminates pixels on a layer.

Exposure property

Lightens or darkens the lighting effects ellipse.

Extract feature

Used to isolate a foreground object from its background. This (plug-in) feature requires a separate installation, and may not be installed on your computer.

Extrude filters

Used to convert an image into pyramids or blocks.

Fade options

Brush settings that determine how and when brushes fade toward the end of their strokes.

Fading type

An effect in which the type appears to originate in darkness and then gradually gets brighter, or vice versa.

Fastening point

An anchor within the marquee. When the marquee pointer reaches the initial fastening point, a small circle appears on the pointer, indicating that you have reached the starting point.

Feather

A method used to control the softness of a selection's edges by blurring the area between the selection and the surrounding pixels.

Filter Gallery

A feature that lets you see the effects of each filter before applying it.

Filters

Used to alter the look of an image and give it a special, customized appearance by applying special effects, such as distortions, changes in lighting, and blurring.

Flattening

Merges all visible layers into one layer, named the Background layer, and deletes all hidden layers, greatly reducing file size.

Flow

Brush tip setting that determines how much paint is sprayed while the mouse button is held.

Font

Characters with a similar appearance.

Font family

Represents a complete set of characters, letters, and symbols for a particular typeface. Font families are generally divided into three categories: serif, sans serif, and symbol.

Foreground color

Used to paint, fill, and stroke selections. The default foreground color is black.

Frame

An individual image that is used in animation.

Frame delay

In an animation sequence, the length of time that each frame appears.

Freeform Pen tool

Acts like a traditional pen or pencil, and automatically places *both* the anchor points and line segments wherever necessary to achieve the shape you want.

Freeze

To protect areas within an image from being affected by Liquify tools.

Fuzziness

Similar to tolerance, in that the lower the value, the closer the color pixels must be to be selected.

Gamut

The range of displayed colors in a color model.

Gloss Contour

A Bevel and Emboss setting that determines the pattern with which light is reflected.

Gloss property

Controls the amount of surface reflectance on the lighted surfaces.

Gradient fill

A type of fill in which colors appear to blend into one another. A gradient's appearance is determined by its beginning and ending points. Photoshop contains five gradient fill styles.

Gradient presets

Predesigned gradient fills that are displayed in the Gradient picker.

Graphics tablet

An optional hardware peripheral that enables use of pressure-sensitive tools, create programmable menu buttons, and maneuver faster in Photoshop.

Grayscale image

Can contain up to 256 shades of gray. Pixels can have brightness values from 0 (black) to white (255).

Grayscale mode

Uses up to 256 shades of gray, assigning a brightness value from 0 (black) to 255 (white) to each pixel.

Guides

Horizontal and vertical lines that you create to help you align objects. Guides appear as light blue lines.

Handles

Small boxes that appear along the perimeter of a selected object and are used to change the size of an image.

HDR (High Dynamic Range) Image

An image that is used in motion pictures, special effects, 3D work, and high-end photography, and stores pixel values that span the whole tonal range.

Hexadecimal values

Sets of three pairs of letters or numbers that are used to define the R, G, and B components of a color.

Highlight Mode

A Bevel and Emboss setting that determines how pigments are combined.

Histogram

A graph that displays the frequency distribution of colors and is used to make adjustments in the input and output levels.

History panel

Contains a record of each action performed during a Photoshop session. Up to 1000 levels of Undo are available through the History panel (20 levels by default).

Hotspot

Area within an object that is assigned a URL. This area can then be clicked to jump to the associated web address.

HTML

Hypertext Markup Language (HTML) is the language used for creating web pages.

Hue
The color reflected from/transmitted through an object and expressed as a degree (between 0° and 360°). Each hue is identified by a color name (such as red or green).

ICC profile
Created for specific devices and embedded in an image, and used to define how colors are interpreted by a specific device. ICC stands for International Color Consortium.

Image-editing program
Used to manipulate graphic images that can be reproduced by professional printers using full-color processes.

Image map
An area composed of multiple hotspots; can be circular, rectangular, or polygonal.

Intellectual property
An image or idea that is owned and retained by legal control.

Jitter
The randomness of dynamic brush tip elements such as size, angle, roundness, hue, saturation, brightness, opacity, and flow.

Kerning
Controlling the amount of space between two characters.

Keyboard shortcuts
Combinations of keys that can be used to work faster and more efficiently.

Kuler
A web-hosted application that lets you create, save, share, and download color-coordinated themes for use in images. It can be accessed from a browser, the desktop, or Adobe products such as Photoshop or Illustrator.

Landscape orientation
An image with the long edge of the paper at the top and bottom.

Layer
A section within an image on which objects can be stored. The advantage: Individual effects can be isolated and manipulated without affecting the rest of the image. The disadvantage: Layers can increase the size of your file.

Layer comp
A variation on the arrangement and visibility of existing layers within an image; an organizational tool.

Layer group
An organizing tool you use to group layers on the Layers panel.

Layer mask
Can cover an entire layer or specific areas within a layer. When a layer contains a mask, an additional thumbnail appears on the Layers panel.

Layers panel
Displays all the layers within an active image. You can use the Layers panel to create, delete, merge, copy, or reposition layers.

Layer style
An effect that can be applied to a type or image layer.

Layer thumbnail
Contains a miniature picture of the layer's content, and appears to the left of the layer name on the Layers panel.

Leading
The amount of vertical space between lines of type.

Libraries
Storage units for brushes.

Lighten Only option
Replaces dark pixels with light pixels.

Lighting Effects filter
Applies lighting effects to an image.

Link
Clickable text, graphic, or object that hyperlinks to a specific website and opens that website in a browser window.

Liquify feature
Applies distortions to layers using distinct tools in the Liquify dialog box.

Liquify session
The period of time from when you open the Liquify dialog box to when you close it.

List mode
The default display of actions in which all action detail can be viewed.

Logo
A distinctive image used to identify a company, project, or organization. You can create a logo by combining symbols, shapes, colors, and text.

Lossless
A file-compression format in which no data is discarded.

Lossy
A file format that discards data during the compression process.

Luminosity
The remaining light and dark values that result when a color image is converted to grayscale.

Magic Eraser tool
Used to erase areas in an image that have similar-colored pixels.

Magic Wand tool
Used to choose pixels that are similar to the ones where you first click in an image.

Marquee
A series of dotted lines indicating a selected area that can be edited or dragged into another image.

Mask
A feature that lets you protect or modify a particular area; created using a marquee.

Match Color command
Allows you to replace one color with another.

Material property
Controls parts of an image that reflect the light source color.

Matte
A colorful box placed behind an object that makes the object stand out.

Menu bar
Contains menus from which you can choose Photoshop commands.

Merging layers
Process of combining multiple image layers into one layer.

Mesh
A series of horizontal and vertical gridlines that are superimposed in the Liquify preview window.

Modal control
Dialog boxes that are used in an action, and are indicated by an icon on the Actions panel.

Mode
Represents the amount of color data that can be stored in a given file format, and determines the color model used to display and print an image.

Model
Determines how pigments combine to produce resulting colors; determined by the color mode.

Monitor calibration
A process that displays printed colors accurately on your monitor.

Monotype spacing
Spacing in which each character occupies the same amount of space.

Morph
To blend multiple images in the animation process. Short for *metamorphosis*.

Motion Blur filter
Adjusts the angle of the blur, as well as the distance the blur appears to travel.

Multiple-image layout
Layout (generated in Adobe Bridge) that features more than one image.

Noise filters
Used to add or remove pixels with randomly distributed color levels.

Non-destructive editing
Alterations to an image that are *not* permanent and can be edited.

None
Anti-aliasing setting that applies no anti-aliasing, resulting in jagged edges.

Normal blend mode
The default blending mode.

Opacity
Determines the percentage of transparency. Whereas a layer with 100% opacity will obstruct objects in the layers beneath it, a layer with 1% opacity will appear nearly transparent.

Open path

A path that comprises two distinct endpoints, such as an individual line.

Optical center

The point around which objects on the page are balanced; occurs approximately 3/8ths from the top of the page.

Optimized image

An image whose file size has been reduced without sacrificing image quality.

Options bar

Displays the settings for the active tool. The options bar is located directly under the Application bar, but can be moved anywhere in the workspace for easier access.

Orientation

Direction an image appears on the page: portrait or landscape.

Other filters

Allow you to create your own filters, modify masks, or make quick color adjustments.

Outline type

Type that is mathematically defined and can be scaled to any size without its edges losing their smooth appearance. (Also known as a *vector font*.)

Out-of-gamut indicator

Indicates that the current color falls beyond the accurate print or display range.

Panels

Floating windows that can be moved and are used to modify objects. Panels contain named tabs, which can be separated and moved to another group. Each panel contains a menu that can be viewed by clicking the list arrow in its upper-right corner.

Panel well

An area where you can assemble panels for quick access.

Path

One or more straight or curved line segments connected by anchor points used to turn the area defined within an object into an individual object.

Path component

One or more anchor points joined by line segments.

Path Selection tool

Used to select an entire path.

Paths panel

Storage area for paths.

Pen tool

Used to draw a path by placing anchor points along the edge of another image or wherever you need them to draw a specific shape.

Picture package

Shows multiple copies of a single image in various sizes, similar to a portrait studio sheet of photos.

Pixel

Each dot in a bitmapped image that represents a color or shade.

Pixel aspect ratio

A scaling correction feature that automatically corrects the ratio of pixels displayed for the monitor in use. Prevents pixels viewed in a 16:9 monitor (such as a widescreen TV) from looking squashed in a 4:3 monitor (nearly-rectangular TV).

Pixelate filters

Used to sharply define a selection.

Plug-ins

Additional programs—created by Adobe and other developers—that expand the functionality of Photoshop.

Points

Unit of measurement for font sizes. Traditionally, one inch is equivalent to 72.27 points. The default Photoshop type size is 12 points.

Portrait orientation

An image with the short edge of the paper at the top and bottom.

PostScript

A programming language created by Adobe that optimizes printed text and graphics.

Preferences

Used to control the Photoshop environment using your specifications.

Preset Manager

Allows you to manage libraries of preset brushes, swatches, gradients, styles, patterns, contours, and custom shapes.

Profile

Defines and interprets colors for a color management system.

Properties color swatch

Changes the ambient light around the lighting spotlight.

Proportional spacing

The text spacing in which each character takes up a different amount of space, based on its width.

Quick Selection tool

Tool that lets you paint to make a selection from the interior using a brush tip, reducing rough edges and blockiness.

Radial Blur filter

Adjusts the amount of blur and the blur method (Spin or Zoom).

Rasterize

Converts a type layer to an image layer.

Rasterized shape

A shape that is converted into a bitmapped object. It cannot be moved or copied and has a much smaller file size.

Red Eye effect

Photographic effect in which eyes within photographs look red.

Reference point

Center of the object from which distortions and transformations are measured.

Refine Edge option

Button found on the options bar of a variety of tools that allows you to improve the size and edges of a selection.

Relief

The height of ridges within an object.

Render filters

Transform three-dimensional shapes and simulated light reflections in an image.

Rendering intent

The way in which a color-management system handles color conversion from one color space to another.

Resolution

Number of pixels per inch.

Resulting color

The outcome of the blend color applied to the base color.

RGB image

Image that contains three color channels (one each for red, green, and blue).

Rulers

Onscreen markers that help you precisely measure and position an object. Rulers can be displayed using the View menu.

Sampling

A method of changing foreground and background colors by copying existing colors from an image.

Sans serif fonts

Fonts that do not have tails or strokes at the end of characters; commonly used in headlines.

Saturation

The strength or purity of the color, representing the amount of gray in proportion to hue (measured as a percentage from 0% [gray], to 100% [fully saturated]). Also known as *chroma*.

Save As

A command that lets you create a copy of the open file using a new name.

Scale

The size relationship of objects to one another.

Scanner

An electronic device that converts print material into an electronic file.

Screening back

An illusory effect in which type appears to fade into the imagery below it. Also known as *screening*.

Script

Creates external automation of Photoshop from an outside source, such as JavaScript. Also called *scripting*.

Selection

An area in an image that is surrounded by a selection marquee and can then be manipulated.

Serif fonts

Fonts that have a tail, or stroke, at the end of some characters. These tails make it easier for the eye to recognize words; therefore, serif fonts are generally used in text passages.

Shading
Bevel and Emboss setting that determines lighting effects.

Sharpness
An element of composition that draws the viewer's eye to a specific area.

Shadow Mode
Bevel and Emboss setting that determines how pigments are combined.

Shape
A vector object that keeps its crisp appearance when it is resized and, like a path, can be edited.

Shape layer
A clipping path or shape that can occupy its own layer.

Sharp
Anti-aliasing setting that displays type with the best possible resolution.

Sharpen More filter
Increases the contrast of adjacent pixels and can focus blurry images.

Size
Determines the clarity of a drop shadow.

Sketch filters
Used to apply a texture or create a hand-drawn effect.

Slice
A specific area within an image to which you can assign special features, such as a link, or animation.

Smart Blur filter
Adjusts the quality, radius, and threshold of a blur.

Smart Guides
A feature that displays vertical or horizontal guides that appear automatically when you draw a shape or move an object and are helpful in its positioning.

Smart Filter
A filter applied to a Smart Object and allows for nondestructive editing of the filter(s).

Smart Object
A combination of objects that has a visible indicator in the bottom-right corner of the layer thumbnail. Makes it possible to scale, rotate, and wrap layers without losing image quality.

Smooth
Anti-aliasing setting that gives type more rounded edges.

Snapshot
A temporary copy of an image that contains the history states made up to that point. You can create multiple snapshots of an image, and you can switch between snapshots.

Source
The image containing the color that will be matched.

Splash screen
A window that displays information about the software you are using.

Spot channel
Designed to provide a channel for additional inks, also called a spot color channel. A spot channel is added to an image using the Channels panel.

Spot color
A method of defining a difficult or unique color that couldn't otherwise be easily re-created by a printer.

Spread
Determines the width of drop shadow text.

Spring-loaded keyboard shortcuts
Shortcut keyboard combinations that *temporarily* change the active tool.

State
An entry on the History panel, or the individual steps in an action in the Actions panel.

Status bar
The area located at the bottom of the program window (Win) or the image window (Mac) that displays information such as the file size of the active window and a description of the active tool.

Step
Measurement of fade options that can be any value from 1–9999, and equivalent to one mark of the brush tip.

Stop
In an action, a command that interrupts playback or includes an informative text

message for the user, so that other operations can be performed.

Stroking the edges
The process of making a selection or layer stand out by formatting it with a border.

Strong
Anti-aliasing setting that makes type appear heavier, much like the bold attribute.

Structure
A Bevel and Emboss setting that determines the size and physical properties of the object.

Style
Eighteen predesigned styles that can be applied to buttons.

Stylize filters
Used to produce a painted or impressionistic effect.

Subtractive colors
A color system in which the full combination of cyan, magenta, and yellow absorb all color and produce black.

Swatches panel
Contains available colors that can be selected for use as a foreground or background color. You can also add your own colors to the Swatches panel.

Symbol fonts
Used to display unique characters (such as $, ÷, or ™).

Symmetrical balance
When objects are placed equally on either side of an imaginary vertical line in the center of the page.

Target
When sampling a color, the image that will receive the matched color.

Texture filters
Used to give the appearance of depth or substance.

Thaw
To remove protection from a protected area in an image so it can be affected by Liquify tools.

This Layer slider
Used to specify the range of pixels that will be blended on the active layer.

Threshold
The Normal mode when working with bitmapped images. The threshold is the starting point for applying other blending modes.

Thumbnail
Contains a miniature picture of the layer's content, appears to the left of the layer name, and can be turned on or off.

Title bar
Displays the program name and filename of the open image. The title bar also contains buttons for minimizing, maximizing, and closing the image.

Tolerance
The range of pixels that determines which pixels will be selected. The lower the tolerance, the closer the color is to the selection. The setting can have a value from 0–255.

Tonal values
Numeric values of an individual color that can be used to duplicate a color. Also called *color levels*.

Tone
The brightness and contrast within an image.

Tools panel
Contains tools for frequently used commands. On the face of a tool is a graphic representation of its function. Place the pointer over each button to display a ScreenTip, which tells you the name or function of that button.

Tracking
The insertion of a uniform amount of space between characters.

Transform
To change the shape, size, perspective, or rotation of an object or objects on a layer.

Transform box
A rectangle that surrounds an image and contains handles that can be used to change dimensions. Also called a *bounding box*.

Tweening
The process of selecting multiple frames, then inserting transitional frames between them. This effect makes frames appear to blend into one another and gives the animation a more fluid appearance.

Twirl filter
Applies a circular effect.

Type

Text, or a layer containing text. Each character is measured in points. In PostScript measurement, one inch is equivalent to 72 points. In traditional measurement, one inch is equivalent to 72.27 points.

Type spacing

Adjustments you can make to the space between characters and between lines of type.

Underlying Layer slider

Used to specify the range of pixels that will be blended on lower visible layers.

URL

Uniform Resource Locator, a web address.

User-slice

A slice created by you. A user-slice has a solid-line border.

Vanishing Point filter

Used to maintain perspective as you drag objects around corners and into the distance.

Vector data

A shape or path that will not lose its crisp appearance if resized or reshaped.

Vector font

Fonts that are vector-based type outlines, which means that they are mathematically defined shapes.

Vector graphic

Image made up of lines and curves defined by mathematical objects.

Vector mask

Makes a shape's edges appear neat and defined on a layer.

Version Cue

A file versioning and management feature of the Adobe Creative Suite.

Video filters

Used to restrict colors to those acceptable for television reproduction and smooth video images.

Vignette

A feature in which the border of a picture or portrait fades into the surrounding color at its edges.

Vignette effect

A feature that uses feathering to fade a marquee shape.

Warping type

A feature that lets you create distortions that conform to a variety of shapes.

Web Photo Gallery

Contains a thumbnail index page of all exported images, the actual JPEG images, and any included links.

Web-safe colors

The 216 colors that can be displayed on the web without dithering.

Wind filter

Conveys the feeling of direction and motion on the layer to which it is applied.

Work path

A path when it is first created, but not yet named.

Working space

Tells the color management system how RGB and CMYK values are interpreted.

Workspace

The entire window, from the Application bar at the top of the window, to the status bar at the bottom border of the program window.

Workspace switcher

Button on the Application bar that lets you switch between defined workspaces.

Written annotation

Text similar to a sticky note that is attached to a file.

I N D E X

Photoshop Chapter Opener Art Credits

Chapter	Art credit for opening pages
Chapter 1	© Philip and Karen Smith/Digital Vision/Getty Images
Chapter 2	© Jeff Rotman/Digital Vision/Getty Images
Chapter 3	© Paul Souders/Photodisc/Getty Images
Chapter 4	© Plush Studios/Digital Vision/Getty Images
Chapter 5	© David Tipling/Digital Vision/Getty Images
Chapter 6	© David Newham/Alamy
Chapter 7	© Josephine Marsden/Alamy
Chapter 8	© Radius Images/Alamy
Chapter 9	© Christopher Scott/Alamy
Chapter 10	© Radius Images/Alamy
Chapter 11	© Darryl Leniuk/Lifesize/Getty Images
Chapter 12	© Dimitri Vervitsiotis/Digital Vision/Getty Images
Chapter 13	© Veer
Chapter 14	© Barbara Peacock/Photodisc/Getty Images
Chapter 15	© Stuart Westmorland/Digital Vision/Getty Images
Chapter 16	© Nick Norman/National Geographic Image Collection/Getty Images
Appendix	© Georgette Douwma/Photodisc/Getty Images
Data Files/Glossary/Index	© Veer